MW00834485

Federal Tax Research

Federal Tax Research

Second Edition

Joni Larson
PROFESSOR OF LAW
THOMAS M. COOLEY LAW SCHOOL

Dan Sheaffer
PROFESSOR OF LAW
THOMAS M. COOLEY LAW SCHOOL

CAROLINA ACADEMIC PRESS
Durham, North Carolina

Copyright © 2011
Joni Larson
Dan Sheaffer
All Rights Reserved

Library of Congress Cataloging-in-Publication Data

Larson, Joni.
  Federal tax research / Joni Larson, Dan Sheaffer. -- 2nd ed.
    p. cm.
  Includes bibliographical references and index.
  ISBN 978-1-59460-857-5 (alk. paper)
  ISBN 978-1-5310-2001-9 (pbk)

  1. Taxation--Law and legislation--United States--Legal research. I. Sheaffer, Dan. II.
Title.
  KF241.T38L37 2011
  343.7304072--dc22

                              2010049470

            CAROLINA ACADEMIC PRESS
                    700 Kent Street
             Durham, North Carolina 27701
              Telephone (919) 489-7486
                  Fax (919) 493-5668
                  www.cap-press.com

        Printed in the United States of America
                    2020 Printing

Contents

Federal Tax Research

Chapter 1

Introduction

Federal Tax Research

- *How is federal tax research different from other types of research?*
- *How is federal tax research like other types of research?*
- *Are there special tools available to the tax researcher?*

Kevin walked into the firm's lunchroom and joined the other interns sitting at the large table. He let out a long, exasperated sigh.

"What's wrong?" Kari asked, setting her lunch out before her on the table.

"I got an assignment from Taxler."

"Taxler the 'Taxman'! You have got to be kidding!"

"I don't even know where to start," Kevin lamented. "The world of tax is all a big mystery to me. This is too much! Do you think it would look horrible on my résumé to have clerked here for only one month?"

"Don't you think you are being just a little dramatic?" Sam asked. "Research is research. A good attorney can research any issue."

"I couldn't disagree more." Kari said, setting down her sandwich. "Sam, have you ever heard of Revenue Rulings? Competent authority? BNA Portfolios? Do you know the authoritative weight of a Tax Court Memorandum Opinion?"

"Uh, actually, no," Sam said, suddenly looking very interested in his tuna salad.

"Don't worry, Kevin," Kari said. "I've done tax research before and can help you get started."

Kevin let out a long sigh. But this time it was a sigh of relief.

A. Discussion

Tax research has a lot in common with other types of legal research. As in other areas, the facts must be established, the issues identified, the relevant law ascertained, the law applied to the facts, and the conclusions or recommendations summarized and communicated.

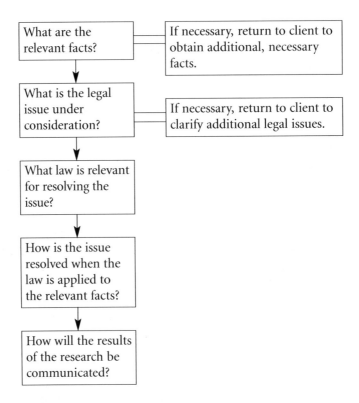

The researcher must have a clear understanding of all relevant facts. If there are any gaps in the facts needed to resolve the issue, the researcher must return to the client for additional information. At a minimum, the researcher must make it clear to the client that the advice will be based on any facts provided by the client. Any alteration in the facts could potentially lead to a different legal conclusion.

The researcher must understand what issue the client needs resolved. If, after the researcher has begun his research, an issue not previously considered comes to light, he may need to return to the client to refine the issue or obtain additional factual information.

The law relevant for providing advice to the client will depend on the issue under consideration. The United States Constitution authorizes Congress to enact a federal income tax. Issues may arise regarding whether a particular tax is constitutional or how the tax should be interpreted or applied in light of constitutional provisions.

In some circumstances, the researcher might begin with an evaluation of statutory authority. Most often in tax research the relevant statutory authority is the Internal Revenue Code. If the statute is clear, the researcher's job is done. If the statute is not clear,

the next step might be to consider the legislative history of the statute. When Congress enacts tax legislation, it will almost always follow the same process. The bill will begin in the House Ways and Means Committee, then be considered by the Senate Finance Committee, and finally have any differences resolved in a conference committee. Each committee that considers the bill will prepare a committee report, explaining the bill that was put forward by that committee. If the bill passes through Congress and is signed into law by the president, it becomes part of the Public Law and is incorporated into the Internal Revenue Code. Unlike other areas of law, once the measure becomes law, an additional report is often created by the Staff of the Joint Committee on Taxation, explaining the law.

The researcher may be assisted in his attempt to interpret the Code by considering regulations issued by the Internal Revenue Service (IRS). There are different types of regulations: proposed, final, and temporary. Each type of regulation has a different implication which must be understood in order to determine the impact the regulation has on the researcher's issue.

The researcher may begin his research with a survey of relevant case law. Courts interpret the statutes enacted by Congress and the regulations issued by the IRS. In the tax arena, there are three separate trial level forums: the United States Tax Court, the U.S. Court of Federal Claims, and district courts. Each trial court has its own strengths and weaknesses that must be understood, both from the perspective of bringing a case to litigation and for evaluating the weight to be given to the court's opinion.

Trial level opinions can be appealed to one of thirteen separate courts of appeals. These appellate courts may or may not agree with the resolution of the issue by the trial court. In addition, the appellate courts may not agree with each other on the resolution of the same issues. The researcher must understand which opinions control the resolution of his issue and which are merely advisory. Of course, any opinions rendered by the Supreme Court will be binding on all taxpayers, unless a statute has subsequently changed the state of the law. In all situations, the researcher must evaluate the weight to be given any relevant opinion he locates. Finally, cite checking opinions is just as important when conducting tax research as when conducting other types of research.

As part of his research, the researcher may also consider various documents generated by the IRS. To assist taxpayers in understanding and applying the Internal Revenue Code, the IRS issues publicly available documents setting forth how it interprets various tax provisions. The issues are set forth in a generic, non-taxpayer specific manner. The researcher must understand the variety of documents made available by the IRS, how to locate them, and to what extent he can rely on the position taken by the IRS in the document.

The IRS will also give guidance directly to individual taxpayers on their specific tax issues. Once the taxpayer's personal information is redacted, the taxpayer-specific guidance is made available to the public. The researcher must understand the situations in which this type of advice is rendered, how to locate the advice, and whether he can rely on the advice.

Finally, the IRS generates a variety of documents as part of carrying out its duty of enforcing the Code. While these documents were not intended to assist the public in understanding the Code, they can provide a wealth of information. The researcher must be aware of the types of internal documents that are generated by the IRS, how they can be helpful in resolving a legal issue, how they can be located, and to what extent they would be persuasive authority for a position taken by a taxpayer. Finally, if an internal document (or any other type of IRS document) has not been released to the public, the researcher must understand the tools he has at his finger tips for obtaining that document.

With so many resources available to the researcher, the prospect of conducting tax research could be overwhelming. Commercial publishers have come to the rescue by providing treatises that organize the various types of information. Some treatises organize the information by Code section; others organize the information by topic; and some treatises cover only very narrow areas of tax law, but cover them in great depth. Because international taxation may involve understanding tax provisions of other countries and understanding how the United States and other countries have resolved any differences, the researcher is often required to consult resources that would not be consulted for domestic tax research.

In addition to treatises, law reviews, seminar and tax conference materials, journals, and other publications provide a wealth of information on specific tax issues. The researcher can utilize the articles in a variety of ways, from a tool to beginning research to a way of keeping current on hot tax topics.

Tax research is like any other type of research in that the researcher should have a plan of how to approach it. What is the exact issue the researcher is considering? Does the researcher need additional information on the subject in order to properly conduct more specific research? Is the issue one of statutory construction? Will the issue be resolved by judicial interpretation of a provision? What is the best source for beginning the research?

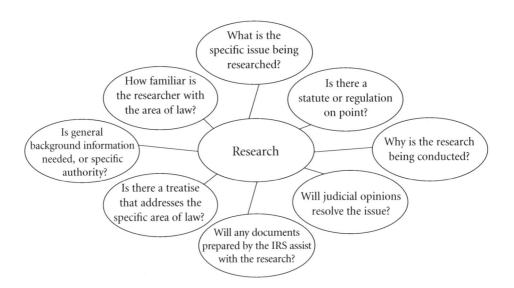

By focusing his search and understanding what type of information the researcher is seeking, he can avoid using the "shotgun" approach, wasting valuable time in searching multiple sources, rather than in just the best sources. In addition, while tax research is often an iterative process, with new issues coming to light as the researcher gains additional knowledge, the researcher should take care to avoid becoming sidetracked on irrelevant issues.

Once the research is concluded, the researcher must record the results. He may prepare a memorandum to a partner or business associate, draft a letter to the client, or prepare a tax opinion. He may draft a protest letter, a petition, or a brief. For whatever document the researcher is preparing, he must understand the relevant attributes of the document and what implications they have on how he drafts the document. However,

regardless of the document being drafted, good writing practices applicable in other areas of law are just as applicable in tax law. The researcher should use persuasive writing, demonstrate good grammar skills, be effective in his means of communicating the information, and give attention to the intended audience. In addition, he must understand and take into consideration any requirements imposed upon him by the IRS in providing the advice to a client.

The remainder of this book explores in greater detail the various aspects of tax research. It concludes with a discussion of the various documents the researcher may be called upon to draft.

B. Problems

1. In what substantive areas do you currently conduct research? Do you expect to be conducting research in other areas in the future?

2. What do you believe is the most difficult part of conducting research?

3. What resources, whether traditional books or electronic, will you have available to you to conduct your research?

4. When you have concluded your research, what form does the final product usually take? Memorandum? Letter to the client? Brief? Something else?

Chapter 2 *Highest Level*

The Constitution of the United States

Constitution

- *Do tax issues involve constitutional issues?*
- *Where can the constitution be found?*
- *What role do constitutional issues play in the Tax Court?*

Jason took his seat for the seminar. It was advertised as an in-depth tax seminar, one that would teach attorneys and CPAs how to completely eliminate an individual's federal income tax. Jason paged through the materials. They were filled with draft trusts, information on how to set up bank accounts and trusts in countries that were classified as tax havens, and lists of resident agents in the same locations.

Jason turned more pages and saw charts containing rows of numbers, always resulting in a net tax liability of zero. The only thing that came into Jason's mind was, *If it looked too good to be true, it probably was.* He sat back and waited for the tax-shelter promoter to begin his pitch. Jason was curious about how the promoter would explain how a result of zero tax liability was justified in all instances.

Contents

A. Key Terms

After completing this chapter, you should be familiar with the following key terms:

➤ Constitution of the United States

➤ Sixteenth Amendment

B. Discussion

1. The Constitution = *Highest primary authority*

The authority of Congress to impose tax is found in the Constitution of the United States. Specifically, the Constitution gives Congress the authority "to lay and collect Taxes, Duties, Imposts and Excises."[1] This provision has been interpreted as giving Congress a very broad power of taxation.

The uniformity clause provides that "all Duties, Imposts and Excises shall be uniform throughout the United States."[2] This clause has been interpreted as requiring that the same tax regime apply regardless of the locale of the taxpayer. In other words, the tax code that applies to the residents of Alaska must be the same tax code that applies to the residents of Florida.

---

1. Article I, section 8.
2. Article I, section 8, clause 1

If the tax constitutes a "direct tax," the Constitution imposes the additional requirement that it "be apportioned among the several States"[3] and that "[n]o capitation, or other direct, Tax shall be laid, unless in Proportion to the Census or Enumeration herein before directed to be taken."[4] The courts have interpreted these provisions as requiring that any direct tax be apportioned among the states based on their respective populations.

The first income tax was enacted in 1862 to fund the Civil War; it expired in 1872. Another income tax was enacted in 1894. However, in *Pollock v. Farmers' Loan & Trust Co.*, the Supreme Court held that the tax was unconstitutional because it was a direct tax that was not apportioned among the states according to population.[5]

A corporate income tax was passed in 1909 and held to be constitutional.[6] The Court found that the tax was an excise tax and not a prohibited direct income tax. Similarly, the Supreme Court found that the estate and gift tax was an indirect tax and upheld it as constitutional.[7]

Returning to the income tax, in response to *Pollack*, in 1913 the Sixteenth Amendment to the Constitution was ratified. The courts have found all subsequent income tax codes to be constitutional. *valid*

Sixteenth Amendment:

The Congress shall have power to lay and collect taxes on income, from whatever source derived, without apportionment among the several States, and without regard to any census or enumeration.

---

2. Unsuccessful Constitutional Arguments

a. Tax Protestors

not having any serious purpose or value.

Taxpayers who are opposed to paying income taxes have put forth a number of arguments based on the constitutionality of the income tax code to support their position that they owe no taxes. Taxpayer challenges based on the constitutionality of the Code are generally not well grounded in the law and are frivolous in nature. Nevertheless, taxpayers continuously raise constitutional arguments challenging the validity of the Code. Such arguments have been repeatedly rejected by the courts. Below is a brief discussion of a few of the more common arguments.

Wages are not income. Some taxpayers have argued that wages are not income. In essence, the taxpayer is arguing that there is an even exchange—work for income. As such, there is no accession to wealth by the taxpayer and, thus, no income. The Tax Court has repeatedly rejected this argument.

---

3. Article I, section 2, clause 3.

4. Article I, section 9, clause 4.

5. 157 U.S. 429 (1895) (holding that unapportioned tax on income from real property was unconstitutional); 158 U.S. 601 (1895) (holding that tax on income from personal property was unconstitutional and rejecting entire tax).

6. *Flint v. Stone Tracy Co.*, 220 U.S. 107 (1911).

7. *Knowlton v. Moore*, 178 U.S. 41 (1900).

Case on Point:

Rowlee v. Commissioner
80 T.C. 1111, 1119–20, 1122 (1983)

Section 61(a) ... states that "gross income means all income from whatever source derived, including (but not limited to) * * * compensation for services." Petitioner has admitted that he exchanged his labor for the amounts paid to him by his employers during the taxable year. He argues that taxation of the amounts paid to him in exchange for his labor is a tax on the "source" of income and not on the income itself. This "taxation on source" argument is spurious; the tax is imposed on the money he receives for his services, not on the performance of those services.... Finally, petitioner claims that he did not have any taxable income or "gain" because the value of his labor was the same as (or more than) the payment he received for it.

Petitioner's position has been repeatedly rejected by this and other courts....

[I]it is clear that wages, salaries, and any other things of value received in exchange for work performed are income within the meaning of the Sixteenth Amendment to the United States Constitution, and the Internal Revenue Code. The etymology of the word "income" reveals that it is a compound word meaning "that which comes in." Whether or not something is income does not depend on whether what comes in is received in exchange for something else.

The Sixteenth Amendment was not properly ratified. Using a variety of theories, such as clerical issues in ratifying the resolution, procedural errors, and an allegation that Ohio was not a state, some taxpayers have argued that the Sixteenth Amendment to the Constitution was not properly ratified. This argument has been uniformly rejected by the courts. It is worth noting that there is some academic debate about whether the income tax is even a direct tax. To the extent it is not a direct tax, it is not subject to the apportionment requirement and would not depend on the passage of the Sixteenth Amendment to be constitutional.

Payment of tax is voluntary. Some taxpayers have argued that the payment of income tax is voluntary or that the amount of tax required to be paid can be reduced by a conscientious objection. There is no support in the Code for allowing a taxpayer who has religious or moral beliefs in conflict with the use to which the tax dollars are put to not pay taxes. Furthermore, the Code specifically provides that all taxpayers are required to pay income taxes. Thus, both arguments have been rejected.

Quote:

"If you think paying taxes is voluntary, you may end up doing voluntary time in federal prison."

Patrick Dunne, *Can't Just Say "No" to Filing, Paying Income Tax*, Hous. Chron., April 14, 1995, at 35.

The gold standard is no longer used. Some taxpayers have argued that, for the income tax to be valid, it must be computed on the gold standard that was in place when the Sixteenth Amendment was ratified. Because the gold standard is no longer used, the argument is that the income tax is invalid. Courts have uniformly rejected this argument.

The income tax violates the Fifth Amendment. Some taxpayers have argued that requiring a taxpayer to file a return under the penalties of perjury requires a taxpayer to be

swearing a false oath

a witness against himself and that such a requirement violates the Fifth Amendment to the Constitution.

> **Fifth Amendment:**
>
> No person shall be held to answer for a capital, or otherwise infamous crime, unless on a presentment or indictment of a Grand Jury, except in cases arising in the land or naval forces, or in the Militia, when in actual service in time of War or public danger; nor shall any person be subject for the same offense to be twice put in jeopardy of life or limb; nor shall be compelled in any criminal case to be a witness against himself, nor be deprived of life, liberty, or property, without due process of law; nor shall private property be taken for public use, without just compensation.

The Fifth Amendment protects an accused taxpayer, or a taxpayer facing possible criminal prosecution, from being compelled to testify against himself or provide evidence needed to prosecute the taxpayer for a crime. The protection may be invoked whenever a taxpayer reasonably believes his testimony could "furnish a link in the chain of evidence needed to prosecute" him for a crime.[8]

The privilege only protects an accused, or a taxpayer facing possible criminal prosecution, from being compelled to provide evidence of a testimonial or communicative nature. Because an income tax return requests information necessary to compute the tax liability, and not facts needed to pursue a criminal prosecution, courts have uniformly held that an argument based on the Fifth Amendment will not support the taxpayer's position that he is not required to file an income tax return.

> **Practice Note:**
>
> A comprehensive list of frivolous arguments can be found on the IRS's website, www.irs.gov, under "The Truth About Frivolous Tax Arguments." It addresses frivolous arguments about the legality of not paying taxes or filing returns and frivolous arguments in collection due process cases. It sets forth the arguments, then provides the law proving the claims false. Finally, it discusses the applicable penalties for pursuing frivolous tax arguments.

b. Legitimate Constitutional Challenges

Even though traditional tax protestor-type arguments have been uniformly rejected by the courts many, many times, that does not mean that no legitimate constitutional arguments ever arise in tax disputes. Several legitimate constitutional arguments have been made challenging classifications or distinctions within the Code. However, even legitimate constitutional arguments face an arduous burden. → challenging.

It has been long established that Congress has a great deal of latitude when creating distinctions and classifications within the Code. However, when Congress exercises such broad authority, it often leads to constitutional challenges of such distinctions or classifications based on the equal protection component of the Fifth Amendment and/or the First Amendment. Below is a brief discussion of First and Fifth Amendment arguments challenging distinctions and classifications within the Code.

---

8. *Acock, Schlegel Architects, Inc. v. Commissioner*, 97 T.C. 352, 358 (1991), *quoting Hoffman v. United States*, 341 U.S. 479, 486 (1951).

A distinction or classification violates the equal protection clause of the Fifth Amendment. Section 104(a)(2) draws a distinction between damages arising out of physical injuries and those arising out of emotional injuries; it provides an exclusion from gross income for damages received on account of a physical injury but not for damages arising solely out of emotional distress.[9] The United States Court of Appeals for the Sixth Circuit has examined whether the Code's distinction between physical and emotional injuries violates the equal protection component of the Fifth Amendment.[10] The Sixth Circuit held that the distinction between physical and emotional injuries was rationally related to government purposes of providing for a uniform policy and reducing litigation and, therefore, that the distinction did not violate the Fifth Amendment.

Generally, a statutory provision that does not "'interfere with the exercise of a fundamental right, such as freedom of speech, or employ a suspect classification, such as race'... is constitutional as long as it bears a rational relationship to a legitimate government purpose."[11] Further, as alluded to above, Congress has particularly broad discretion in adopting distinctions or classifications within the Code. A Code distinction or classification that does not interfere with a fundamental right or employ a suspect classification is presumed to have a rational basis if there are any conceivable facts supporting such position. The burden is on the taxpayer "to negate every conceivable basis which might support it."[12]

A distinction or classification violates the First Amendment. Even when a fundamental right, such as freedom of speech, is involved, a distinction or classification will not be subject to strict scrutiny[13] unless it can be demonstrated that the distinction or classification is infringing on such a right.

First Amendment:

Congress shall make no law respecting an establishment of religion, or prohibiting the free exercise thereof; or abridging the freedom of speech, or of the press; or the right of the people peaceably to assemble, and to petition the Government for a redress of grievances.

Taxpayers on several occasions have challenged whether Code distinctions based on lobby activities violate the right to free speech under the First Amendment.[14] The Code has traditionally denied tax-exempt status to organizations that engage in lobbying activities and has disallowed tax deductions for lobbying expenses.[15] Taxpayers have asserted that these Code provisions violate the First Amendment right to freedom of speech.

The Supreme Court held that denial of tax-exempt status for such organizations and denial of deductions for lobbying expenses does not infringe on any First Amendment rights.

---

9. I.R.C. § 104(a)(2). This subsection provides that gross income does not include "the amount of any damages (other than punitive damages) received (whether by suit or agreement and whether as lump sums or as periodic payments) on account of personal physical injuries or physical sickness."

10. *Young v. U.S.*, 332 F.3d 893 (6th Cir. 2003)

11. *Young*, 332 F.3d at 895 (*quoting Regan v. Taxation with Representation of Wash.*, 461 U.S. 540, 547 (1983)).

12. *Young*, 332 F.3d at 896 (*quoting Madden v. Kentucky*, 309 U.S. 83, 88 (1940)).

13. Under "strict scrutiny" review, a law will only withstand a Constitutional challenge if the government can demonstrate that the law is narrowly tailored to promote a compelling governmental interest. *See, e.g., Simon & Schuster, Inc. v. New York State Crime Victims Bd.*, 502 U.S. 105 (1991).

14. *See e.g., Cammarano v. U.S.*, 358 U.S. 498 (1959); *Regan v. Taxation with Representation of Wash.*, 461 U.S. 540 (1983).

15. *See* I.R.C. §§ 501(h), 162(e).

Rather, it reflects Congress's choice not to subsidize lobbying activities.[16] As a result, the Court has not applied strict scrutiny analysis under such circumstances and has found such distinctions to be constitutional.[17]

3. Successful Constitutional Arguments

The summary above is not intended to give the impression that taxing statutes are always found to be constitutional. As recently as 1998, a district court held that a federal excise tax was unconstitutional.

On December 29, 1981, Congress created the Black Lung Disability Trust Fund. An excise tax on coal was enacted to fund the trust.[18] The excise tax applied to all sales of American coal, regardless of whether the coal was sold in the United States or abroad.

The Export clause of the Constitution provides that "No Tax or Duty shall be laid on Articles exported from any State."[19] Thus, the district court held that the excise tax, as applied to exports of coal, was unconstitutional.[20] The district court's holding was consistent with prior holdings striking down excise taxes on exports.

Even more recently, the Court of Appeals for the District of Columbia initially held an income tax provision unconstitutional.[21] In the underlying action, the taxpayer complained to the authorities about environmental hazards on her employer's land. In response, the employer "blacklisted" her. She suffered mental and physical injuries as a result of the blacklisting. In an administrative proceeding she was awarded compensatory damages with no amount of the award allocable to lost wages or diminished earning capacity. The taxpayer argued that the award was excludable from gross income.[22] The Circuit Court held that Section 104(a)(2) was unconstitutional to the extent it permitted the taxation of an award for a non-physical injury, such as mental distress and loss of reputation, when such amounts were not related to lost wages or earnings.[23] However, on a motion for rehearing, the court reversed itself and held that gross income included compensatory damages for non-physical injuries and that Congress had the power to tax such damages.[24]

4. Constitutional Issues and the Tax Court

Congress created the Board of Tax Appeals as an administrative board of the Treasury Department in the Revenue Act of 1924. It subsequently had many transformations and in 1969 was elevated to a regular judicial court under Article 1 of the United States Constitution. Consistent with becoming a regular judicial court, it received the same powers

---

16. *Cammarano, supra; Regan, supra.*
17. *Cammarano, supra; Regan, supra.*
18. I.R.C. § 4121.
19. *See* Article 1, Section 9, clause 5 of the Constitution.
20. *Ranger Fuel Corp. v. United States,* 33 F. Supp. 2d 466 (E. Dist. Va. 1998).
21. *Murphy v. United States,* 460 F.3d 79 (D.C. Cir. 2006).
22. See generally I.R.C. § 104(a)(2).
23. *Murphy,* 460 F.3d at 81, 92.
24. *Murphy v. United States,* 493 F.3d 170, 171, 180–86 (D.C. Cir. 2007).

regarding contempt and the carrying out of its writs and orders as other federal courts. The status of the Tax Court as an Article I court has been upheld as constitutional.[25]

No right to a jury trial. A taxpayer has no right to a jury trial in the Tax Court. This position has been uniformly upheld.

Seventh Amendment:

In Suits at common law, where the value in controversy shall exceed twenty dollars, the right of trial by jury shall be preserved, and no fact tried by a jury shall be otherwise re-examined in any court of the United States, than according to the rules of the common law.

Because there was no common law action against the sovereignty, the Seventh Amendment does not apply to suits against the United States. Because the Tax Court hears only suits filed by taxpayers against the Commissioner of the Internal Revenue Service, there is no constitutional right to a jury trial in the Tax Court.[26]

Status of Special Trial Judges. In 1943, Congress gave the presiding judge of the Tax Court the authority to designate a commissioner to assist him with fact finding. In 1969, as part of the Tax Reform Act, this authority was expanded and commissioners where given the authority to write summary opinions in cases involving $1,000 or less. In 1986, Congress further expanded the role of the commissioner and changed his title from "commissioner" to "special trial judge." Now, the chief judge may appoint to special trial judges any—

- Declaratory judgment proceeding;
- Proceeding under small case provisions;
- Proceeding where neither the amount of the deficiency placed in dispute nor the amount of any claimed overpayment exceeds $50,000;
- Proceeding under the collection due process provisions; or
- Other proceeding which the chief judge may designate.

The Supreme Court has held that the appointment of and assignment of cases to special trial judges is constitutional.[27]

5. Penalties for Frivolous Positions

Regardless of any constitutional positions taken by the taxpayer, the IRS is prohibited from designating the taxpayer as a "tax protestor."[28] However, to encourage taxpayers to file correct income tax returns and combat the continuing flow of tax protester-type arguments, the Code has provisions that penalize a taxpayer for taking a frivolous position on his income tax return or before a court.

---

25. *See Ex parte Bakelite Corp.*, 279 U.S. 438, 451–52 (1929) (holding that Congress may create legislative courts); *Nash Miami Motors, Inc. v. Commissioner*, 358 F.2d 636 (5th Cir. 1966), *cert. denied*, 385 U.S. 918 (1966); *Burns, Stix Friedman & Co. v. Commissioner*, 57 T.C. 392 (1971). For a further discussion of Article I and Article III courts, *see* Chapter 5, *Judicial Opinions.*
26. *Masat v. Commissioner*, 784 F.2d 573 (5th Cir. 1986).
27. *Freytag v. Commissioner*, 501 U.S. 868 (1991).
28. Sec. 3707, IRS Restructuring and Reform Act of 1998, P.L. 105-206.

> **Quote:**
>
> "Like moths to a flame, some people find themselves irresistibly drawn to the tax pro-
> testor movement's illusory claim that there is no legal requirement to pay federal in-
> come tax. And, like moths, these people sometimes get burned."
>
> *United States v. Sloan*, 939 F.2d 499, 499–500 (7th Cir. 1991).

Civil penalties. If a taxpayer files a tax return that does not contain information sufficient to calculate the tax liability or contains information that on its face indicates the
tax liability is substantially incorrect and such information is based on a frivolous position or a desire to impede administration of the tax law, a $5,000 penalty can be im-
posed.[29]

A penalty can be imposed if the taxpayer fails to timely file a tax return or pay the tax[30]
or fails to pay estimated taxes.[31] A penalty can be imposed if the taxpayer files a return
that contains an underpayment attributable to negligence or disregard of the rules, a substantial understatement of tax, substantial valuation misstatement, substantial overstatement of pension liabilities, or substantial estate or gift tax valuation understatement.[32]
If any portion of an underpayment is attributable to fraud, a penalty of 75 percent of the
underpayment attributable to fraud may be imposed.[33]

A penalty of up to $25,000 can be imposed if it appears the taxpayer instituted the
proceedings before the Tax Court primarily to cause delay, the taxpayer's position was
frivolous, or the taxpayer failed to pursue available administrative remedies.[34] If the taxpayer brings a frivolous or groundless action in a court besides the Tax Court, the maximum penalty is $10,000.[35]

Criminal penalties. Any taxpayer who willfully attempts to evade or defeat tax may be
found guilty of a felony and fined not more than $100,000 or imprisoned not more than
five years or both.[36] A taxpayer who fails to pay estimated taxes may be found guilty of a
misdemeanor and fined not more than $25,000 or imprisoned not more than one year,
or both.[37]

If a taxpayer willfully supplies false or fraudulent information on his Form W-4, he may
be liable for a penalty of up to $25,000 or imprisonment of up to a year, or both.[38] A tax-
payer who willfully makes and subscribes any return, statement, or other document under
the penalties of perjury or willfully aids or assists in or advises the preparation of a return,
affidavit, or other document which is fraudulent or is false in any material matter may be
found guilty of a felony and fined not more than $100,000 or imprisoned not more than
three years, or both.[39]

If a taxpayer attempts to intimidate or impede the enforcement of the Code through
force or threat of force, including through threatening letters or communications, he may

---

29. I.R.C. § 6702.
30. I.R.C. § 6651.
31. I.R.C. § 6654.
32. I.R.C. § 6662.
33. I.R.C. § 6663.
34. I.R.C. § 6673(a).
35. I.R.C. § 6673(b).
36. I.R.C. § 7201.
37. I.R.C. § 7203.
38. I.R.C. § 7203.
39. I.R.C. § 7206.

be fined up to $5,000, imprisoned up to three years, or both. A threat of force includes threats of bodily harm to an IRS employee or his family.[40]

IRS Notice on Point:[41]

Notice 2010-33

I. Purpose

Positions that are the same as or similar to the positions listed in this notice are identified as **frivolous** for purposes of the **penalty** for a "**frivolous** tax return" under section 6702 (a) of the Internal Revenue Code and the **penalty** for a "specified **frivolous** submission" under section 6702 (b). Persons who file a purported return of tax, including an original or amended return, based on one or more of these positions are subject to a **penalty** of $5,000 if the purported return of tax does not contain information on which the substantial correctness of the self-assessed determination of tax may be judged or contains information that on its face indicates the self-assessed determination of tax is substantially incorrect. Likewise, persons who submit a "specified submission" (namely, a request for a collection due process hearing or an application for an installment agreement, offer-in-compromise, or taxpayer assistance order) based on one or more of the positions listed in this notice are subject to a **penalty** of $5,000. The **penalty** may also be applied if the purported return or any portion of the specified submission is not based on a position set forth in this notice, yet reflects a desire to delay or impede the administration of Federal tax laws for purposes of section 6702(a)(2)(B) or 6702(b)(2)(A)(ii). The **penalty** will be imposed only when the **frivolous** position or desire to delay or impede the administration of Federal tax laws appears on the face of the return, purported return, or specified submission, including any attachments to the return or submission.

II. Background

Section 407 of Tax Relief and Health Care Act of 2006, Pub. L. No. 109-432, 120 Stat. 2922, 2960–62 (2006), amended section 6702 to increase the amount of the **penalty** for **frivolous** tax returns from $500 to $5,000 and to impose a **penalty** of $5,000 on any person who submits a "specified **frivolous** submission." A submission is a "specified **frivolous** submission" if it is a "specified submission" (defined in section 6702(b)(2)(B) as a request for a hearing under section 6320 or 6330 or an application under section 6159, 7122 or 7811) and any portion of the submission (i) is based on a position identified by the Secretary as **frivolous** or (ii) reflects a desire to delay or impede administration of the Federal tax laws. Section 6702 was further amended to add a new subsection (c) requiring the Secretary to prescribe, and periodically revise, a list of positions identified as **frivolous**. Notice 2007-30, 2007-14 I.R.B. 883, contained the prescribed list. Notice 2007-30 was modified and superseded by Notice 2008-14, 2008-4 I.R.B. 310, which added **frivolous** positions to the prescribed list. This notice revises the list in Notice 2008-14 to add additional positions identified as **frivolous**. The positions that have been added are found in paragraphs 21, 22, and 27.

III. Discussion

Positions that are the same as or similar to the following are **frivolous**.

---

40. I.R.C. §7212.
41. For a discussion on what a "Notice" is, see Chapter 6, *Public Guidance from the Office of Chief Counsel.*

(1) Compliance with the internal revenue laws is voluntary or optional and not required by law, including arguments that:

- (a) Filing a Federal tax or information return or paying tax is purely voluntary under the law, or similar arguments described as **frivolous** in Rev. Rul. 2007-20, 2007-1 C.B. 863.

- (b) Nothing in the Internal Revenue Code imposes a requirement to file a return or pay tax, or that a person is not required to file a tax return or pay a tax unless the Internal Revenue Service responds to the person's questions, correspondence, or a request to identify a provision in the Code requiring the filing of a return or the payment of tax.

- (c) There is no legal requirement to file a Federal income tax return because the instructions to Forms 1040, 1040A, or 1040EZ or the Treasury regulations associated with the filing of the forms do not display an OMB control number as required by the Paperwork Reduction Act of 1980, 44 U.S.C. § 3501 *et seq.*, or similar arguments described as **frivolous** in Rev. Rul. 2006-21, 2006-1 C.B. 745.

- (d) Because filing a tax return is not required by law, the Service must prepare a return for a taxpayer who does not file one in order to assess and collect tax.

- (e) A taxpayer has an option under the law to file a document or set of documents in lieu of a return or elect to file a tax return reporting zero taxable income and zero tax liability even if the taxpayer received taxable income during the taxable period for which the return is filed, or similar arguments described as **frivolous** in Rev. Rul. 2004-34, 2004-1 C.B. 619.

- (f) An employer is not legally obligated to withhold income or employment taxes on employees' wages.

- (g) Only persons who have contracted with the government by applying for a governmental privilege or benefit, such as holding a Social Security number, are subject to tax, and those who have contracted with the government may choose to revoke the contract at will.

- (h) A taxpayer may lawfully decline to pay taxes if the taxpayer disagrees with the government's use of tax revenues, or similar arguments described as **frivolous** in Rev. Rul. 2005-20, 2005-1 C.B. 821.

- (i) An administrative summons issued by the Service is *per se* invalid and compliance with a summons is not legally required.

(2) The Internal Revenue Code is not law (or "positive law") or its provisions are ineffective or inoperative, including the sections imposing an income tax or requiring the filing of tax returns, because the provisions have not been implemented by regulations even though the provisions in question either (a) do not expressly require the Secretary to issue implementing regulations to become effective or (b) expressly require implementing regulations which have been issued.

(3) A taxpayer's income is excluded from taxation when the taxpayer rejects or renounces United States citizenship because the taxpayer is a citizen exclusively of a State (sometimes characterized as a "natural-born citizen" of a "sovereign state"), that is claimed to be a separate country or otherwise not subject to the laws of the United States. This position includes the argument that the United States does not include all or a part of the physical territory of the 50 States and instead consists of only places such as the District of Columbia, Commonwealths and Territories (*e.g.*, Puerto Rico),

and Federal enclaves (*e.g.*, Native American reservations and military installations), or similar arguments described as **frivolous** in Rev. Rul. 2004-28, 2004-1 C.B. 624, or Rev. Rul. 2007-22, 2007-1 C.B. 866.

(4) Wages, tips, and other compensation received for the performance of personal services are not taxable income or are offset by an equivalent deduction for the personal services rendered, including an argument that a taxpayer has a "claim of right" to exclude the cost or value of the taxpayer's labor from income or that taxpayers have a basis in their labor equal to the fair market value of the wages they receive, or similar arguments described as **frivolous** in Rev. Rul. 2004-29, 2004-1 C.B. 627, or Rev. Rul. 2007-19, 2007-1 C.B. 843.

(5) United States citizens and residents are not subject to tax on their wages or other income derived from sources within the United States, as only foreign-based income or income received by nonresident aliens and foreign corporations from sources within the United States is taxable, and similar arguments described as **frivolous** in Rev. Rul. 2004-30, 2004-1 C.B. 622.

(6) A taxpayer has been untaxed, detaxed, or removed or redeemed from the Federal tax system though the taxpayer remains a United States citizen or resident, or similar arguments described as **frivolous** in Rev. Rul. 2004-31, 2004-1 C.B. 617.

(7) Only certain types of taxpayers are subject to income and employment taxes, such as employees of the Federal government, corporations, nonresident aliens, or residents of the District of Columbia or the Federal territories, or similar arguments described as **frivolous** in Rev. Rul. 2006-18, 2006-1 C.B. 743.

(8) Only certain types of income are taxable, for example, income that results from the sale of alcohol, tobacco, or firearms or from transactions or activities that take place in interstate commerce.

(9) Federal income taxes are unconstitutional or a taxpayer has a constitutional right not to comply with the Federal tax laws for one of the following reasons:

- (a) The First Amendment permits a taxpayer to refuse to pay taxes based on religious or moral beliefs.
- (b) A taxpayer may withhold payment of taxes or the filing of a tax return until the Service or other government entity responds to a First Amendment petition for redress of grievances.
- (c) Mandatory compliance with, or enforcement of, the tax laws invades a taxpayer's right to privacy under the Fourth Amendment.
- (d) The requirement to file a tax return is an unreasonable search and seizure contrary to the Fourth Amendment.
- (e) Income taxation, tax withholding, or the assessment or collection of tax is a "taking" of property without due process of law or just compensation in violation of the Fifth Amendment.
- (f) The Fifth Amendment privilege against self-incrimination grants taxpayers the right not to file returns or the right to withhold all financial information from the Service.
- (g) The Ninth Amendment exempts those with religious or other objections to military spending from paying taxes to the extent the taxes will be used for military spending.
- (h) Mandatory or compelled compliance with the internal revenue laws is a form of involuntary servitude prohibited by the Thirteenth Amendment.

- (i) Individuals may not be taxed unless they are "citizens" within the meaning of the Fourteenth Amendment.
- (j) The Sixteenth Amendment was not ratified, has no effect, contradicts the Constitution as originally ratified, lacks an enabling clause, or does not authorize a non-apportioned, direct income tax.
- (k) Taxation of income attributed to a trust, which is a form of contract, violates the constitutional prohibition against impairment of contracts.
- (l) Similar constitutional arguments described as **frivolous** in Rev. Rul. 2005-19, 2005-1 C.B. 819.

* * *

(46) Any position described as **frivolous** in any revenue ruling or other published guidance in existence when the return adopting the position is filed with or the specified submission adopting the position is submitted to the Service.

Returns or submissions that contain positions not listed above, which on their face have no basis for validity in existing law, or which have been deemed **frivolous** in a published opinion of the United States Tax Court or other court of competent jurisdiction, may be determined to reflect a desire to delay or impede the administration of Federal tax laws and thereby subject to the $5,000 **penalty.**

The list of **frivolous** positions above will be periodically revised as required by section 6702 (c).

IV. Effective Date

This Notice is effective for submissions made and issues raised after April 7, 2010. For submissions made and issues raised between January 14, 2008 and April 7, 2010, Notice 2008-14 applies.

V. Effect on Other Documents

Notice 2008-14 is modified and superseded.

VI. Drafting Information

The principal author of this Notice is Emily M. Lesniak, Office of the Associate Chief Counsel, Procedure and Administration. For further information contact Emily M. Lesniak at 202-622-4940 (not a toll-free number).

6. Where Can the Constitution Be Found?

The Constitution can be found in Volume One of the United States Code. It can also be found at various websites.

C. Main Points

- The Constitution gives Congress the authority to impose tax.
- A federal tax must be uniform.
- The federal income tax is constitutional.

- The courts have repeatedly rejected many constitutional arguments taxpayers have raised in an attempt to avoid paying income tax.
- Civil and criminal penalties may be imposed if a taxpayer takes a frivolous or unsupportable position on his income tax return or before a court.
- Where can the Constitution be found?

Constitution

Title	Publisher	Comments
United States Code	Government Printing Office	Located in Volume One.
United States Code Annotated	West	Located at the beginning of the set.
United States Code Service Lawyers Edition	LexisNexis	Located at the beginning of the set.
On-line: • www.gpoaccess.gov • www.thomas.loc.gov • www.archives.gov	• Government Printing Office • The Library of Congress • U.S. National Archives & Records Administration	• www.gpoaccess.gov/constitution/index.html • http://loc.gov/law/help/usconlaw/index.php • http://www.archives.gov/exhibits/charters/constitution.html

D. Related Articles for Further Reading

- Jason A. Derr, *"Taxnapping": How* Murphy v. IRS *Used Direct Taxation to Steal the Tax Reform Debate*, 12 Barry L. Rev. 21 (2009).
- Yoseph Edrey, *Constitutional Review and Tax Law: An Analytical Framework*, 56 Am. U.L. Rev. 1187 (2007).
- Stephen W. Mazza and Tracy A. Kaye, *Section IV: Constitutional and Administrative Law: Restricting the Legislative Power to Tax in the United States*, 54 Am. J. Comp. L. 641 (2006).
- Burgess J.W. Raby and William L. Raby, *Frivolity, Tax Practitioners, and the Tax Law*, Tax Notes 561 (January 31, 2005).
- Erik M. Jensen, *Interpreting the Sixteenth Amendment (By Way of the Direct Tax Clauses)*, 21 Const. Comm. 355 (2004).
- James L. Wittenback, A *Synopsis of "The Truth About Frivolous Tax Arguments,"* Tax Notes 977 (August 30, 2004).
- Erik M. Jensen, *The Constitution Matters in Taxation*, 2003 TNT 155–21.
- Calvin H. Johnson, *Purging Out* Pollock: *The Constitutionality of Federal Wealth or Sales Taxes*, Tax Notes 1723 (December 30, 2002).
- Erik M. Jensen, *The Taxing Power, the Sixteenth Amendment, and the Meaning of "Incomes,"* 33 Ariz. St. L. J. 1057 (2001).
- Bruce Ackerman, *Taxation and the Constitution*, 99 Colum. L. Rev. 1 (1999).

- Calvin H. Johnson, *The Constitutional Meaning of "Apportionment of Direct Taxes,"* Tax Notes, Aug. 3, 1998, at 591.

- Erik M. Jensen, *The Apportionment of "Direct Taxes": Are Consumption Taxes Constitutional?*, 97 Colum. L. Rev. 2334 (1997).

- Ellen E. Sward, *Legislative Courts, Article III, and the Seventh Amendment*, 77 North Carolina Law Review 1037 (1997).

- John O. McGinnis and Michael B. Rapparport, *The Rights of Legislators and the Wrongs of Interpretation: A Further Defense of the Constitutionality of Legislative Supermajority Rules*, 4 Duke L.J. 327 (1997).

E. Problems

1. The source of the congressional power of taxation is:
   a. The Sixteenth Amendment to the Constitution.
   b. The Constitution.
   c. The Commerce Clause of the Constitution.
   d. The Sixteenth Amendment together with the Constitution.

2. Wages are not taxable if the taxpayer can establish the following:
   a. That the wages did not constitute an accession to wealth.
   b. That he objects to taxes being collected to pay for any war effort.
   c. That he has opted out of the voluntary tax system.
   d. None of the above; wages are taxable.

3. If a taxpayer has embezzled money:
   a. He is excused from filing an income tax return based on the Fifth Amendment privilege against self-incrimination.
   b. He is not liable for any income tax as the tax applies only to income received from legal sources.
   c. He may be liable for tax penalties if he fails to properly report his income, including the embezzled money.
   d. If he fails to report the income, he can be charged with embezzlement or evading income tax, but not both.

4. Visit the IRS website (www.irs.gov) and locate information on frivolous tax positions. Based on that information, identify which of the following arguments are considered frivolous:
   a. The Sixteenth Amendment is invalid because it was not properly ratified.
   b. Wages are not income because there is no accession to wealth; the value of what you give up is equal to the value of what you receive.
   c. Only employees of the federal government are liable for the federal income tax.
   d. The payment of tax is voluntary; thus a taxpayer can elect not to pay.
   e. Only foreign-source income is taxable.

5. Locate Article 1 of the Constitution. Locate Article 3 of the Constitution. Recall that the United States Tax Court is a court created under Article 1 of the Constitution. What courts can you identify as having been created under Article 3 of the Constitution?

6. Consider *Ontario Power Generation Inc. v. United States*, 369 F.3d 1298 (Fed. Cir. 2004).

   a. What constitutional provision was at issue?
   b. Why was the provision relevant to the issue before the court?
   c. What did the court hold on that issue?

7. Consider *Cammarano v. United States*, 358 U.S. 498 (1959), and *Speiser v. Randall*, 357 U.S. 513 (1958).

   a. What constitutional challenge do the cases have in common?
   b. Why didn't the Supreme Court apply the same level of scrutiny in both cases?

8. Jim, a very wealthy individual, wants to challenge the constitutionality of the United States progressive tax rate system. Jim claims that the distinctions in tax rates based on income level violate the equal protection component of the Fifth Amendment. What must Jim demonstrate in order to be successful in his challenge?

9. An agent from the IRS Criminal Investigation Division appears at Mr. Markbe's place of business. The agent has information that Mr. Markbe has been storing cash received from the sale of stolen car parts in a safe deposit box located on the premises. The agent explains that, to the extent Mr. Markbe has received an accession to wealth from the sale of stolen car parts, he has gross income that he is required to report. Not to do so could result in criminal and/or civil penalties. The agent has requested permission to search the business premises. He also explains that he is only interested in tax violations. Any crime directly related to the sale of stolen car parts is outside his jurisdiction. Mr. Markbe, a long time client of yours, has called you for advice. You only handle the client's business and tax affairs. Can you identify any potential constitutional issues?

10. Ms. Witherspoon walks into your office. She has been your client for many years. She tells you that she has just come from a tax seminar on how to reduce income tax liability. The presenter at the seminar stated that any taxpayer who was opposed to war efforts could reduce his or her tax payments by the amount that otherwise would be allocated to war efforts. To assist the participants in properly calculating the portion of the tax payment that would be allocable to war efforts, the presenter offered to sell materials with step-by-step, easy-to-follow instructions. Ms. Witherspoon wants to know if she should purchase the materials, or if, instead, you could do the calculation for her. What do you tell her?

11. Mr. Benedetti filed an income tax return where the amounts were all zeros, from income to net taxable income to tax liability. After the IRS issued a statutory notice of deficiency, Mr. Benedetti filed a petition in the Tax Court contesting the deficiency. He argued to the court that wages were property and that property did not constitute gross income for tax purposes. Should Mr. Benedetti be liable under section 6673 for maintaining a frivolous position?

12. Mr. Valenti was a professional gambler. Before the Tax Court he argued that the government's refusal to allow gambling losses from his gambling business violated the Equal Protection Clause of the Constitution. Should Mr. Valenti be liable under section 6673 for maintaining a frivolous position?

13. Mr. and Mrs. Sochia argued before the Tax Court that the Code violates various amendments to the Constitution and that tax returns that contain no information, but instead claim the Fifth Amendment privilege, are valid. Mr. and Mrs. Sochia also argued before the Tax Court that section 61(a) of the Code is incompatible with the

Sixteenth Amendment of the Constitution. Should Mr. and Mrs. Sochia be liable for a penalty under section 6673(a) because their position is frivolous or groundless? Would your answer be influenced by the fact that Mr. and Mrs. Sochia had made the same arguments, and the Tax Court had rejected the same arguments, on two previous occasions? How much of a penalty would you impose?

14. Is the income tax a "direct tax" under the Constitution?

Chapter 3

statutory law

Federal Public Law

Federal Public Law

- *What is federal public law?*

- *How does a bill become law?*

- *What happens when a bill becomes public law?*

- *What weight does the court give legislative history?*

- *Where can public law and its history be found?*

Alex read the Code section from beginning to end one more time. He knew that Congress had amended it, and that certain portions of the old provisions were grandfathered in. What he didn't know was where the information on the grandfather provision was. And, he needed to find out in order to determine if his client had a tax concern or not.

Finally, giving up searching on his own, he headed for the law firm's library. Perhaps the staff librarian could help him.

After Alex explained to George what he was looking for, George asked, "Have you checked the Public Laws?"

Alex just stared at him, wondering if George thought he hadn't even checked the Code before coming to him with a question. "Well," he answered slowly, "I checked the Internal Revenue Code, if that is what you mean."

"There is more to the law than what you will find in the Internal Revenue Code. The Public Laws have all sorts of provisions that never make it into the Code, but can have a huge impact." Alex's stomach turned just a bit as he considered the implications of this fact. "Here, let me show you," George said as he turned down the next aisle of books.

Contents

A. Key Terms

After completing this chapter, you should be familiar with the following key terms:

➤ Joint Committee on Taxation *provide significant amount of assistance*
➤ Congressional Record
➤ Bill Number
➤ House Ways and Means Committee
➤ Report of the Ways and Means Committee
➤ Committee Print
➤ Senate Finance Committee
➤ Report of the Finance Committee
➤ Joint Explanatory Statement of the Conference Committee
➤ Report of the Conference Committee
➤ Blue Book
➤ Public Law Number
➤ United States Statutes at Large
➤ United States Code
➤ Non-codified Provision

B. Discussion

1. What Is Federal Public Law?

The applicable tax laws are contained in the public law. The public law most often re-lied upon by tax attorneys and accountants is codified in the Internal Revenue Code. Also, attorneys and accounts may rely upon the Employee Retirement Income Security Act (ERISA), relating to the regulation of retirement plans; the Federal Bankruptcy Law; or

other federal laws. However, not all public law is codified; such provisions cannot be found in the United States Code and are often referred to as "noncodified provisions." To understand and interpret the relevant public laws, both codified and noncodified, the researcher should be familiar with the process by which a bill becomes a law and where such laws can be found.

2. The Origin of Federal Public Law— How a Bill Becomes Law

The Constitution grants Congress the power "to lay and collect Taxes, Duties, Imposts and Excises."[1] In addition, it provides that all bills for raising revenue must originate in the House of Representatives.[2] Accordingly, the legislative trail of a law begins in the House of Representatives. Along the way, the Staff of the Joint Committee on Taxation provides a significant amount of assistance.

Quote:

School House Rock
Listen Here I'm Just a Bill

Boy: Whew! You sure gotta climb a lot of steps to get to this Capitol Building here in Washington. But I wonder who that sad little scrap of paper is?

Bill: I'm just a bill.
Yes, I'm only a bill.
And I'm sitting here on Capitol Hill.
Well, it's a long, long journey
To the capital city.
It's a long, long wait
While I'm sitting in committee,
But I know I'll be a law some day
At least I hope and pray that I will
But today I am still just a bill.

Boy: Gee, Bill, you certainly have a lot of patience and courage.

Bill: Well, I got this far. When I started I wasn't even a bill, I was just an idea. Some folks back home decided they wanted a law passed, so they called their local Congressman, and he said, "You're right, there oughta be a law." Then he sat down and wrote me out and introduced me to Congress. And I became a bill, and I'll remain a bill until they decide to make me a law.

I'm just a bill
Yes I'm only a bill,
And I got as far as Capitol Hill.
Well, now I'm stuck in committee
And I'll sit here and wait

---

1. Art. 1, sec. 8.
2. Art. 1, sec. 7.

While a few key Congressmen discuss
and debate
Whether they should let me be a law.
How I hope and pray that they will,
But today I am still just a bill.

Boy: Listen to those Congressmen arguing! Is all that discussion and debate about you?

Bill: Yeah, I'm one of the lucky ones. Most bills never even get this far. I hope they decide to report on me favorably, otherwise I may die.

Boy: Die?

Bill: Yeah, die in committee. Ooh, but it looks like I'm gonna live! Now I go to the House of Representatives, and they vote on me.

Boy: If they vote yes, what happens?

Bill: Then I go to the Senate and the whole thing starts all over again.

Boy: Oh no!

Bill: Oh yes!
I'm just a bill
Yes, I'm only a bill
And if they vote for me on Capitol Hill
Well, then I'm off to the White House
Where I'll wait in a line
With a lot of other bills
For the president to sign
And if he signs me, then I'll be a law.
How I hope and pray that he will,
But today I am still just a bill.

Boy: You mean even if the Whole Congress says you should be a law, the president can still say no?

Bill: Yes, that's called a veto. If the president vetoes me, I have to go back to Congress and they vote on me again, and by that time you're so old …

Boy: By that time it's very unlikely that you'll become a law. It's not easy to become a law, is it?

Bill: No!
But how I hope and pray that I will,
But today I am still just a bill.

Congressman: He signed you, Bill! Now you're a law!

Bill: Oh yes!!!

Schoolhouse Rock Site, www.schoolhouserock.tv/Bill.html (last visited April 3, 2010)

The **Joint Committee on Taxation** is a non-partisan, statutorily-created body made up of five members of the House Ways and Means Committee and five members of the Senate Finance Committee.[3] Of the five members from each Committee, three are

---

3. I.R.C. §§ 8001–8005, 8021–8023.

from the majority party and two are from the minority party.[4] During the first session of a Congress, the Chairman of the Joint Committee is the Chairman of the House Ways and Means Committee; during the second session of a Congress, the Chairman is the Chairman of the Senate Finance Committee. The Joint Committee on Taxation has a variety of statutorily defined duties,[5] including providing revenue estimates for all tax legislation considered by either the House or the Senate.[6] Nevertheless, it meets infrequently.

The Joint Committee has a permanent Staff headed by the Chief of Staff of the Joint Committee.[7] The Staff is involved at every stage of the legislative process, from development and analysis of proposals to preparing a statutory draft to preparing a description of the bill. The Staff advises Congress, generally, and committees as necessary.

> The Joint Committee on Taxation is a non-partisan, statutorily-created body made up of five members of the House Ways and Means Committee and five members of the Senate Finance Committee. The Staff of the Joint Committee is involved at every stage of the legislative process, from development and analysis of proposals to preparing a statutory draft to preparing a description of the bill.
>
> Additional information on the Joint Committee on Taxation can be found at www.jct.gov.

In the House of Representatives, the representative sponsoring a tax bill introduces the bill by placing it in the "hopper." The bill is given the designation "H.R." followed by a number. Usually a bill is assigned a number chronologically according to the order in which it is introduced in the two-year term. However, members may ask the bill clerk to reserve a particular number for assignment to his bill. The designation is retained throughout the life of the bill.

> **Example:**
> - The Jobs and Growth Tax Act of 2003 was designated "H.R. 2."
> - The Economic Growth and Tax Relief Reconciliation Act of 2001 was designated "H.R. 1836."
> - The Internal Revenue Service Restructuring and Reform Act of 1998 was designated "H.R. 2676."

When the bill is introduced, the sponsoring member can give introductory remarks. If approval is requested and given, the introductory remarks are printed in the Congressional Record.

The Congressional Record is an account of the proceedings and debates of the House and Senate.[8] In general, the Record reflects a verbatim account of the members' words. Statements and speeches not actually read or spoken during a session but included in the Congressional Record are identified by the use of a "bullet" symbol. The Congressional

---

4. I.R.C. § 8002(a).

5. *See, e.g.,* I.R.C. § 8022, 6405.

6. Section 201(g), as amended by the Balanced Budget and Emergency Deficit Control Act of 1985, P.L. 99-177, 99 Stat. 1037.

7. I.R.C. § 8004.

8. The Congressional Record is governed by 44 U.S.C. §§ 901–910.

Record is published daily and bound with an index and history of bills and resolutions at the conclusion of each session of the Congress.

> The **Congressional Record**, published by the government daily, contains an almost verbatim account of the proceedings and debates of the House and Senate.

Items printed in the Congressional Record include items such as:

- Introductory remarks;
- Referrals to committees;
- Committee Reports;
- Floor debates; and
- Conference Reports.

The House and the Senate report their proceedings in separate portions of the Record, and each controls the contents of what is reported.

Once a bill is introduced, it is referred to the appropriate standing committee. Because the House Ways and Means Committee has primary jurisdiction over tax matters, the bill is referred to that Committee. After receiving the bill, the Committee may:

- Consider the bill and report (approve) it with or without amendments or recommendation; *by Vote*
- Consider, partially or entirely rewrite, and then report the bill; *by Vote*
- Consider and reject the bill; or *by Vote*
- Refuse to consider the bill. *by Vote*

In considering the bill, the Committee may hold hearings, which are generally open to the public. A transcript of each hearing is prepared. Witnesses may appear and testify; however, a witness is usually required to file a written statement of his proposed testimony prior to testifying and, at the hearing, may provide only a summary of that testimony. Any witness testimony (prepared or actual) is printed in the hearing record, which is included in the Congressional Record.

The Staff of the Joint Committee on Taxation may prepare a hearing pamphlet. The pamphlet would set forth a variety of matters, including the current law, a description of the bill, the proposed changes, and a revenue estimate. The Staff may also include various factors the Ways and Means Committee may want to consider. Finally, the Staff will attend the hearings and answer questions, brief Representatives and their staff on issues, and assist Representatives in preparing for taking testimony at hearings.

Example:

The following is an example of a document prepared by the Staff of the Joint Committee on Taxation to assist the Ways and Means Committee in considering a bill:

[JOINT COMMITTEE PRINT]

TAX REFORM PROPOSALS
IN CONNECTION WITH
COMMITTEE ON WAYS AND MEANS MARKUP

Prepared by the Staff
of the
Joint Committee on Taxation

September 26, 1985

JCS-11-85

U.S. GOVERNMENT PRINTING OFFICE

INTRODUCTION

This document [1] provides a summary description of tax reform proposals in connection with the markup by the Committee on Ways and Means, beginning on September 25, 1985.

The document, in columnar form for each item, includes present law (Col. 2), the President's tax reform proposal (Col. 3), and a possible option (Col. 4).

Part I describes individual income tax provisions. Part II describes provisions relating to the tax treatment of capital income. Part III describes corporate tax provisions and ESOPs. Part IV describes tax shelter-related provisions. Part V describes minimum tax provisions. Part VII describes foreign-related tax provisions. Part VII describes provisions related to tax-exempt bonds. Part VIII describes provisions relating to the taxation of financial institutions. Part IX describes accounting-related tax provisions. Part X describes tax provisions relating to insurance products and companies. Part XI describes pensions and deferred compensation and fringe benefits. Part XII describes income taxation of trusts and estates and the generation-skipping transfer tax. Finally, Part XIII describes provisions relating to taxpayer compliance and tax administration.

[1] This document may be cited as follows: Joint Committee on Taxation, *Tax Reform Proposals in Connection With Committee on Ways and Means Markup* (JCS-11-85), September 26, 1985.

For sale by the Superintendent of Documents, U.S. Government Printing Office
Washington, D.C. 20402

IV. TAX SHELTERS

Item	Present Law	President's Proposal	Possible Option
A. At-Risk Rules	The loss limitation at-risk rules limit the losses in excess of income with respect to an activity, which individuals and closely held corporations may deduct, to the amount the taxpayer has actually invested in the activity, including borrowed amounts to the extent the taxpayer is personally liable to repay or has pledged other non-financed property (except property used in the activity as security, and has not borrowed the funds from a person with an interest in the activity other than as a creditor. Closely held corporations engaged in certain equipment leasing activities and in certain active business activities are excepted from the rules. The at-risk rules apply to all activities except the holding of real estate.	The exception for the activity of holding real estate would be repealed. *Effective date.*—The proposal would be effective with respect to losses attributable to property acquired after December 31, 1985.	Same as President's proposal.
B. Investment Interest			
1. General limitation	The deduction for investment interest of noncorporate taxpayers is limited to the sum of $10,000, plus net investment income, plus certain deductible expenditures in excess of rental income from net lease property. Interest deductions not allowed due to this limitation carry over to future years.	The deduction for all nonbusiness interest of noncorporate taxpayers would be limited to the sum of: interest on debt secured by the taxpayer's principal residence to the extent of its value, plus $3,000, plus net investment income, plus certain deductible expenditures in excess of rental income from net lease property.	Modify the President's proposal to provide that the deduction for all nonbusiness interest in excess of net investment income plus certain deductible expenditures in excess of rental income from net lease property) of noncorporate taxpayers is limited to the greater of (i) interest on debt secured by the taxpayer's principal residence to the extent of its fair market value, or (ii) $20,000. Housing cooperatives may qualify under (i) subject to appropriate limitations.
2. Interest subject to limitation	Investment interest subject to the limitation is interest on debt to purchase or carry investment property. The treatment of interest expense to acquire stock of S corporations or an interest in limited partnerships is not entirely clear under present law.	Nonbusiness interest subject to the limitation is broader than present-law investment interest, and would mean all interest not incurred in a trade or business, including the taxpayer's share of interest of S corporations in whose management he does not actively participate, and the taxpayer's share of interest expense of limited partnerships in which he is a limited partner.	Same as the President's proposal, except that investment interest also includes the taxpayer's share of interest expense of certain trusts and other entities in which he is a limited entrepreneur.

IV. TAX SHELTERS—(Continued)

Item	Present Law	President's Proposal	Possible Option
3. Investment income defined	Net investment income means investment income net of investment expense. Investment income means interest, dividends, rents, royalties, short-term capital gain from disposition of investment property and depreciation recapture not from conduct of a trade or business. Investment expense means deductible investment expenses (other than interest), except that straight line (not accelerated) depreciation over useful life, and cost (not percentage) depletion are used in calculating investment expenses.	Investment income is expanded to include the same income items as present law plus the taxpayer's share of all income of S corporations in whose management the taxpayer does not actively participate and his share of all income of limited partnerships in which the taxpayer is a limited partner. Investment expense would be determined the same as under present law, except that the Treasury report RCRS depreciation schedule would be substituted for present-law straight-line depreciation.	Same as President's proposal except that investment income also includes the taxable portion of long-term capital gain and the taxpayer's share of income of certain trusts and other entities in which he is a limited entrepreneur; and investment expense also includes the depreciation and depletion the taxpayer actually utilized rather than RCRS depreciation or cost depletion, so that the net investment income portion of the limitation reflects the taxpayer's actual net investment income subject to tax.
4. Net leases	Property subject to net lease is treated as an investment, unless the trade or business deductions exceed 15 percent of the rental income.	Same as present law.	Modify the President's proposal to provide that, to the extent the taxpayer performs personal services in lieu of incurring deductible expenses with respect to directly owned leased property in certain circumstances, the value of such services may be included with the actual trade or business deductions in determining whether such deductions exceed 15 percent of the rental income.
5. Rental property	Interest on rental property used for both business and personal purposes (e.g., a vacation home, in some circumstances) is not subject to the interest limitation. Expenses of such rental property are generally allocated to business use in the ratio of the number of days the property is rented at a fair rental to the number of days the property is used in the taxable year.	A portion of interest on business rental property used by the taxpayer for both business and personal purposes (e.g., a vacation home in some circumstances) is treated as business interest not subject to the limitation, in the ratio of the number of days the property is rented at a fair rental to the number of days in the taxable year.	Retain present law regarding allocation of expenses of rental property used for both business and personal purposes, and apply the present law allocation ratio, in lieu of the ratio of the President's proposal, to determine the portion of business interest subject to the limitation.
6. Effective date		*Effective date.*—The limitation would be effective for interest paid or incurred in taxable years beginning on or after January 1, 1986, regardless of when the obligation was incurred. The first phase-in rule is that the $10,000 limit under present law would be reduced to $3,000 for taxable years beginning on or after January 1, 1988. The second phase-in rule is that interest not subject to the limitation under present law, but which would be subject to the expanded limitation, would become subject to the limitation ratably (10 percent p.r year) over 10 years commencing with taxable years beginning in 1986. Thus, 100 percent of interest subject to the expanded limitation would have become subject to it in taxable years commencing in 1995.	*Effective date.*—Generally the same as the President's proposal, except that the first phase-in rule does not apply.

After the hearings, the **Ways and Means Committee** "marks up" the bill. When the mark-up is complete, the Ways and Means Committee, in conjunction with its staff and often the Staff of the Joint Committee on Taxation, prepares the **Report of the Ways and Means Committee.** The report will include, among other items, the language of the bill as agreed to by the Committee and an explanation of the provisions. House Ways and Means Committee reports are numbered by chamber (H.R.), Congressional term, and assigned a number chronologically according to the order in which it is filed with the Clerk of the House during the two-year term.

Example:

H.R. Rep. No. 105-364 refers to a report filed in the House of Representatives during the 105th term of Congress; it was the 364th report to have been filed during that two-year term.

Each term of Congress stretches over two years. Thus, the Congressional term does not reflect the year in which the report was filed. The following chart lists the recent terms of Congress and the years covered by the term:

Term of Congress	Years
112th	2011–2012
111th	2009–2010
110th	2007–2008
109th	2005–2006
108th	2003–2004
107th	2001–2002
106th	1999–2000
105th	1997–1998
104th	1995–1996
103rd	1993–1994
102nd	1991–1992
101st	1989–1990
100th	1987–1988

Practice Note:

The years that a term of Congress covers can be determined by using the following formulas:

Through 1999: (term x 2) – 112 = year (and previous year)
2000 and forward: (term x 2) – 212 = year (and previous year)

For example:
The 105th term covers the years 1998 and 1997.
(105 x 2) – 112 =
210 – 112 = 98
1998 and 1997

The 108th term covers the years 2004 and 2003.
(108 x 2) – 212 =
216 – 212 = 2004
2004 and 2003

The report of the Ways and Means Committee must contain:

• The Committee's recorded vote;

• Oversight findings and recommendations;

• Estimate of the costs that would be incurred in carrying out the bill in the fiscal year reported and in each of the following five fiscal years;

• An estimate and comparison prepared by the Congressional Budget Office;

- A summary of any oversight findings and recommendations made by the Government Operations Committee;
- A detailed analytical statement as to the bill's potential inflationary impact on prices and costs; and
- If the bill repeals or amends any statute, the report must contain a section that shows the proposed deletions and insertions.

Any committee member may file a supplemental opinion, minority opinion, or additional views to the committee's report.

Each report is accompanied by an explanatory statement which generally includes:

- A summary of the origin of the bill and its background;
- The objectives of the bill;
- The hearings and other steps taken by the committee;
- A section-by-section analysis describing what each section of the bill provides; and
- A discussion of the amendments to the bill adopted by the subcommittee and full committee.

Example:

The following is a portion of Report No. 105-364, part 1, of the House Ways and Means Committee. It relates to H.R. 2676:

105TH CONGRESS *1st Session*	HOUSE OF REPRESENTATIVES	REPT. 105–364 Part 1

INTERNAL REVENUE SERVICE RESTRUCTURING AND REFORM ACT OF 1997

OCTOBER 31, 1997.—Committed to the Committee of the Whole House on the State of the Union and ordered to be printed

Mr. ARCHER, from the Committee on Ways and Means, submitted the following

R E P O R T

[To accompany H.R. 2676]

[Including cost estimate of the Congressional Budget Office]

together with

ADDITIONAL AND DISSENTING VIEWS

The Committee on Ways and Means, to whom was referred the bill (H.R. 2676) to amend the Internal Revenue Code of 1986 to restructure and reform the Internal Revenue Service, and for other purposes, having considered the same, report favorably thereon with an amendment and recommend that the bill as amended do pass.

CONTENTS

59–006

33

Subcommittee on Oversight.—The Subcommittee on Oversight held public hearings on IRS-related topics in 1997 as follows:

Annual Report of the Internal Revenue Service Taxpayer Advocate (February 25, 1997).

"High-Risk" Programs Within the Jurisdiction of the Committee on Ways and Means (March 4, 1997).

IRS Budget for Fiscal Year 1998 and the 1997 Tax Return Filing Season (March 18, 1997).

Electronic Federal Tax Payment System (April 16, 1997).

Report of the National Commission on Restructuring the Internal Revenue Service (July 24, 1997).

Recommendations of the National Commission on Restructuring the Internal Revenue Service to Expand Electronic Filing of Tax Returns (September 9, 1997).

Recommendations of the National Commission on Restructuring the Internal Revenue Service on Taxpayer Protections and Rights (September 26, 1997).

In addition, the Subcommittee on Oversight submitted recommendations on October 20, 1997, to the Full Committee relating to (1) electronic filing and (2) taxpayer rights and protections. These Subcommittee recommendations are the basis for the provisions in Title II and Title III, respectively, of the Committee bill. Chairman Archer had directed the Subcommittee on Oversight to review these two areas of the Commission's report and to make recommendations to the Full Committee.

II. EXPLANATION OF THE BILL

TITLE I. EXECUTIVE BRANCH GOVERNANCE

A. CREATION OF IRS OVERSIGHT BOARD

(sec. 101 of the bill and sec. 7802 of the Code)

PRESENT LAW

Under present law, the administration and enforcement of the internal revenue laws are performed by or under the supervision of the Secretary of the Treasury.[3]

Present law imposes standards of ethical conduct on Federal employees in order to avoid conflicts of interest. Criminal penalties are imposed on violations of these standards. In some cases, less strict standards apply to special government employees than to regular, full-time Federal government employees. In general, a special government employee is an individual who is expected to serve no more than 130 days during any 365-day period.

In general, the ethical conduct rules (1) prohibit a Federal employee from accepting compensation for representing clients before the agency in which the employee serves or against the United States;[4] (2) prohibit a Federal employee from acting as agent or attorney for anyone in a claim against the United States;[5] (3) impose post-employment restrictions on senior employees in order to pro-

---

[3] Code sec. 780(a).
[4] 18 U.S.C. sec. 203.
[5] 18 U.S.C. sec. 205.

34

hibit the unfair use of prior Government employment;[6] and (4) prohibit a Federal employee from participating personally and substantially in matters that affect his or her own financial interest or that of persons with certain relationships to the employee.[7]

In the case of a special government employee who serves less than 60 days in the preceding 365 days, the restrictions in (1) and (2) above only apply with respect to matters in which the special government employee personally and substantially participated in his or her official capacity.

One of the post-employment restrictions prohibits senior government employees from representing parties other than the United States before their former department or agency for one year after employment. This restriction does not apply to special government employees who serve less than 60 days in the final 1-year period of service.

Federal government employees compensated at certain pay grades are subject to public financial disclosure requirements. Special government employees who serve less than 60 days in a year are not subject to the public financial disclosure requirements, but are subject to confidential financial disclosure requirements.

REASONS FOR CHANGE

The Committee believes that a well-run IRS is critical to the operation of our tax system. Public confidence in the IRS must be restored so that our system of voluntary compliance will not be compromised. The Committee believes that most Americans are willing to pay their fair share of taxes, and that public faith in the IRS is key to maintaining that willingness.

The National Commission on Restructuring the IRS (the "Restructuring Commission"), which conducted a year-long study of the IRS, found that a number of factors contribute to current IRS management problems, including the following. While the Treasury is responsible for IRS oversight, it has generally provided little consistent strategic oversight or guidance to the IRS. The Secretary and Deputy Secretary have many other broad responsibilities, and generally leave the IRS largely independent. The average tenure of an IRS Commissioner is under 3 years, as is the average tenure of senior Treasury officials responsible for IRS oversight. Many of the issues that need to be addressed by the IRS will require expertise in various areas, particularly management and technology.

The Restructuring Commission concluded that "problems throughout the IRS cannot be solved without focus, consistency and direction from the top. The current structure, which includes Congress, the President, the Department of the Treasury, and the IRS itself, does not allow the IRS to set and maintain consistent long-term strategy and priorities, nor to develop and execute focused plans for improvement. Additionally, the structure does not ensure that the IRS budget, staffing and technology are targeted toward achieving organizational success."

The Committee shares the concerns of the Commission, and agrees that fundamental change in IRS management and oversight

---

[6] 18 U.S.C. sec. 207.
[7] 18 U.S.C. sec. 208.

35

is essential. The Committee believes that a new management structure that will bring greater expertise in more areas, focus, and continuity will help the IRS on the path toward becoming an efficient, responsive, and respected agency that always acts appropriately in carrying out its functions.

The Committee believes that private sector input is a necessary part of any new management structure. The Committee believes that the ethics rules applicable to special government employees (without regard to exceptions for length of service or pay grade) should be applied to the private sector members of the new IRS management. These rules will enhance the ability of such members to demonstrate impartiality in the performance of their duties, while not unduly restricting the available pool of potential candidates.

The Committee is aware that the taxpaying public may never relish contacts with the agency responsible for collecting taxes. Nevertheless, by establishing a new management structure that will better enable the IRS to develop and fulfill long-term goals, the Committee believes that the IRS will be able to gain public support, and will make contacts with the IRS as infrequent and as pleasant as possible. The Committee is also aware that changes being made to IRS management structure are not the final step, and that continued oversight of the IRS, by Congress as well as the Administration, is necessary in order to ensure long-term progress.

EXPLANATION OF PROVISION

Duties, responsibilities, and powers of the IRS Oversight Board

The bill provides for the establishment within the Treasury Department of the Internal Revenue Service Oversight Board (referred to as the "Board"). The general responsibilities of the Board are to oversee the Internal Revenue Service (the "IRS") in its administration, management, conduct, direction, and supervision of the execution and application of the internal revenue laws. The Board has no responsibilities or authority with respect to (1) the development and formulation of Federal tax policy relating to existing or proposed internal revenue laws, (2) law enforcement activities of the IRS, including compliance activities such as criminal investigations, examinations, and collection activities,[8] and (3) specific procurement activities of the IRS (e.g., selecting vendors or awarding contracts). As discussed more fully in Part B., below, the Board also has the authority to recommend candidates for IRS Commissioner to the President, and to recommend removal of the Commissioner. The members of the Board do not have authority to receive confidential taxpayer return information.[9]

The Board has the following specific responsibilities: (1) to review and approve strategic plans of the IRS, including the establishment

---

[8] This provision is not intended to limit the Board's authority with respect to the review and approval of strategic plans and the budget of the Commissioner or to preclude the Board from review of IRS operations generally.

[9] The bill does not affect the extent to which the Secretary of the Treasury (or the Deputy Secretary) and the IRS Commissioner have authority to receive confidential taxpayer return information under present law by virtue of such positions. Any request for information that cannot be disclosed to Board members and any contact relating to a specific taxpayer made by a private-life Board member or the union representative to an employee of the IRS must be reported by such employee to the Secretary and Joint Committee on Taxation.

After reported out of the Ways and Means Committee, the bill is scheduled for consideration on the House floor. However, a matter reported by the Ways and Means Committee may not be considered in the House until the third calendar day (excluding Saturdays, Sundays, and legal holidays) on which the report has been available to the members of the House. Thus, on occasion, where the matter is to be considered before the three-day time period has elapsed, the explanation will be prepared by the Staff of the Committee and published as a "**Committee Print**," rather than as a report. The House is not required to wait three days to consider a bill accompanied by a Print.

On the House floor, any proposed amendments to the bill must come within the House's strict germaneness requirements for floor amendments. After consideration, the House can recommit the bill to the Ways and Means Committee or pass the bill. A transcript of the House proceeding is reported in the Congressional Record.

If the bill passes, even though commonly still referred to as a bill, technically at this point the bill becomes an Act of the House of Representatives. It is then referred to the Senate.

Practice Note:

Important income and related tax bills for the current year that have been introduced, but not yet become law, can be found in Volume 19 of the CCH's Federal Standard Tax Reporter. With respect to each covered bill, it will list all actions taken and portions of the language proposed in the bill. Additional sources are discussed in Chapter 10, *Researching the Issue.*

The progress of a bill can also be tracked on-line through the following sources:

- thomas.loc.gov
- WestLaw
  CQBILLANLY
- Lexis
  Legal/Federal Legal/U.S./Archived Bill Text and Tracking

In the Senate, the bill follows substantially the same process as it did in the House. First, it is referred to a committee. All revenue bills are referred to the Senate Finance Committee. After receiving the bill, the Senate Finance Committee may:

- Consider the bill and report (approve) it with or without amendments or recommendation;
- Consider, partially or entirely rewrite, and then report the bill;
- Consider and reject the bill; or
- Refuse to consider the bill.

In considering the bill, the Senate Finance Committee may hold hearings, which are generally open to the public. A transcript of each hearing is prepared and the hearing record is included in the Congressional Record. As with the Ways and Means Committee, the Staff of the Joint Committee on Taxation will attend hearings, answer questions, brief members and their staff on issues, and assist members in preparing for taking testimony at hearings.

After the hearings, the Senate Finance Committee "marks up" the bill. If the changes to the bill are substantial, the Senate may delete the House bill in its entirety and substi-

tute its own text.[9] When the mark-up is complete, the committee and its staff prepare an explanation of the proposal, referred to as the **Report of the Senate Finance Committee.** The report must include:

- The estimated budget effects of the bill;
- The Committee's recorded vote; and
- Regulatory impact that might be incurred in carrying out the provisions.

The accompanying Explanation will:

- Include the legislative background of the bill;
- Describe the purposes and scope of the bill;
- Explain the committee revisions;
- Note proposed changes in existing law; and
- Usually include the views of the executive branch agencies consulted.

A Senate Finance Committee report is numbered by chamber (S.), Congressional term, and assigned a number chronologically according to the order in which it is filed with the Clerk of the Senate during the two-year tem.

Example:

- On May 15, 2001, the Senate Finance Committee favorably reported its version of H.R. 1836. The report was numbered S.Rep. No. 107-30. The report was printed by the 107th term of Congress and was the 30th report printed by the Senate.

- On April 22, 1998, an amendment in the nature of a substitute for H.R. 2676 was reported by the Senate Finance Committee. The report was numbered S.Rep. No. 105-174. The report was printed by the 105th term of Congress and was the 174th report printed by the Senate.

---

9. It is possible for the Senate Finance Committee to not formally consider the House version of the bill, but instead to approve its own version, originating in the Senate, of the bill. In such situations, the approved bill will be numbered in the Senate.

Example:

The following is a portion of Report No. 105-174 of the Finance Committee. It relates to H.R. 2676:

Calendar No. 341

105TH CONGRESS		REPORT
2d Session	SENATE	105–174

INTERNAL REVENUE SERVICE RESTRUCTURING AND REFORM ACT OF 1998

APRIL 22, 1998.—Ordered to be printed

Mr. ROTH, from the Committee on Finance,
submitted the following

REPORT

[To accompany H.R. 2676]

The Committee on Finance, to which was referred the bill (H.R. 2676) to amend the Internal Revenue Code of 1986 to restructure and reform the Internal Revenue Service, and for other purposes, having considered the same, reports favorably thereon with an amendment and recommends that the bill as amended do pass.

CONTENTS

8

II. EXPLANATION OF THE BILL

TITLE I. EXECUTIVE BRANCH GOVERNANCE AND MANAGEMENT OF THE IRS

A. IRS RESTRUCTURING AND CREATION OF IRS OVERSIGHT BOARD

1. IRS mission and restructuring (secs. 1001 and 1002 of the bill)

Present Law

IRS mission statement

The IRS mission statement provides that:

> The purpose of the Internal Revenue Service is to collect the proper amount of tax revenue at the least cost; serve the public by continually improving the quality of our products and services; and perform in a manner warranting the highest degree of public confidence in our integrity and fairness.

IRS organizational plan

Under Reorganization Plan No. 1 of 1952, the Internal Revenue Service ("IRS") is organized into a 3-tier geographic structure with a multi-functional National Office, Regional Offices, and District Offices. A number of IRS reorganizations have occurred since then, but no major changes have been made to the basic 3-tier structure. Presently, as a result of a 1995 reorganization, there is a Regional Commissioner, a Regional Counsel and a Regional Director of Appeals for each of the following 4 regions: (1) the Northeast Region (headquartered in New York); (2) the Southeast Region (Atlanta); (3) the Midstates Region (Dallas); and (4) the Western Region (San Francisco). There are 33 District Offices, 10 service centers, and 3 computing centers.

Reasons for Change

The Committee believes that a key reason for taxpayer frustration with the IRS is the lack of appropriate attention to taxpayer needs. At a minimum, taxpayers should be able to receive from the IRS the same level of service expected from the private sector. For example, taxpayer inquiries should be answered promptly and accurately; taxpayers should be able to obtain timely resolutions of problems and information regarding activity on their accounts; and taxpayers should be treated fairly and courteously at all times. The Commissioner of Internal Revenue has indicated his interest in improving customer service. The Committee believes that taxpayer service is of such importance that the Committee should not only support the Commissioner's efforts, but also mandate that a key part of the IRS mission must be taxpayer service.

The Commissioner has announced a broad outline of a plan to reorganize the structure of the IRS in order to help make the IRS more oriented toward assisting taxpayers and providing better taxpayer service. Under this plan, the present regional structure would be replaced with a structure based on units that serve particular groups of taxpayers with similar needs. The Commissioner

9

has currently identified four different groups of taxpayers with similar needs: individual taxpayers, small businesses, large businesses, and the tax-exempt sector (including employee plans, exempt organizations and State and local governments). Under this structure, each unit would be charged with end-to-end responsibility for serving a particular group of taxpayers. The Commissioner believes that this type of structure will solve many of the problems taxpayers encounter now with the IRS. For example, each of the 33 district offices and 10 service centers are now required to deal with every kind of taxpayer and every type of issue. The proposed plan would enable IRS personnel to understand the needs and problems affecting particular groups of taxpayers, and better address those issues. The present-law structure also impedes continuity and accountability. For example, if a taxpayer moves, the responsibility for the taxpayer's account moves to another geographical area. Further, every taxpayer is serviced by both a service center and at least one district. Thus, many taxpayers have to deal with different IRS offices on the same issues. The proposed structure would eliminate many of these problems.

The Committee believes that the current IRS organizational structure is one of the factors contributing to the inability of the IRS to properly serve taxpayers and the proposed structure would help enable the IRS to better serve taxpayers and provide the necessary level of services and accountability to taxpayers. The Committee supports the Commissioner in his efforts to modernize and update the IRS and believes it appropriate to provide statutory direction for the reorganization of the IRS.

Explanation of Provision

The IRS is directed to revise its mission statement to provide greater emphasis on serving the public and meeting the needs of taxpayers.

The IRS Commissioner is directed to restructure the IRS by eliminating or substantially modifying the present-law three-tier geographic structure and replacing it with an organizational structure that features operating units serving particular groups of taxpayers with similar needs. The plan is also required to ensure an independent appeals function within the IRS. As part of ensuring an independent appeals function, the reorganization plan is to prohibit ex parte communications between appeals officers and other IRS employees to the extent such communications appear to compromise the independence of the appeals officers. The legality of IRS actions will not be affected pending further appropriate statutory changes relating to such a reorganization (e.g., eliminating statutory references to obsolete positions).

Effective Date

The provision is effective on the date of enactment.

After being reported out of the Senate Finance Committee, the bill and accompanying report are scheduled for consideration on the Senate floor. On occasion, rather than preparing a report, the staff of the Finance Committee will prepare a committee print.

Unlike the House, the Senate has no general germaneness rules for floor amendments. After consideration, the Senate can recommit the bill to the Finance Committee or pass the bill. A transcript of the Senate proceedings is reported in the Congressional Record.

Example:

The following is a portion of a transcript of the Senate proceedings for June 23, 1986, during the Senate's consideration of H.R. 3838. In this portion of the transcript, Senator Mitchell offers an amendment to the bill:

V-37   **Low-Income Housing Credit**   §42[1986]pg. 31

BACKGROUND

Senate Discussion

132 Congressional Record S8146
June 23, 1986

Editor's Note: During Senate consideration of H.R. 3838 on June 23, 1986, Senator Mitchell (D-Me.) offered Amendment No. 2153 to amend various provisions of the bill with respect to low-income housing while maintaining revenue neutrality. The Senate discussion leading to adoption of the amendment is presented below.

S 8146

AMENDMENT NO. 2153

(Purpose: To amend various provisions of the bill with respect to low-income housing while maintaining revenue neutrality.)
Mr. MITCHELL. Mr. President, on behalf of myself and Senators KENNEDY, COHEN, CHAFEE, CRANSTON, D'AMATO, DECONCINI, DIXON, DODD, GORE, HOLLINGS, INOUYE, KERRY, LEVIN, MATHIAS, RIEGLE, SARBANES, SIMON, BINGAMAN, and MOYNIHAN I send an amendment to the desk and ask for its immediate consideration.

The PRESIDING OFFICER (Mr. McCONNELL). The amendment will be stated.
The assistant legislative clerk read as follows:

The Senator from Maine [Mr. MITCHELL], for himself and others, proposes an amendment numbered 2153.

Mr. MITCHELL. Mr. President, I ask unanimous consent that reading of the amendment be dispensed with.

The PRESIDING OFFICER. Without objection, it is so ordered.
The amendment is as follows:
On page 2252, strike out lines 17 through 22, and insert in lieu thereof the following:
"(B) BASIS REDUCTIONS.—The basis determined under subparagraph (A) shall be reduced by the allocable amount of—
"(i) the rehabilitation credit allowed under section 38, and
"(ii) the amount of any Federal grant or equivalent assistance described in clause (i), (ii), or (iii) of subsection (f)(4)(A).
On page 2254, between lines 23 and 24, insert the following new paragraph:
"(3) EXCEPTION FOR CERTAIN EXISTING FEDERALLY ASSISTED PROJECTS.—
"(A) IN GENERAL.—A qualified low-income housing project shall be considered to comply with paragraph (1) even though such project has previously been placed in service (other than by the taxpayer or a related person to such taxpayer, as defined in section 461(I)(6)) such project—
"(i) is acquired by the taxpayer from any person other than such a related person,

"(ii) is placed in service by such taxpayer at least 15 years after such project was last placed in service, and
"(iii) is described in subparagraph (B).
"(B) EXISTING FEDERALLY ASSISTED QUALIFIED LOW-INCOME HOUSING PROJECT.—A project is described in this subparagraph if such project is substantially assisted, financed, or operated with respect to the taxpayer only under—
"(i) section 8 of the United States Housing Act of 1937,
"(ii) section 221(d)(3) or 236 of the National Housing Act of 1934, or
"(iii) section 515 of the Housing Act of 1949.

S 8147

as in effect on the date of the enactment of the Tax Reform Act of 1986.
"(C) APPLICABLE CREDIT RATE ALLOWED.—In the case of any project described in subparagraph (B), the applicable credit rate with respect to any occupied residential rental unit shall be the rate described in subsection (a)(2)(A)(ii).
"(D) WAIVER OF 15-YEAR RULE.—Upon application by the taxpayer to the Secretary (in such manner as the Secretary shall prescribe), the Secretary after consultation with the Secretary of Housing and Urban Development or the Secretary of Agriculture (with respect to any project described in subparagraph (B)(iii)) may waive the 15-year requirement in subparagraph (A) based on his determination that such waiver is necessary to avert—
"(i) an assignment of the mortgage secured by property in the project to the Department of Housing and Urban Development or the Farmers Home Administration and a claim against the mortgage insurance fund with respect to such mortgage, or
"(ii) other circumstances, to the extent established by regulations prescribed by the Secretary.
On page 2255, line 6, insert before the period a comma and the following: "or in the case of a project described in subsection (c)(3)(B) the date such project is placed in service."
On page 2258, strike out lines 1 through 9, and insert in lieu thereof the following:
"(1) MINIMUM SET-ASIDE REQUIREMENT.—
"(A) IN GENERAL.—The project meets the requirements of this paragraph if 20 percent or more of the residential rental units

in such project (as determined in the manner described in subsection (b)(1)(A)), are occupied by individuals whose income is 50 percent or less of area median gross income. Such requirements must be met within 12 months of the date a building or rehabilitation expenses are placed in service.
"(B) EXISTING FEDERALLY ASSISTED PROJECTS.—In the case of a project described in subsection (c)(3)(B), subparagraph (A) shall apply by substituting '50 percent' for '20 percent'.
On page 2259, line 2, insert before the period the following: ", other than, in the case of a project described in subsection (c)(3)(B), any such obligation issued to a previous owner before the date of the enactment of the Tax Reform Act of 1986 and taken subject to or assumed by the taxpayer".
On page 2259, line 7, strike out the period and insert a comma and "other than—
"(A) in the case of a qualified low-income housing project described in subsection (c)(1)—
"(i) any assistance under the Urban Development Action Grant program under title I of the Housing and Community Development Act of 1974,
"(ii) any assistance under the Community Development Block Grant program under such title,
"(iii) a development or rental rehabilitation program under section 17 of the United States Housing Act of 1937,
"(B) in the case of any residential rental unit in a building within a qualified low-income housing project described in subsection (c)(1) occupied by individuals described in subsection (a)(1)(B)(i)—
"(i) a moderate rehabilitation program under section 8 of the United States Housing Act of 1973, or
"(ii) section 515 of the Housing Act of 1949, and
"(C) in the case of a qualified low-income housing project described in subsection (c)(3), the programs described in subparagraph (B), thereof.

For purposes of the preceding sentence, programs described in subparagraph (A) and (B) shall be included as in effect on the date of the enactment of the Tax Reform Act of 1986.
On page 2261, strike out lines 12 through 23, and insert in lieu thereof the following:
"(5) RESIDENTIAL RENTAL UNITS.—No residential rental unit shall be included in subsection (a)(1)(B) if—

§42

"(A) such unit is not suitable for occupancy, or

"(B) any portion of the qualifying basis of which is reduced for casualty loss, except to the extent replaced by reconstruction.

"(6) LIMITATION ON CREDIT.—No credit shall be allowed with respect to any residential rental unit unless any payment under section 8 of the United States Housing Act of 1937 with respect to such unit or any occupants thereof is limited to an amount no greater than the excess of—

"(A) 30 percent of 50 percent of the area median gross income, over

"(B) 30 percent of the income of the individuals occupying such unit.

On page 2264, line 15, strike the end quotation marks.

On page 2264, between lines 15 and 16, insert:

"(i) APPLICATION OF AT-RISK RULES.—

"(1) IN GENERAL.—In determining the qualifying basis of any property for purposes of this section—

"(A) section 46(c)(8) (other than subparagraph (D)(iv)(I) thereof) and section 47(d)(1) shall apply, and

"(B) for purposes of such section, the credit base with respect to such property shall be the qualifying basis.

"(2) SPECIAL RULES FOR DETERMINING QUALIFIED PERSON.—For purposes of paragraph (1)—

"(A) IN GENERAL.—In computing the amount of qualified nonrecourse financing with respect to property with respect to which a credit is allowable under this section, the determination of whether an organization—

"(i) which is exempt from taxation under section 501(c)(3) or (4), and

"(ii) 1 of the exempt purposes of which includes the fostering of low-income housing,

is a qualified person (within the meaning of section 46(c)(8)(D)(iv)) shall be made without regard to whether such organization is actively and regularly engaged in the business of lending money or is a person described in section 46(c)(8)(D)(iv)(II) if the requirements of subparagraphs (B) through (D) are met.

"(B) FINANCING SECURED BY PROPERTY.—The requirements of this subparagraph are met with respect to any financing if such financing is secured by the property described in subparagraph (A), except that this subparagraph shall not apply in the case of property described in subsection (a)(1)(B)(ii) if—

"(i) a security interest in such property is not permitted by a Government agency holding or insuring the mortgage secured by such property, and

"(ii) the proceeds from such financing (if any) are applied to acquire or improve such property.

"(C) PORTION OF PROPERTY ATTRIBUTABLE TO FINANCING.—The requirements of this subparagraph are met with respect to any financing if, in the taxable year in which such financing is taken into account in determining qualifying basis, not more than 60 percent of the basis of such property is attributable to such financing (reduced by the principal and interest of any governmental financing which is part of a wraparound mortgage involving such financing).

"(D) REPAYMENT OF PRINCIPAL AND INTEREST.—The requirements of this subparagraph are met with respect to any financing if such financing is fully repaid before the earliest of—

"(i) the date on which such financing matures, or

"(ii) 90 days following the close of the qualified compliance period (within the

meaning of subsection (g)(1)) with respect to such property, or

"(iii) the date of the refinancing of such financing or the sale of the property to which such financing relates.

"(3) PRESENT VALUE OF FINANCING.—If the rate of interest on any financing described in paragraph (2)(A) (determined by taking into account government subsidies) is less than the rate which is 1 percent below the applicable Federal rate as of the time such financing is incurred, then the qualifying basis of property to which such financing relates shall be the present value of the amount of such financing, using as the discount rate such applicable Federal rate.

"(4) Failure to fully repay.—To the extent that the requirements of paragraph (2)(D) are not met, then the amount of tax of the taxpayer for the taxable year in which such failure occurs shall be increased by an amount equal to the applicable portion of the credit under this section with respect to such property, increased by an amount of interest for the period—

"(i) beginning with the due date for the filing of the return of tax imposed by chapter 1 for the first taxable year for which such credit was allowable, and

"(ii) ending with the due date for the taxable year in which such failure occurs.

determined by using the underpayment rate and method under section 6621."

On page 2230, strike lines 18 through 20, and insert: applicable percentage of the portion of the passive activity loss or credit which is attributable to a pre-1987 interest and which (but for this subsection) would have been disallowed under subsection (a).

On page 2230, in the matter following line 23, strike the end quotation marks.

On page 2230, after the matter following line 23, insert:

"(3) PORTION OF LOSS OR CREDIT ATTRIBUTABLE TO PRE-1987 INTERESTS.—

"(A) IN GENERAL.—The portion of the passive activity loss for any taxable year which is attributable to pre-1987 interests shall be the amount which bears the same ratio to such passive activity loss as—

"(i) the amount by which the aggregate losses for such taxable year from all pre-1987 interests exceeds the aggregate income for such taxable year from all such interests (determined after the application of subsection (c)), bears to

"(ii) such passive activity loss.

A similar rule shall apply in the case of a passive activity credit.

"(B) PRE-1987 INTEREST.—The term 'pre-1987 interest' means any interest in a passive activity held by a taxpayer on the date of the enactment of the Tax Reform Act of 1986, and at all times thereafter."

On page 1557, line 25, insert after the period the following new sentence: "For purposes of this subparagraph, the deferral of income to partners for a period of 3 months or less shall not be treated as a business purpose."

On page 1559, between lines 6 and 7, insert:

"(2) BUSINESS PURPOSE.—Section 1378(b) (defining required year) is amended by adding at the end thereof the following new flush sentence:

S 8148

"For purposes of paragraph (2), the deferral of income to shareholders for a period of 3

months or less shall not be treated as a business purpose."

On page 1559, line 7, strike "(2)" and insert "(3)".

On page 1559, line 20, insert after the period the following new sentence: "For purposes of this paragraph, the deferral of income to shareholders for a period of 3 months or less shall not be treated as a business purpose."

The PRESIDING OFFICER. Under the provision order, the amendment of the Senator from Maine will be considered for 1 hour, to be equally divided. Who yields time?

Mr. MITCHELL. I yield myself such time as is necessary.

Mr. President, this is an amendment to the portion of the committee bill which provides a new tax credit for investment in the development and preservation of affordable housing for low-income American families.

I thank the chairman of the Finance Committee for his help in developing this amendment. I am pleased that we were able to reach agreement on the amendment's provisions and that I can offer the amendment today with Senator PACKWOOD's support.

The housing crisis facing low-income Americans has reached a level unmatched since the Great Depression. Over half of the 8.4-million renter households with incomes below $7,000 per year are paying more than one-half their income for rent. Homelessness, overcrowding, and high-rent burdens are all manifestations of the same crisis—too little affordable housing for the very families most in need of it.

The Tax Code has for many years contained incentives to assist in the development and preservations of housing. Tax incentives for homeowners are traditional and massive, favoring upper- and middle-income taxpayers. Tax deductions for mortgage interest, property tax deductions and other provisions favoring homeownership produce revenue losses of $40 billion to $50 billion annually. Tax incentives for low-income rental housing produce revenue losses of between $1 billion and $2 billion annually.

Congress and successive administrations have long recognized the necessity of using tax incentives to attract private capital to low-income housing development and rehabilitation. These provisions recognize that absent some incentives, investment in low-income housing is a fundamentally uneconomic activity.

The committee bill recognized the need for such investment. It would replace current law tax incentives with a new and innovative tax credit for investment in affordable low-income housing.

The tax credit is highly targeted. The full credit is available only for units which actually serve very low-income families—those with incomes below 50 percent of the area median, adjusted for family size. A lesser credit

---

Where there are differences between the House and Senate versions of a bill, and neither chamber will accept the other's version of the bill and the differences cannot be resolved informally between the House and the Senate, the bill is sent to conference committee.[10] The **conference committee** is composed of members of the House and Senate, referred to as managers, appointed by the House Speaker and presiding officer of the Senate. Generally, the meetings of the conference committee are open to the public.

---

10. If there are differences between the bill passed by the House and that passed by the Senate, referral to the Conference Committee is unnecessary if the House recedes from its disagreement to Senate amendments to the House bill or the Senate recedes from its amendments to the House bill.

In preparing a bill for conference, the Staff of the Joint Committee may prepare a side-by-side revenue table for all provisions in both bills as well as a side-by-side document describing all the provisions in both bills. The Chief of Staff of the Joint Committee may attend the hearing and describe the contents of the two bills, with the Staff assisting in developing possible compromise proposals on matters in conference.

The role of the managers is to resolve the differences between the House and Senate. The managers can consider only those portions of the bill on which there was disagreement. However, if the Senate has amended the House's version by striking the entire bill language and substituting its own version, there is total disagreement and the entire bill is negotiable.

Example:

The following is an explanation by the conference committee considering what was to become the Jobs and Growth Tax Act of 2003. The committee notes that, after the bill was passed by the House, the Senate amended the bill by striking all of the House bill and inserting substitute text. Thus, the entire bill was subject to disagreement.

JOINT EXPLANATORY STATEMENT OF THE COMMITTEE OF CONFERENCE

The managers on the part of the House and the Senate at the conference on the disagreeing votes of the two Houses on the amendment of the Senate to the bill (H.R. 2), to provide for reconciliation pursuant to section 201 of the concurrent resolution on the budget for fiscal year 2004, submit the following joint statement to the House and the Senate in explanation of the effect of the action agreed upon by the managers and recommended in the accompanying conference report:

The Senate amendment struck all of the House bill after the enacting clause and inserted a substitute text.

The House recedes from its disagreement to the amendment of the Senate with an amendment that is a substitute for the House bill and the Senate amendment. The differences between the House bill, the Senate amendment, and the substitute agreed to in conference are noted below, except for clerical corrections, conforming changes made necessary by agreements reached by the conferees, and minor drafting and clarifying changes.

If a bill has been extensively amended by the conference committee, the managers may incorporate the changes into an amendment, which acts as a substitute, or introduce a "clean" bill.

When a majority of managers from each chamber reach agreement, the committee and its staff prepare a conference report. Part of the conference report is the new language of the bill. The committee and its staff also prepare a **Joint Explanatory Statement of the Conference Committee** that explains the final action taken by the managers.

The report must be sufficiently detailed and explicit to inform the House and Senate as to the effect that the amendments and propositions in the report will have upon the measure to which the amendments or proposition relate. Generally, it will set forth the present law, the provisions in the House bill, amendments proposed by the Senate,

and the agreement reached in conference. The explanation functions like a committee report.

The conference report must be signed by a majority of managers from the House and the Senate. No minority views are included, however a majority of the managers may, in the explanatory statement, indicate exceptions taken or objections raised by certain managers who signed with the majority.

A report prepared by the conference committee is printed by the House and numbered by chamber (H.R.) and Congressional term in the order in which it was filed with the Clerk of the House during the two-year term. Although printing is also required in the Senate, generally such printing requirement is waived. Thus, conference reports are almost always numbered as H.R. Reports.

Example:

- The Conference Report for the Jobs and Growth Tax Relief Reconciliation Act of 2003 is designated H.R. Conf. Rep. No. 108-126. The report was printed by the 108th term of Congress and was the 126th report printed by the House of Representatives.

- The Conference Report for the Economic Growth and Tax Reconciliation Act of 2001 is designated H.R. Conf. Rep. No. 107-84. The report was printed by the 107th term of Congress and was the 84th report printed by the House of Representatives.

Example:

The following is a portion of Report No. 105-599 of the Conference Committee. It relates to H.R. 2676:

105TH CONGRESS 2d Session	HOUSE OF REPRESENTATIVES	REPORT 105–599

INTERNAL REVENUE SERVICE RESTRUCTURING AND REFORM ACT OF 1998

CONFERENCE REPORT

TO ACCOMPANY

H.R. 2676

JUNE 24, 1998.—Ordered to be printed

U.S. GOVERNMENT PRINTING OFFICE
WASHINGTON : 1998

49–287

105TH CONGRESS 2d Session	HOUSE OF REPRESENTATIVES	REPORT 105–599

INTERNAL REVENUE SERVICE RESTRUCTURING AND REFORM ACT OF 1998

JUNE 24, 1998.—Ordered to be printed

Mr. ARCHER, from the committee of conference, submitted the following

CONFERENCE REPORT

[written by the congress]

[Most authoritative report]

[Read only this while research]

[To accompany H.R. 2676]

The committee of conference on the disagreeing votes of the two Houses on the amendment of the Senate to the bill (H.R. 2676) to amend the Internal Revenue Code of 1986 to restructure and reform the Internal Revenue Service, and for other purposes, having met, after full and free conference, have agreed to recommend and do recommend to their respective Houses as follows:

That the House recede from its disagreement to the amendment of the Senate, and agree to the same with an amendment, as follows:

In lieu of the matter proposed to be inserted by the Senate amendment, insert the following:

SECTION 1. SHORT TITLE; AMENDMENT OF 1986 CODE; WAIVER OF ESTIMATED TAX PENALTIES; TABLE OF CONTENTS.

(a) SHORT TITLE.—*This Act may be cited as the "Internal Revenue Service Restructuring and Reform Act of 1998".*

(b) AMENDMENT OF 1986 CODE.—*Except as otherwise expressly provided, whenever in this Act an amendment or repeal is expressed in terms of an amendment to, or repeal of, a section or other provision, the reference shall be considered to be made to a section or other provision of the Internal Revenue Code of 1986.*

(c) WAIVER OF ESTIMATED TAX PENALTIES.—*No addition to tax shall be made under section 6654 or 6655 of the Internal Revenue Code of 1986 with respect to any underpayment of an installment required to be paid on or before the 30th day after the date of the enactment of this Act to the extent such underpayment was created or increased by any provision of this Act.*

(d) TABLE OF CONTENTS.—*The table of contents for this Act is as follows:*

JOINT EXPLANATORY STATEMENT OF THE COMMITTEE OF CONFERENCE

The managers on the part of the House and the Senate at the conference on the disagreeing votes of the two Houses on the amendment of the Senate to the bill (H.R. 2676) to amend the Internal Revenue Code of 1986 to restructure and reform the Internal Revenue Service, and for other purposes, submit the following joint statement to the House and the Senate in explanation of the effect of the action agreed upon by the managers and recommended in the accompanying conference report:

The Senate amendment struck all of the House bill after the enacting clause and inserted a substitute text.

The House recedes from its disagreement to the amendment of the Senate with an amendment that is a substitute for the House bill and the Senate amendment. The differences between the House bill, the Senate amendment, and the substitute agreed to in conference are noted below, except for clerical corrections, conforming changes made necessary by agreements reached by the conferees, and minor drafting and clerical changes.

TITLE I. REORGANIZATION OF STRUCTURE AND MANAGEMENT OF THE IRS

A. IRS Restructuring and Creation of IRS Oversight Board

1. IRS mission and restructuring (secs. 1001 and 1002 of the Senate amendment)

Present Law

IRS mission statement

The IRS mission statement provides that:

The purpose of the Internal Revenue Service is to collect the proper amount of tax revenue at the least cost; serve the public by continually improving the quality of our products and services; and perform in a manner warranting the highest degree of public confidence in our integrity and fairness.

IRS organizational plan

Under Reorganization Plan No. 1 of 1952, the Internal Revenue Service ("IRS") is organized into a 3-tier geographic structure with a multi-functional National Office, Regional Offices, and District Offices. A number of IRS reorganizations have occurred since then, but no major changes have been made to the basic 3-tier structure. Currently, as a result of a 1995 reorganization, there is a Regional Commissioner, a Regional Counsel and a Regional Director of Appeals for each of the following 4 regions: (1) the Northeast Region (headquartered in New York); (2) the Southeast Region

194

(Atlanta); (3) the Midstates Region (Dallas); and (4) the Western Region (San Francisco). There are 33 District Offices, 10 service centers, and 3 computing centers.

House Bill

No provision.

Senate Amendment

Under the Senate amendment, the IRS is directed to revise its mission statement to provide greater emphasis on serving the public and meeting the needs of taxpayers.

The IRS Commissioner is directed to restructure the IRS by eliminating or substantially modifying the present-law three-tier geographic structure and replacing it with an organizational structure that features operating units serving particular groups of taxpayers with similar needs. The plan is also required to ensure an independent appeals function within the IRS. As part of ensuring an independent appeals function, the reorganization plan is to prohibit ex parte communications between appeals officers and other IRS employees to the extent such communications appear to compromise the independence of the appeals officers. The legality of IRS actions will not be affected pending further appropriate statutory changes relating to such a reorganization (e.g., eliminating statutory references to obsolete positions).

Effective date.—The provision is effective on the date of enactment.

Conference Agreement

The conference agreement follows the Senate amendment.

Effective date.—The provision is effective on the date of enactment.

2. Establishment and duties of IRS Oversight Board (sec. 101 of the House bill and sec. 1101 of the Senate amendment)

Present Law

Under present law, the administration and enforcement of the internal revenue laws are performed by or under the supervision of the Secretary of the Treasury.[1] The Secretary has delegated the responsibility to administer and enforce the Internal Revenue laws to the Commissioner of Internal Revenue ("Commissioner"). The Commissioner has the final authority of the IRS concerning the substantive interpretation of the tax laws as reflected in legislative and regulatory proposals, revenue rulings, letter rulings, and technical advice memoranda. The duties of the Chief Counsel of the IRS are prescribed by the Secretary. The Secretary has delegated authority over the Chief Counsel to the General Counsel of the Treasury. The General Counsel has delegated authority to serve as the legal adviser to the Commissioner to the Chief Counsel.

---

[1] Code sec. 7801(a).

Conference reports are published in the Congressional Record. They are then brought before the House and Senate for final action where they must be acted upon as a whole, and no amendments may be made by either house. Accordingly, the first chamber to act has three options:

- Adopt
- Reject
- Recommit (return to conference for further deliberation).

When the first chamber to act adopts the conference report, the conference committee is dissolved. The other chamber then must either accept or reject the report in its entirety.

If passed by both chambers, the president has 10 days, excluding Sundays, to sign. The president can:

- Sign the measure into law;
- Disapprove, subject to the ability of Congress during the session to override the veto by a 2/3 vote of the members present and voting in each House;
- If no action is taken in 10 days, the bill becomes law; or
- If the final adjournment of a Congress takes place before the ten-day period ends and the president does not sign, the legislation dies. This process is referred to as a pocket veto. Congress has no opportunity to override a pocket veto.

If passed into law, the bill becomes a public law.

Practice Note:

To easily find a Public Law and its legislative history, look in the third and fourth volume of the Cumulative Bulletin for the year in which the Act became law.

Generally, after a major piece of tax legislation is passed into law, the Staff of the Joint Committee on Taxation prepares a "General Explanation." This report is often referred to as the "**Blue Book**," due to the traditionally blue cover of the book, and is published as a committee print. For minor pieces of tax legislation, the Staff may prepare a summary of the legislation.

The **Blue Book** is an explanation of tax legislation prepared by the Staff of the Joint Committee on Taxation after enactment of tax legislation.

Example:

The following is a portion of the Blue Book discussing H.R. 2676:

[JOINT COMMITTEE PRINT]

Move than one bill

GENERAL EXPLANATION OF
TAX LEGISLATION ENACTED IN 1998

least authoritative because the report is prepared by the standing committee who is helping the Congress.

PREPARED BY THE STAFF

OF THE

JOINT COMMITTEE ON TAXATION

NOVEMBER 24, 1998

U.S. GOVERNMENT PRINTING OFFICE

52–240   WASHINGTON : 1998   JCS–6–98

For sale by the U.S. Government Printing Office
Superintendent of Documents, Congressional Sales Office, Washington, DC 20402
ISBN 0-16-057773-X

INTRODUCTION

This pamphlet,[1] prepared by the staff of the Joint Committee on Taxation in consultation with the staffs of the House Committee on Ways and Means and Senate Committee on Finance, provides an explanation of tax legislation enacted in 1998.

A committee report on legislation issued by a Congressional committee sets forth the committee's explanation of the bill as it was reported by that committee. In some instances, a committee report does not serve as an explanation of the final provisions of the legislation as enacted. This is because the version of the bill adopted by the conference committee may differ significantly from the versions of the bill reported by committee or passed by the House and the Senate. The material contained in this pamphlet is prepared so that Members of Congress, tax practitioners, and other interested parties can have a detailed explanation of the final tax legislation enacted in 1998 in one publication.

Part One of the pamphlet is an explanation of the provisions of the Surface Transportation Revenue Act of 1998 (Title IX of H.R. 2400, P.L. 105–178) relating to the extension and revision of the Highway Trust Fund excise taxes. Part Two is an explanation of the Internal Revenue Service Restructuring and Reform Act of 1998 (H.R. 2676, P.L. 105–206). Part Three is an explanation of the revenue provisions of the Tax and Trade Relief Act of 1998 (Division J of the Omnibus Consolidated and Emergency Supplemental Appropriations Act, 1999, H.R. 4328, P.L. 105–277). Part Four is an explanation of the revenue provision in the Ricky Ray Hemophilia Relief Fund Act of 1998 (sec. 103(h) of H.R. 1023, P.L. 105–369). The Appendix provides estimates of the budget effects of revenue legislation enacted in 1998 for the fiscal year period, 1999–2007.

The first footnote in each part gives the legislative history of each of the 1998 Acts.

---

[1] This pamphlet may be cited as follows: Joint Committee on Taxation, *General Explanation of Tax Legislation Enacted in 1998* (JCS–6–98), November 24, 1998.

PART TWO: INTERNAL REVENUE SERVICE RESTRUCTURING AND REFORM ACT OF 1998 (H.R. 2676)[14]

TITLE I. REORGANIZATION OF STRUCTURE AND MANAGEMENT OF THE IRS

A. IRS Restructuring and Creation of IRS Oversight Board

1. IRS mission and restructuring (secs. 1001 and 1002 of the Act)

Prior Law

IRS mission statement

Under prior law, the Internal Revenue Service ("IRS") mission statement provided that:

> The purpose of the Internal Revenue Service is to collect the proper amount of tax revenue at the least cost; serve the public by continually improving the quality of our products and services; and perform in a manner warranting the highest degree of public confidence in our integrity and fairness.

IRS organizational plan

Under Reorganization Plan No. 1 of 1952, the IRS is organized into a 3-tier geographic structure with a multi-functional National Office, Regional Offices, and District Offices. A number of IRS reorganizations have occurred since then, but no major changes have been made to the basic 3-tier structure. A 1995 reorganization provided for a Regional Commissioner, a Regional Counsel and a Regional Director of Appeals for each of the following 4 regions: (1) the Northeast Region (headquartered in New York); (2) the Southeast Region (Atlanta); (3) the Midstates Region (Dallas); and (4) the Western Region (San Francisco). There were 33 District Offices, 10 service centers, and 3 computing centers.

Reasons for Change

The Congress believed that a key reason for taxpayer frustration with the IRS is the lack of appropriate attention to taxpayer needs. Taxpayers should be able to receive from the IRS the same level

---

[14] P.L. 105–206. H.R. 2676 was reported by the House Committee on Ways and Means on October 31, 1997 (H. Rept. 105–364, Part I). The House passed the bill on November 5, 1997, and added (as new Title VI) the provisions of H.R. 2645 ("Tax Technical Corrections Act of 1997") as previously reported by the Committee on Ways and Means (H. Rept. 105–356, October 29, 1997).

H.R. 2676 was reported, as amended, by the Senate Committee on Finance on April 22, 1998 (S. Rept. 105–174), and was passed by the Senate, as amended, on May 7, 1998. The conference report on H.R. 2676 was filed on June 24, 1998 (H. Rept. 105–599). The House passed the conference report on June 25, 1998, and the Senate passed it on July 9, 1998.

H.R. 2676 was signed by the President on July 22, 1998.

17

of service expected from the private sector. For example, taxpayer inquiries should be answered promptly and accurately; taxpayers should be able to obtain timely resolutions of problems and information regarding activity on their accounts; and taxpayers should be treated fairly and courteously at all times. The Commissioner of Internal Revenue has indicated his interest in improving customer service. The Congress believed that taxpayer service is of such importance that the Congress should not only support the Commissioner's efforts, but also mandate that a key part of the IRS mission must be taxpayer service.

The Commissioner announced a broad outline of a plan to reorganize the structure of the IRS in order to help make the IRS more oriented toward assisting taxpayers and providing better taxpayer service. Under this plan, the present regional structure would be replaced with a structure based on units that serve particular groups of taxpayers with similar needs. The Commissioner preliminarily identified four different groups of taxpayers with similar needs: individual taxpayers, small businesses, large businesses, and the tax-exempt sector (including employee plans, exempt organizations and State and local governments). Under this structure, each unit would be charged with end-to-end responsibility for serving a particular group of taxpayers. The Commissioner believed that this type of structure will solve many of the problems taxpayers encounter now with the IRS. For example, each of the 33 district offices and 10 service centers were required to deal with every kind of taxpayer and every type of issue. The proposed plan would enable IRS personnel to understand the needs and problems affecting particular groups of taxpayers, and better address those issues. The prior-law structure also impeded continuity and accountability. For example, if a taxpayer moved, the responsibility for the taxpayer's account moved to another geographical area. Further, every taxpayer was serviced by both a service center and at least one district. Thus, many taxpayers had to deal with different IRS offices on the same issues. The proposed structure would eliminate many of these problems.

The Congress believed that the former IRS organizational structure was one of the factors contributing to the inability of the IRS to properly serve taxpayers and the proposed structure would help enable the IRS to better serve taxpayers and provide the necessary level of services and accountability to taxpayers. The Congress supported the Commissioner in his efforts to modernize and update the IRS and believed it appropriate to provide statutory direction for the reorganization of the IRS.

Explanation of Provision

The IRS is directed to revise its mission statement to provide greater emphasis on serving the public and meeting the needs of taxpayers.

The IRS Commissioner is directed to restructure the IRS by eliminating or substantially modifying the three-tier geographic structure and replacing it with an organizational structure that features operating units serving particular groups of taxpayers with similar needs. The plan is also required to ensure an independent appeals function within the IRS. As part of ensuring an

18

independent appeals function, the reorganization plan is to prohibit ex parte communications between appeals officers and other IRS employees to the extent such communications appear to compromise the independence of the appeals officers. The legality of IRS actions is not affected pending further appropriate statutory changes relating to such a reorganization (e.g., eliminating statutory references to obsolete positions).

Effective Date

The provision is effective on the date of enactment.

Revenue Effect

The provision is estimated to have no effect on Federal fiscal year budget receipts.

2. Establishment and duties of IRS Oversight Board (sec. 1101 of the Act and sec. 7802 of the Code)

Present and Prior Law

The administration and enforcement of the internal revenue laws are performed by or under the supervision of the Secretary of the Treasury.[15] The Secretary has delegated the responsibility to administer and enforce the Internal Revenue laws to the Commissioner. The Commissioner has the final authority of the IRS concerning the substantive interpretation of the tax laws as reflected in legislative and regulatory proposals, revenue rulings, letter rulings, and technical advice memoranda. The duties of the Chief Counsel of the IRS are prescribed by the Secretary. Under prior law, the Secretary delegated authority over the Chief Counsel to General Counsel of the Treasury, and the General Counsel delegated authority to serve as the legal adviser to the Commissioner to the Chief Counsel.

Federal employees are subject to rules designed to prevent conflicts of interest or the appearance of conflicts of interest. The rules applicable to any particular employee depend in part on whether the employee is a regular, full-time Federal Government employee or a special government employee, the length of service of the employee and the pay grade of the employee. A "special government employee" is, in general, an officer or employee of the executive or legislative branch of the U.S. government who is appointed or employed to perform (with or without compensation) for not to exceed 130 days during any period of 365 days, temporary duties either on a full-time or intermittent basis. Violations of the ethical conduct rules are generally punishable by imprisonment for up to 1 year (5 years in the case of wilful conduct), a civil fine, or both. The amount of the fine with respect to each violation cannot exceed the greater of $50,000 or the compensation received by the employee in connection with the prohibited conduct.

Under the ethical conduct rules, all Federal Government employees (including special government employees) are precluded from participating in a matter in which the employee (or a related party)

---

[15] Code section 7801(a).

3. When a Bill Becomes a Public Law

When a bill becomes a public law, it is transmitted to the National Archives and Records Administration (NARA) where it is given a public law number by the Director, Office of the Federal Register. A public law is numbered by Congressional term and assigned a number chronologically according to the order in which it was filed with NARA. The chronological numbering restarts at the beginning of each term of Congress.

Example:

- The IRS Restructuring and Reform Act of 1998 is designated as Public Law No. 105-206. The Act was the 206th Act passed by the 105th term of Congress.
- The Economic Growth and Tax Relief Reconciliation Act of 2001 is designated as Public Law No. 107-16. The Act was the 16th Act passed by the 107th term of Congress.

The public law is then published in the Statutes at Large. The **United States Statutes at Large** are a permanent collection of the laws of each term of Congress. The laws are organized chronologically, based on when they were enacted. The Title of the bill is retained on the bill and published. However, the title is not considered to be part of the enacted statute. The relevant Statute at Large is cited based on the volume and page number on which the provision is found.

Example:

The Economic Growth and Tax Relief Reconciliation Act of 2001, Pub. L. No. 107-16 begins on 115 Stat. 38; it is located in the 115 volume, beginning on page 38.

115 STAT. 38   PUBLIC LAW 107–16—JUNE 7, 2001

Public Law 107–16
107th Congress

An Act

June 7, 2001
[H.R. 1836]

To provide for reconciliation pursuant to section 104 of the concurrent resolution on the budget for fiscal year 2002.

Be it enacted by the Senate and House of Representatives of the United States of America in Congress assembled,

Economic Growth
and Tax Relief
Reconciliation
Act of 2001.
26 USC 1 note.

SECTION 1. SHORT TITLE; REFERENCES; TABLE OF CONTENTS.

(a) SHORT TITLE.—This Act may be cited as the "Economic Growth and Tax Relief Reconciliation Act of 2001".

(b) AMENDMENT OF 1986 CODE.—Except as otherwise expressly provided, whenever in this Act an amendment or repeal is expressed in terms of an amendment to, or repeal of, a section or other provision, the reference shall be considered to be made to a section or other provision of the Internal Revenue Code of 1986.

(c) TABLE OF CONTENTS.—The table of contents of this Act is as follows:

PUBLIC LAW 107–16—JUNE 7, 2001   115 STAT. 39

(1) escrow accounts or settlement funds established pursuant to the settlement of the action entitled "In re: Holocaust Victim Assets Litigation," (E.D.N.Y.) C.A. No. 96–4849,

(2) funds to benefit eligible individuals or their heirs created by the International Commission on Holocaust Insurance Claims as a result of the Agreement between the Government of the United States of America and the Government of the Federal Republic of Germany concerning the Foundation "Remembrance, Responsibility, and Future," dated July 17, 2000, or

(3) similar funds subject to the administration of the United States courts created to provide excludable restitution payments to eligible individuals (or eligible individuals' heirs or estates).

(e) EFFECTIVE DATE.—

(1) IN GENERAL.—This section shall apply to any amount received on or after January 1, 2000.

(2) NO INFERENCE.—Nothing in this Act shall be construed to create any inference with respect to the proper tax treatment of any amount received before January 1, 2000.

TITLE IX—COMPLIANCE WITH CONGRESSIONAL BUDGET ACT

26 USC 1 note.

SEC. 901. SUNSET OF PROVISIONS OF ACT.

(a) IN GENERAL.—All provisions of, and amendments made by, this Act shall not apply—

(1) to taxable, plan, or limitation years beginning after December 31, 2010, or

(2) in the case of title V, to estates of decedents dying, gifts made, or generation skipping transfers, after December 31, 2010.

(b) APPLICATION OF CERTAIN LAWS.—The Internal Revenue Code of 1986 and the Employee Retirement Income Security Act of 1974 shall be applied and administered to years, estates, gifts, and transfers described in subsection (a) as if the provisions and amendments described in subsection (a) had never been enacted.

Approved June 7, 2001.

LEGISLATIVE HISTORY—H.R. 1836:

HOUSE REPORTS: No. 107–84 (Comm. of Conference).
CONGRESSIONAL RECORD, Vol. 147 (2001):
    May 16, considered and passed House.
    May 17, 21–23, considered and passed Senate, amended.
    May 25, House agreed to conference report.
    May 26, Senate agreed to conference report.
WEEKLY COMPILATION OF PRESIDENTIAL DOCUMENTS, Vol. 37 (2001):
    June 7, Presidential remarks.

Beginning in 1975, at the conclusion of the Public Law a footnote reference includes information on the legislative history, such as the bill number, Conference Committee Report number, dates the bill was passed by the House and Senate, and location of such information in the Congressional Record.

> The **United States Statutes at Large** are a permanent collection, in chronological order, of the laws passed by each term of Congress.

Each section of the Public Law will amend a current Code provision, amend the Code by adding a new Code provision, or contain a provision which is not codified. The 1939 Internal Revenue Code was replaced by the 1954 Internal Revenue Code. And the 1954 Internal Revenue Code was replaced by the 1986 Internal Revenue Code.[11] Thus, currently, any amendments to the Code are amendments to the Internal Revenue Code of 1986.

The Internal Revenue Code of 1986, as amended, is reflected in the United States Code. The **United States Code** is prepared by the Law Revision Counsel of the House of Representatives and is a consolidation of the laws of the United States, arranged by subject matter in 50 titles. The law is set forth as amended by the Public Law. New editions are published every six years and supplements are published after the conclusion of each session of Congress.

> The **United States Code** sets forth the permanent codified laws of the United States according to subject matter. The Internal Revenue Code is located in Title 26. In the **United States Code Annotated**, each Code section is annotated with court opinions or other important documents that interpret or otherwise analyze or apply that Code section.

> **Practice Note:**
>
> The Public Law sets forth changes that must be made to the current law.
>
> The United States Code sets forth the law, taking into account any changes required by the Public Laws.

The United States Code is divided into Titles. The Internal Revenue Code is contained in Title 26. Title 26 is further broken down as follows:

Subtitle
    Chapter
        Subchapter
        Part
            Subpart
                Section
                    Subsection

---

11. In Code Volume 1 of CCH Standard Federal Tax Reporter, Cross-reference Table 1, sections of the 1939 Code are cross-referenced to the 1954 and 1986 Code. In Cross-reference Table 2 sections of the 1986 Code are cross-referenced to the 1939 Code.

Example:

Section 162 (trade or business expenses) is found in Title 26, Subtitle A, Chapter 1, Subchapter B, Part VI.

Subtitles, chapters, and sections run continuously through Title 26; neither chapters nor sections begin anew with each new subtitle or subpart, respectively. Thus, for example, in Title 26 there is one Subtitle B, one Chapter 11, and one section 165.

Subtitles:

A	Income Taxes
B	Estate and Gift Taxes
C	Employment Taxes
D	Miscellaneous Excise Taxes
E	Alcohol, Tobacco, and Certain Other Excise Taxes
F	Procedure and Administration
G	The Joint Committee on Taxation
H	Financing and Presidential Election Campaigns
I	Trust Fund Code
J	Coal Industry Health Benefits
K	Group Health Plan Requirements

Chapters:

1. Normal Taxes and Surtaxes
2. Tax on Self-Employment Income
3. Withholding of Tax on Nonresident Aliens and Foreign Corporations
6. Consolidated Returns
11. Estate Tax
12. Gift Tax
13. Tax on Generation-Skipping Transfers
14. Special Valuation Rules
21. Federal Insurance Contribution Act
22. Railroad Retirement Tax Act
23. Federal Employment Tax Act
23A. Railroad Unemployment Repayment Tax
24. Collection of Income Tax at Source on Wages
25. General Provisions Relating to Employment Taxes
31. Retail Excise Taxes
32. Manufacturers Excise Taxes
33. Facilities and Services
34. Policies Issued by Foreign Insurers
35. Taxes on Wages
36. Certain Other Excise Taxes
38. Environmental Taxes
39. Registration Required Obligations
40. General Provisions Relating to Occupational Taxes
41. Public Charities
42. Private Foundations and Certain Other Tax-Exempt Organizations
44. Qualified Investment Entities

46. Golden Parachute Payments
47. Certain Group Health Plans
51. Distilled Spirits, Wines, and Beer
52. Tobacco Products and Cigarette Papers and Tubes
53. Machine Guns, Destructive Devices, and Certain Other Firearms
54. Greenmail
55. Structured Settlement Factoring Transactions
61. Information and Returns
62. Time and Place for Paying Tax
63. Assessment
64. Collection
65. Abatements, Credits, and Refunds
66. Limitations
67. Interest
68. Additions to the Tax, Additional Amounts, and Assessable Penalties
69. General Provisions
70. Jeopardy, Receiverships, Etc.
71. Transferees and Fiduciaries
72. Licensing and Registration
73. Bonds
74. Closing Agreements and Compromises
75. Crimes, Other Offenses, and Forfeitures
76. Judicial Proceedings
77. Miscellaneous Provisions
78. Discovery of Liability and Enforcement of Title
79. Definitions
80. General Rules
91. Organization and Membership of the Joint Committee
95. Presidential Election Campaign Fund
96. Presidential Primary Matching Payment Account
98. Trust Fund Code
99. Coal Industry Health Benefits
100. Group Health Plan Requirements

In contrast, subchapters begin anew with each new Chapter; parts begin anew with each new subchapter; and subparts begin anew with each new part. Nevertheless, some areas of the Code are so closely connected with the subchapter in which the relevant provisions are contained that the area is commonly referred to by the subchapter.

Areas of Law in Chapter 1 Often Referred to by Subchapter:

Subchapter	Area of Law
C	Corporate Distributions and Adjustments ("C Corporations")
D	Deferred Compensation
E	Accounting Periods and Methods of Accounting
F	Exempt Organizations
H	Banking Institutions
I	Natural Resources
J	Estate, Trusts, Beneficiaries and Decedents

		("Trusts and Estates")
K		Partners and Partnerships
L		Insurance Companies
M		Regulated Investment Companies
S		Tax Treatment of S Corporations and Their Shareholders ("S Corporations")
V		Title 11 Cases

Code sections can be further broken down into subsections (lower case letters), paragraphs (numbers), subparagraphs (capital letters), and clauses (lower case roman numerals).

Example:

A reference to section 165(h)(2)(A)(i) is to

    Section 165
    Subsection h
    Paragraph 2
    Subparagraph A
    Clause i

To the extent the Public Law does not require the addition of a codified law or amendment to an existing codified law, the law is not reflected in the United States Code.

Non-codified provisions (sometimes referred to as off-code provisions) are public laws that are not codified in the United States Code.

Such provisions may include anything from simple matters, such as the effective date of a provision or a grandfather provision, to matters as complex as the tax treatment of an entity.

Example:

Section 3201(c) of Pub. L. 105-206 provides:

- Not later than 190 days after the date of the enactment of this Act, the Secretary of the Treasury shall develop a separate form with instructions for use by taxpayers in applying for relief under section 6015(a) of the Internal Revenue Code of 1986, as added by this section.

- The Federal Home Loan Mortgage Corporation (FHLMC) originally was exempt from federal income tax. Sec. 177 of Pub. L. No. 98-369 provided that, effective January 1, 1985, the FHLMC would be subject to tax.

---

4. Early History of the United States Tax System

The early development of the United States tax system was largely based on the need for revenue to finance wars. After the Revolutionary War, Congress imposed excise taxes to pay debts incurred in the war. The excise taxes were on items such as tobacco, legal documents, refined sugar and spirits. The first direct tax was imposed during the 1790s

to finance skirmishes with France. It was a recurring tax on land, houses, estates, and slaves. The tax was imposed based on the value of the item that gave rise to taxation. The tax was short-lived being abolished in 1802. However, with the outbreak of the War of 1812 the country was once again in need of additional revenue. As a result tariffs were raised and additional excise taxes were levied.

New taxes were not needed until 1861. The need for revenue to fund the Civil War resulted in the Revenue Act of 1861. The 1861 Act introduced a three percent tax on income. The income tax was imposed on income over $800. However, the revenue raised by three percent income tax was not sufficient to fund the war. In 1862 Congress passed the precursor to our current graduated rate system. The 1862 Act levied a tax on income up to $10,000 at three percent and income over $10,000 was subject to taxation at five percent The act also introduced the standard deduction and other deductions for certain expenses and losses.

Prior to 1874, U.S. statutes, including revenue statutes, were contained in an assortment of acts passed by Congress. In 1873, codification of U.S. statutes was undertaken. The codification was approved by Congress June 22, 1874. Originally, internal revenue statutes were codified in Title 35.

In 1894, a flat rate federal income tax was introduced. However, in 1895 the Supreme Court of the United States found the income tax to be unconstitutional. With an income tax being held unconstitutional, Congress was forced to impose additional taxes on items such as beer and increased tariffs to fund the Spanish American War.

By 1913 the Country had come to terms with the need for an income tax and the 16th amendment to the Constitution was adopted. That same year Congress adopted a graduated income tax with rates ranging from one percent to seven percent. The 16th Amendment was passed just in time for World War I. The 1916 Revenue Act was passed to fund World War I. The Act increased the lowest marginal income tax rate from one percent to two percent and the highest marginal rate was increased to 15 percent. Tax rates were increased again, dramatically, in 1917. For example, the highest marginal rate was increased to 77 percent. Once the war ended and the roaring 20s began, tax rates were quickly reduced. The lowest marginal rate was decreased to one percent and the highest rate declined to 25 percent. However, the decline in tax rates would not last. The great depression brought about several tax increases to combat declining federal revenue. A two-percent Social Security tax was also introduced during the 1930s. The tax was levied on salary or wage income up to $3,000.

On February 10, 1939, Congress made sweeping changes to the United States tax provisions. The United States tax statutes were re-codified as the "Internal Revenue Code" and issued as title 26 of the United States Code. The re-codified statute was eventually named the "Internal Revenue Code of 1939."

World War II once again brought about dramatic increases in the graduated rates of taxation. For example, Taxpayers with income over $1 million were subject to a 94 percent tax rate. Once the war ended the rates were greatly reduced. However, at least one tax reform that took place during the war continues through today. During World War II Congress introduced an income tax withholding system. The withholding tax reduced tax collection issues for the Bureau of Internal Revenue.

Internal Revenue Code of 1954 and Introduction of Social Security and Medicare. The 1950s brought about reorganization of the Internal Revenue Service and a major revision to the Internal Revenue Code of 1939. Prior to 1954 the Internal Revenue Service was known as the "Bureau of Internal Revenue." The reorganization of the Internal Revenue Service was not in name only. Prior to the 1950s, employment within the "Bureau of Internal Revenue" was largely based on patronage—career professionals replaced the patronage

system. As part of the Internal Revenue Service reorganization, the Internal Revenue Code of 1939 was reorganized by Congress on August 16, 1954. The reorganization of the Code changed the lettering and number of the sections and subtitles of the Code. For example, the current Code Section 61 (definition of gross income) was Section 22 prior to the change made by the 1954 Code.

The modern Social Security system began its evolution during the 1950s. Since 1956 Social Security benefits have steadily increased. In 1965, the Medicare and Medicaid systems were introduced. The introduction of Medicare and Medicaid and increases in Social Security benefits necessitated increases in payroll taxes. The two percent Social Security payroll tax increased to six-percent by 1960 and ultimately to 12.3 percent in 1980.

Internal Revenue Code of 1986. The 1986 Tax Act made major substantive changes to the United States tax system. It was not a re-codification of the 1954 Code; however, it did change the name of the 1954 Code to the "Internal Revenue Code of 1986." The 1986 act introduced several new international tax provisions that added to the complexity of operating abroad. For individuals, some of the major changes included the elimination of deductions for state and local tax and for interest on most personal loans. The 1986 Act also lowered the top marginal rates for individuals and corporations, reduced the number of graduated rate brackets, and increased the standard deduction and personal exemption and indexed them for inflation.

5. What Weight Does the Court Give Legislative History?

In interpreting a Code section, the courts will look first to the language of the statute. The words will be interpreted by considering the provision as a whole. The Supreme Court has stated that there is—

> no more persuasive evidence of the purpose of a statute than the words by which the legislature undertook to give expression to its wishes. Often these words are sufficient in and of themselves to determine the purpose of the legislation. In such cases, we have followed their plain meaning.[12]

However, if the meaning of the words would lead to an absurd result or the results are at odds with the policy of the legislation considered as a whole, the court will follow the purpose, rather than the literal words, of the statute. Thus, unequivocal evidence of a clear legislative intent may sometimes override a plain meaning interpretation and lead to a different result. The courts will also look to legislative intent if the meaning of the statute is ambiguous.

Quote:

"When I use a word it means just what I choose it to mean—neither more nor less."

Lewis Carroll, ALICE'S ADVENTURES IN WONDERLAND AND THROUGH THE LOOKING GLASS 169 (Bantan Classic 1981) (1986).

---

12. *United States v. American Trucking Assoc.*, 310 U.S. 534, 543 (1940).

Legislative intent can be ascertained by considering the words in connection with the context, the general purposes of the statute in which it was found, and the occasion and circumstances of its use. The language of the proposed statute; reports of the Ways and Means, Finance, and Conference Committee; and disagreements between chambers eventually worked out in conference will all be considered in determining legislative intent.

Case on Point:

Sundstrand Corp. v. Commissioner
98 T.C. 518, 542 (1992)

We look first to the statutory language to interpret section 1481. *Reiter v. Sonotone Corp.*, 442 U.S. 330, 337 (1979). In interpreting statutory language, "we must not be guided by a single sentence or members of a sentence, but look to the provisions of the whole law, and to its object and policy." *United States v. The Heirs of Boisdore*, 49 U.S. (8 Howard) 113, 121 (1849). As explained in *Helvering v. Stockholms Enskilda Bank*, 293 U.S. 84, 93–94 (1934):

> The intention of the lawmaker controls in the construction of taxing acts as it does in the construction of other statutes, and that intention is to be ascertained, not by taking the word or clause in question from its setting and viewing it apart, but by considering it in connection with the context, the general purposes of the statute in which it is found, the occasion and circumstances of its use, and other appropriate tests for the ascertainment of the legislative will.

For this purpose, explanatory legislative history may be referred to in interpreting the meaning of statutory language.

Statements made during floor debates are only relevant in discerning legislative intent if the proposals debated were enacted into legislation or the debates otherwise shed light on intent in enacting the provision at issue.

Case on Point:

First Chicago Corp. v. Commissioner
96 T.C. 421, 436 (1991)

Petitioner, however, asks us to focus upon what it considers to be part of the legislative history concerning the Revenue Act of 1918, ch. 18, 40 Stat. 1057. During floor debate of a 1918 Revenue Act predecessor of the current foreign tax credit sections, one Senator proposed the aggregation of related domestic taxpayers in order to meet the majority voting requirements (which was required at that time). The proposal did not, however, find its way into enacted legislation, and, to date, has not appeared as part of the statutory language. To the extent one would consider this to be material in the legislative history, it should not be denominated as a reflection of congressional intent because it reflects the view or proposal of only one Senator and, more importantly, was not incorporated in the resulting legislation. Accordingly, we find no express or implied congressional intent to include consolidated shareholdings or aggregation of shareholdings in order to meet the 10-percent-or-more threshold for application of section 902.

Because the General Explanation of the Staff of the Joint Committee on Taxation is prepared by the Committee's staff members (as opposed to the legislators) and is prepared

after the legislation is enacted, the courts have held that the explanation does not directly represent the views of the legislators or an explanation that was available to the legislators when acting on the bill.

Case on Point:

Birth v. Commissioner
92 T.C. 769, 773 (1989)

n.4 Although the Blue Book "does not directly represent the views of the legislators or an explanation available to them when acting on the bill," *McDonald v. Commissioner*, 764 F.2d 322, 336–337 n.25 (5th Cir. 1985), affg. a Memorandum Opinion of this Court, and is technically not considered part of the legislative history of the Tax Reform Act of 1986, we recognize that a Blue Book explanation was previously relied upon by the Supreme Court in its analysis of another tax statute. See *FPC v. Memphis Light, Gas, & Water Div.*, 411 U.S. 458, 471–472 (1973).

Furthermore, the General Explanation technically is not a part of the legislative history. However, while the General Explanation, standing alone without any direct evidence of legislative intent, is not unequivocal evidence of legislative intent, the General Explanation has been relied upon and has been held to be entitled to great respect.

Quote:

"It is not enough merely that hard and objectionable or absurd consequences, which probably were not within the contemplation of the framers, are produced by an act of legislation. Law enacted with good intention, when put to the test, frequently, and to the surprise of the law maker himself, turn out to be mischievous, absurd or otherwise objectionable. But in such case the remedy lies with the law making authority, and not with the courts."

Crooks, Collector of the Internal Revenue Service v. Harrelson, 282 U.S. 55 (1930).

---

6. Where Can Public Laws and Legislative History Be Found?

Public Laws and legislative history can be grouped based on the term of Congress, or include all the relevant law and history of just one Act, or many Acts can be broken down into individual sections of the Act and those sections grouped based on the Internal Revenue Code section each section of the public law amends.

➤ Sources Grouped by Term of Congress (Or By Year)

The following sources publish Public Laws and related legislative history based on the term of Congress that passed the Act or by the year in which the Act was passed:

♦ Congressional Record

The Congressional Record includes all legislative history from introductory remarks to committee reports to the language of the bill that was passed by the House and Senate. The Congressional Record has an index organized by subjects and organizations, by titles, by bill numbers, by Superintendent of Documents Classification Numbers, by Re-

ports and Documents (including House and Senate Reports), and by personal name. It also has a Reference Bibliography.

♦ **Statutes at Large**

The Statutes at Large are organized by Congressional term. For each term of Congress, the laws are organized chronologically by Public Law number. Beginning in 1975, at the conclusion of the Public Law a footnote reference includes information on the legislative history, such as the bill number, Conference Committee Report number, dates the bill was passed by the House and Senate, and location of such information in the Congressional Record.

♦ **Cumulative Bulletin**

The Cumulative Bulletin is organized by year, but published twice a year. For each year, when applicable, the third and fourth volumes contain information on laws that directly impact the Internal Revenue Code.[13] The Cumulative Bulletin includes the following information:

- A cross-reference table for each Public Law enacted that year, organized by Internal Revenue Code section. For each Public Law it lists those Internal Revenue Code sections that are affected by the Public Law and the affecting section of the Public Law;

---

13. The first and second volumes include consolidations of the Internal Revenue Bulletins.

Example:

The following is the last page of Public Law 105–106. Note the reference to the legislative history in the footnote:

112 STAT. 868   PUBLIC LAW 105–206—JULY 22, 1998

23 USC 101 note.   **SEC. 9016. EFFECTIVE DATE.**

This title and the amendments made by this title shall take effect simultaneously with the enactment of the Transportation Equity Act for the 21st Century. For purposes of all Federal laws, the amendments made by this title shall be treated as being included in the Transportation Equity Act for the 21st Century at the time of the enactment of such Act, and the provisions of such Act (including the amendments made by such Act) (as in effect on the day before the date of enactment of this Act) that are amended by this title shall be treated as not being enacted.

Approved July 22, 1998.

LEGISLATIVE HISTORY—H.R. 2676:
HOUSE REPORTS: Nos. 105–364, Pt. 1 (Comm. on Ways and Means) and 105–599
    (Comm. of Conference).
SENATE REPORTS: No. 105–174 (Comm. on Finance).
CONGRESSIONAL RECORD:
    Vol. 143 (1997): Nov. 5, considered and passed House.
    Vol. 144 (1998): May 4–7, considered and passed Senate, amended.
        June 25, House agreed to conference report.
        July 7–9, Senate considered and agreed to conference report.
WEEKLY COMPILATION OF PRESIDENTIAL DOCUMENTS, Vol. 34 (1998):
    July 22, Presidential remarks.

○

Example:

The following is a portion of a cross-reference table that lists those Internal Revenue Code sections that are affected by the Public Law and the affecting section of the Public Law:

1986 Code Sections Added, Amended, or Repealed by Public Laws

The following sections of the Internal Revenue Code 1986 are affected by the Public Laws listed below.

P.L. 105-178
Transportation Equity Act for the 21st Century

1986 Code Section	Act Section
1	9001(a)
40	9003(b)(3)
	9003(a)(3), (b)(1)
132	9010(c)(3)
	9010(c)(1), (2)
	9010(b)(3)
	9010(b)(1), (2)
	9010(a)(2)
	9010(a)(1)
172	9007(b)
	9007(a)
4041	9006(a)
	9003(b)(2)(A)
	9003(a)(1)(A), (B)
	9002(a)(1)(A)-(C)
	9008
4051	9002(a)(1)(D)
4071	9002(a)(1)(E)
4081	9003(b)(2)(B), (C)
	9003(a)(1)(C)
	9002(a)(1)(F)
4091	9003(b)(2)(D)
	9003(a)(1)(D)
4221	9002(b)(1)
4481	9002(a)(1)(G)
4482	9002(a)(1)(H)
4483	9002(b)(2)
6156	9002(a)(2)(B)
6412	9002(a)(2)(A)
6421	9009(c)
	9009(b)(3)
	9006(b)(1)
6427	9009(a)-(b)(2)
	9006(b)(2)
	9003(a)(2)
9501	9011(b)(3)
9503	9011(b)(1), (2)
	9005(e)
	9005(a)
9503	9004(c), (d)
	9004(b)(2)
	9004(b)(1)
	9004(a)(2)
	9004(a)(1)
	9002(f)
	9002(e)(2)

1986 Code Section	Act Section
	9002(c)(3)-(e)(1)
	9002(c)(1), (2)(A)
9504	9004(b)-(d)
9511	9011(a)

P.L. 105-206
Internal Revenue Service
Restructuring and Reform Act of 1998

1986 Code Section	Act Section
1	6007(f)(1)
	6005(d)(1)
	6001(b)
	6001(a)
	5001(b)
	5001(a)(1)-(4)
	1(a)
	6024
	3000
21	6004(a)(1)
23	6018(h)
	6018(f)(1)
	6008(d)(6)
24	6003(a)
25	6008(d)(7)
32	6021(c)
	6021(a), (b)
	6010(p)(1), (2)
	6003(b)
34	6023(32)
	6023(24)(B)
39	6010(n)
42	6004(g)(5)
45A	6023(1)
49	6004(g)(6)
50	6004(g)(7)
55	6006(a)
	6005(d)(2)
57	6005(d)(3)
59	6023(2)
	6011(a)
66	3201(b)
72	6023(3), (4)
	6005(c)(1)
	6004(d)(3)(B
	3436(b)
	3436(a)
101	6010(o)(3)(B)

- A cross-reference table for each Public Law enacted that year, organized by Public Law section. For each Public Law it lists those Public Law sections that affect an Internal Revenue Code section and the Internal Revenue Code Section affected;
- The language of the Public Law as published in the Statutes at Large, including the footnote reference with information on the legislative history of the Act, such as the bill number, Conference Report number, dates the bill was passed by the House and Senate, and location of such information in the Congressional Record;

Example:

The following is a portion of the Public Law as published in the Cumulative Bulletin:

PUBLIC LAW 105–206—JULY 22, 1998   112 STAT. 689

TITLE I—REORGANIZATION OF STRUCTURE AND MANAGEMENT OF THE INTERNAL REVENUE SERVICE

Subtitle A—Reorganization of the Internal Revenue Service

SEC. 1001. REORGANIZATION OF THE INTERNAL REVENUE SERVICE.   26 USC 7801 note.

(a) IN GENERAL.—The Commissioner of Internal Revenue shall develop and implement a plan to reorganize the Internal Revenue Service. The plan shall—

(1) supersede any organization or reorganization of the Internal Revenue Service based on any statute or reorganization plan applicable on the effective date of this section;

(2) eliminate or substantially modify the existing organization of the Internal Revenue Service which is based on a national, regional, and district structure;

(3) establish organizational units serving particular groups of taxpayers with similar needs; and

(4) ensure an independent appeals function within the Internal Revenue Service, including the prohibition in the plan of ex parte communications between appeals officers and other Internal Revenue Service employees to the extent that such communications appear to compromise the independence of the appeals officers.

(b) SAVINGS PROVISIONS.—

(1) PRESERVATION OF SPECIFIC TAX RIGHTS AND REMEDIES.— Nothing in the plan developed and implemented under subsection (a) shall be considered to impair any right or remedy, including trial by jury, to recover any internal revenue tax alleged to have been erroneously or illegally assessed or collected, or any penalty claimed to have been collected without authority, or any sum alleged to have been excessive or in any manner wrongfully collected under the internal revenue laws. For the purpose of any action to recover any such tax, penalty, or sum, all statutes, rules, and regulations referring to the collector of internal revenue, the principal officer for the internal revenue district, or the Secretary, shall be deemed to refer to the officer whose act or acts referred to in the preceding sentence gave rise to such action. The venue of any such action shall be the same as under existing law.

(2) CONTINUING EFFECT OF LEGAL DOCUMENTS.—All orders, determinations, rules, regulations, permits, agreements, grants, contracts, certificates, licenses, registrations, privileges, and other administrative actions—

(A) which have been issued, made, granted, or allowed to become effective by the President, any Federal agency or official thereof, or by a court of competent jurisdiction, in the performance of any function transferred or affected by the reorganization of the Internal Revenue Service or any other administrative unit of the Department of the Treasury under this section; and

(B) which are in effect at the time this section takes effect, or were final before the effective date of this section

- Ways and Means Committee Report;

- Senate Finance Committee Report;

- Conference Report;

    → 3 *Legislative history*.

- Occasionally, additional explanatory information prepared by the Staff of the Joint Committee on Taxation;

- Occasionally, the General Explanation of the Staff of the Joint Committee on Taxation ("Blue Book").

♦   **U.S. Code Congressional and Administrative News**

The U.S. Code Congressional and Administrative News (USCCAN) is organized by Congressional term. For each term it includes:

- The language of the Public Law as published in the Statutes at Large, including the footnote reference with information on the legislative history of the Act, such as the bill number, Conference Committee Report number, dates the bill was passed by the House and Senate, and location of such information in the Congressional Record.

- Following the Public Laws, the USCCAN includes some of the legislative history such as committee reports, conference reports, joint explanatory statements, statements by legislative leaders on major bills and any Signing Statements by the President. The legislative history is organized chronologically by Public Law number and includes additional relevant information such as the bill number, the dates of consideration and passage, and a cross-reference to the Congressional Record.

- A cross-reference table organized by Internal Revenue Code section. For each Code section it lists the section of the public law that amended the Code section and cross-references to the Statutes at Large.

- A table reflecting the legislative history, including bill numbers; Senate, House, and committee report numbers; and dates of passage by the House and Senate.

Example:

The following is a portion of a table reflecting the legislative history, including bill numbers; Senate, House, and committee report numbers; and dates of passage by the House and Senate:

TABLE 4—LEGISLATIVE HISTORY

Public Law No. 107–	Date App.	Stat. Page	Bill No.	Report No. 107– House	Report No. 107– Senate	Comm. Reporting House	Comm. Reporting Senate	Cong. Rec. Vol.(2001) Dates of Passage House	Cong. Rec. Vol.(2001) Dates of Passage Senate
1	Feb. 15	3	HJR 7	none	none	none	none	Feb. 06	Feb. 06
2	Mar. 13	4	HR 559	none	none	none	none	Feb. 14	Feb. 15
3	Mar. 13	5	S 279	none	none	none	none	Feb. 07	Feb. 14
4	Mar. 16	6	HJR 19	none	none	none	none	Feb. 28	Mar. 01
5	Mar. 20	7	SJR 6	none	none	none	none	Mar. 06	Mar. 07
6	Apr. 12	8	HR 132	none	none	none	none	Feb. 07	Mar. 21
7	Apr. 12	9	HR 395	none	none	none	none	Feb. 06	Mar. 21
8	May 11	10	HR 256	2	none	J	none	Feb. 28	Apr. 26
9	May 24	11	S 700	none	none	none	none		May 09
10	May 28	17	HR 428	none	none	none	none	Apr. 24	May 09
11	May 28	19	HR 1696	none	none	none	none	May 15	May 21
12	May 30	20	HR 802	15	none	J	none	Mar. 22	May 14
			(HR 39)						May 14
13	June 03	24	HR 581	35	none	R	none	May 09	May 24
14	June 05	25	HR 801	27	none	VA	none	Mar. 27	May 24
15	June 05	37	HR 1727	65	none	WM	none	May 15	May 22
16	June 07	38	HR 1836	none	none	none	none	May 16	May 23
17	June 26	151	HR 1914	none	none	none	none	June 06	June 08
18	July 05	152	S 1029	none	none	none	none	June 20	June 13
19	July 10	153	S 657	none	none	none	none	June 25	June 19
20	July 24	155	HR 2216	102	none	App	none	June 20	July 10
				148		Conf			
			(S 1077)	none	33	none	App		
21	July 26	194	S 360	none	none	none	none	July 17	
22	July 26	196	S 1190	none	none	none	none	July 23	July 18
23	Aug. 03	198	S 468	none	none	none	none	July 23	May 24
			(HR 621)	none	none	none	none	Feb. 28	
24	Aug. 03	199	HR 1954	107	none	IR	none	July 26	July 27
			(S 1218)	none	none	none	none		July 25
25	Aug. 13	201	HR 2213	111	none	Agr	none	June 26	
			(S 1246)	none	none	none	none		
26	Aug. 17	206	HR 2131	119	none	IR	none	July 10	July 23
			(S 1021)	none	none	none	none		
27	Aug. 20	207	HR 93	none	none	none	none	Jan. 30	
28	Aug. 20	208	HR 271	122	none	R	none	July 23	
			(S 230)	none	21	none	ENR		
29	Aug. 20	209	HR 364	none	none	none	none	Mar. 14	
30	Aug. 20	210	HR 427	151	none	R	none	July 23	
			(S 254)	none	23	none	ENR		
31	Aug. 20	213	HR 558	none	none	none	none	Feb. 28	
			(S 757)	none	none	none	none		May 24
32	Aug. 20	214	HR 821	none	none	none	none	Mar. 14	
33	Aug. 20	215	HR 988	166	none	TI	none		
34	Aug. 20	216	HR 1183	none	none	none	none	June 05	
35	Aug. 20	217	HR 1753	none	none	none	none	June 20	
36	Aug. 20	218	HR 2043	none	none	none	none	June 05	
37	Sept. 18	219	HR 2882	none	none	none	none	Sept. 13	Sept. 13
38	Sept. 18	220	HR 2888	none	none	none	none	Sept. 14	
			(S 1426)	none	none	none	none		Sept. 14
39	Sept. 18	222	SJR 22	none	none	none	none	Sept. 13	Sept. 12
			(HJR 61)	none	none	none	none		Sept. 13
40	Sept. 18	224	SJR 23	none	none	none	none	Sept. 14	Sept. 14
			(HJR 64)	none	none	none	none		Sept. 14
41	Sept. 18	226	HR 2133	none	none	none	none		Aug. 03
			(S 1046)	none	none	none	none		Aug. 03

◆   **Reporter Services**

CCH Standard Federal Tax Reporter and RIA United States Tax Reporter (Income Taxes) may include the language of a Public Law passed during the current year. In CCH, the information is found in Volume 19 and in RIA the information is found in Volume 16.

➤   **Source Addressing Individual Public Laws**

◆   **Supplemental Publications**

Supplemental publications include all the relevant law and history for just one Act. In addition, they include other explanatory information about the Act intended to be practical and helpful to the practitioner.

Publishers such as CCH, RIA, and Mertens provide supplemental publications following the passage of tax legislation. Generally, the publications include:

- The Internal Revenue Code provisions, as amended by the Act;
- Committee reports and other related materials;
- Summary of the act provisions;
- Explanation of the act provisions;
- Commentary and analysis of the law provided by editors, practitioners, and academics;
- Non-code provisions;
- Many cross-reference tables such as tables listing effective dates; Code sections added, amended, or repealed; provisions of other Acts that were amended; sections of the Act that do not amend Code sections (non-code provisions); and sections of the Act and the Code sections they modify.

Practice Note:

Supplemental Publications are an excellent, practical, and comprehensive source of information on a Public Law. A wide variety of information, such as the Code as amended by the Act, non-code provisions, explanations of the changes, commentaries on and examples demonstrating the changes, planning opportunities, and relevant legislative history are included in one source.

For example, CCH prepared "Law, Explanation and Analysis" for the Economic Growth and Tax Relief Reconciliation Act of 2001.

➤   **Changes Organized by Code Section**

The Acts can be broken down into individual sections of the Act and those sections grouped based on the Internal Revenue Code section the Act section amends. Thus, the changes made to a particular Code section over time can be traced.

◆   **Tax Management Primary Sources**

Series V of Tax Management Primary Sources begins with the Internal Revenue Code as enacted in 1986. For selected Code sections it show changes made by Public Laws subsequent to the Tax Reform Act of 1986.

Legislative history for the Internal Revenue Code prior to 1986 is contained in Series I (Tax Reform Act of 1969 through 1975), Series II (Tax Reform Act of 1976 through 1977), Series III (Revenue Act of 1978 through Miscellaneous Revenue Act of 1980), and

Series IV (Economic Recovery Act of 1981 up to, but not including, the Tax Reform Act of 1986) of Primary Sources.

Series V includes:

- Master Table of Contents which lists all Public Laws that have amended a Code section;

Example:

The following is a portion of the Master Table of Contents:

MASTER TABLE OF CONTENTS—Section References to IRC (V–180) 1

MASTER TABLE OF CONTENTS

Section References are to the Internal Revenue Code

> Boldface entries indicate the pages are located in Series V of Primary Sources. All other entries direct the reader to Series I, II, III, or IV Primary Sources. The Roman numeral at the left of an entry designates which series of Primary Sources contains the legislative history for that statute. Interim Supplements are filed in front of the Master Table of Contents.

§1 —Tax Imposed
  (V) Legislative History — P.L. 99-514
    (1986) . . . .§1[1986] pg. 1
  (V) Legislative History — P.L. 100-647
    (1988) . . . .§1[1988] pg. 1
  (V) Legislative History — P.L. 101-239
    (1989) . . . .§1[1989] pg. 1
  (V) Legislative History — P.L. 101-508
    (1990) . . . .§1[1990] pg. 1
  (V) Legislative History — P.L. 103-66
    (1993) . . . .§1[1993] pg. 1
  (V) Legislative History — P.L. 104-188
    (1996) . . . .§1[1996] pg. 1
  (V) Legislative History — P.L. 105-34
    (1997) . . . .§1[1997] pg. 1
  (V) Legislative History — P.L. 105-34
    (1997) . . . .§221[1997] pg. 1
  (V) Legislative History — P.L. 105-206
    (1998) . . . . .221§[1998] pg. 1
  (V) Legislative History — P.L. 105-277
    (1998) . . . .§221[1998] pg. 5
    (V)Legislative History — P.L. 105-206
    (1998) . . . .§1[1998] pg. 1
  (V) Legislative History — P.L. 105-277
    (1998) . . . . §1[1998] pg. 15

§2 —Definitions and Special Rules
  (IV) Statute — P.L. 97-448 (1982) . . . .§2[1982] pg. 1
    Legislative History . . . .§2[1982] pg. 2
  (IV) Statute — P.L. 98-368 (1984) . . . .§2[1984] pg. 1
    Legislative History . . . .§152[1984] pg. 3
  (V) Legislative History — P.L. 99-514
    (1986) . . . .§2[1986] pg. 1
  (V) Legislative History — P.L. 100-647
    (1988) . . . . §2[1986] pg. (i)
  (V) Legislative History — P.L. 104-117
    (1996) . . . . §2[1986] pg. (ii)
  (V) Legislative History — P.L. 106-21
    (1999) . . . . §2[1986] pg. (ii)

§3 —Tax Tables for Individuals
  (V) Legislative History — P.L. 99-514
    (1986) . . . .§3[1986] pg. 1

§4 —Rules for Optional Tax
  (I) Statute — P.L. 83-591 (1954) . . . . §4[1954-68].2
    Legislative History . . . .§4[1954-68].4
  (I) Statute — P.L. 88-272 (1964) . . . . §4[1954-68].6
    Legislative History . . . .§4[1954-68].7
  (I) Statute — P.L. 91-172 (1969) . . . . §4.2
    Legislative History . . . . §4.6
  (I) Statute — P.L. 92-178 (1971) . . . .§4[1971].2
    Legislative History . . . . §4[1971].4

§5 —Cross References Relating to Individuals
  (V) Legislative History — P.L. 99-514
    (1986) . . . .§5[1986] pg. 1

§11 —Tax Imposed
  (V) Legislative History — P.L. 99-514
    (1986) . . . . §11[1986] pg. 1
  (V) Legislative History — P.L. 100-203
    (1987) . . . . §11[1987] pg. 1
  (V) Legislative History — P.L. 100-647
    (1988) . . . . §11[1988] pg. 1
  (V) Legislative History — P.L. 103-66
    (1993) . . . . §11[1993] pg. 1

§12 —Cross References Relating to Tax on Corporations
  (V) Legislative History — P.L. 99-514
    (1986) . . . . §12[1986] pg. 1

§15 —Effect of Changes
  (V) Legislative History — P.L. 99-514
    (1986) . . . . §15[1986] pg. 1
  (V) Legislative History — P.L. 100-647
    (1988) . . . . §15[1988] pg. 1
  (V) Legislative History — P.L. 101-508
    (1990) . . . .§15[1986] pg. (ii)

Boldface entries indicate the pages are located in Series V of Primary Sources. All other entries direct the reader to Series I, II, III, or IV of Primary Sources. See supplements on preceding pages for most recent Code section entries.

12/19/01   © 2001 Tax Management Inc., a subsidiary of The Bureau of National Affairs, Inc.

- Summaries of the legislative history of tax Acts including extensive bibliographies to related materials;

Example:

The following is a sample of a summary of legislative history. It discusses the Personal Responsibility and Work Opportunity Reconciliation of 1996:

TAS:1102	**Personal Responsibility and Work Opportunity Reconciliation Act of 1996**	V-127

credit to offset the costs of legal adoptions, as well as the earned income tax credit program provisions.

The conference agreement contained a package of changes designed to improve EITC compliance and target the benefits to needy working families, while a Senate proposal to deny inflation adjustment of EITC benefits to childless workers was dropped.

According to Joint Committee on Taxation staff estimates, the adoption tax credit proposal included in the welfare bill would cost about $1.8 billion over seven years.

The House approved the conference report on July 31, 1996, by a vote of 328-101, and Senate approval came late Aug. 1, 1996, in a bipartisan vote of 78-21.

On Aug. 22, 1996, President Clinton signed the bill (P.L. 104-193) because "the current system is broken" and because the bill was the "best chance we will have for a long, long time to complete the work of ending welfare as we know it by moving people from welfare to work, demanding responsibility and doing better by children."

Related Documents

H.R. 4, introduced on January 4, 1995, by Rep. E. Clay Shaw (R-Fla.)
H.R. 3734, introduced on June 27, 1996, by Rep. John Kasich (R-Ohio).
S. 1956, introduced on July 16, 1996, by Sen. Pete Domenici (R-N.M.)
H.R. Rep. 104-651, House Budget Committee report to accompany H.R. 3734, filed June 27, 1996.

H.R. Rep. 104-725, Conference Committee report to accompany H.R. 3734, filed July 30, 1996.

Congressional Record, Vol. 142, as follows:

June 27, 1996, pgs. H7105, H7106, — House Budget Committee report filed; Introductory information;

July 17, 1996, pg. H7745 — House debate on H.R. 3734;

July 18, 1996, pgs. H7796, H7820, H7903, H7907, H7990 — Further House debate; amendments and text of bill; House passage of H.R. 3734;

July 23, 1996, pg. S8532 — Senate passage of H.R. 3734 and request for conference;

July 24, 1996, pg. H8319 — House disagrees to Senate amendment and agrees to go to conference;

July 30, 1996, pg. H8829 — Conference Committee report (H.R. Rep. 104-725) submitted in the House; explanatory statement;

July 31, 1996, pgs. H9403, H9424 — Conference report considered, agreed to in the House;

Aug. 1, 1996, pgs. S9322, S9337, S9344, S9387, S9415 — Conference report considered, agreed to in the Senate;

Sept. 4, 1996, pg. H10019 — Presented to the President (Aug. 9, 1996).

Reprinted with permission by Tax Management Inc., a subsidiary of The Bureau of National Affairs, Inc.

LEGISLATIVE HISTORY SUMMARY OF
THE PERSONAL RESPONSIBILITY AND WORK OPPORTUNITY RECONCILIATION ACT OF 1996
P.L. 104-193, 104th Congress, 2nd Session, Aug. 22, 1996

In January 1995, after regaining control of both houses of Congress during the 1994 Federal elections, Republican lawmakers made a written commitment to the American people called the "Contract With America" aimed at restoring the faith and trust of the American people in their government. This "contract" assured that within the first 100 days of the 104th Congress, certain major reforms would be debated and voted on.

Among the reform measures included in the "Contract With America" was a proposal to overhaul the nation's welfare system. This proposal was introduced on Jan. 4, 1995, as H.R. 4 by Rep. E. Clay Shaw (R-Fla.)

The House Ways and Means Subcommittee on Human Resources held a series of topical hearings on Jan. 13, 20, 23, 27, and 30, 1995, on a variety of welfare reform issues, including costs of welfare, role of entitlements, and block grants; illigitimacy and welfare; welfare dependency and welfare-to-work programs; and changing eligibility for supplemental security income.

On Jan. 9, 1996, President Clinton vetoed H.R. 4 because it did "too little to move people from welfare to work" with insufficient assistance for child care, health care, incentives for states that put welfare recipients into jobs, and scant cushion for states when economic downturns call for increased federal help.

On June 27, 1996, Rep. John Kasich (R-Ohio) introduced the fiscal 1997 budget resolution (H.R. 3734) which originally called for three separate reconciliation bills, the first of which would include Medicaid and welfare, the second Medicare, and the third tax cuts.

On the same day, the House Budget Committee filed a report on H.R. 3734 (H.R. Rep. 104-651).

In the Senate, on July 16, 1996, the Budget Committee approved the first of three unnumbered budget reconciliation bills for fiscal 1997, which proposed comprehensive Medicaid and welfare reforms designed to produce savings of nearly $125 billion over six years. Sen. Pete Domenici (R-N.M.) subsequently introduced the measure on the Senate floor July 18, as S. 1956.

On July 18, 1996, the House passed H.R. 3734 by a vote of 256-170. The bill contained a proposal to scale back cuts in the earned income tax credit from the previously proposed level of $5 billion to $1.6 billion over six years. The decision to trim the original cuts proposed in the EITC reflected an effort by Republican leaders to win the president's approval of their welfare bill.

Also on July 18, the Senate began debate on the Republican reconciliation bill (S. 1956) that originally contained both welfare reform and Medicaid proposals. The debate focused exclusively on the proposed changes to the welfare system, including changes to the earned income tax credit. Those changes primarily involved adding income

from tax-exempt interest for calculation of adjusted gross income and lowering the amount of taxable investment income that would disqualify an individual from receiving EITC benefits.

At the request of Senate Republican Leader Bob Dole (R-Kans.), the Medicaid provisions were stripped from the reconciliation bill in order to focus on sending the president a welfare reform package he could sign into law and that the Republicans could take credit for. The Senate passed the bill on July 23, 1996, by a vote of 74-24.

House, Senate Provisions Vary

As passed by the House, H.R. 3734 proposed to save $1.6 billion over six years largely from allowing the Internal Revenue Service to employ expedited procedures in correcting EITC claims in cases where there is an incorrect or missing taxpayer identification number. The bill also contained provisions to deny EITC benefits to individuals without valid Social Security numbers.

The House changes in the EITC were not included in the Senate welfare reform bill, which proposed to cut the program by $4.2 billion over six years.

The Senate bill contained both of those provisions, but added a modification of the definition of adjusted gross income to be used for phasing out benefits. Specifically, the Senate proposal would have disregarded net capital losses, and net losses from trusts and estates, non-business rents and royalties, and businesses in the calculation of adjusted gross income. Income to be included was defined as tax-exempt interest income and non-taxable distributions from pensions, annuities, and individual retirement arrangements.

The Senate Republican welfare reform bill set a five-year lifetime limit on welfare payments to families, and proposed far-reaching changes in the current welfare system by replacing the entitlement status of the program with block grants.

Finally, the Senate bill proposed to reduce the threshold of "disqualified income" — the maximum amount of unearned income a beneficiary can have before becoming ineligible for the EITC — from $2,350 to $2,200 and would have indexed that threshold for inflation after 1996. In total, the Senate EITC proposals would have brought in an estimated $4.9 billion over six years.

Agreement Reached; Clinton Signs Bill

House and Senate negotiators met July 25, 1996, and agreed to a compromise budget reconciliation bill (H.R. 3734) making welfare reforms (H.R. Rep. 104-725). During conference committee debate, an amendment was offered by the Senate which would provide a $5,000 tax

- The following may be included after each Code section:
  - Sections of Public Laws that have amended the Code section;
  - Relevant portions of the Ways and Means, Senate Finance, and Conference Committee reports;
  - Relevant portions of the General Explanation of the Staff of the Joint Committee on Taxation;
  - Relevant portions of other documents prepared by the Staff of the Joint Committee on Taxation;
  - Budget Committee Reports;
  - Informal reports;
  - Hearing transcripts

Practice Note:

Tax Management Primary Sources has extensive and comprehensive legislative history organized by Code section.

♦ **Reporter Services**

CCH Standard Federal Tax Reporter and RIA United States Tax Reporter are organized based on Code section. A small amount of legislative history, generally the portion of the conference report relevant to the Code section, is included after the Code section.

C. Summary

Introductory Remarks, Hearing Transcripts, House and Senate Proceeding Transcripts

Title	Publisher	Comments
Congressional Record	Government Printing Office	Substantial amount of information.
Cumulative Bulletin	Government Printing Office	Information is organized by year in which Public Law was enacted.
Tax Management Primary Sources	BNA	Information is organized based on Code section.
Seidman's Legislative History of the Federal Income Tax Laws 1959–1939	Prentice-Hall	Committee reports, hearing, debates for selected legislation from 1986–1939.
Tax Notes	Tax Analyst	Information on current congressional debates and hearing.
On-line: www.gpoaccess.gov	Government Printing Office	

Ways and Means, Finance, and Conference Committee Reports

Title	Publisher	Comments
Congressional Record	Government Printing Office	Reports are organized based on the term of Congress.
USCCAN	West Group	Reports are organized based on the term of Congress.
Cumulative Bulletin	Government Printing Office	Located in the third or fourth volume of the Cumulative Bulletin for the year in which the Act was passed.
Standard Federal Tax Reporter	CCH	Some legislative history (usually only relevant portions of the conference committee report) is included, organized by Code section.
United States Tax Reporter	RIA	Some legislative history (usually only relevant portions of the conference committee report) is included, organized by Code section.
Tax Management Primary Sources	BNA	Extensive legislative history is included, organized by Code section.
Various supplemental publications	CCH/RIA/ Mertens	Some legislative history (usually only relevant portions of the conference committee report) is included.
On-line: • thomas.loc.gov • www.house.gov/jct • www.house.gov • www.senate.gov • www.gpoaccess.gov • WestLaw • Lexis		

General Explanation of the Staff of the Joint Committee on Taxation — Blue Book

Title	Publisher	Comments
General Explanation of the Joint Committee on Taxation	Government Printing Office	Referred to as the "Blue Book" due to its traditionally blue cover.
Statutes at Large	Government Printing Office	Organized chronologically by Public Law number.
Cumulative Bulletin	Government Printing Office	Not always included, but if it is, will be located in the third or fourth volume of the Cumulative Bulletin for the year in which the Act was passed.
On-line: • www.house.gov/jct		

Public Laws

Title	Publisher	Comments
Statutes at Large	Government Printing Office	Organized by term of Congress.
USCCAN	West Group	Organized by term of Congress.
Cumulative Bulletin	Government Printing Office	Located in the third or fourth volume of the Cumulative Bulletin for the year in which the Act was passed.
Standard Federal Tax Reporter	CCH	Generally located in Volume 9 for the year in which the Act was passed.
United States Tax Reporter	RIA	Generally located in Volume 16 for the year in which the Act was passed.
On-line: • WestLaw • Lexis • www.gpoaccess.gov		

Internal Revenue Code

Title	Publisher	Comments
United States Code	Government Printing Office	Includes Amendments that include sections of Public Law that have amended the Code section and cross-references to relevant Public Law numbers and Statute at Large numbers.
United States Code Annotated	West Publishing Co.	Includes Historical and Statutory Notes that include sections of Public Law that have amended the Code section and cross-references to relevant Public Law numbers and Statute at Large numbers.
United States Code Service	LexisNexis	
Internal Revenue Code	CCH	Includes sections of Public Law that have amended the Code section and cross-references to relevant Public Law numbers.
Internal Revenue Code	RIA	Includes sections of Public Law that have amended the Code section and cross-references to relevant Public Law numbers.
Internal Revenue Code	Mertens	Includes sections of Public Law that have amended the Code section and cross-references to relevant Public Law numbers.
On-line: • www.irs.gov • www.gpoaccess.gov • www.law.cornell.edu	Government Printing Office Cornell University Law School	• www.gpoaccess.gov/uscode/index.html • www.law.cornell.edu/uscode/26

Selected Internet Sources

Office of the Clerk	www.clerkweb.house.gov
The Hill	www.hillnews.com
House of Representatives	www.house.gov
Senate	www.senate.gov
White House	www.whitehouse.gov
Joint Committee on Taxation	www.house.gov/jct
Government Printing Office	www.gpoaccess.gov

D. Related Articles for Further Reading

- Brian Ladin, *The Plain Meaning Rule: Justice's Version of Tough Love*, TAX NOTES (July 5, 2004).

- Mary L. Heen, *Plain Meaning, the Tax Code, and Doctrinal Incoherence*, 48 HASTINGS L.J. 771 (1997).

- John F. Coverdale, *Text as Limit: A Plea for a Decent Respect for the Tax Code*, 71 TUL. L. REV. 1501 (1997).

- Donna D. Adler, *A Conversational Approach to Statutory Analysis: Say What You Mean & Mean What You Say*, 66 MISS. L.J. 37 (1996).

- Deborah A. Geier, *Interpreting Tax Legislation: The Role of Purpose*, 2 FLA. TAX REV. 492 (1995).

- Robert Thornton Smith, *Interpreting the Internal Revenue Code: A Tax Jurisprudence*, 72 TAXES 527 (1994).

- Michael Livingston, *What's Blue and White and Not Quite So Good as a Committee Report: General Explanations and the Role of "Subsequent" Tax Legislative History*, 11 AM. J. TAX POL'Y 91 (1994).

- Deborah A. Geier, *Commentary: Textualism and Tax Cases*, 66 Temple L. Rev. 445 (1993).

- Michael Livingston, *Congress, the Courts, and the Code: Legislative History and the Interpretation of Tax Statutes*, 69 TEX. L. REV. 819 (1991).

- James B. Lewis, *Viewpoint: The Nature and Role of Tax Legislative History*, 68 TAXES 442 (1990).

- Bradford L. Ferguson, Frederic W. Hickman, Donald C. Lubick, *Reexamining the Nature and Role of Tax Legislative History in Light of the Changing Realities of the Process*, 67 TAXES 804 (1989).

- Lawrence Zelenak, *Thinking About Nonliteral Interpretations of the Internal Revenue Code*, 64 N.C.L. REV. 623 (1986).

E. Problems

1. Non-code provisions are:

   a.   Public Laws.
   b.   Legislative history.
   c.   Provisions outside the Internal Revenue Code.
   d.   Public Laws not codified in the United States Code.

2. What Committee is involved in every stage of the legislative process?

   a.   Finance Committee.
   b.   Joint Committee on Taxation.
   c.   Ways and Means Committee.
   d.   Tax Committee.

3. When a bill is introduced, it is assigned a number:

   a.   Based on the date it is introduced.
   b.   Based on the number of bills introduced by the sponsoring Congressman.
   c.   Based on the political party sponsoring the bill.
   d.   Based on the chronological order in which it is introduced during the two year term.

4. The United States Code is:

   a.   A compilation of the Public Laws.
   b.   A compilation of the laws of the United States, arranged by subject matter in titles.
   c.   A compilation of legislative history.
   d.   A compilation of important committee reports.

5. The Congressional Record contains:

   a.   An almost verbatim account of the proceedings and debates of the House and Senate, published daily.
   b.   Summaries of committee meetings.
   c.   Compilations of bills passed by Congress.
   d.   None of the above.

6. When a bill concerning a tax matter is introduced, it is generally referred to:

   a.   The Senate Finance Committee.
   b.   The Joint Committee on Taxation.
   c.   The Ways and Means Committee.
   d.   The Conference Committee.

7. A Committee Print can be used:

   a.   If a matter is to be considered without a three-day time period having elapsed.
   b.   If the committee votes in favor of the bill.
   c.   If the committee has made revisions to the bill.
   d.   If the report reflects compromises between the Ways and Means Committee and the Finance Committee.

8. The United States Statutes at Large contain:

   a. Public laws.
   b. Summaries of committee debates.
   c. Summaries of floor debates.
   d. Summaries of testimony given before committees.

9. A report issued by the Senate Finance Committee is assigned a number based on:

   a. The order in which it was introduced into Congress.
   b. The order in which it was considered by the Senate Finance Committee.
   c. The order in which it was considered by the Senate as a whole.
   d. The order in which it was filed with the Clerk of the Senate during the two-year term.

10. Where there are differences between the House and Senate versions of a bill that cannot be resolved informally, the bill is sent to:

    a. Conference Committee.
    b. The Joint Committee on Taxation.
    c. The Ways and Means Committee.
    d. The Finance Committee.

11. The Blue Book provides:

    a. A summary of legislation.
    b. A compilation of the public laws passed during a specific time frame.
    c. A summary of legislative history.
    d. None of the above.

12. Conference Reports are almost always numbered as:

    a. Senate Reports.
    b. House Reports.
    c. Congressional Reports.
    d. Joint Committee Reports.

13. If both chambers adopt a conference report, the president can:

    a. Sign the measure into law.
    b. Disapprove, subject to the ability of Congress during the session to override the veto by 2/3 vote of the members present and voting in each House.
    c. By not taking any action in 10 days, allow the bill to become law.
    d. Any of the above.

14. Public Law can be found in all of the following locations, except:

    a. Cumulative Bulletin.
    b. U.S.C.C.A.N.
    c. Federal Reporter.
    d. United States Statutes at Large.

15. With respect to the legislative process:

    a. Describe the process.
    b. What documents are generated by the legislative process that might indicate the intent of the legislators?
    c. What other sources might provide the intent of the legislators?

RIA Checkpoint

16. What is the Blue Book? Who prepares it?

17. If you had to locate the legislative history of a particular act, where would you look? Why? *lage = 71 54 or 71*

18. What is the difference between a committee report and a committee print?

19. With respect to the Jobs and Growth Tax Relief Reconciliation Act of 2003, provide the following information:

    a. Bill number.
    b. The name of the legislator who introduced the bill.
    c. Number for the report filed by the House Ways and Means Committee.
    d. Did any Congressman file a supplemental or minority opinion?
    e. Was a report filed by the Senate Finance Committee?
    f. Number for the report filed by the Conference Committee.
    g. Public Law number.
    h. Citation in the Statutes at Large for section 302 of the Act.

20. What information is included in the Statutes at Large?

21. What is the relationship between the Statutes at Large and the United Stated Code?

22. What is the difference between the United States Code and the United States Code Annotated?

23. Are all public laws included in the United States Code?

RIA Checkpoint

24. If you had to track changes made to a particular Code provision over a certain period of time, where would you look? Why? *P = 79*

25. With respect to section 121 of the Internal Revenue Code, provide the following information:

    a. Which Public Laws have amended section 121?
    b. What years did the term of Congress that amended section 121 cover?
    c. What is the effect of section 901 of Public Law No. 107-16?
    d. What was the language of section 121 prior to amendment by section 6005(e)(3) of Public Law No. 105-34?
    e. When did each of the changes become effective?

26. With respect to section 721 of the Internal Revenue Code, provide the following information:

    a. Title in which it is located.
    b. Subtitle in which it is located.
    c. Chapter in which it is located.
    d. Subchapter in which it is located.
    e. Part in which it is located.
    f. Subpart in which it is located.

Register on Taxnotes website for this kind of research

27. Read section 469(c)(1).

    a. What is the definition of a passive activity?
    b. Under what Public Law was section 469 enacted?
    c. What information does the Statutes at Large contain about what a passive activity is?
    d. What information does the Finance Committee Report include about what a passive activity is?
    e. What information, if any, does the Ways and Means Committee Report include about what a passive activity is?
    f. Is the legislative history supported by the language of the Act?

28. Who are the current members of the Joint Committee of Taxation? Who is the Chief of Staff?

29. You have been closely following a tax bill that has a provision in it that would have a negative tax impact on a tax planning technique one of your clients intends to utilize. The planning technique is somewhat aggressive. The tax bill ultimately becomes a public law. However, the provision that would have had a negative impact on your client was removed during mark-up. Does the fact the provision was dropped from the final version of the bill have any precedential value? *NO, because it is not yet a law.*

30. Is the General Explanation of the Staff of the Joint Committee on Taxation part of the legislative history? Why or why not? What deference *some* do courts give the General *NO* Explanation of the Staff of the Joint Committee? What result if the General Explanation differs from the explanation provided in the Conference Report. *See Alen III v. Commissioner,* 118 TC 1 (1995). *because not written by Congress.*

31. If you had to support a position you wanted to take:

    a. When could you use legislative history as support? *when words are ambiguous*
    b. How would you use legislative history as support? *By refering to reports.*
    c. What would you do if it appeared the legislative history did not support the position you wanted to take? *Try to convince the court.*

32. Read *Gitlitz v. Commissioner,* 182 F.3d 1143 (10th Cir. 1999).

    a. What was the issue before the court?
    b. What statutory language was at issue?
    c. Do you believe the statutory language is clear or ambiguous?
    d. Is it relevant whether the statutory language is clear or ambiguous? Why or why not?
    e. What result did the court reach? Why? (See also *Gitlitz v. Commissioner,* 531 U.S. 206 (2001).)

what is legislative history?

→ Legislative history is a legal term used to describe the purpose or intent during the process of making a legislative bill.

Chapter 4

Must Read article reading assigned for Supplementary reading to Chapter 4 on canvas.

Treasury Regulations

Regulations

• *What types of regulations are there?*

• *How are regulations issued?*

• *What weight does each type of regulation have?*

• *What is the effective date of a regulation?*

• *How are regulations numbered?*

• *Which regulations is the IRS working on now?*

• *Where can I find treasury decisions and regulations?*

Mary had been in the library since arriving at work that morning. After pouring over book after book, she spotted Ned, a friendly and knowledgeable senior associate, entering the library. She decided he might be able to help her, so walked over to talk to him.

"I am having a terrible time with some research," Mary began.

"What are you working on?"

"My client wants to know if he can take the loss from the sale of corporate stock," Mary explained.

"That doesn't seem to be that complicated of a question. Exactly what is giving you all the trouble?"

"The stock was held as part of a consolidated group."

"Oh," groaned Ned. "Now, I understand. As I am sure you know, the bulk of the law in the consolidated return area is found in the regulations. Miles and miles of regulations, I might add. Did you try there?"

"As a matter of fact, I did. And, that is what is causing me all the problems. I found a regulation that seemed to be on point. But, the more I looked into it, the more I thought it wasn't consistent with what other areas of tax law allowed. I guess what I am trying to say is that I think the IRS went beyond what Congress intended it to do when it issued this regulation. How do I know if my client is bound by the regulation or whether we can challenge it? And, if we can challenge it, what burden will we have to meet?"

"All good questions. Let's see if we can answer some of them," Ned responded as he took a seat at her research table.

Contents

A. Key Terms

After completing this chapter, you should be familiar with the following key terms:

➤ Legislative Regulation

➤ Interpretative Regulation

➤ Treasury Decision

➤ Federal Register

➤ Notice of Proposed Rule Making

➤ Proposed Regulation

➤ Final Regulation

➤ Temporary Regulation

➤ Code of Federal Regulations

B. Discussion

is administrative

Regulations are issued to assist the public in interpreting and understanding the Internal Revenue Code. Section 7805 gives the Secretary of the Treasury Department general authority to issue such regulations. The Secretary of the Treasury is the head of the Treasury Department and a member of the president's cabinet. The Internal Revenue Service, and more particularly its legal representatives in the Office of Chief Counsel, assists the Secretary in carrying out this responsibility by drafting the regulations. The Internal Revenue Service is an agency located within the Treasury Department. The Office of Chief Counsel is its legal arm.

A tax practitioner may not always agree with the IRS's interpretation of a Code section. In such situations, to properly advise his client, the practitioner must discern how much weight a court would give to the regulation. This, in turn, depends on what type of regulation is at issue, legislative or interpretative.

1. Types of Regulations — Legislative and Interpretative

Legislative regulations. In some instances, the language of the statute instructs the Secretary to issue regulations to carry out the intent of the statute. Congress may include such language in a statute when spelling out the exact criteria of a provision in a statute would be too cumbersome or complex or when the IRS is in a better position through practical experience or exposure to delineate the parameters of a particular statutory provision.

Example:

The following is a Code a section calling for legislative regulations:

Section 2663. Regulations

The Secretary shall prescribe such regulations as may be necessary or appropriate to carry out the purposes of this chapter [Tax on Generation-Skipping Transfers], including—

(1) such regulations as may be necessary to coordinate the provisions of this chapter with the recapture tax imposed under section 2032A(c),

(2) regulations (consistent with the principles of chapters 11 and 12) providing for the application of this chapter in the case of transferors who are nonresidents not citizens of the United States, and

(3) regulations providing for such adjustments as may be necessary to the application of this chapter in the case of any arrangement which, although not a trust, is treated as a trust under section 2652(b).

When Congress has specifically instructed the Secretary in the statute to issue regulations, any such regulations are considered legislative regulations.

A **legislative regulation** is one that is issued pursuant to a specific congressional delegation to the Secretary.

Legislative regulations are given the highest level of judicial deference. A court will follow a legislative regulation unless it is arbitrary, capricious, or manifestly contrary to the authorizing statute.[1] A regulation is contrary to the statute if it is outside the scope of the authority that has been delegated by the statute.

---

1. *Chevron U.S.A. Inc. v. Natural Res. Def. Council, Inc.*, 467 U.S. 837, 844 (1984); *Carlos v. Commissioner*, 123 T.C. 275, 280 (2004).

Case on Point: *flux*

Chevron U.S.A. Inc. v. Natural Resources Defense Council, Inc.
467 U.S. 837, 843–44 (1984)

If Congress has explicitly left a gap for the agency to fill, there is an express delegation of authority to the agency to elucidate a specific provision of the statute by regulation. Such legislative regulations are given controlling weight unless they are arbitrary, capricious, or manifestly contrary to the statute.

In many situations, even though the statute instructs the IRS to issue regulations, it has not yet done so. The impact of this lack of guidance depends on what the regulations were intended to do. If the statute requires the IRS to issue regulations on "how" a statute should apply (i.e., "The Secretary shall prescribe regulations as may be necessary or appropriate to carry out the purpose of this section …"), in the absence of regulations the substance of the statutory provision still must be implemented.

Case on Point:

Estate of Maddox v. Commissioner
93 T.C. 228, 233 (1989)

Some 13 years have now passed since the Congress provided that the Secretary "shall" prescribe the regulations, and at this writing he has not even submitted any proposed regulations. The situation is similar to the one we faced in *Occidental Petroleum Corp. v. Commissioner*, 82 T.C. 819, 829 (1984), and *First Chicago Corp. v. Commissioner*, 88 T.C. 663, 669 (1987), aff'd. 842 F.2d 180 (7th Cir. 1988), where the regulations there called for had not been issued some 8 and 11 years, respectively, after enactment of the statute. We repeated in *First Chicago* our critical comment in *Occidental* upon this "sorry situation." See 88 T.C. at 669 and 82 T.C. at 829 n.6. However, as was the case in *Occidental* and *First Chicago*, we must do the best we can with the statutory provision (subsection (g)) now before us in the absence of pertinent regulations, since, in our view, the Secretary cannot deprive a taxpayer of rights which the Congress plainly intended to confer simply by failing to promulgate the required regulations.

If the statute requires the IRS to issue regulations on "whether" a provision applies (i.e., the Secretary "shall prescribe such regulations as may be necessary or appropriate … which provide that certain items of gross income will not be taken into account in determining income or loss from any activity …"), unless regulations are issued that allow the taxpayer the treatment contemplated by the statute, such treatment cannot be read into the statutory provision. If the IRS has issued regulations, but not addressed the specific area desired by the taxpayer, unless the IRS's position in the regulation is contrary to the plain meaning of the statute, a court is not free to replace that clear language with its own interpretation.[2]

Interpretative regulations. If the statute does not specifically direct the Secretary to issue regulations, the Secretary still has the authority to issue interpretative regulations. Section 7805(a) gives the Secretary the general authority to issue "all needful rules and regulations for the enforcement" of the Code.

---

2. See, e.g., *Hillman v. Commissioner*, 263 F.3d 338 (4th Cir. 2001), rev'g and remanding 114 T.C. 103 (2000).

> Section 7805 provides:
>
> (a) Authorization. Except where such authority is expressly given by this title to any person other than an officer or employee of the Treasury Department, the Secretary shall prescribe all needful rules and regulations for the enforcement of this title, including all rules and regulations as may be necessary by reason of any alteration of law in relation to internal revenue.

Regulations issued under this authority are called interpretative (or interpretive) regulations.

> **Example:**
>
> The following are examples of interpretative regulations:
>
> Treas. Reg. § 1.61-1 Gross income.
>
> (a) General definition. Gross income means all income from whatever source derived, unless excluded by law. Gross income includes income realized in any form, whether in money, property, or services. Income may be realized, therefore, in the form of services, meals, accommodations, stock, or other property, as well as in cash. Section 61 lists the more common items of gross income for purposes of illustration. For purposes of further illustration, § 1.61-14 mentions several miscellaneous items of gross income not listed specifically in section 61. Gross income, however, is not limited to the items so enumerated.
>
> * * *
>
> Treas. Reg. § 1.213-1 Medical, dental, etc., expenses.
>
> (a) Allowance of deduction. (1) Section 213 permits a deduction of payments for certain medical expenses (including expenses for medicine and drugs). Except as provided in paragraph (d) of this section (relating to special rule for decedents) a deduction is allowable only to individuals and only with respect to medical expenses actually paid during the taxable year, regardless of when the incident or event which occasioned the expenses occurred and regardless of the method of accounting employed by the taxpayer in making his income tax return. Thus, if the medical expenses are incurred but not paid during the taxable year, no deduction for such expenses shall be allowed for such year.

> An **interpretative regulation** is one issued pursuant to the general authority given the Secretary under section 7805(a).

An interpretative regulation is given less deference than a legislative regulation.[3] Nevertheless, the court will follow an interpretative regulation as long as it implements the Congressional mandate in some way.[4] If Congress has directly spoken to the question at issue, and the intent of Congress is clear, the regulation must give effect to the Congressional intent. If Congress has not spoken directly to the question at issue, the court will

---

3. *Chevron U.S.A., Inc., v. Natural Res. Def. Council, Inc.* 467 U.S. 837, 843–44 (1984); *United States v. Vogel Fertilizer Co.*, 45 U.S. 16, 24 (1982); *Robinson v. Commissioner*, 119 T.C. 44, 68 (2002).
4. *Mayo Foundation for Medical Education and Research v. United States*, ___ U.S. ___ (2011).

not determine which potential interpretation is the best, the taxpayer's or the IRS's; rather it will limit itself to determining only whether the IRS's interpretation is reasonable. A regulation is considered reasonable if it is consistent with the statutory language and the statute's origin and purpose. A statute's legislative history is often considered in determining its purpose.[5]

Case on Point:

Tutor-Saliba Corp. v. Commissioner
115 T.C. 1, 8 (2000)

[4]We are mindful that the choice among reasonable statutory interpretations is for the executive branch of Government and not the courts. See *National Muffler Dealers Association, Inc. v. United States*, 440 U.S. 472, 488 (1979). The issue is whether the Secretary's interpretation of the statute is a reasonable one, not whether it is the best or only one. See *Brown v. United States*, 890 F.2d 1329, 1338 (5th Cir. 1989). When the regulation implements in some reasonable manner the congressional intent underlying a provision, courts are not at liberty to strike down the regulation merely because the taxpayer offers a more attractive statutory interpretation. See id.

Given the frequency with which Congress makes changes to the Internal Revenue Code, the IRS has been unable to keep regulations current with the Code as amended by Congress. Care should be given when considering a regulation to assure that the regulation is not providing an interpretation of the Code as it existed prior to being amended. Specifically, the date the relevant Code provision was enacted should be compared with the date the relevant regulation was filed in the Federal Register.

Practice Note:

Regulatory compilations offered by CCH provide references to Treasury Decisions and the dates they were filed following each regulation. This information provides a quick reference to the age of the regulation. In addition, to the extent relevant, CCH lists cautions at the beginning of the regulation alerting the reader if the regulation has not been updated since the Code section was amended.

Furthermore, the fact that no regulation has been issued to interpret a particular Code provision or that a regulation has not been updated to reflect a change in the Code bears no interpretive weight.

Case on Point:

Speckling v. Commissioner
117 T.C. 95, 105, 111 (2001)

Petitioners contend further that respondent's failure to amend section 1.931-1, Income Tax Regs., to exclude Johnston Island from the list of possessions for which section 931 applies, shows that respondent believes that old section 931 remained in force for the years in issue. Petitioners further argue that section 1.931-1, Income Tax Regs, is not inconsistent with the statute because the conditions required by Congress for the effectuation of the amendments to old section 931 have not yet occurred....

---

5. *NationsBank of N.C., N.A. v. Variable Annuity Life Ins. Co.*, 513 U.S. 251, 257 (1995).

We do not agree with petitioners that respondent's failure to amend section 1.931-1, Income Tax Regs., supports petitioners' position. As the Supreme Court recently observed regarding another unamended regulation provision: "The Treasury's relaxed approach to amending its regulations to track Code changes is well documented. * * * The absence of any amendment * * * is more likely a reflection of the Treasury's inattention than any affirmative intention on its part to say anything at all." United Dominion Indus., Inc. v. United States, 532 U.S. ___, 121 S. Ct. 1934, 1942–1943 (June 4, 2001).

Figure 4.1 Types of Regulations

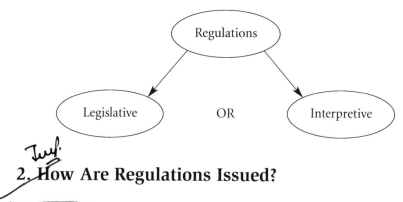

2. How Are Regulations Issued?

If the IRS is issuing a legislative regulation, it must comply with the Administrative Procedures Act (APA). If issuing an interpretative regulation, it is not required to follow the APA, but generally does anyway. Thus, effectively, both types of regulations follow one process. The requirement that the APA must be followed when issuing a legislative regulation generally is only important if the taxpayer intends to make an argument that the procedures were not correctly followed, rendering the regulation invalid.

Under the APA, regulations are issued by a two-step process. First, the regulation is issued in proposed form. Then, after the public has been given an opportunity to provide input and at least 30 days have passed, the regulation can be issued in its final form. Given the pace at which the IRS processes regulations, there is generally substantially more than 30 days separating issuance of the proposed regulation from issuance in final form.

Proposed regulations. The issuance of a proposed regulation is announced by a notice of proposed rulemaking, which is published in the Federal Register as a Treasury Decision. If the IRS intends to offer a public hearing on the proposed regulation, a notice of public hearing will also be filed.

The **Federal Register** is a daily publication published by the Office of the Federal Register, National Archives and Records Administration. It provides a uniform system for making available to the public regulations and legal notices issued by Federal agencies. It is available on-line at www.access.gpo.gov/nara.

The **notice of proposed rulemaking** will include a statement of the time, place, and nature of the public rulemaking proceedings; reference to the legal authority under which the rule is proposed; and either the terms or substance of the proposed rule or a de-

scription of the subjects and issues involved. In addition to the proposed language, the notice will include a preamble which may contain valuable information related to the proposed regulation. Specifically, it will contain:

- A summary of the proposed Treasury Decision;
- Dates by which written comments and requests for hearings must be submitted;
- Address for submitting submissions;
- Name and telephone number for person to contact for additional information;
- Background of proposed Treasury Decision;
- Explanation of the provisions;
- If already determined, information on the hearing place and date; and
- Proposed amendments to the regulation.

While the information given in the preamble is given little weight by the court, it provides a wealth of information to the taxpayer or practitioner, such as the reason for the proposed regulation or proposed change to an existing regulation.

Example:

The following is an example of a notice of proposed rule making:

DEPARTMENT OF THE TREASURY

Internal Revenue Service (IRS)

26 CFR Part 301

[REG-131739-03]

RIN 1545-BC45

Substitute for Return

70 FR 41165

DATE: Monday, July 18, 2005

ACTION: Notice of proposed rulemaking by cross-reference to temporary regulations.

SUMMARY: In the Rules and Regulations section of this issue of the Federal Register, the IRS is issuing temporary regulations relating to the IRS preparing or executing returns for persons who fail to make required returns. The text of those regulations also serves as the text of these proposed regulations.

EFFECTIVE DATE: Written or electronically generated comments and requests for a public hearing must be received by October 17, 2005.

ADDRESSES: Send submissions to: CC:PA:LPD:PR (REG-131739-03), Room 5203, Internal Revenue Service, PO Box 7604, Ben Franklin Station, Washington, DC 20044. Submissions may be hand delivered Monday through Friday between the hours of 8 a.m. and 4 p.m. to: CC:PA:LPD:PR (REG-131739-03), Courier's Desk, Internal Revenue Service, 1111 Constitution Avenue, NW, Washington, DC. Alternatively, taxpayers may submit comments electronically via the IRS Internet site at http://www.irs.gov/regs or via the Federal eRulemaking Portal at http://www.regulations.gov (IRS and REG-131739-03).

FOR FURTHER INFORMATION CONTACT: Concerning the proposed regulations, Tracey B. Leibowitz, (202) 622-4940; concerning submissions of comments and re-

quests for a public hearing, Treena Garrett of the Regulations Unit at (202) 622-7180 (not toll-free numbers).

SUPPLEMENTARY INFORMATION:

Background and Explanation of Provisions

Temporary regulations in the Rules and Regulations section of this issue of the **Federal Register** amend 26 CFR part 301 relating to section 6020. The temporary regulations retain the method by which an internal revenue officer or employee prepares a return under section 6020(a). Further, the temporary regulations provide that a document (or set of documents) signed by an authorized internal revenue officer or employee is a return under section 6020(b) if the document (or set of documents) identifies the taxpayer by name and taxpayer identification number, contains sufficient information from which to compute the taxpayer's tax liability, and the document (or set of documents) purport to be a return under section 6020(b). A Form 13496, "IRC Section 6020(b) Certification," or any other form that an authorized internal revenue officer or employee signs and uses to identify a document (or set of documents) containing the information set forth above as a section 6020(b) return, and the documents identified, constitute a valid section 6020(b) return. The text of those regulations also serve as the text of these proposed regulations. The preamble to the temporary regulations explains the amendments.

Special Analyses

It has been determined that this notice of proposed rulemaking is not a significant regulatory action as defined in Executive Order 12866. Therefore, a regulatory assessment is not required. It also has been determined that section 553(b) of the Administrative Procedure Act (5 U.S.C. chapter 5) does not apply to these regulations, and, because these regulations do not impose a collection of information on small entities, the Regulatory Flexibility Act (5 U.S.C. chapter 6) does not apply. Pursuant to section 7805(f) of the Internal Revenue Code, this notice of proposed rulemaking will be submitted to the Chief Counsel for Advocacy of the Small Business Administration for comment on their impact.

Comments and Requests for a Public Hearing

Before these proposed regulations are adopted as final regulations, consideration will be given to any written (a signed original and 8 copies) and electronic comments that are submitted timely to the IRS. The IRS and Treasury specifically request comments on the clarity of the proposed regulations and how they can be made easier to understand. All comments will be available for public inspection and copying. A public hearing will be scheduled if requested in writing by any person that timely submits comments. If a public hearing is scheduled, notice of the date, time, and place for the public hearing will be published in the Federal Register.

Drafting Information

The principal author of these regulations is Tracey B. Leibowitz, of the Office of the Associate Chief Counsel (Procedure and Administration), Administrative Provisions and Judicial Practice Division.

List of Subjects in 26 CFR Part 301

Employment taxes, Estate taxes, Excise taxes, Gift taxes, Income taxes, Penalties, Reporting and recordkeeping requirements.

Proposed Amendments to the Regulations

Accordingly, 26 CFR part 301 is proposed to be amended to read as follows:

PART 301 — PROCEDURE AND ADMINISTRATION

Paragraph 1. The authority citation continues to read, in part, as follows:

Authority: 26 U.S.C. 7805 * * * Par. 2. Section 301.6020-1 is added to read as follows:

§ 301.6020-1 Returns prepared or executed by the Commissioner or other internal revenue officers.

[The text of proposed § 301.6020-1 is the same as the text of § 301.6020-1T published elsewhere in this issue of the Federal Register].

Mark E. Matthews,

Deputy Commissioner for Services and Enforcement.

[FR Doc. 05-14085 Filed 7-15-05; 8:45 am]

BILLING CODE 4830-01-P

The IRS assigns a project number to each regulation. While the numbering system has varied over the years, currently the project number begins with "REG," is followed by a number, followed by a dash and the year the project was opened.

Once a notice of proposed rulemaking has been filed, a taxpayer can submit his data, views, or arguments regarding the proposal to the IRS. Any such submitted comments are available for public inspection. Thus, a person interested in the proposal can follow and consider comments submitted by others.

In addition to providing written comments, a person may want to speak at the public hearing on the proposed regulation. To do so, he must first file his written comments with the IRS and then submit an outline of his presentation (within the timeline set forth in the notice of proposed rulemaking). The outline must include the topics the person wishes to discuss and the amount of time he intends to devote to each topic. At the hearing, the person generally will be limited to a discussion of matters relating to his written comments and to questions and answers connected with the comments. However, as the IRS already has the written comments, the oral comments should not be a repetition of what was contained in the written comments.

Prior to the hearing, the IRS will prepare an agenda containing the order of all presenters and the time allotted to each presentation. As a general rule, no speaker will be allocated more than 10 minutes. After all the presenters listed on the agenda have spoken, if time permits and others attending the hearing find they want to make a comment, they will be allowed to do so.

Representatives from the IRS and Treasury Department assigned to the regulation project who are on the hearing panel generally only listen to the oral comments. The hearing is not intended as a forum to debate the merits of the proposed regulation.

Final regulations. After taking into consideration the comments received from interested parties, three things can occur. First, infrequently, the IRS will withdraw the proposed regulation by issuing a notice of withdrawal.

Example:

The following is a notice of withdrawal of proposed regulations:

Announcement 2000-63, 2000-2 C.B. 149

Bad Debt Reserves of Thrift Institutions

AGENCY: Internal Revenue Service (IRS), Treasury.

ACTION: Withdrawal of proposed regulations.

SUMMARY: This document withdraws proposed regulations amending the income tax regulations. This action is taken to remove from the IRS' inventory of regulations projects certain proposed regulations that will not be published in final form because under a subsequent amendment the underlying statute does not apply to taxable years beginning after December 31, 1995.

DATES: These proposed regulations are withdrawn July 12, 2000.

FOR FURTHER INFORMATION CONTACT: Craig Wojay, of the Office of Assistant Chief Counsel, Financial Institutions and Products, Internal Revenue Service, 1111 Constitution Ave., NW, Washington, DC 20224. Telephone (202) 622-3920, (not a toll-free number).

SUPPLEMENTARY INFORMATION:

Background

This document withdraws certain proposed regulations previously published in the Federal Register (FI-42-90, 1992-1 C.B. 1072 [57 F.R. 1232]) by the IRS. These proposed regulations, §§ 1.593-12, 1.593-13, and 1.593-14, are being withdrawn because under a subsequent amendment the underlying statute, section 593, does not apply subsections (a), (b), (c), and (d) to taxable years beginning after December 31, 1995.

Drafting Information

The principal author of this withdrawal notice is Craig Wojay, Office of the Assistant Chief Counsel (Financial Institutions and Products) within the Office of the Chief Counsel, IRS. However, other personnel from the IRS and the Treasury Department participated in developing the withdrawal notice.

* * * *

Withdrawal of Proposed Amendments to the Regulations

Accordingly, under the authority of 26 U.S.C. 7805, the proposed rulemaking that was published in the Federal Register on Monday, January 13, 1992 (57 F.R. 1232) is withdrawn.

Robert E. Wenzel, *Deputy Commissioner of Internal Revenue.*

(Filed by the Office of the Federal Register on July 11, 2000, 8:45 a.m., and published in the issue of the Federal Register for July 12, 2000, 65 F.R. 42900)

2. Second, the IRS can make no changes and issue the proposed regulation as a final regulation by filing a Treasury Decision in the Federal Register. Finally, the IRS can make changes it deems necessary to the proposed regulation based on comments received from the public.

3. Under the third scenario, if the final regulation differs substantially from the proposed regulation, the IRS will be required to provide another notice and comment period. For example, if interested parties could not reasonably have anticipated the final regulation from the proposed regulation or if the final regulation deviates too sharply from the proposed regulation, another notice and comment period is necessary.

However, merely adopting a new position in the final regulation does not mandate another notice and comment period. For example, even if the final regulation differs substantially from the proposed regulation, if it is in character with the proposed regulation and is a logical outgrowth of the notice and comments on the proposed rule, no subsequent notice and comment period is required. The test for whether another notice and

comment period is required is whether the purposes of notice and comment have been adequately served—did commentators have a fair opportunity to present their views on the final plan in a way that the IRS might find convincing. If the proposed regulation fairly apprises interested persons of subjects and issues that may be addressed in the final regulation, no additional notice and comment period is required and the final regulation can be filed as a Treasury Decision in the Federal Register.

The preamble of the Treasury Decision for the final regulation generally will discuss any comments received and why they were followed or rejected. It also may provide any other relevant information, such as effective dates, whether the regulation is understood to be interpretive or legislative, which IRS division drafted the regulations, and the objective of the regulation.

Temporary Regulations. By statute, temporary regulations are a hybrid form of regulation. They are treated the same as a final regulation[6] that has been through the notice and comment period even though they are in fact issued without a notice and comment period. However, at the same time it issues the temporary regulation, the IRS must issue the regulation as a proposed regulation and follow the same notice and comment procedures, just as it would with any other proposed regulation.

> **Example:**
> Treas. Reg. § 1.469-2T is a temporary regulation that addresses passive activity losses under section 469.

The IRS issues a temporary regulation when it wants to provide immediate guidance to the public without waiting for a notice and comment period. Temporary regulations are issued most often when Congress has passed new legislation and the public needs immediate guidance on implementing the legislation. For temporary regulations issued after November 20, 1988, the IRS has three years from issuance of the temporary regulation to process it from its proposed form into a final regulation. If it fails to do so, the temporary regulation will expire and no longer be given the same effect as a final regulation. If the temporary regulation was issued on or before November 20, 1988, it remains effective, even if it never becomes a final regulation.

> **Section 7805 provides:**
> (e) Temporary regulations.
>
>   (1) Issuance. Any temporary regulation issued by the Secretary shall also be issued as a proposed regulation.
>
>   (2) 3-year duration. Any temporary regulation shall expire within 3 years after the date of issuance of such regulation.

As with final and proposed regulations, the preamble of a Treasury Decision containing a temporary regulation can contain valuable information.

---

6. *Robinson v. Commissioner,* 119 T.C. 44, 68 (2002); *Peterson Marital Trust v. Commissioner,* 102 T.C 790, 797 (1994), aff'd, 78 F.3d 795 (2d Cir. 1996).

Figure 4.2 Summary of Procedure for Issuing Regulations

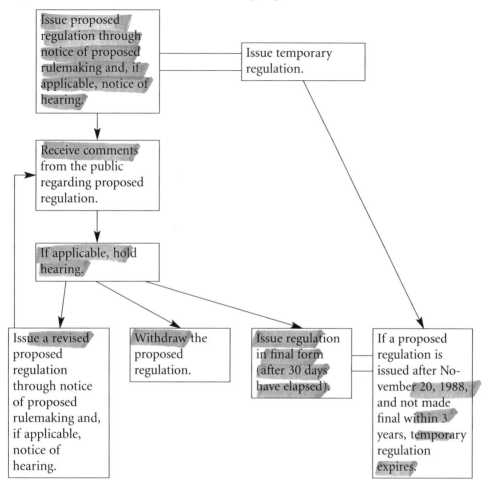

3. What Weight Is Given to Proposed and Temporary Regulations?

Proposed regulations. Because a proposed regulation is nothing more than a proposed interpretation of a Code section advocated by the IRS, courts do not give it any judicial deference; it is treated merely as a position advanced by the IRS. However, as a practical matter, if the proposed regulation closely follows the legislative history of the provision and the IRS's interpretation has been consistent over a number of years, a court generally will use it as a guide in interpreting the Code provision.

Case on Point:

Tax and Accounting Software Corporation v. United States
301 F.3d 1254, 1260–61 (10th Cir. 2002)

The respect that is owed to an agency position ... is based on the "body of experience and informed judgment" that agencies have in the interpretation, enforcement, and im-

> plementation of the statutes for which they are responsible. Christensen, 529 U.S. at 587, 120 S. Ct. 1655; Skidmore, 323 U.S. at 140, 65 S. Ct. 161. The respect owed to the agency interpretation "will depend upon the thoroughness evident in its consideration, the validity of its reasoning, [and] its consistency with earlier and later pronouncements." Skidmore, 323 U.S. at 140.
>
> The government's position regarding the "discovering information" requirement has been consistent in §41(d)(1) litigation, [citations omitted], but it has changed significantly as the government has developed regulations to implement §41(d)(1).... [W]e conclude that the government's position is not entitled to substantial deference.

Temporary regulations. In general, for three years a temporary regulation is given the same weight as a final regulation. However, as noted above, if the temporary regulation was issued after November 20, 1988, and the proposed form of the regulation is not made final, the temporary regulation expires and is given the same weight as a proposed regulation—a proposed interpretation advocated by the IRS. If issued before November 20, 1988, the temporary regulation continues to have the same weight as a final regulation.

4. When Are Regulations Effective?

Based on section 7805(b), in general regulations will not be given retroactive effect. Rather, they are effective on the earliest of the following dates:

- Date the regulation was filed in the Federal Register;
- If the regulation is a final regulation, the date any proposed or temporary regulation to which the final regulation relates was filed in the Federal Register; or
- Date any notice that substantially described the expected contents of the regulation (whether temporary, proposed, or final) was issued.

In certain situations, however, a regulation can have retroactive effect. These situations include:

- If the regulation was filed or issued within 18 months of the date of the enactment of the statutory provision to which the regulation relates;
- The regulation is designed to prevent abuse by taxpayers;
- The regulation corrects a procedural defect in the issuance of a prior regulation;
- The regulation applies to internal Treasury Department policies, practices, or procedures;
- Congress has authorized the IRS to prescribe the effective date; or
- The taxpayer is given an opportunity to elect to apply a new regulation retroactively.

Example:

T.D. 8629 provides the following as part of the preamble:

Transitional Relief

The proposed regulations provide that they will be effective for taxable years of a partnership beginning on or after the date final regulations are published. The preamble

to the proposed regulations requests comments on whether transitional relief is necessary for partnerships that qualified for an exclusion under Notice 88-75. Many commentators suggested some form of transitional relief, ranging from 180 days to a permanent grandfather provision.

The final regulations provide that, for partnerships that were actively engaged in an activity before December 4, 1995, the regulations apply for taxable years beginning after December 31, 2005. This ten-year grandfather provision is similar to the grandfather rule provided on the enactment of section 7704. The final regulations provide that this transitional relief expires if the partnership adds a substantial new line of business within the meaning of § 1.7704-2. The transitional relief is not affected by a termination of the partnership under section 708(b)(1)(B). Finally, partnerships subject to transitional relief may continue to rely on Notice 88-75 for guidance.

5. How Are Regulations Numbered?

Each regulation issued by a Treasury Decision is given a number. The number before the period reflects the "part" of the Code of Federal Regulations (CFR) in which the regulation is contained and indicates the type of regulation, such as income tax, estate and gift tax, or excise tax.

The **Code of Federal Regulations** is a codification of the general and permanent rules published in the Federal Register by the Executive departments and agencies of the federal government. The Code is divided into 50 titles which represent broad areas subject to federal regulation. Each title is divided into chapters that usually bear the name of the issuing agency. Each chapter is further subdivided into parts covering specific regulatory areas.

The Code of Federal Regulations is a Special Edition of the Federal Register and is published by the Office of the Federal Register, National Archives and Records Administration.

Title 26 is Internal Revenue. It is updated once a year, usually by April 1.

Guide to common types of tax regulations:

1.	income tax
20.	estate tax
25.	gift tax
26.	generation-skipping transfer tax
31.	employment taxes
54.	pension excise taxes
301.	procedure and administration
601.	procedural rules

The number after the period indicates the Code section to which the regulation relates. There is one exception to this rule, and that is for the procedural rules contained in regulations beginning with section 601. Because these regulations relate to the operation of the IRS, rather than provide an interpretation of the Code, the number following 601 and the period does not refer to a Code section.

Example:

Treasury regulation § 601.107 addresses the functions of the Criminal Investigation Division. Subsection (a) provides:

General. Each district has a Criminal Investigation function whose mission is to encourage and achieve the highest possible degree of voluntary compliance with the internal revenue laws by: enforcing the statutory sanctions applicable to income, estate, gift, employment, and certain excise taxes through the investigation of possible criminal violations of such laws and the recommendation (when warranted) of prosecution and/or assertion of the 50 percent ad valorem addition to the tax; developing information concerning the extent of criminal violations of all Federal tax laws (except those relating to alcohol, tobacco, narcotics, and firearms); measuring the effectiveness of the investigation process; and providing protection of persons and of property and other enforcement coordination as required.

The number after the dash indicates the sequential order of the regulation issued under that Code section. A "T" following the number indicates the regulation is a temporary regulation.

Examples:

Treasury regulation § 1.61-4 is an income tax regulation. It interprets Code section 61 and is the fourth regulation interpreting that Code section.

Treasury regulation § 20.2031-2 is an estate tax regulation. It interprets Code section 2031 and is the second regulation interpreting that Code section.

Treasury regulation § 1.469-5T is a temporary income tax regulation. It interprets Code section 469.

There is no correlation between the number after the dash and the subsection or other subdivision of the Code it is interpreting. However, for some Code sections that contain extensive regulations, a regulation may contain a cross reference between subsequent regulations and topics.

Example:

Treasury regulation § 1.704-1(b)(0) contains the following cross-reference information:

Heading	Section
Cross-references	1.704-1(b)(0)
In general	1.704-1(b)(1)
Basic principles	1.704-1(b)(1)(i)
Effective dates	1.704-1(b)(1)(ii)
Generally	1.704-1(b)(1)(ii)(a)
Foreign tax expenditures	1.704-1(b)(1)(ii)(b)
Effect of other sections	1.704-1(b)(1)(iii)
Other possible tax consequences	1.704-1(b)(1)(iv)
Purported allocations	1.704-1(b)(1)(v)
Section 704(c) determinations	1.704-1(b)(1)(vi)
Bottom line allocations	1.704-1(b)(1)(vii)
Substantial economic effect	1.704-1(b)(2)
Two-part analysis	1.704-1(b)(2)(i)

Economic effect	1.704-1(b)(2)(ii)
Fundamental principles	1.704-1(b)(2)(ii)(a)
Three requirements	1.704-1(b)(2)(ii)(b)
Obligation to restore deficit	1.704-1(b)(2)(ii)(c)
Alternate test for economic effect	1.704-1(b)(2)(ii)(d)
Partial economic effect	1.704-1(b)(2)(ii)(e)
Reduction of obligation to restore	1.704-1(b)(2)(ii)(f)
Liquidation defined	1.704-1(b)(2)(ii)(g)
Partnership agreement defined	1.704-1(b)(2)(ii)(h)
Economic effect equivalence	1.704-1(b)(2)(ii)(i)

The letters, numbers, and letters that follow the dash and number represent paragraphs, subparagraphs, and subdivisions, respectively.

Example:

Treas. Reg. § 1.704-1(f)(5)(i) is a reference to:

-1:   the first regulation interpreting section 704
(f):   paragraph f
(5):   subparagraph 5
(i):   subdivision i

6. Which Regulations Is the IRS Working On?

The IRS and the Treasury Department's Office of Tax Policy decide in which specific areas to focus its attention and issue regulations, rulings, or other public guidance. Those items are listed on the Guidance Priority List, or Business Plan. To decide which projects are included on the list, the IRS now seeks input internally and from the public. Once an item is included on the list, the expectation is that the guidance will be published during that fiscal year. The list is updated periodically.

Practice Note:

The Department of Treasury and the Internal Revenue Service invite public comment on recommendations for items that should be included on the Guidance Priority List. Comments can be provided by mail, hand delivery, or e-mail. See for example Notice 2009-43, 2009-1 C.B. 1037.

Quick Find:

The Guidance Priority List can be obtained from the IRS website at www.irs.gov.

7. Where Can Treasury Decisions and Regulations Be Found?

Treasury Decisions containing Proposed, Temporary, and Final Regulations can be found in the Federal Register. The Federal Register is cited by volume and page number.

> **Example:**
> TD 9105 can be found at 69 FR 5. "69" is the volume of the Federal Register and "5" is the page number.

They can also be found in the Internal Revenue Bulletin and later in the Cumulative Bulletin. They are listed by Treasury Decision number and the Cumulative Bulletin reflects on the spine the Treasury Decision numbers included in that volume.

Similar to the manner in which the Internal Revenue Code is issued through Public Laws, with the actual statutory provisions enacted by the Public Laws distilled and contained in Title 26, regulations are issued through Treasury Decisions, with the actual regulations distilled and contained in the Code of Federal Regulations. The regulations are organized sequentially by Code section in Title 26 of the Code of Federal Regulations. Thus, regulation § 20.2055-3 comes before regulation § 1.7520-3.

The regulations can also be found in multi-volume sets prepared by various commercial tax publishers such as CCH, RIA, and Mertens. In some of the commercial volumes, following each regulation is the Treasury Decision, citation to Federal Register, and date of promulgation. Regulations are also included in CCH, RIA, and Mertens treatises.

C. Main Points

Types of Regulations:

- Regulations are either legislative or interpretative.
- A legislative regulation is one issued pursuant to a specific congressional delegation to the Secretary.
- An interpretative regulation is one issued pursuant to the general authority given the Secretary under section 7805(a).
- A legislative regulation is given the highest level of judicial deference and a court will follow it unless it is arbitrary, capricious, or manifestly contrary to the authorizing statute.
- A court will follow an interpretative regulation as long as it is consistent with Congressional intent.

Issuance of Regulations:

- A regulation is issued in proposed form at least 30 days before it is issued in final form.
- When a regulation is issued in proposed form, the IRS accepts comments from the public on the proposed regulation.
- After considering the comments, the IRS can either withdraw the proposed regulation, issue the regulation as a final regulation, or make changes to the proposed regulation and re-issue it is as a proposed regulation.

Weight Given to Proposed and Temporary Regulations:

- A proposed regulation is not given any judicial deference.
- A temporary regulation is given the same weight as a final regulation.

- If not made final within three years from the date of issuance, a temporary regulation may expire and have the same weight as a proposed regulation.

When Regulations Are Effective:

- In general, a final regulation is effective on the date any proposed or temporary regulation to which the final regulation relates was filed in the Federal Register.

Regulations the IRS Is Working On:

- The IRS is working on regulations identified in the Business Plan.

Where Can Treasury Decisions and Regulations Be Found?

Item	Location	Comments
Treasury Decisions	• Federal Register • Internal Revenue Bulletin • Cumulative Bulletin • Various commercial publishers • On-line: • www.irs.gov	

Regulations	• Code of Federal Regulations (CFR)
	• Various commercial publishers, such as CCH, RIA, and Mertens
	• USCCAN, Chapter 16, includes a listing of all regulations in effect as of January 1 of that year
	• On-line:
	  • www.irs.gov
	  • www.access.gpo.gov
	  • www.law.cornell.edu
		• After each regulation, some commercial publishers include the applicable T.D. number, Federal Register citation, and the date it was filed.
		
		• www.access.gpo.gov/cfr/index.html
		• www.law.cornell.edu/cfr/cfr.php?title=26

D. Related Articles for Further Reading

- Kristin E. Hickman, *The Need for Mead: Rejecting Tax Exceptionalism in Judicial Deference*, 90 Minn. L. Rev. 1537 (2006).

- Ellen P. Aprill, *The Interpretive Voice*, 38 Loy. L.A. L. Rev. 2081 (2005).

- Gregg D. Polsky, *Can Treasury Overrule the Supreme Court?*, 84 B.U.L. Rev. 185 (2004).

- John F. Coverdale, *Chevron's Reduced Domain: Judicial Review of Treasury Regulations and Revenue Rulings After Mead*, 55 Admin. L. Rev. 39 (2003).

- Naftali Z. Dembitzer, *Beyond the IRS Restructuring and Reform Act of 1998: Perceived Abuses of the Treasury Department's Rulemaking Authority*, 52 Tax Law. 501 (1999).

E. Problems

1. Treas. Reg. § 1.267-1 is what type of regulation?
   - a. Income tax.
   - b. Estate tax.
   - c. Employment tax.
   - d. Generation-skipping transfer tax.

2. Regulations can be:
   - a. Interpretative or legislative.
   - b. Interpretative and procedural.
   - c. Legislative and procedural.
   - d. Procedural and mandatory.

3. A final regulation:
   - a. Is binding on taxpayers.
   - b. Is a legislative regulation.
   - c. Sets forth the IRS's position, but is not binding on taxpayers.
   - d. Is a type of proposed regulation.

4. A legislative regulation is:
   - a. Issued by Congress.
   - b. One issued pursuant to a specific congressional delegation to the Secretary.
   - c. Issued pursuant to I.R.C. § 7805(a).
   - d. Interpretative only.

5. An interpretative regulation is:
   - a. Issued by Congress.
   - b. One issued pursuant to a specific congressional delegation to the Secretary.
   - c. Issued pursuant to I.R.C. § 7805(a).
   - d. Mandated by Congress.

6. Regulations are effective:
   - a. On the date filed in the Federal Register.
   - b. On the date the proposed or temporary regulation to which the final regulation relates was filed in the Federal Register.
   - c. On the date any notice that substantially described the expected contents of the regulation was issued.
   - d. Any of the above.

7. A proposed regulation:
   - a. Is binding on taxpayers.
   - b. Is a legislative regulation.
   - c. Sets forth the IRS's position, but is not binding on taxpayers.
   - d. Is a type of final regulation.

8. A temporary regulation:
   - a. Is a hybrid form of regulation.
   - b. Must also be issued as a proposed regulation.
   - c. Is given the same weight as a final regulation.
   - d. All of the above.

9. Consider I.R.C. § 2032A(g). What type of regulations should be issued under this provision?

10. Locate Proposed Treasury Regulation § 1.102-1(f). *[handwritten: Go to RIA checkpoint / a) Click on Preamble / b) ? c) ? / d) It depends]*

   a. When was it issued?
   b. Where is it located in the Federal Register?
   c. Has the regulation ever been made final?
   d. What weight would the court give to the regulation?

11. Read Treas. Reg. § 1.48-12(b)(3)(iii). To what extent does the definition of "internal structural framework" apply?

12. Locate Notice of Proposed Rulemaking at 56 FR 14,034.

   a. To what extent is Treas. Reg. § 1.469-7 considered a legislative regulation?
   b. What is the effective date of the regulation?
   c. What options does the taxpayer have in the notice with respect to electing out of provisions?
   d. How could the information be useful for tax planning purposes?

13. Locate Treas. Reg. § 1.469-2(f)(6). *[handwritten: Go to RIA checkpoint]*

   a. Is the regulation a legislative regulation? How do you know? *[handwritten: a) Interp. div.]*
   b. What can you find out about the history of this regulation?
   c. What information is contained in the preamble?
   d. Why is that information relevant?
   e. When might you use that information?

14. What position did the government take in Notice 2003-72, 2003-44 I.R.B. 964?

15. Examine Temp. Treas. Reg. § 1.861-13T.

   a. What date was the regulation issued?
   b. What weight will the court give the regulation?

16. To which regulations would a court give more deference, the regulations issued under I.R.C. § 469(l) or those issued under I.R.C. § 103?

17. Does Treas. Reg. § 25.2518-2(c) relate to an income tax, estate tax, or gift tax Code section? Can you make such determination without looking at the content of the regulation? *[handwritten: Gift tax]*

18. Consider the "check-the-box" regulations (Treas. Reg. § 301.7701-1 et seq.; T.D. 8697). Before the regulations were issued, the relevant test for determining whether an entity was a partnership or a corporation was found in *Morrissey v. Commissioner*, 296 U.S. 344 (1935).

   a. How did the "check-the-box" regulations change the test for determining if an entity is a partnership or a corporation?
   b. Are the "check-the-box" regulations interpretive or legislative?
   c. When the IRS issued the regulations, did it exceed its authority? Are the regulations valid?

19. If you had to support a position you wanted to take:

   a. When could you use information contained in the preamble as support?
   b. How would you use the preamble as support?
   c. What would you do if it appeared the preamble did not support the position you wanted to take?

Chapter 5

Judicial Opinions

Judicial Opinions

- *What is the role of the trial courts?*
- *What is the role of the appellate courts?*
- *Where can the court opinions be found?*

Walking into the spare conference room, Lon spotted Kate, the firm's newest associate, seated before a table strewn with cases, a puzzled look on her face. "How is it going on your research for the home office deduction?" he asked.

"Great, and not so great."

"What does that mean?" Lon asked with a chuckle.

"I have a number of cases that address the criteria for taking a home office deduction," Kate said.

"That's great!" Lon exclaimed. "That means you can write up your memo to the partner and be out of here to enjoy what's left of the weekend!"

Well," Kate said hesitantly. "Having the cases and knowing what they all mean are two different things. I know that the ultimate in case law authority is the Supreme Court, but what about all these other courts? I don't think that I understand the relationship between the district court and the Tax Court. Which opinion is more authoritative? And, where does the Court of Federal Claims fit into all this? To top it all off, I have some T.C. Memorandum Opinions and some opinions that are not Memorandum Opinions. Why does the Tax Court issue two types of opinions?" She let out a long sigh. "Until I understand the bigger picture, I don't think I will know which of these cases will be authority for my position. Until I know that, I can't even begin to write the memo, much less finish it."

"Oh, it's not that bad. Let me walk you through it," Lon said as he took a seat at the table.

Contents

A. Key Terms

After completing this chapter, you should be familiar with the following key terms:

➤ United States Tax Court

➤ Court of Federal Claims

➤ United States District Courts

➤ United States Bankruptcy Courts

➤ Circuit Courts of Appeals

➤ United States Supreme Court

➤ Tax Court regular opinion

➤ T.C. Memorandum Opinion

➤ Tax Court reviewed opinion

➤ Tax Court Summary Opinion

➤ Decision under Rule 155

➤ *Golsen* Rule

➤ Action on Decision

➤ Acquiescence

➤ Acquiescence in Result Only

➤ Nonacquiescence

B. Discussion

If the IRS proposes changes to the taxpayer's income tax return which would increase the taxpayer's tax liability and the taxpayer does not agree with the proposed changes, there are three possible trial courts to which the taxpayer can go to have his case heard—the Tax Court, the Court of Federal Claims, or federal district court. Procedurally, a case pursued in the Tax Court is at a different stage in the administrative process than a case pursued in the Court of Federal Claims or district court. Nonetheless, because the taxpayer is the party who initiates the lawsuit, which court hears the dispute is determined largely by the taxpayer.

> **Practice Note:**
> With a few limited exceptions, in tax litigation the taxpayer is always the party bringing the suit—the petitioner or complainant.

To bring an action in the Tax Court, the taxpayer must file a petition generally within 90 days from the date the statutory notice of deficiency was mailed to him.[1] The notice of deficiency will include the date determined by the IRS to be the last day on which the taxpayer may timely file a petition with the Tax Court. The taxpayer does not pay the tax prior to filing suit.

> **Practice Note:**
> The receipt of a statutory notice of deficiency and non-payment of the deficiency noted on the notice are required for the Tax Court to have jurisdiction of the case.

To bring an action in the Court of Federal Claims or district court, all tax liabilities must be assessed (an assessment is a bookkeeping entry noting the liability of the taxpayer) and paid.[2] Next, the taxpayer must file a claim for refund with the IRS for the amount he believes he overpaid.[3] If the IRS denies the refund claim, he can file suit in the Court of Federal Claims or district court. He has two years from the date the IRS issues the notice of disallowance of the claim for refund to file suit. If the taxpayer does not want to wait until he receives the notice of disallowance, he may file if 6 months have passed from the date the claim for refund was filed.[4]

The court in which the taxpayer decides to bring his suit will depend in part on the characteristics of the trial courts and in part on the taxpayer's individual circumstances. Once the taxpayer has made his decision and the trial-level proceedings are concluded, the losing party can appeal the decision to the applicable circuit court of appeals.[5] From the circuit court of appeals, the next level of judicial review is the United States Supreme Court.[6] The relationship of the courts is set forth in Figure 5.1.

---

1. I.R.C. §§ 6212, 6213.
2. *Flora v. United States*, 362 U.S. 145 (1960).
3. I.R.C. § 7422.
4. I.R.C. § 6532.
5. I.R.C. § 7482; 28 U.S.C. § 1291.
6. 28 U.S.C. § 1291.

Figure 5.1

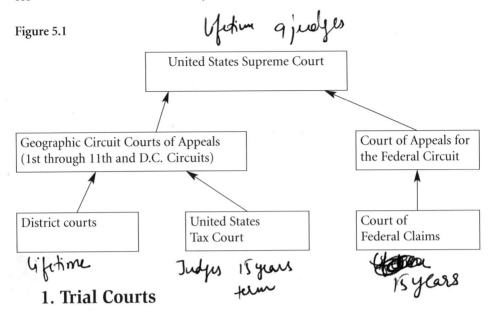

1. Trial Courts

a. Tax Court

The **United States Tax Court** is a specialized court that hears only tax cases.[7] While it currently is a court established under Article I of the United States Constitution,[8] it was not always a judicial court. It began in 1924 as an administrative board of the Treasury Department and was called the Board of Tax Appeals. Then, in 1939, it became an agency of the Executive Branch. In 1942, the name was changed to the Tax Court of the United States, but it remained an administrative court. Finally, in 1969, it was removed from the Executive Branch and established as a regular judicial court under Article I of the United States Constitution. As a regular judicial court, it received the same powers regarding contempt and the carrying out of writs and orders as other federal courts. Its jurisdiction currently extends to hearing tax disputes concerning notices of deficiency, notices of transferee liability, certain types of declaratory judgment, readjustment and adjustment of partnership items, review of the failure to abate interest, administrative costs, worker classification, relief from joint and several liability on a joint return, and review of certain collection actions.

Section 7441. Status

There is hereby established, under article I of the Constitution of the United States, a court of record to be known as the United States Tax Court. The members of the Tax Court shall be the chief judge and the judges of the Tax Court.

Practice Note:

The United States Tax Court has its own rules of practice and procedure. They can be obtained from the Tax Court website at www.ustaxcourt.gov under Rules, or by writing:

---

7. See I.R.C. §6213.
8. I.R.C. §7441.

Administrative Office
United States Tax Court
400 Second Street, N.W.
Washington, D.C. 20217

Enclose a check or money order to "Clerk, United States Tax Court" in the amount of $30.

The Tax Court is composed of 19 judges, plus any retired judges acting under recall to duty. Each judge is appointed by the president, confirmed by the Senate, and serves a 15-year term.[9] Because the Tax Court hears only tax cases, the judges are specialists in tax law.

The Tax Court judges elect a Chief Judge who serves a two-year term.[10] The Chief Judge may designate persons to act as Special Trial Judges in particular cases.[11]

The Tax Court is located in Washington, D.C., but the judges travel to locations throughout the country. Hearings and trials are held before a single judge, and no jury trial is available.[12]

The **United States Tax Court** is a specialized federal trial court that hears only tax cases.

---

9. I.R.C. §7443.
10. I.R.C. §7444.
11. I.R.C. §7443A.
12. I.R.C. §7445.

Practice Note:

The Tax Court holds hearings and trials in the following cities:

Alabama	Illinois	Montana	South Dakota
Birmingham	Chicago	Billings*	Aberdeen*
Mobile	Peoria*	Helena	
			Tennessee
Alaska	Indiana	Nebraska	Knoxville
Anchorage	Indianapolis	Omaha	Memphis
			Nashville
Arizona	Iowa	Nevada	
Phoenix	Des Moines	Las Vegas	Texas
		Reno	Dallas
Arkansas	Kansas		El Paso
Little Rock	Wichita*	New Mexico	Houston
		Albuquerque	Lubbock
California	Kentucky		San Antonio
Fresno*	Louisville	New York	
Los Angeles		Albany*	Utah
San Diego	Louisiana	Buffalo	Salt Lake City
San Francisco	New Orleans	New York City	
	Shreveport*	Syracuse*	Vermont
Colorado			Burlington*
Denver	Maine	North Carolina	
	Portland*	Winston-Salem	Virginia
Connecticut			Richmond
Hartford	Maryland	North Dakota	Roanoke*
	Baltimore	Bismarck*	
District of Columbia			Washington
Washington, D.C.	Massachusetts	Ohio	Seattle
	Boston	Cincinnati	Spokane
Florida		Cleveland	
Jacksonville	Michigan	Columbus	West Virginia
Miami	Detroit		Charleston
Tallahassee*		Oklahoma	
Tampa	Minnesota	Oklahoma City	Wisconsin
	St. Paul		Milwaukee
Georgia		Oregon	
Atlanta	Mississippi	Portland	Wyoming
	Jackson		Cheyenne*
		Pennsylvania	
Hawaii	Missouri	Philadelphia	
Honolulu	Kansas City	Pittsburgh	
	St. Louis		
Idaho		South Carolina	
Boise		Columbia	
Pocatello*			

* Only small tax case trials are heard at these locations.

Practice Note:

To practice before the United States Tax Court, the representative need not be an attorney. However, he must be admitted to the Tax Court Bar and enter an appearance in the Tax Court case. A power of attorney is not required.

Practice Note:

An opinion and a decision are two different documents that serve two different purposes. The Tax Court issues an "opinion." The opinion sets forth the reason for its decision in the case. The Tax Court files a "decision." A decision is a document that sets forth the taxpayer's deficiency as determined by the Tax Court; it contains no explanation for the computations. Below is an example of a Tax Court decision.

UNITED STATES TAX COURT

JOHN and JANE DOE,	)
	)
Petitioners,	)
v.	) Docket No. 22-22
	)
COMMISSIONER OF INTERNAL REVENUE,	)
	)
Respondent.	)

DECISION

Pursuant to agreement of the parties in this case, it is

ORDERED and DECIDED: That there is a deficiency in income tax due from Petitioners for taxable year 1996 in the amount of $2,622.00; and

That there is an addition to tax due from Petitioners for taxable year 1996, under the provisions of I.R.C. §6651(a)(1), in the amount of $320.75.

Judge.

Entered:

* * * * *

It is hereby stipulated that the Court may enter the foregoing Decision in this case.

It is further stipulated that interest will be assessed as provided by law on the deficiency and addition to tax due from Petitioners.

It is further stipulated that, effective upon the entry of this decision by the Court, Petitioners waive the restrictions contained in I.R.C. §6213(a) prohibiting assessment and collection of the deficiency and addition to tax (plus statutory interest) until the decision of the Tax Court becomes final.

Because the Tax Court is a national trial court and its opinions could be appealed to any of the geographical circuit courts of appeal, depending on where the taxpayer resides or has its principal place of business,[13] the Tax Court judge may be presented with a legal issue on which the circuits are in disagreement or on which some circuits have disagreed

---

13. I.R.C. §7482.

with a position previously taken by the Tax Court. In such situations, the Tax Court will apply the **Golsen rule**, derived from *Golsen v. Commissioner*, 54 T.C. 742 (1970). Under this rule, the Tax Court follows the opinion of the circuit court to which the taxpayer could appeal. Thus, similarly situated taxpayers could be given different treatment in the Tax Court if they could appeal their case to different circuits and there is a split on the issue in the circuits.

> Under the **Golsen rule**, the Tax Court follows the opinion of the circuit court to which the taxpayer could appeal.

After the judge hears the case, he prepares an opinion, setting forth his findings of fact and conclusions of law. Once written, the Tax Court judge's opinion is reviewed by the Chief Judge.[14] When the Chief Judge considers it advisable, the opinion is also officially reviewed by the entire court.[15] Generally, such review happens only if the opinion proposes to invalidate a regulation, overrule a published Tax Court case, or reconsider an issue appealable to a circuit court of appeals that has not addressed the issue where the Tax Court has been reversed by a different court of appeals on that issue.

> **Section 7460 Provisions of Special Application to Divisions**
>
> (a) Hearings, Determinations, and Reports. A division shall hear, and make a determination upon, any proceeding instituted before the Tax Court and any motion in connection therewith, assigned to such division by the chief judge, and shall make a report of any such determination which constitutes its final disposition of the proceeding.
>
> (b) Effect of Action by a Division. The report of the division shall become the report of the Tax Court within 30 days after such report by the division, unless within such period the chief judge has directed that such report shall be reviewed by the Tax Court. Any preliminary action by a division which does not form the basis for the entry of the final decision shall not be subject to review by the Tax Court except in accordance with such rules as the Tax Court may prescribe. The report of a division shall not be a part of the record in any case in which the chief judge directs that such report shall be reviewed by the Tax Court.

The Tax Court issues three types of opinions. It publishes only those opinions it considers as containing legal principles useful as precedent. Such cases are referred to as **regular opinions** and, of all the Tax Court opinions, are the most authoritative. Summary opinions are issued under the small case procedures, discussed below. The remainder of the opinions, memorandum opinions, are not officially published by the Tax Court. Such opinions do not set forth any new law, but are helpful in illustrating particular factual situations or demonstrating how the court applies a particular rule of law. They are published by commercial publishers.

> **Practice Note:**
>
> **Court reviewed opinions** can be identified by the notation of "Reviewed by Court" after the decision line and the inclusion of concurring and/or dissenting opinions at the end of the opinion.

---

14. I.R.C. §§ 7459, 7460.
15. I.R.C. § 7460(b).

A special, simplified Tax Court procedure is available for small tax cases. The procedure may apply where the disputed tax, including additions to tax and penalties, for the year is $50,000 or less. It is also available in the case of an innocent spouse proceeding where the amount of relief requested does not exceed $50,000 and collection due process proceedings where the amount of unpaid tax does not exceed $50,000. At any time prior to trial, the taxpayer, with the concurrence of the court, can elect to have the small tax case procedures apply.[16]

Practice Note:

Once the election is made, a small tax case contains an "S" after the docket number and, generally, is referred to as an "S case."

Trials of small tax court cases are conducted as informally as possible, usually by a Special Trial Judge. The rules of evidence are relaxed, with the court admitting any evidence it deems to have probative value. The judge's opinion will be issued as a **summary opinion**, which is not officially published and may not be cited as precedent for any other case. Neither party can appeal the decision.

Summary of Types of Tax Court Opinions:

Regular Tax Court opinions: Present important legal issues. Some regular Tax Court opinions will be reviewed by the entire court.

Memorandum opinions: Apply well-established legal principles to a factual situation.

Summary opinions: Issued in cases tried under the small case procedures and have no precedential value.

Quick Find:

Tax Court Opinions

Opinions issued by the Tax Court, whether regular, memorandum, or summary, can be obtained from the court's website at www.ustaxcourt.gov.

Regular tax court opinions also can be found in the Tax Court Reporter. Memorandum opinions can also be found in Memorandum Decisions, published by both CCH and RIA.

Rule 155. At the end of an opinion, oftentimes the court will note that the "Decision will be entered under Rule 155." "**Rule 155**" refers to Tax Court Rule 155 which requires the parties to reach an agreement as to the amount of the taxpayer's liability that is due after taking into consideration the holdings in the judge's opinion. Sometimes the parties disagree as to the exact manner in which the liability should be computed and return to the judge for an opinion on the correct method.

b. Court of Federal Claims

The **U.S. Court of Federal Claims** began as the U.S. Court of Claims in 1855. In 1982, the Court of Claims was abolished and replaced by the U.S. Claims Court. In 1992, the court was renamed the U.S. Court of Federal Claims.

---

16. I.R.C. § 7463.

Years	Name
1855–1982	U.S. Court of Claims
1982–1992	Claims Court
1992–present	U.S. Court of Federal Claims

The Court of Federal Claims is a trial court composed of 16 judges. Each judge is appointed by the president, confirmed by the Senate, and serves a 15-year term. The court has jurisdiction over all monetary claims against the Federal government, one of which is tax refunds.[17] The chief judge is selected by the president to serve until the age of 70 or until another chief judge is chosen. Retired judges may serve as senior judges on assigned cases.[18] The judges are not specialists in technical tax law.

Like the Tax Court, the Court of Federal Claims is a national court located in Washington, D.C., and the judges travel to locations throughout the country.[19] Hearings and trials are held before a single judge, and no jury trial is available.[20]

The Court of Federal Claims is required to follow only the opinions of the Federal Circuit Court of Appeals.[21] Opinions of the geographical Circuit Courts of Appeals that have ruled on similar issues have no precedential value, regardless of whether it is the circuit in which the taxpayer works or resides.

The **Court of Federal Claims** is a specialized federal trial court that hears only monetary claims against the federal government, including tax refunds.

Quick Find:

Opinions of the Court of Federal Claims

Opinions issued by the Court of Federal Claims can be obtained from the court's website at www.cofc.uscourts.gov.

The opinions can also be found in either:

CCH's U.S.T.C. (U.S. Tax Cases) or
RIA's A.F.T.R. (American Federal Tax Reports).

---

c. District Court

United States district courts are trial courts located throughout the United States that hear legal issues on any matter that could arise under the United States Code, including tax issues.[22] Therefore, the judges are not tax specialists.

There are a total of 94 federal judicial districts. Within the United States there are 89, with at least one district in each state, the District of Columbia, and the Commonwealth of Puerto Rico. Three territories, Guam, the Virgin Islands, and the Northern Mariana Islands, also have district courts.

---

17. 28 U.S.C. §§ 1346(a)(1), 1491.
18. See 28 U.S.C. §§ 171, 172.
19. 28 U.S.C. §§ 173, 795.
20. 28 U.S.C. § 2402.
21. See 28 U.S.C. § 1295.
22. 28 U.S.C. §§ 132, 1331, 1340.

With the exception of the territorial courts, all district court judges are appointed for life by the president with the advice and consent of the Senate. In each district, the judge who has served on the court the longest and who is under 65 years of age is designated as the chief judge. The chief judge has administrative duties in addition to a caseload.[23] The district court where the taxpayer would file his claim depends on the location in which he lives or conducts business. In district court, either the taxpayer or the government can request a jury trial.[24]

> **District Courts** are trial courts that hear legal issues on any matter that could arise under the United States Code, including tax issues.

A comparison of the three trial courts is set forth in chart 5.1.

> **Quick Find:**
>
> **Opinions of the district courts**
>
> District court opinions addressing tax issues can be found in either:
>
> CCH's U.S.T.C. (U.S. Tax Cases) or
> RIA's A.F.T.R. (American Federal Tax Reports).

d. Bankruptcy Court

Tax issues may also be resolved as part of a bankruptcy proceeding.[25] Federal courts have exclusive jurisdiction over bankruptcy cases, and each of the federal judicial districts includes a **U.S. bankruptcy court** as a unit of the district court. A U.S. bankruptcy judge is a judicial officer of the U.S. district court and is appointed by the majority of judges of the court of appeals. The number of bankruptcy judges is determined by Congress, and each judge serves for a 14-year term.

---

23. 28 U.S.C. §§ 133, 134, 136.
24. 28 U.S.C. §§ 2402, 1346(a)(1).
25. See 11 U.S.C. § 505.

Chart 5.1

	United States Tax Court	District court	Court of Federal Claims
Must the taxpayer prepay the tax in dispute?	No.	Yes.	Yes.
Is a jury trial available?	No.	Yes.	No.
What procedural rules does the court follow?	Tax Court Rules of Practice and Procedure.	Local rules.	Rules of the U.S. Court of Federal Claims.
Which circuit court law is precedential?	Precedent from the circuit court of appeals of the circuit in which the case is brought (generally the circuit in which the taxpayer resided or where the corporation's principal place of business was when the litigation began).	Precedent from the circuit court of appeals of the circuit in which the case is brought (generally the circuit in which the taxpayer resided or where the corporation's principal place of business was when the litigation began).	Precedent from the Court of Appeals for the Federal Circuit.
Expertise of the judge?	Tax expert.	Not a tax expert.	Not a tax expert.
Location of the court?	Various; the court is located in Washington, D.C., but circuit rides.	Various districts.	Various; the court is located in Washington, D.C., but circuit rides.
Are there special rules for small cases?	Yes—small case procedures as outlined in the Code and Tax Court Rules of Practice and Procedure.	No.	No.
Which rules of evidence does the court apply?	Federal Rules of Evidence applicable to trials without a jury in the District Court for the District Court.	Federal Rules of Evidence.	Federal Rules of Evidence.
Who represents the government?	Attorneys from the IRS's Office of Chief Counsel.	Attorneys from the Department of Justice.	Attorneys from the Department of Justice.
Who is the defendant?	Commissioner.	United States.	United States.
Who has the burden of proof?	Generally, the taxpayer.	Generally, the taxpayer.	Generally, the taxpayer.

2. Appellate Courts

a. Circuit Courts of Appeals

In 1891, nine regional courts of appeals were created. In 1893, a regional court of appeals covering the District of Columbia was created. In 1929, the Tenth Circuit was carved from the Eighth Circuit, and in 1981, the Eleventh Circuit was carved from the Fifth Circuit. Now, the 94 judicial districts are organized into the 12 regional circuits, each of which are responsible for reviewing cases appealed from federal district courts located within its circuit and from the Tax Court.[26]

In 1982, Congress established the Court of Appeals for the Federal Circuit, a jurisdictional rather than geographical circuit. A decision of the Court of Federal Claims must be taken to the Court of Appeals for the Federal Circuit.[27]

Practice Note:

The jurisdiction of the geographical circuit courts of appeals is as follows:

District of Columbia
District of Columbia

First Circuit	Fifth Circuit	Ninth Circuit
Maine	Louisiana	Alaska
Massachusetts	Mississippi	Arizona
New Hampshire	Texas	California
Rhode Island		Hawaii
Puerto Rico	Sixth Circuit	Idaho
	Kentucky	Montana
Second Circuit	Michigan	Nevada
Connecticut	Ohio	Oregon
New York	Tennessee	Washington
Vermont		Guam
	Seventh Circuit	N. Mariana Islands
Third Circuit	Illinois	
Delaware	Indiana	
New Jersey	Wisconsin	Tenth Circuit
Pennsylvania		Colorado
Virgin Islands	Eighth Circuit	Kansas
	Arkansas	New Mexico
Fourth Circuit	Iowa	Oklahoma
Maryland	Minnesota	Utah
North Carolina	Missouri	Wyoming
South Carolina	Nebraska	
Virginia	North Dakota	Eleventh Circuit
West Virginia	South Dakota	Alabama
		Florida
		Georgia

---

26. I.R.C. §§ 7482, 7483; 28 U.S.C. § 1291.
27. 28 U.S.C. § 1295.

Figure 5.2

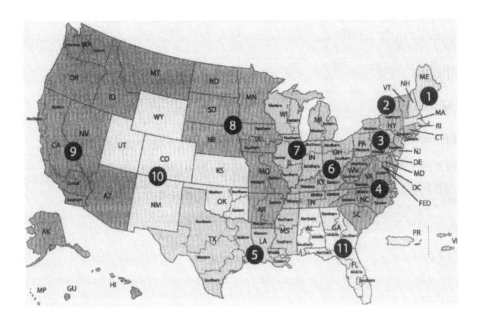

Appellate court judges are appointed for life by the president, with the advice and consent of the Senate. Each court of appeals consists of six or more judges, depending on the caseload of the court. The judge who has served on the court the longest and who is under 65 years of age is designated as the chief judge and performs administrative duties in addition to hearing cases.

Generally, the case is considered by a panel of three judges. If there is a conflict between panels or the issue is of great importance, the judges may sit en banc, where all the judges for that circuit court sit on a panel and decide the case. However, in the Ninth Circuit, where assembling all the judges becomes too cumbersome, en banc panels normally consist of eleven judges. Determinations of the courts of appeals are final unless the U.S. Supreme Court, in its discretion, chooses to review the case by certiorari.

A substantial amount of information, from court rules to judges' biographies to driving directions, can be obtained from each circuit court of appeal's website:

First Circuit Court of Appeals	www.ca1.uscourts.gov
Second Circuit Court of Appeals	www.ca2.uscourts.gov
Third Circuit Court of Appeals	www.ca3.uscourts.gov
Fourth Circuit Court of Appeals	www.ca4.uscourts.gov
Fifth Circuit Court of Appeals	www.ca5.uscourts.gov
Sixth Circuit Court of Appeals	www.ca6.uscourts.gov
Seventh Circuit Court of Appeals	www.ca7.uscourts.gov
Eighth Circuit Court of Appeals	www.ca8.uscourts.gov
Ninth Circuit Court of Appeals	www.ca9.uscourts.gov

Tenth Circuit Court of Appeals	www.ca10.uscourts.gov
Eleventh Circuit Court of Appeals	www.ca11.uscourts.gov
District of Columbia Court of Appeals	www.cadc.uscourts.gov
Federal Circuit Court of Appeals	www.cafc.uscourts.gov
General Information	www.uscourts.gov

Practice Note:

Oral arguments made before the Seventh and Eighth Circuit Courts of Appeals can be heard by going to the court's website.

Quote:

"There is a question whether, having once decided a case, we should change our decision when we are not entirely certain that the result we reached is wrong. One response is that, if the issue could be resolved with that degree of certainty, it is unlikely that we would have decided the case incorrectly the first time. Moreover, if certainty were the standard, we would probably never reverse ourselves. There is actually no clear set of rules that tells us when a case warrants our changing our decision on rehearing. We start with the premise that doing so is not generally desirable, and that it runs contrary to the sense of stability and finality that the law seeks to foster. We also know that it is often better to have a definitive answer, whatever it is, than to have continuing reexaminations or self-questioning.

On the other hand, we judges do not just bury our mistakes, We display them publicly in the Federal Reporters and, while we may then as individuals move on to more decision-making, the opinions we have published continue to haunt indefinitely not just the parties, but often numerous other persons whose affairs and fortunes will be governed by them. Because all of us make hundreds of difficult decisions a year involving complex legal questions, we know that we will make a certain number of errors. All that we can do is try our best to hold them to a minimum. At the same time, if a rehearing is requested and we have a strong sense that we may have erred in the particular case, we should not hesitate to undertake a reexamination of the issue. This is particularly so when significant individual rights or interests are at stake or when a number of parties may be seriously affected by a decision that may be erroneous. Given all of this, our conclusion is that, while we should not ordinarily abandon the decisions we have just reached following full deliberation, we must be willing to take that unusual step—at least in cases of some significance—when ultimately we are fairly persuaded that our decision is in error."

Albertson's Inc. v. Commissioner, 42 F.3d 537, 540 (9th Cir. 1994) (internal footnote omitted).

b. Actions on Decision

If the IRS loses a significant issue in the Tax Court, district court, Court of Federal Claims, bankruptcy court, or circuit court of appeals, it will prepare a legal memorandum on whether to acquiesce or nonacquiesce in the result. The memorandum sets forth the legal issue decided against the IRS, a brief discussion of the facts, and reasons for the acquiescence or nonacquiescence.

There are three potential **Actions on Decision (AOD)**: **acquiescence, acquiescence in result only**, or **nonacquiescence**. An *acquiescence* and *acquiescence in result only* means

that the IRS accepts the holding of the court in a case with the same controlling facts. *Acquiescence* indicates neither approval nor disapproval of the reasons assigned by the court for its conclusions. *Acquiescence in result only* indicates disagreement or concern with some or all of those reasons. *Nonacquiescence* signifies that, although no further review was sought, the IRS does not agree with the holding of the court and, generally, will not follow the decision in disposing of cases involving other taxpayers. With respect to a circuit court opinion, a *nonacquiescence* indicates that the IRS will recognize the precedential impact of the opinion on cases arising within the venue of the deciding circuit, but not follow the holding on a nationwide basis. The IRS can issue an AOD with respect to one issue or portion of an opinion. However, an AOD will not be finalized in those cases in which the IRS has recommended appeal until the litigation has become final.

Quick Find:

AODs can be found on the IRS website, www.irs.gov, in the Electronic Reading Room.

---

c. Supreme Court

The United States Supreme Court is the only court mandated by the Constitution and is the court of last resort. The Supreme Court has original jurisdiction over all disputes involving foreign ministers and interstate disputes, and disputes between the federal and state governments. The Court has jurisdiction over cases originating from any other court if the case involves constitutional issues, federal laws, or maritime treaties and laws.

Article III of the United States Constitution

The judicial power of the United States shall be vested in one Supreme Court, and in such inferior Courts as the Congress may from time to time ordain and establish. The Judges, both of the supreme and inferior Courts, shall hold their Offices during good Behavior, and shall, at stated Times, receive for their Services, a Compensation, which shall not be diminished during their Continuance in Office.

The Supreme Court is comprised of the Chief Justice and eight Associate Justices who are appointed for life by the president and confirmed by the Senate. Each Associate Justice is assigned to serve as Circuit Justice for a circuit court of appeals. The Justice may, but rarely does, sit as a judge of the circuit court.

Practice Note:

The current members of the Supreme Court are:

Chief Justice
John G. Roberts, Jr.

Associate Justices
Antonin Scalia
Anthony M. Kennedy
Clarence Thomas
Ruth Bader Ginsburg
Stephen G. Breyer
Samuel Alito, Jr.
Sonia Sotomayer
Elena Kagan

Practice Note:

Access: The Supreme Court is open to the public from 9 a.m. to 4:30 p.m., Monday through Friday. It is closed on federal holidays.

Courtroom lectures: Courtroom lectures are available in the courtroom every hour on the half-hour from 9:30 a.m. to 3:30 p.m. on days the Court is not sitting. Seating is limited and available on a first-come, first-seated basis. Lecture schedule is posted daily at the Information Desk.

Public sessions: When the court is sitting, public sessions begin at 10:00 a.m. and continue until 3:00 p.m., with a one-hour recess at noon. No public sessions are held on Thursdays or Fridays.

Opinions: Opinions are generally released on Tuesday and Wednesday mornings and on the third Monday of each sitting, when the court takes the bench but no arguments are heard. In May and June, the court sits only to announce orders and opinions.

Library: The library is open to members of the bar of the Court, attorneys for the various federal departments and agencies, and Members of Congress.

Petitions filed: Approximately 10,000 petitions are filed in the course of a Term. Approximately 1,200 applications of various kinds that can be acted upon by a single Justice are filed each year.

The formal session of the Supreme Court lasts from the first Monday in October until the business of the term is completed, usually in late June or July. The court's term is divided into sittings, during which it meets in open session and holds internal conferences, and recesses, during which the justices work behind closed doors as they consider cases and write opinions. Sittings and recesses alternate at approximately two-week intervals.

Oral arguments are generally scheduled on Monday through Wednesday during the sittings. Supreme Court decisions are made by a majority vote. When sitting for oral arguments, the judges are seated by seniority; the Chief Justice sits in the center chair, the most senior Associate Justice on his right, the second most senior Associate Justice on his left, and continuing until all Associate Justices are seated.

Practice Note:

A substantial amount of information, including the court rules, argument calendars, and admission requirements, can be obtained from the U.S. Supreme Court's website at www.supremecourt.gov.

Practice Note:

Oral arguments made before the Supreme Court can be heard by going to www.oyez.org.

---

3. Where Can the Opinions and Actions on Decisions Be Found?

The government publishes the regular opinions of the Tax Court in the Reports of the United States Tax Court. For example, *Hutchinson v. Commissioner* is cited:

116 T.C. 172 (2001)

➤ "116" refers to the volume in which the opinion is found

➤ "172" refers to the page of the volume on which the opinion is found

➤ "2001" refers to the year in which the opinion was issued

Practice Note:

A regular Tax Court opinion will always be cited the same way and is found in only one location:

Hutchinson v. Commissioner, 116 T.C. 172 (2001).

Commercial publishers, primarily CCH and RIA, publish Tax Court Memorandum Opinions in a series called Memorandum Decisions. For example, consider the memorandum opinion of *Doyel v. Commissioner*. When issued by the court, the opinion will contain the following designation:

T.C. Memo. 2004-35.

➤ "2004" refers to the year the opinion was issued

➤ "35" refers to the sequential number of the opinion. This opinion was the 35th issued by the court in 2004.

Both CCH and RIA have their own citation method. In CCH, *Doyel v. Commissioner* would be cited:

87 T.C.M. (CCH) 960.

➤ "87" refers to the volume in which the opinion is found

➤ "960" refers to the page of the volume on which the case is found.

In RIA, *Doyel v. Commissioner* would be cited:

2004 RIA T.C.M. ¶ 55,540.

➤ "2004" refers to the year the opinion was issued

➤ "55,540" refers to the paragraph at which the opinion can be found.

For the majority of the memorandum opinions issued before 2000, RIA used a citation that was a combination of the year and the number of the memorandum opinion. For example, *Peoplefeeders, Inc. v. Commissioner*, which was issued as T.C. Memorandum Opinion 1999-36, contained the RIA citation of T.C.M. (RIA) ¶ 99,036. Notice that "99" refers to the year and "36" refers to the sequential designation of the opinion.

Practice Note:

A memorandum opinion may be found in three different locations and cited three different ways:

Doyel v. Commissioner, T.C. Memo. 2004-35
Doyel v Commissioner, 87 T.C.M. (CCH) 960
Doyel v. Commissioner, 2004 T.C.M. (RIA) ¶ 55,540

While district court, Court of Federal Claims, bankruptcy court, circuit courts of appeals, and Supreme Court opinions can be found in traditional sources (Federal Reporters and Federal Supplements), commercial publishers have compiled opinions that address tax issues from all of these courts into one series. CCH publishes United States

Tax Cases (USTC) and RIA publishes American Federal Tax Reports (AFTR). Note that neither of these publications contains any Tax Court opinions, whether regular or memorandum.

For example, *Fransen v. Commissioner* can be found at 191 F.3d 599 (5th Cir. 1999). It can also be found in CCH's USTC under the following citation:

➤ 99-2 U.S.T.C. (CCH) ¶ 50,882

➤ "99" refers to the volume in which the opinion is found, and the volumes are organized by year

➤ "-2" refers to the fact that this is the second volume issued to cover 1999

➤ "50,882" refers to the paragraph number at which the opinion is found

The same case can be found in RIA's AFTR under the following citation:

84 A.F.T.R.2d (RIA) 6,360

➤ "84" refers to the volume in which the opinion is found

➤ "6,360" refers to the page in the volume at which the opinion is found

---

Practice Note:

A circuit court, district court, Court of Federal Claims, bankruptcy court, and Supreme Court opinion that addresses a tax issue may be found in three different sources and may be cited three different ways:

Fransen v. Commissioner, 191 F.3d 599 (5th Cir. 1999)
Fransen v Commissioner, 99-2 U.S.T.C. (CCH) ¶ 50,882
Fransen v. Commissioner, 84 A.F.T.R.2d (RIA) 6,360

Prior to 1991, the IRS published in the Internal Revenue Bulletin acquiescences or nonacquiescences only in certain regular Tax Court opinions. In 1991, it expanded those it published to include other civil tax cases including Tax Court memoranda, district courts, Claims Court (and subsequently the Court of Federal Claims), and circuit courts of appeals opinions.

The lists published during January through June each year are consolidated in a list published in the first weekly Bulletin in July and in the Cumulative Bulletin for January through June. A consolidated list for each calendar year is published in the first weekly Bulletin for the following January and in the Cumulative Bulletin for the last half of the year in which the various lists were published.

Quick Find:

Actions on Decisions can be found on the IRS website, www.irs.gov, in the Electronic Reading Room.

C. Main Points

Trial courts:

• There are three trial-level courts: the United States Tax Court, the Court of Federal Claims, and district courts.

- The Tax Court hears only tax cases, and the judges are tax specialists.
- The Tax Court issues regular, memorandum, and summary opinions. Regular opinions have the greatest precedential value and summary opinions have no precedential value.
- The Tax Court will follow precedent from the circuit court to which the case could be appealed.
- The Court of Federal Claims hears cases involving monetary claims, and the judges are not tax specialists.
- The Court of Federal Claims follows precedence from the Circuit Court of Appeals for the Federal Circuit.
- District courts hear a wide variety of cases, civil and criminal, and the judges are not tax specialists.
- Bankruptcy judges may be called upon to resolve tax issues.

Appellate courts:

- There are 12 geographical courts of appeals and one jurisdictional court of appeals.
- The Supreme Court is the appellate court of last resort.

Actions on Decisions:

- An *acquiescence* and *acquiescence in result only* indicates the IRS accepts the holding of the court in a case with the same controlling facts.
- An *acquiescence in result only* indicates the IRS disagrees or is concerned with the court's rational.
- A *nonacquiescence* signifies that, although no further review was sought, the IRS does not agree with the holding of the court and, generally, will not follow the decision in disposing of cases involving other taxpayers.
- With respect to a circuit court opinion, a *nonacquiescence* indicates that the IRS will recognize the precedential impact of the opinion on cases arising within the venue of the deciding circuit, but not follow the holding on a nationwide basis.

Where can the court opinions be found?

Item	Location	Publisher
Regular Tax Court Opinions	• Reports of the United States Tax Court • Board of Tax Appeals (1928–1942) • Tax Court website	• General Printing Office • General Printing Office • www.ustaxcourt.gov
Tax Court Memorandum Opinions	• Tax Court Memorandum Decisions • Tax Court Reported and Memorandum Decisions • Tax Court website	• CCH • RIA • www.ustaxcourt.gov
Court of Federal Claims Opinions	• AFTR • USTC • Federal Claims Reporter • Court of Claims Reporter (1982–1992) • Federal Reporter (1930–1932; 1960–1982) • Federal Supplement (1932–1960) • Court of Claims Reports (1863–1982)	• RIA • CCH • West • General Printing Office • West • West • General Printing Office
District Court Opinions	• AFTR • USTC • Federal Supplement	• RIA • CCH • West
Bankruptcy Opinions	• AFTR • USTC • Bankruptcy Reporter	• RIA • CCH • West
Federal Circuit Court of Appeals Opinions	• Federal Reporter • AFTR • USTC	• West • RIA • CCH
Supreme Court Opinions	• AFTR • USTC • United States Reports • Supreme Court Reporter • United States Supreme Court Reports, Lawyers' Edition	• RIA • CCH • Government Printing Office • West • LexisNexis

D. Related Articles for Further Reading

• Danshera Cords, *Administrative Law and Judicial Review of Tax Collection Decisions*, 52 St. Louis L.J. 429 (Winter, 2008).

• Stephen C. Gara, *Challenging the Finality of Tax Court Judgments: When Is Final Not Really Final?*, 20 Akron Tax J. 35 (2005).

• ABA Section of Taxation Report of the Task Force on Judicial Deference, Tax Notes 1231 (September 13, 2004).

- Kathleen Pakenham, *You Better Shop Around: The Status and Authority of Specialty Judges in Federal Tax Cases*, Tax Notes 1527 (June 21, 2004).

- Mark P. Altieri, Jerome E. Apple, Penny Marquette & Charles K. Moore, *Political Affiliation of Appointing President and Outcome of Tax Court Cases*, 84 Judicature 310 (May/June 2001).

- Judge Cohen, *How to Read Tax Court Opinions*, 1 Hous. Bus. & Tax L.J. 1 (2001).

- Daniel M. Schneider, *Empirical Research on Judicial Reasoning: Statutory Interpretation in Federal Tax Cases*, 31 N.M. L. Rev. 325 (2001).

- Leandra Lederman, *Equity and the Article I Court: Is the Tax Court's Exercise of Equitable Powers Constitutional?*, 5 Florida Tax Review 357 (2001).

- Paul E. Treusch, *What to Consider in Choosing a Forum to Resolve an Ordinary Tax Dispute*, 55 Tax Law. 83 (2001).

- James Edward Maule, *Instant Replay, Weak Teams, and Disputed Calls: An Empirical Study of Alleged Tax Court Bias*, 66 Tenn. L. Rev. 351 (1999).

- Mark F. Sommer & Anne D. Waters, *Tax Court Memorandum Opinions—What Are They Worth?*, Tax Notes, July 20, 1998, at 384.

- Judge David Laro, *Panel Discussion: Evolution of the Tax Court as an Independent Tribunal*, 1995 U. Ill. L. Rev. 17 (1995).

- Theodore Tannenwald, Jr., *Tax Court Trials: An Updated View from the Bench*, 47 Tax Law. 587 (1994).

- Judge Arthur L. Nimms III, *Statement Before the Federal Courts Study Committee*, 90 TNT 26-18.

- Harold H. Bruff, *Specialized Courts in Administrative Law*, 43 Admin. L. Rev. 325 (1991).

E. Problems

1. A taxpayer wants to contest the amount of tax he owes. Which of the following is not a trial-level forum?

    a. Tax Court.
    b. Court of Federal Claims.
    c. First Circuit Court of Appeals.
    d. District court.

2. A decision of the Court of Federal Claims is appealable to:

    a. The United States Supreme Court.
    b. The circuit court of appeals in which the taxpayer resides.
    c. The Court of Appeals for the Federal Circuit.
    d. The circuit court of appeals in which the taxpayer does business.

3. The Tax Court hears:

    a. Only tax cases.
    b. All cases, except criminal cases.
    c. Any monetary claims against the federal government.
    d. Only criminal tax cases.

4. The Tax Court issues all of the following types of opinions, except:

   a. Regular opinions.
   b. Circulated opinions.
   c. Memorandum opinions.
   d. Summary opinions.

5. The Tax Court can hear which of the following types of cases?

   a. Worker classification.
   b. Transferee liability.
   c. Failure to abate interest.
   d. All of the above.

6. The Tax Court is established:

   a. Under Article I of the Constitution.
   b. As an agency of the IRS.
   c. Under Article III of the Constitution.
   d   As a tribunal in the Department of Treasury.

7. A jury trial is available in which of the following courts:

   a. First Circuit Court of Appeals.
   b. Tax Court.
   c. District court.
   d. Court of Federal Claims.

8. Which of the following decisions cannot be appealed?

   a. Circuit court of appeals decision.
   b. Decision in a Tax Court case tried under the small tax case procedures.
   c. Decision rendered by the Court of Federal Claims.
   d. Decision rendered by the Federal Circuit Court of Appeals.

9. The Court of Federal Claims hears:

   a. Only tax cases.
   b. All cases, except criminal cases.
   c. Any monetary claims against the federal government.
   d. Only criminal tax cases.

10. District courts can hear:

   a. Only tax cases.
   b. All cases.
   c. Any monetary claims against the federal government.
   d. Only criminal tax cases.

11. The IRS issues the following types of Actions on Decision except:

   a. Acquiescence.
   b. Acquiescence in Result Only.
   c. Nonacquiescence.
   d. Objection.

12. Tax Court opinions can be found in:

   a. Tax Court Reports.
   b. CCH's Memorandum Decisions.
   c. RIA's Memorandum Decisions.
   d. All of the above.

13. District court opinions addressing a tax issue can potentially be found in all of the following locations, except:

   a.   West's Federal Supplement.
   b.   RIA's American Federal Tax Reports.
   c.   CCH's United States Tax Cases.
   d.   West's Federal Reporter.

14. Circuit court opinions addressing a tax issue can potentially be found in all of the following locations, except:

   a.   West's Federal Supplement.
   b.   RIA's American Federal Tax Reports.
   c.   CCH's United States Tax Cases.
   d.   West's Federal Reporter.

15. Supreme Court opinions addressing a tax issue can potentially be found in all of the following locations, except:

   a.   United States Reports.
   b.   RIA's American Federal Tax Reports.
   c.   CCH's United States Tax Cases.
   d.   West's Federal Reporter.

16. Consider *Montgomery v. Commissioner*, 112 T.C. 1 (2004).

   a.   What kind of opinion is it? How do you know?
   b.   Who wrote the majority opinion?
   c.   Who wrote dissenting and concurring opinions?

17. Consider the following cases:

   a.   In *Arnes v. Commissioner*, 102 T.C. 522 (1994):
        i.   What issue was before the court?
        ii.   How did the court resolve the issue?
   b.   In *Arnes v. Commissioner*, 91-1 U.S.T.C. (CCH) 50,207:
        i.   What was the issue before the court?
        ii.   What relationship did the taxpayer in this case have to the taxpayer in the *Arnes v. Commissioner*, 102 T.C. 522 (1994) case?
        iii. How did the court resolve the issue?
        iv.   Given the two cases, did the IRS recover anything from the transaction at issue? Why not? How can such an inconsistency exist?

research notes
mgm 10/17/22

18. Consider *Albertson's Inc. v. Commissioner*, 95 T.C. 415 (1990).

    a. What was the issue before the court?
    b. Who did the court hold for, the government or the taxpayer?
    c. What kind of opinion is this?
    d. Which judge presided over the trial? (hint: information on cases also can be found on the Tax Court's website)
    e. What factual determination did the judge who tried the case make?
    f. Which judge authored the opinion?
    g. Which judge wrote a dissenting opinion?
    h. Were any amicus curiae briefs filed?
    i. What happened on appeal (*Albertson's Inc. v. Commissioner*, 12 F.3d 1529 (9th Cir. 1993))?
    j. What happened on re-hearing (*Albertson's Inc. v. Commissioner*, 42 F.3d 537 (9th Cir. 1994))?
    k. Do you agree with the appellate court's holding? Why or why not?

19. Consider *Hamlett v. Commissioner*, T.C. Memo. 2004-78.

    a. Under what circumstances did the Tax Court cite to Supreme Court opinions?
    b. Under what circumstances did the Tax Court cite to Tax Court regular opinions?
    c. Under what circumstances did the Tax Court cite to Tax Court memorandum opinions?
    d. Under what circumstances would a taxpayer cite to the Supreme Court and Tax Court regular opinions cited in *Hamlett v. Commissioner*?
    e. Under what circumstances would a taxpayer cite to *Hamlett v. Commissioner*?

20. In *Estate of Leavitt v. Commissioner*, 90 T.C. 206 (1988), the Tax Court addressed the extent to which a shareholder in an S corporation was given basis for a loan made to the S corporation.

    a. Did the Fourth Circuit Court of Appeals, the circuit to which the Tax Court decision was appealable, agree with the Tax Court? See *Estate of Leavitt v. Commissioner*, 875 F.2d 420 (4th Cir. 1989).
    b. Did the Eleventh Circuit Court of Appeals agree with the Tax Court? See *Selfe v. United States*, 778 F.2d 769 (11th Cir. 1985).
    c. Did the Tenth Circuit Court of Appeals agree with the Tax Court? See *Uri v. Commissioner*, 949 F.2d 371 (10th Cir. 1991).
    d. If the issue were to be tried in the Tax Court and would be appealable to the Eleventh Circuit Court of Appeals, what law will the Tax Court apply? Why?
    e. You are advising a client on this same issue. The client's case would be tried in the Tax Court and appealable to the Eighth Circuit Court of Appeals. What advice would you give your client?

21. You are conducting some research for a client on when deductions are allowed if the taxpayer claims to be in the tutoring business. A senior partner suggested that you look at *Jeffries v. Commissioner*, T.C. Summary Opinion 2001-143.

    a. Locate the opinion on the Tax Court's website.
    b. What type of opinion is it?
    c. Which judge authored the opinion?
    d. Could the case be cited as authority by the government?
    e. What other use might the government make of the opinion?
    f. What use might you make of the opinion?

22. You are interested in looking at *Apollo Overseas International, Inc. v. Commissioner,* T.C. Memo. 1996-280.

    a. Locate the opinion on the Tax Court's website.
    b. What type of opinion is it?
    c. Which judge authored the opinion?
    d. Can you find the same case in both CCH and RIA's services?
    e. Which service did you prefer using? Why?

23. You have been conducting research on statutory notices of deficiency and when the Commissioner has the burden of proof. You have come across *Estate of Mitchell v. Commissioner,* 250 F.3d 696 (9th Cir. 2001).

    a. Has the government acquiesced in the court's opinion?
    b. What impact does that fact have on your client if he resides in the second circuit?
    c. What impact does that fact have on your client if he resides in the ninth circuit?

24. In *Redlark v. Commissioner,* 106 T.C. 31 (1996) and *Kikalos v. Commissioner,* T.C. Memo. 1998-92, the Tax Court determined that Treas. Reg. 1.163-8T and Treas. Reg. 1.163-9T(b)(2)(i)(A) were an unreasonable interpretation of the Code. The Tax Court was reversed by both the Ninth and the Seventh Circuit Court of Appeals. See *Redlark v. Commissioner,* 141 F.3d 936 (9th Cir. 1998) and *Kikalos v. Commissioner,* 190 F.3d 791 (7th Cir. 1999). The validity of the regulations was again before the court in *Robinson v. Commissioner,* 119 T.C. 44 (2002). Considering the *Robinson* opinion:

    a. What other circuits have agreed with the Ninth and Seventh Circuit Court of Appeals?
    b. To what circuit would the Robinson case be appealable?
    c. Had that circuit addressed the issue of the validity of the regulations?
    d. What result did the Tax Court reach? *Holding*

25. You are interested in looking at *Oliver v. Commissioner,* 138 F.2d 910 (4th Cir. 1943).

    a. Locate the opinion in West's Federal Reporter.
    b. Can you find the same case in both CCH and RIA's services?
    c. Which service did you prefer using? Why?

26. Locate Action on Decision 1991-015.

    a. What was the year and date it was issued?
    b. What was the IRS recommendation?
    c. Why?

27. Your client is an oil and gas producer that owns several pipelines. Consistent with an opinion of the Tenth Circuit Court of Appeals, your client has treated the pipelines as producer assets and depreciated the pipelines over seven years. Your client is located in the Ninth Circuit and is currently under audit. The IRS has issued a notice of deficiency to your client, asserting that the pipelines should have been depreciated over 15 years. If your client challenges the notice of deficiency in the Tax Court, is the Court bound by the Tenth Circuit opinion on such matter? What if your client was located in the Tenth Circuit?

28. Examine *Millard v. Commissioner,* T.C. Memo. 2005-192. Why was the opinion issued as a memorandum opinion?

29. Visit www.oyez.org. Can you locate the oral arguments before the Supreme Court from *Ballard v. Commissioner*? What is your opinion of the oral arguments?

30. When drafting a brief:

    a.   When might you cite to a Tax Court regular opinion?

    b.   When might you cite to a Tax Court memorandum opinion?

    c.   When might you cite to a Tax Court summary opinion?

Chapter 6

Public Guidance from the Office of Chief Counsel

Public Guidance

- *What types of guidance are issued?*

- *Who is responsible for issuing public guidance?*

- *In what areas is the IRS planning on issuing guidance?*

- *Where can the various types of guidance be found?*

Stacey leaned back in her chair and rolled her head from side to side, loosening her tight neck muscles. She let out a heavy sigh and was trying to convince herself to get back to work when she heard a familiar voice behind her.

"You look tense. What are you working on?" Zack had started working at the firm just one week before her, and they had quickly become friends.

"I am working on a memo for one of the senior partners. Where I am having a problem is trying to figure out what else we should tell the client about the tax consequences of a transaction he is planning."

"That doesn't seem too bad."

"In the abstract, it isn't. But, in reality it has been my personal nightmare. I have looked at so many court opinions I have lost count. None of them really talks about this kind of a transaction. But, I don't feel comfortable telling the client only that there is no case law on point. I would like to tell him more about what position we can anticipate the IRS taking on the issue. Too bad it doesn't advertise its position."

"Ahh," Zack said, slowly nodding his head. "But, it does. You just need to know where to look. Let me show you."

Contents

A. Key Terms

After completing this chapter, you should be familiar with the following key terms:

- ➤ Commissioner
- ➤ Office of Chief Counsel
- ➤ Chief Counsel
- ➤ Subject matter jurisdiction
- ➤ Revenue Ruling
- ➤ Revenue Procedure
- ➤ Notice
- ➤ Announcement
- ➤ Action on Decision
- ➤ Acquiescence
- ➤ Acquiescence in Result Only
- ➤ Nonacquiescence
- ➤ Publication
- ➤ Internal Revenue Bulletin
- ➤ Cumulative Bulletin

B. Discussion

The Internal Revenue Service is responsible for the collection of taxes and enforcement of the Internal Revenue Code. To assist the public in understanding the Code, and better be able to comply with its terms, the Office of Chief Counsel and Department of Treasury issue various forms of guidance as to how the government interprets the Code. To understand what types of guidance are issued, it is helpful to understand the organization of the IRS and Office of Chief Counsel.

1. Internal Revenue Service

The Internal Revenue Service is overseen by the **Commissioner**, who is appointed by the president, with the advice and consent of the Senate, for a five-year term. Under the IRS Restructuring and Reform Act of 1998, the IRS was required to organize the agency into units that serve groups of taxpayers with similar needs. Following the mandate, the IRS formed operating divisions. Four are based on the type of taxpayer served:

1) Wage and Investment Division. It serves individuals earning wages who do not file a Schedule C, E, F, or Form 2106.

2) Small Business/Self-Employed Division. It serves individuals filing Schedules C, E, F and Form 2106, corporations and partnerships having assets of less $10 million, estate and gift taxpayers, fiduciary returns, and individuals with international returns.

3) Large Business and International Division. It serves C corporations, S corporations, and partnerships with assets equal to or greater than $10 million. It also includes an International unit.

4) Tax-Exempt and Government Entities Division. It serves the customer segments of Employee Plans, Exempt Organizations, and Government Entities (including Indian Tribal Governments, Federal, State and local Governments, and Tax Exempt Bond issuances).

5) There is also a Criminal Investigation Division. It provides the law enforcement arm of the IRS with its agents participating in many types of criminal cases, including money laundering and illegal source income cases.

Finally, the Office of the National Taxpayer Advocate represents taxpayers' interests and concerns. It is headed by the National Taxpayer Advocate, who is charged with protecting individual taxpayer's rights and reducing the taxpayer's burden. The Taxpayer Advocate is individually accountable to Congress and the taxpayers.

Practice Note:

Based on the Taxpayer Advocate's Report, from June 1, 2007, through May 31, 2008, the ten most litigated issues were:

- Gross income
- Collection due process hearings
- Summons enforcement
- Trade or business expenses

- Accuracy-related penalty
- Civil damages for certain unauthorized collection actions
- Failure to file penalty
- Relief from joint and several liability for spouses
- Frivolous issues penalty
- Family status issues

Figure 6.1

[handwritten: appointed by President for 5 years]

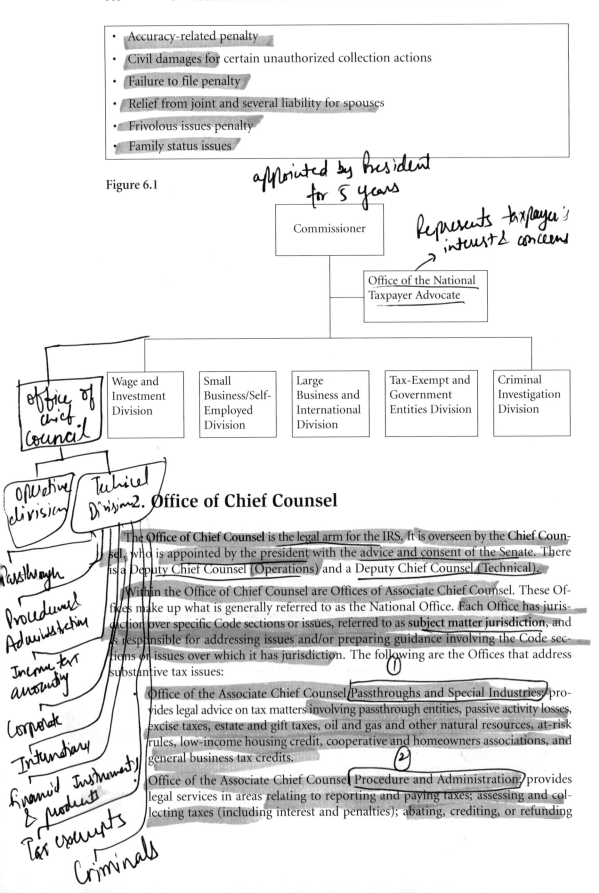

[handwritten: Represents taxpayer's interest & concerns]

[handwritten annotations include: Office of Chief Council; Operative division; Technical Division; Passthrough; Procedural Administration; Income tax annuity; Corporate; Intermediary; Financial Instruments & products; Tax exempts; Criminals]

2. Office of Chief Counsel

The **Office of Chief Counsel** is the legal arm for the IRS. It is overseen by the **Chief Counsel,** who is appointed by the president with the advice and consent of the Senate. There is a Deputy Chief Counsel (Operations) and a Deputy Chief Counsel (Technical).

Within the Office of Chief Counsel are Offices of Associate Chief Counsel. These Offices make up what is generally referred to as the National Office. Each Office has jurisdiction over specific Code sections or issues, referred to as **subject matter jurisdiction**, and is responsible for addressing issues and/or preparing guidance involving the Code sections or issues over which it has jurisdiction. The following are the Offices that address substantive tax issues:

- Office of the Associate Chief Counsel (Passthroughs and Special Industries: provides legal advice on tax matters involving passthrough entities, passive activity losses, excise taxes, estate and gift taxes, oil and gas and other natural resources, at-risk rules, low-income housing credit, cooperative and homeowners associations, and general business tax credits.

- Office of the Associate Chief Counsel (Procedure and Administration: provides legal services in areas relating to reporting and paying taxes; assessing and collecting taxes (including interest and penalties); abating, crediting, or refunding

overassessments or overpayments of tax; bankruptcy; summonses and information gathering; federal tax liens and levies.

- Office of the Associate Chief Counsel Income Tax and Accounting: provides advice on tax matters involving recognition and timing of income and deductions of individuals and corporations, sales and exchanges, capital gains and losses, accounting methods and periods, depreciation, installment sales, long-term contracts, inventories, and alternative minimum tax.

- Office of the Associate Chief Counsel Corporate: provides advice on matters involving corporate organizations, reorganizations, liquidations, spin-offs, transfers to controlled corporations, distributions to shareholders, debt vs. equity determinations, bankruptcies, and consolidated return issues affecting affiliated groups of corporations that file consolidated returns.

- Office of the Associate Chief Counsel International: provides advice on all international and foreign tax matters, including all matters relating to the activities of non-United States persons or entities within the United States, involving international provisions of the United States revenue laws, arising from bilateral and multilateral tax treaties and agreements to which the United States is a party, and all foreign revenue laws that pertain to tax matters in the United States.

- Office of the Associate Chief Counsel Financial Institutions and Products: provides advice on the taxation of financial institutions and tax matters involving financial institutions and the taxation of financial products such as insurance companies, products, and annuities; commercial banks and thrift institutions; regulated investment companies and real estate investment trusts; equity and debt securities, discount premium obligations, options, forwards, futures contracts, financial derivatives; tax exempt bonds, asset securitization; and financial strategies.

- Office of the Associate Chief Counsel Tax Exempt and Government Entities: provides legal advice on employment taxes and taxes on self-employment income, executive compensation, exempt organizations, employee benefit plans, Indian tribal governments, and federal, state, and local governments.

- Office of the Associate Chief Counsel Criminal Tax: provides legal advice with respect to substantive criminal matters (*e.g.*, tax, currency, and money laundering crimes), criminal procedure and investigative matters (*e.g.*, administrative and grand jury investigations, undercover operations, electronic surveillance, search warrants, and forfeitures), and referral of cases to the Department of Justice for prosecution or commencement of judicial forfeitures.

The Associate Chief Counsel for each Office reports to the Deputy Chief Counsel (Technical). A Healthcare Counsel also reports to the Deputy Chief Counsel (Technical). The Office of Chief Counsel also includes a field component, or the Division Counsel Offices. Each Office is responsible for representing the Commissioner in litigation before the United States Tax Court and related matters. While the Headquarters of each Division is located in Washington, D.C., there are many local, or field, offices throughout the United States. The Divisions mirror those of the IRS, being organized by the taxpayer served.

- Office of Division Counsel, Wage and Investment Division. It is responsible for providing legal services to the Wage and Investment Division on tax matters involving wage earning and investing taxpayers who do not file Schedules C, E, F or

Form 2106. The Division does not have dedicated attorneys or other legal staff to litigate cases with respect to Wage and Investment taxpayers or the collection of taxes. Rather, the Division partners with the Office of Division Counsel (Small Business/Self-Employed) for such matters.

- Office of Division Counsel, Small-Business/Self-Employed Division. It provides legal advice, litigation services, and litigation support services on tax matters involving small business taxpayers and provides assistance to the Commissioner (Small Business/Self-Employed), Taxpayer Advocate's Office, Division Counsel (Wage & Investment), and the Campuses (Service Centers).

- Office of Division Counsel, Large Business and International Division. It provides legal advice, litigation services, and litigation support services on tax matters involving subchapter C corporations, subchapter S corporations, and partnerships with assets of $10 million or greater to the Commissioner of Large and Mid-Sized Business. It also provides advice on international and foreign tax matters.

- Office of Division Counsel, Tax Exempt and Government Entities Division. It provides legal advice on employment taxes and taxes on self-employment income, executive compensation, exempt organizations, employee benefit plans, Indian tribal governments, and federal, state, and local governments.

- Office of Division Counsel, Criminal Tax. It provides legal advice and litigation support services with respect to substantive criminal matters (*e.g.*, tax, currency, and money laundering crimes), criminal procedure and investigative matters (*e.g.*, administrative and grand jury investigations, undercover operations, electronic surveillance, search warrants, and forfeitures), and referral of cases to the Department of Justice for prosecution or commencement of judicial forfeitures.

The Divisions are further broken down into Areas. There also is an Office of the Associate Chief Counsel for General Legal Services. It provides legal advice, litigation services, and litigation support services on non-tax matters such as disclosure, employment, and ethics issues. The Division Counsel of each Division reports to the Deputy Chief Counsel (Operation).

The Counsel to the National Taxpayer Advocate has direct jurisdiction and responsibility for issues relating to the scope of the Taxpayer Advocate Service's authority. Because the Counsel to the National Taxpayer Advocate does not have a field component, the Office of the Division Counsel (Small Business/Self-Employed) provides legal advice and support to the field components of the Taxpayer Advocate Service. *See* Figure 6.2.

Figure 6.2

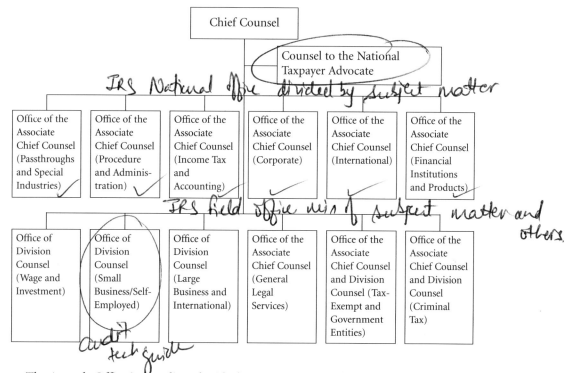

The Appeals Office is not aligned with the operating units, but rather is divided into two parts, the east and the west. It functions as an independent, alternative dispute resolution forum for any taxpayer contesting a compliance action taken by the IRS. It ensures all taxpayers receive an impartial review of their cases after an examination of a return is complete or collection action is proposed. A substantial number of cases are resolved through the appeals process.

3. Public Guidance

The Office of Chief Counsel can issue a variety of types of guidance, all aimed at giving the public additional information about how the IRS interprets and intends to apply the Code and, therefore, how it expects the public to interpret and apply the Code. The specific purpose the guidance is to serve will dictate the form in which it is issued, *e.g.,* Revenue Ruling, Revenue Procedure, Notice, Announcement, or Publication. Because such guidance addresses an issue set forth in a non-taxpayer specific format, it is intended to be relied upon by all taxpayers to whom it might apply.

a. Revenue Rulings

A **revenue ruling** gives guidance on how the IRS will treat a particular transaction by applying the Code, regulations, and any related statutes or tax treaties to a specific factual situation. They generally follow one basic format. First, the ruling sets forth the issues to be analyzed. Next, it sets forth a brief statement of non-taxpayer specific facts. It

follows with a short analysis of the issue presented, primarily by setting forth the applicable Code sections and regulations. It ends with the conclusion for each issue presented.

> **Revenue Rulings** explain the government's view of the tax consequences of a particular, non-taxpayer specific transaction.

Revenue rulings are issued exclusively by the National Office. Because they are considered interpretive law, no notice and comment period is required under the Administrative Procedure Act. While a draft or preliminary Revenue Ruling is occasionally presented for comment, such an occurrence is rare.

Example:

Below is an example of a Revenue Ruling.

Rev. Rul. 99-58
1999-2 C.B. 701

Continuity of interest on repurchase of issuer's shares. This ruling holds that an open market repurchase of shares through a broker has no effect on continuity of interest in a potential reorganization.

ISSUE

What is the effect on continuity of interest when a potential reorganization is followed by an open market reacquisition of P's stock?

FACTS

T merges into P, a corporation whose stock is widely held, and is publicly and actively traded. P has one class of common stock authorized and outstanding. In the merger, T shareholders receive 50 percent common stock of P and 50 percent cash. Viewed in isolation, the exchange would satisfy the continuity of interest requirement of § 1.368-1(e) of the Income Tax Regulations. However, in an effort to prevent dilution resulting from the issuance of P shares in the merger, P's preexisting stock repurchase program is modified to enable P to reacquire a number of its shares equal to the number issued in the acquisition of T. The number of shares repurchased will not exceed the total number of P shares issued and outstanding prior to the merger. The repurchases are made following the merger, on the open market, through a broker for the prevailing market price. P's intention to repurchase shares was announced prior to the T merger, but the repurchase program was not a matter negotiated with T or the T shareholders. There was not an understanding between the T shareholders and P that the T shareholders' ownership of P stock would be transitory. Because of the mechanics of an open market purchase, P does not know the identity of a seller of P stock, nor does a former T shareholder who receives P stock in the merger and subsequently sells it know whether P is the buyer. Without regard to the repurchase program, a market exists for the newly-issued P stock held by the former T shareholders. During the time P undertakes its repurchase program, there are sales of P stock on the open market, which may include sales of P shares by former T shareholders.

LAW AND ANALYSIS

Requisite to a reorganization under the Internal Revenue Code is a continuity of interest as described in § 1.368-1(e). Section 1.368-1(b). The general purpose of the continuity of interest requirement is "to prevent transactions that resemble sales from qualifying for nonrecognition of gain or loss available to corporate reorganizations."

Section 1.368-1(e)(1)(i). To achieve this purpose, the regulation provides that a proprietary interest in the target corporation is not preserved to the extent that, "in connection with the potential reorganization, ... stock of the issuing corporation furnished in exchange for a proprietary interest in the target corporation in the potential reorganization is redeemed." Id. However, for purposes of the continuity requirement, "a mere disposition of stock of the issuing corporation received in the potential reorganization to persons not related ... to the issuing corporation is disregarded." Id. The regulation provides that all facts and circumstances will be considered in determining whether, in substance, a proprietary interest in the target corporation is preserved.

Under the facts set forth above, continuity of interest is satisfied. There was not an understanding between the T shareholders and P that the T shareholders' ownership of the P shares would be transitory. Further, because of the mechanics of an open market repurchase, the repurchase program does not favor participation by the former T shareholders. Therefore, even if it could be established that P has repurchased P shares from former T shareholders in the repurchase program, any such purchase would be coincidental. The merger and the stock repurchase together in substance would not resemble a sale of T stock to P by the former T shareholders and, thus, the repurchase would not be treated as "in connection with" the merger. Under the facts presented, a sale of P stock on the open market by a former T shareholder during the repurchase program will have the same effect on continuity of interest as a mere disposition to persons not related to P.

HOLDING
Under the facts presented, the open market repurchase of shares through a broker has no effect on continuity of interest in the potential reorganization.

DRAFTING INFORMATION
The principal author of this revenue ruling is Marie C. Milnes-Vasquez of the Office of Assistant Chief Counsel (Corporate). For further information regarding this revenue ruling, contact Ms. Milnes-Vasquez on (202) 622-7770 (not a toll-free call).

In the past, topics for Revenue Rulings were derived from requests for private letter rulings.[1] Currently, however, there is no direct relationship between topics selected for guidance and private letter ruling requests. Rather, the decision of what issue to address in a Revenue Ruling depends on the area in which the government perceives the public needs the most guidance.

Generally, revenue rulings apply retroactively. In addition, a subsequent revenue ruling may amplify, clarify, distinguish, modify, obsolete, revoke, supersede, supplement, or suspend a prior ruling. Thus, the tax researcher must make sure that no other actions have been taken since the revenue ruling was issued. In addition, the tax researcher should consider the impact of legislation, regulations, court opinions, rulings, and procedures issued subsequent to the revenue ruling before applying it.

Practice Note:

The IRS uses the following terms:

Amplified — describes a situation where no change is being made in a prior published position, but the prior position is being extended to apply to a variation of the fact

---

1. For information on private letter rulings, *see* Chapter 7, *Taxpayer-Specific Guidance From the Office of Chief Counsel.*

situation set forth therein. Thus, if an earlier ruling held that a principle applied to A, and the new ruling holds that the same principle also applies to B, the earlier ruling is amplified.

Clarified—used in those instances where the language in a prior ruling is being made clear because the language has caused, or may cause, some confusion. It is not used where a position in a prior ruling is being changed.

Distinguished—describes a situation where a ruling mentions a previously published ruling and points out an essential difference between them.

Modified—used where the substance of a previously published position is being changed. Thus, if a prior ruling held that a principle applied to A but not to B, and the new ruling holds that it applies to both A and B, the prior ruling is modified because it corrects a published position.

Obsoleted—describes a previously published ruling that is not considered determinative with respect to future transactions. This term is most commonly used in a ruling that lists previously published rulings that are obsoleted because of changes in law or regulations. A ruling may also be obsoleted because the substance has been included in regulations subsequently adopted.

Revoked—describes situations where the position in the previously published ruling is not correct and the correct position is being stated in the new ruling.

Superseded—describes a situation where the new ruling does nothing more than restate the substance and situation of a previously published ruling. Thus, the term is used to republish under the 1986 Code and regulations the same position published under the 1939 Code and regulations. The term is also used when it is desired to republish in a single ruling a series of situations, names, etc., that were previously published over a period of time in separate rulings. If the new ruling does more than restate the substance of a prior ruling, a combination of terms is used. For example, modified and superseded describes a situation where the substance of a previously published ruling is being changed in part and is continued without change in part and it is desired to restate the valid portion of the previously published ruling in a new ruling that is self contained. In this case the previously published ruling is first modified and then, as modified, is superceded.

Supplemented—used in situations in which a list, such as a list of the names of countries, is published in a ruling and that list is expanded by adding further names in subsequent rulings. After the original ruling has been supplemented several times, a new ruling may be published that includes the list in the original ruling and the additions, and supersedes all prior rulings in the series.

Suspended—used in rare situations to show that the previous published rulings will not be applied pending some future action such as the issuance of new or amended regulations, the outcome of cases in litigation, or the outcome of a Service Study.

Revenue rulings do not have the force and effect of regulations, but may be relied upon by a taxpayer if his facts and circumstances are substantially the same. A ruling is merely the position of the IRS on a particular issue. It may be helpful in interpreting a statute, but is not binding on the court; it will be given no special deference by the courts and is only as persuasive as the reasoning and precedents upon which it relies.

Case on Point:

Halliburton Company v. Commissioner
100 T.C. 216, 216, 231–32, 234 (1993),
aff'd, 25 F.3d 1043 (5th Cir. 1994)

The issue presented for decision is whether a profit sharing plan sponsored by Halliburton Co. (Halliburton) experienced a partial termination under section 411(d)(3) for the plan year ending on December 31, 1986....

Respondent urges that we should apply the significant number test to determine whether a partial termination of the Halliburton Plan occurred, while Halliburton argues that such test should not be applied. In *Tipton & Kalmbach*, we specifically reserved for another day the decision on whether the significant number test should be used to determine whether a plan has experienced a partial termination. *Tipton & Kalmbach, Inc. v. Commissioner*, 83 T.C. at 160 n.5.

The significant number test first appeared in respondent's revenue rulings on the partial termination issue. The test was first announced in a 1972 revenue ruling, which was superseded by a 1981 ruling reaffirming the test. Rev. Rul. 81-27, 1981-1 C.B. 228, superseding Rev. Rul. 72-510, 1972-2 C.B. 223....

Because the significant number test was announced in a revenue ruling, it is entitled to no special deference. *Higgins v. Commissioner*, 312 U.S. 212, 215 (1941); *Helvering v. New York Trust*, 292 U.S. 455 (1934); *Stark v. Commissioner*, 86 T.C. 243, 250–51 (1986). As has been stated by the Court of Appeals for the Fifth Circuit, the court to which an appeal in the instant case would lie:

> a [revenue] ruling is merely the opinion of a lawyer in the agency and must be accepted as such. It may be helpful in interpreting a statute, but it is not binding on the Secretary [of the Treasury] or the courts. It does not have the effect of a regulation or a Treasury Decision. [*Stubbs, Overbeck & Associates v. United States*, 445 F.2d 1142, 1146–1147 (5th Cir. 1971.)]

Accordingly, a ruling or other interpretation by the Commissioner is only as persuasive as her reasoning and the precedents upon which she relies. *Gordon v. Commissioner*, 88 T.C. 630, 635 (1987); *Reinhardt v. Commissioner* 85 T.C. 511, 520 (1985); *Wolfers v. Commissioner*, 69 T.C. 975, 989 (1978); *Hartman v. Commissioner*, 34 T.C. 1085 (1960), aff'd per curiam 296 F.2d 726 (2d Cir. 1961).

The rationale for the significant number test, however, is not readily apparent....

The other test used to measure the drop in plan participation for purposes of considering whether a partial termination has occurred is the significant percentage test. Such test was also first announced in one of the Commissioner's revenue rulings, Rev. Rul. 72-439, 1972-2 C.B. 223....

After due consideration, we apply the significant percentage test in the instant case, rather than the significant number test. Doing so appears to us to be more consistent with the overall nature of the partial termination inquiry, an inquiry which focuses on the effect that a reduction in participation has on the plan as a whole.

To the extent the IRS's position is favorable to the taxpayer, but inconsistent with legal precedent, it will be considered a concession by the IRS.

Read this one for exam

Case on Point:

Rauenhorst v. Commissioner
119 T.C. 157, 169–73 (2002)

We are convinced that respondent, in this case, is arguing against the principles which he states in Rev. Rul. 78-197, *supra*....

Respondent's quotation from the Blake opinion makes his position patently clear. Respondent is disavowing Rev. Rul. 78-197, *supra*, in this case. When respondent's arguments are boiled down to their essential elements, he argues against the validity of the bright-line test of Rev. Rul. 78-197, *supra*.

The Commissioner has neither revoked nor modified Rev. Rul. 78-197, *supra*, in response to the comments in Blake. Indeed, the Commissioner has continued to rely on Rev. Rul. 78-197, *supra*, in issuing his private letter rulings. See, e.g., Priv. Ltr. Rul. 2002-30-004 (July 26, 2002). Moreover, the Commissioner has in a private letter ruling dismissed the statements made in *Blake v. Commissioner, supra* at 480–481, as "dicta", and stated that "Rev. Rul. 78-197 remains in effect, however" despite the statements made in that case....

Although we do not question the validity of the opinions of this Court and the Courts of Appeals upon which respondent relies, we are not prepared to allow respondent's counsel to argue the legal principles of those opinions against the principles and public guidance articulated in the Commissioner's currently outstanding revenue rulings.

We agree with respondent that revenue rulings are not binding on this Court, or other Federal courts for that matter. See *Frazier v. Commissioner*, 111 T.C. 243, 248 (1988); *N. Ind. Pub. Serv. Co. v. Commissioner*, 105 T.C. 341, 350 (1995), affd. 115 F.3d 506 (7th Cir. 1997). However, we cannot agree that the Commissioner is not bound to follow his revenue rulings in Tax Court proceedings. Indeed, we have on several occasions treated revenue rulings as concessions by the Commissioner where those rulings are relevant to our disposition of the case. *Walker v. Commissioner*, 101 T.C. 537, 550–551 (1993); *Burleson v. Commissioner*, T.C. Memo. 1994-364. In *Phillips v. Commissioner*, 88 T.C. 529 (1987), a Court-reviewed opinion, we stated:

> Respondent's position in this case directly contradicted his long-standing and clearly articulated administrative position as set forth in Rev. Rul. 72-539, 1972-2 C.B. 634, and reiterated in Rev. Rul. 83-183, 1983-2 C.B. 220. Respondent's counsel may not choose to litigate against the officially published rulings of the Commissioner without first withdrawing or modifying those rulings. The result of contrary action is capricious application of the law. * * * [*Phillips v. Commissioner*, 88 T.C. at 534; citation omitted.]....

While this Court may not be bound by the Commissioner's revenue rulings, and in the appropriate case we could disregard a ruling or rulings as inconsistent with our interpretation of the law, see *Stark v. Commissioner*, 86 T.C. 243, 251 (1986), in this case it is respondent who argues against the principles stated in his ruling and in favor of our previous pronouncements on this issue. The Commissioner's revenue ruling has been in existence for nearly 25 years, and it has not been revoked or modified. No doubt taxpayers have referred to that ruling in planning their charitable contributions, and, indeed, petitioners submit that they relied upon that ruling in planning the charitable contributions at issue. Under the circumstances of this case, we treat the Commissioner's position in Rev. Rul. 78-197, 1978-1 C.B. 83, as a concession. Accordingly, our decision is limited to the question whether the charitable donees were legally obligated or could be compelled to sell the stock warrants at the time of the assignments.

Through Chief Counsel Notice CC-2002-043, attorneys in the Office of Chief Counsel are reminded that they are required to follow legal positions established by published guidance in papers filed in the Tax Court or in defense or suit letters[2] sent to the Department of Justice.

Notice CC-2002-043

Purpose

The purpose of this notice is to remind Chief Counsel attorneys of the requirement to follow legal positions established by published guidance in papers filed in the Tax Court or in defense or suit letters sent to the Department of Justice. This notice also establishes a requirement that all briefs, trial memoranda and motions to be filed in the Tax Court or letters to the Department of Justice that seek to distinguish a position set forth in published guidance shall be subject to national office review prior to filing in the Tax Court or transmission to the Department of Justice.

Discussion

It has been a longstanding policy of the Office of Chief Counsel that we are bound by our published positions, whether in regulations, revenue rulings, or revenue procedures, and that we will not argue to the contrary. Accordingly, we do NOT take positions in litigation, TAMs, PLRs, CCAs, advisory opinions, *etc.*, inconsistent with a position that the Service has taken in published guidance or even if there are plans to revoke, change or clarify the position taken in the published guidance. The policy applies regardless of the age of the guidance and regardless of whether courts have chosen to follow the published position. So long as the published guidance remains on the books, the Office of Chief Counsel will follow it. Counsel can, however, take positions inconsistent with prior informal advice, such as TAMs, CCAs, *etc.*, but should never take a position inconsistent with published guidance or proposed regulations. Our adherence to the Internal Revenue Code and our published guidance in articulating our litigation position was recently reiterated by the Chief Counsel in the Roles Memo issued on August 26, 2002.

Sometimes reasonable minds can differ over whether we can effectively distinguish the position we want to take in our current case from an existing published position. Also, attorneys will encounter rulings that appear outdated or inconsistent with well established case law. In those situations, attorneys should bring the ruling or other published guidance to the attention of the Associate office with subject matter jurisdiction so that the Associate can consider whether to revoke or modify the published guidance or whether the published guidance can be distinguished in a particular case. Accordingly, as stated above, effective immediately, all briefs, motions, trial memoranda and letters that seek to distinguish a litigation position from a published guidance position must be reviewed by the national office prior to filing with the Tax Court or sending to the Department of Justice, regardless of the issue or amount involved.

Again, our litigating positions should be derived from, and consistent with, the Internal Revenue Code and our published guidance. A reading of the Roles Memo and Tax Court opinions where the Court has found that respondent argued contrary to published guidance should make us sensitive to that principle. *See Rauenhorst v. Com-*

---

2. Defense or suit letters are letters from the Office of Chief Counsel to the Department of Justice requesting that the Department of Justice defend against a tax related lawsuit filed against the United States in district court or the Court of Federal Claims.

missioner, 119 T.C. No. 9 (Oct. 7, 2002); *Walker v. Commissioner*, 101 T.C. 537 (1993); *Phillips v. Commissioner*, 88 T.C. 529 (1987).

Any questions regarding the matters contained herein should be directed to George Bowden of Procedure and Administration at (202) 622-3400.

b. Revenue Procedures

Who issued? → Office of Chief Counsel

In contrast to a revenue ruling, a revenue procedure does not address substantive issues. Rather, it is a statement of procedure that affects the rights or duties of taxpayers; it is published to announce practices and procedures for public guidance. Revenue procedures may also be based on internal management documents which should be a matter of public knowledge even though not necessarily affecting the rights or duties of the public.

Revenue Procedures give the public guidance on procedural rules.

Example:

Below is an example of a Revenue Procedure.

you

Rev. Proc. 89-21
1989-1 C.B. 842

21st Revenue Procedure

SECTION 1. PURPOSE

This revenue procedure makes available a sample form of declaration of trust that meets the requirements for a charitable remainder annuity trust as described in section 664(d)(1) of the Internal Revenue Code.

SEC. 2. BACKGROUND

The Internal Revenue Service receives and responds to requests for rulings dealing with the qualification of trusts as charitable remainder trusts and the availability of deductions for contributions made to such trusts. In many of these requests, the trust instruments and charitable objectives are very similar. Consequently, in order to provide a service to taxpayers and to save the time and expense involved in requesting and processing a ruling on a proposed charitable remainder annuity trust, taxpayers who make transfers to a trust that substantially follows the sample trust instrument contained herein can be assured that the Service will recognize the trust as meeting all of the requirements of a charitable remainder annuity trust, provided the trust operates in a manner consistent with the terms of the trust instrument and provided it is a valid trust under applicable local law.

SEC. 3. SCOPE AND OBJECTIVE

The sample declaration of trust made available by section 4 of this revenue procedure meets all of the applicable requirements under section 664(d)(1) of the Code for an inter vivos charitable remainder annuity trust providing for annuity payments during one life, followed by distribution of the trust assets to the charitable remainder beneficiary, if the trust document also creates a valid trust under local law. If the trust instrument makes reference to this revenue procedure and adopts a document substantially similar to the sample, the Service will recognize the trust as satisfying all of the applicable requirements of section 664(d)(1) of the Code and the corresponding regu-

lations. Moreover, for transfers to a qualifying charitable remainder annuity trust, the remainder interest will be deductible under sections 170(f)(2)(A) and 2522(c)(2)(A) for income and gift tax purposes, respectively. Therefore, it will not be necessary for a taxpayer to request a ruling as to the qualification of a substantially similar trust, and the Service generally will not issue such a ruling. See Rev. Proc. 89-19, page 00, this Bulletin. The Service, however, will continue to issue rulings to taxpayers who create trusts that are not substantially similar.

SEC. 4. SAMPLE CHARITABLE REMAINDER ANNUITY TRUST

On this day of , 19 , I, (hereinafter referred to as "the Donor") desiring to establish a charitable remainder annuity trust, within the meaning of Rev. Proc. 89-21 and section 664(d)(1) of the Internal Revenue Code (hereinafter referred to as "the Code") hereby create the Charitable Remainder Annuity Trust ("the Trust") and designate as the initial Trustee.

1. *Funding of Trust.* The Donor transfers to the Trustee the property described in Schedule A, and the Trustee accepts such property and agrees to hold, manage and distribute such property of the Trust under the terms set forth in this Trust instrument.

2. *Payment of Annuity Amount.* The Trustee shall pay to [a living individual] (hereinafter referred to as "the Recipient") in each taxable year of the Trust during the Recipient's life an annuity amount equal to [*at least five*] percent of the net fair market value of the assets of the Trust as of this date. The annuity amount shall be paid in equal quarterly amounts from income and, to the extent income is not sufficient, from principal. Any income of the Trust for a taxable year in excess of the annuity amount shall be added to principal. If the net fair market value of the Trust assets is incorrectly determined, then within a reasonable period after the value is finally determined for Federal tax purposes, the Trustee shall pay to the Recipient (in the case of an undervaluation) or receive from the Recipient (in the case of an overvaluation) an amount equal to the difference between the annuity amount(s) properly payable and the annuity amount(s) actually paid.

3. *Proration of the Annuity Amount.* In determining the annuity amount, the Trustee shall prorate the same on a daily basis for a short taxable year and for the taxable year of the Recipient's death.

4. *Distribution to Charity.* Upon the death of the Recipient, the Trustee shall distribute all of the then principal and income of the Trust (other than any amount due Recipient or Recipient's estate under paragraphs 2 and 3, above) to (hereinafter referred to as the Charitable Organization). If the Charitable Organization is not an organization described in sections 170(c), 2055(a), and 2522(a) of the Code at the time when any principal or income of the Trust is to be distributed to it, then the Trustee shall distribute such principal or income to such one or more organizations described in sections 170(c), 2055(a), and 2522(a) as the Trustee shall select in its sole discretion.

5. *Additional Contributions.* No additional contributions shall be made to the Trust after the initial contribution.

6. *Prohibited Transactions.* The income of the Trust for each taxable year shall be distributed at such time and in such manner as not to subject the Trust to tax under section 4942 of the Code. Except for the payment of the annuity amount to the Recipient, the Trustee shall not engage in any act of self-dealing, as defined in section 4941(d), and shall not make any taxable expenditures, as defined in section 4945(d). The Trustee shall not make any investments that jeopardize the charitable purpose of the Trust,

within the meaning of section 4944, or retain any excess business holdings, within the meaning of section 4943.

7. *Successor Trustee.* The Donor reserves the right to dismiss the Trustee and to appoint a successor Trustee.

8. *Taxable Year.* The taxable year of the Trust shall be the calendar year.

9. *Governing Law.* The operation of the Trust shall be governed by the laws of the State of . However, the Trustee is prohibited from exercising any power or discretion granted under said laws that would be inconsistent with the qualification of the Trust under section 664(d)(1) of the Code and the corresponding regulations.

10. *Limited Power of Amendment.* The Trust is irrevocable. However, the Trustee shall have the power, acting alone, to amend the Trust in any manner required for the sole purpose of ensuring that the Trust qualifies and continues to qualify as a charitable remainder annuity trust within the meaning of section 664(d)(1) of the Code.

11. *Investment of Trust Assets.* Nothing in this Trust instrument shall be construed to restrict the Trustee from investing the Trust assets in a manner that could result in the annual realization of a reasonable amount of income or gain from the sale or disposition of Trust assets.

IN WITNESS WHEREOF and [TRUSTEE] by its duly authorized officer have signed this agreement the day and year first above written.

[DONOR]

[TRUSTEE]

By

[Acknowledgements, Witnesses, etc.]

SEC. 5. APPLICATION

The Service will recognize a trust as meeting all of the requirements of a qualified charitable remainder unitrust under section 664(d)(2) of the Code if the trust instrument makes reference to this document and is substantially similar to the sample provided in section 4, provided the trust operates in a manner consistent with the terms of the trust instrument and provided it is a valid trust under applicable local law. A trust that contains substantive provisions in addition to those provided by section 4 (other than provisions necessary to establish a valid trust under applicable local law) or that omits any of these provisions will not necessarily be disqualified, but neither will it be assured of qualification under the provisions of this revenue procedure.

SEC. 6. EFFECTIVE DATE

This revenue procedure is effective for ruling requests received in the National Office after February 27, 1989, the date of publication of this revenue procedure in the Internal Revenue Bulletin.

DRAFTING INFORMATION

The principal author of this revenue procedure is John McQuillan of the Office of Assistant Chief Counsel (Passthroughs and Special Industries). For further information regarding this revenue procedure, contact John McQuillan on (202) 535-9540 (not a toll-free call).

A revenue procedure does not have the force and effect of a regulation, but may be relied upon by a taxpayer if his facts and circumstances are substantially the same. How-

ever, as with a revenue ruling, a revenue procedure may be amplified, clarified, distinguished, modified, obsoleted, revoked, superseded, supplemented, or suspended by subsequent rulings. These terms are defined the same as set forth above.

Practice Note:

The first revenue procedure issued each year always sets forth the procedures for submitting a private letter ruling request; the second revenue procedure always sets forth the procedure for submitting a technical advice memorandum request.

The procedures set forth in a revenue procedure are merely directory, not mandatory. Thus, if the IRS takes an action that is contrary to a revenue procedure, the action is not invalidated because it is contrary to the revenue procedure. Similarly, a revenue procedure is not independent authority for a position taken by the IRS.

Case on Point:

Security Bank of Minnesota v. Commissioner
98 T.C. 33, 43 (1992)

Our decision is unaffected by respondent's publication of Rev. Proc. 90-37, 1990-2 C.B. 361, which provides that certain taxpayers, including banks, may obtain expeditious consent to change their accounting method to report interest on short-term loans to customers to accord with section 1281. That procedure is merely consistent with respondent's argument in this case and is not independent authority for respondent's position.

Practice Note:

The IRS has identified the distinction between revenue rulings and revenue procedures as follows:[3]

- Revenue rulings and revenue procedures are issued only by the National Office. Both provide information and guidance to taxpayers, Service personnel, and others concerned.

- A revenue ruling sets forth statements of IRS position or interprets the law with respect to particular tax issues. A revenue procedure is used to announce statements of procedure or general instructive information.

- Generally, a revenue ruling states an IRS position and a revenue procedure provides instructions concerning an IRS position that enables taxpayers to achieve a particular result.

- A revenue ruling ordinarily does not include a statement of IRS practice or procedure, and a revenue procedure does not ordinarily include a statement of IRS position on a substantive tax issue. When a matter involves both a statement of IRS position on a substantive tax issue and a statement of practice or procedure, it normally requires the issuance of both a revenue ruling and a revenue procedure. They will be issued simultaneously and be cross-referenced.

---

3. Chief Counsel Directives Manual 32.2.2.4.

Issued by Office of Chief council

c. Notices and Announcements

Notices and announcements are public pronouncements containing guidance on matters of general importance. They may be used for a variety of purposes, including to announce new provisions of tax law affecting a large number of taxpayers, publicize future guidance, or to alert taxpayers to the enforcement position the IRS will take on a tax shelter. In general, they have only immediate or short-term value.

In the past, notices have been considered more important than announcements as announcements were not included in the Cumulative Bulletin. Now, both notices and announcement are included in the Cumulative Bulletin.

Example:

Below is an example of a Notice.

Notice 2004-13
2004-12 I.R.B. 631

Common Mistakes on Tax Returns

The purpose of this notice is to alert taxpayers about common mistakes made by individuals while preparing their federal income tax returns. These mistakes may result in taxpayers failing to fully pay their correct tax liabilities. In addition, these mistakes may result in delays in processing returns and receiving any refunds. Taxpayers should carefully read all the instructions to the tax forms and schedules and review their entire return before filing. In addition, e-filing, either through the Service's Free File Program at www.irs.gov or through a tax professional, will help reduce errors and speed refunds. Taxpayers who e-file and use direct deposit will receive their refunds in as little as two weeks.

Additional taxpayer resources, including answers to frequently asked questions, also can be found at www.irs.gov. Taxpayers can learn more about common mistakes and find an error checklist on page 60 of the Instructions to the 2003 Form 1040 Federal Income Tax Return; this information also is available at TeleTax Topic 303 on the internet at www.irs.gov and from the toll-free TeleTax number, 1-800-829-4477.

1. Choosing the wrong filing status. Taxpayers should confirm that the filing status (i.e., single, married filing jointly, married filing separately, head of household, qualifying widower) selected on the return is correct. For example, taxpayers often incorrectly claim "head of household" filing status without meeting the requirements for that status. In addition to delaying the processing of the return and any refund, designating the wrong filing status on a return also may affect a taxpayer's eligibility for the Earned Income Credit. The Instructions to the 2003 Form 1040 provide detailed information to assist taxpayers in choosing their correct filing status.

2. Failing to include or using incorrect social security numbers. The names and social security numbers for the taxpayer, taxpayer's spouse, dependents, and qualifying children for the Earned Income Credit or Child Tax Credit must be included on the return exactly as they appear on the social security cards.

3. Failing to use the correct forms and schedules. Taxpayers should review the instructions to all applicable forms and schedules to be sure they have correctly used, and accurately completed, each form or schedule.

4. Failing to sign and date the return. Taxpayers must sign and date their return under penalties of perjury. If the return is not signed, it will not be accepted as filed by the Service. Both spouses must sign a joint return.

5. Claiming ineligible dependents. Taxpayers may claim a person as a dependent only if that person meets the legal definition of a dependent. Taxpayers should consult the Instructions to Form 1040 to confirm whether a person qualifies as a dependent. Each dependent must have a valid social security number, which must be included on the tax return. The failure to include a dependent's name and social security number, or claiming an ineligible dependent, may result in an underpayment of tax and/or a denial of the Earned Income Credit.

6. Failing to file for the Earned Income Credit. Taxpayers should review carefully the eligibility requirements for the Earned Income Credit, including income limits, before filing returns. For example, many military families may qualify for the Earned Income Credit because supplemental payments and combat pay are exempt from the income calculations. Detailed instructions for claiming and computing the Earned Income Credit are contained in the Instructions to the Form 1040, Fact Sheet 2004-8, in Publication 596 and through links at 1040 Central at www.irs.gov.

7. Improperly claiming the Earned Income Credit. Taxpayers must have a qualifying amount of earned income to claim the Earned Income Credit. For example, a taxpayer whose sole income is from the receipt of disability payments does not have qualifying earned income and is ineligible for the Earned Income Credit. Detailed instructions for claiming and computing the Earned Income Credit are contained in the Instructions to the Form 1040, Fact Sheet 2004-8, and Publication 596, and through links at 1040 Central at www.irs.gov.

8. Failing to pay and report domestic payroll taxes. Taxpayers employing household workers, such as a house cleaner, an in-home caregiver, or a nanny, must pay and report payroll taxes for those individuals where the payments exceed certain threshold amounts. Failure to pay and report payroll taxes may result in the assessment of additional tax due, interest on the unpaid amounts, and penalties. The Instructions to the Form 1040, Publication 926 (Household Employer's Tax Guide), and Publication 15-A (Employer's Supplemental Tax Guide) contain detailed information to assist taxpayers in determining whether an individual providing household help is a household employee for whom the taxpayer must pay and report payroll taxes.

9. Failing to report income because it was not included on a Form W-2, Form 1099 or other information return. Taxpayers must report all income, even if the income was not reported on a third-party reporting statement such as a Form W-2, Form 1099, or other similar statement. Failure to report all income may result in the assessment of additional tax due, interest on the unpaid amounts, and penalties.

10. Treating employees as independent contractors. Employers may not treat an employee as an "independent contractor" to avoid paying and reporting payroll taxes. Employers who improperly treat an employee as an independent contractor may be liable for additional tax due, interest on the unpaid amounts, and penalties. Publication 15-A (Employer's Supplemental Tax Guide) contains detailed information to assist taxpayers in determining whether an individual is an employee or an independent contractor.

11. Failing to file a return when due a refund. Taxpayers must file a return to claim a refund of withheld taxes when a refund is due. Taxpayers will forfeit refunds of withheld tax if a return requesting a refund is not filed within three years of the due date.

12. Failing to check liability for the alternative minimum tax. Taxpayers should determine whether the alternative minimum tax, or AMT, applies. If the taxpayer is liable for AMT, the Service may reduce or deny a requested refund or may assess any additional tax due, interest on the unpaid amounts and penalties.

This notice was authored by the Office of Associate Chief Counsel (Procedure and Administration), Administrative Provisions and Judicial Practice Division. For further information regarding this revenue ruling, contact that office on (202) 622-7800 (not a toll-free call).

Example:

Below is an example of an Announcement.

Announcement 2004-16

2004-13 I.R.B. 668

Revision of Form 3115

Form 3115, Application for Change in Accounting Method, and its instructions have been revised. This December 2003 revision is the current Form 3115 and replaces the May 1999 version of the Form 3115.

In general, a taxpayer requesting a change in accounting method must complete and file a current Form 3115. *See* section 8.06 of Rev. Proc. 97-27, 1997-21 I.R.B. 10 (as modified and amplified by Rev. Proc. 2002-19, 2002-13 I.R.B. 696, as amplified and clarified by Rev. Proc. 2002-54, 2002-35 I.R.B. 432). See also Rev. Proc. 2002-9, 2002-3 I.R.B. 327 (as modified and clarified by Announcement 2002-17, 2002-8 I.R.B. 561, modified and amplified by Rev. Proc. 2002-19, 2002-13 I.R.B. 696, and amplified, clarified and modified by Rev. Proc. 2002-54, 2002-35 I.R.B. 432). To allow a reasonable transition period to the December 2003 Form 3115, the Service will accept either the May 1999 Form 3115 or the December 2003 Form 3115 through May 31, 2004, except where the use of the December 2003 Form 3115 is specifically required in guidance published by the IRS. Taxpayers filing Forms 3115 after May 31, 2004, must use the December 2003 Form 3115. The Service encourages taxpayers to use the December 2003 Form 3115 prior to June 1, 2004.

When requesting a change in accounting method, the applicant must provide the requested information to be eligible for approval of the requested accounting method change. The applicant may be required to provide information specific to the accounting method change such as an attached statement. The applicant must provide all information relevant to the requested accounting method change, even if not specifically requested by the Form 3115.

The December 2003 Form 3115 and instructions may be downloaded or ordered using the IRS website, www.irs.gov, and will be available at many local IRS offices. In addition, the December 2003 Form 3115 and instructions may be ordered by telephone by calling 1-800-TAX FORM (1-800-829-3676).

EFFECT OF THE DECEMBER 2003 FORM 3115 ON OTHER DOCUMENTS

* * *

For further information regarding this announcement contact Brenda D. Wilson on (202) 622-4800 (not a toll-free call).

d. Actions on Decision

If the IRS looses a significant issue in the Tax Court, district court, Court of Federal Claims, bankruptcy court, or circuit court of appeals, it will prepare a legal memorandum on whether to acquiesce or nonacquiesce in the result. The memorandum sets forth

the legal issue decided against the IRS, a brief discussion of the facts, and reasons for the acquiescence or nonacquiescence.

There are three potential **Actions on Decision (AOD): acquiescence, acquiescence in result only**, or **nonacquiescence**. An *acquiescence* and *acquiescence in result only* means that the IRS accepts the holding of the court in a case with the same controlling facts. *Acquiescence* indicates neither approval nor disapproval of the reasons assigned by the court for its conclusions. *Acquiescence in result only* indicates disagreement or concern with some or all of those reasons. *Nonacquiescence* signifies that, although no further review was sought, the IRS does not agree with the holding of the court and, generally, will not follow the decision in disposing of cases involving other taxpayers. With respect to a circuit court opinion, a *nonacquiescence* indicates that the IRS will recognize the precedential impact of the opinion on cases arising within the venue of the deciding circuit, but not follow the holding on a nationwide basis. The IRS can issue an AOD with respect to one issue or portion of an opinion. However, an AOD will not be finalized in those cases in which the IRS has recommended appeal until the litigation has become final.

Quick Find:

AODs can be found on the IRS website, www.irs.gov, in the Electronic Reading Room.

---

e. Publications

The IRS has prepared a large number of pamphlets, called **publications**, covering a broad range of issues. They are prepared to assist taxpayers in understanding the Code. The publications rarely contain citations to the Code or regulations, but rather explain the Code in simple, layperson terms. They are intended for guidance purposes only and do not have the force and effect of law.

Practice Note:

Publications can be found on the IRS website at www.irs.gov. or ordered by calling 1-800-829-3676.

Example:

Publication 1, *Your Rights as a Taxpayer.*

Publication 17, *Your Federal Income Tax.*

Publication 587, *Business Use of Your Home.*

Publication 1542, *Per Diem Rates.*

---

4. Internal Revenue Bulletin and Cumulative Bulletin

The **Internal Revenue Bulletin** (IRB) is published weekly. It is the authoritative instrument for the publication of official rulings and procedures issued by the IRS as well as other tax documents of interest to taxpayers and tax practitioners. It is divided into four parts:

1. 1986 Code. This part includes rulings and decisions based on provisions of the 1986 Code.

2. Treaties and Tax Legislation. This part is broken into two subparts, Subpart A which includes Tax Conventions and Subpart B which includes legislation and related Committee Reports.

3. Administrative, Procedural, and Miscellaneous. To the extent practicable, pertinent cross references to these subjects are contained in the other Parts and Subparts. It also includes Bank Secrecy Act Administrative Rulings and Bank Secrecy Act Administrative Rulings issued by the Department of the Treasury's Office of the Assistant Secretary (Enforcement).

4. Items of General Interest. This part includes notices of proposed rulemakings, disbarment and suspension lists, and announcements.

The first bulletin for each month includes finding lists and a cumulative topical index for the matters published during the preceding months. The material is indexed according to the following categories:

- Employee Plans
- Employment Tax
- Estate Tax
- Excise Tax
- Exempt Organizations
- Gift Tax
- Income Tax

Twice a year, the IRS compiles the weekly IRB into the **Cumulative Bulletin**. Prior to 1998, the IRB was reorganized, with announcements removed, and published as the Cumulative Bulletin. Beginning in July 1997, the Cumulative Bulletin is composed of reprints of the weekly IRB. Volume 1 contains the IRB from week 1 through the IRB from week 26. Volume 2 contains the IRB from week 27 through the IRB from week 52. Public laws are published in Volume 3. The finding lists and indexes are cumulated and published in the Bulletin of the succeeding semi-annual period. Beginning in 1998, the Cumulative Bulletin includes a list of Code sections affected by actions included in the Cumulative Bulletin.

Practice Note:

Currently, the documents published in the Cumulative Bulletin include:

- Announcements
- Congressional committee reports
- Court opinions
- Delegation orders
- Executive orders
- Notices
- Proposed regulations
- Public laws
- Prohibited transaction exemptions
- Railroad Retirement quarterly rate
- Revenue procedures

- Revenue rulings
- Social Security Contribution and Benefit Base; Domestic Employee Coverage Threshold
- Statement of procedural rules
- Tax Conventions
- Treasury Decisions
- Treasury Department orders

5. In What Areas Is the IRS Planning on Issuing Public Guidance?

Watch video 10 mints before ending

The IRS and the Treasury Department's Office of Tax Policy decide in which specific areas to focus their attention and issue regulations, rulings, or other public guidance. Those items are listed on the Guidance Priority List, or Business Plan. To decide which projects are included on the list, the IRS now seeks input internally and from the public. Once an item is included on the list, the expectation is that the guidance will be published during that fiscal year (ending June 30). The list is updated periodically.

> **Practice Note:**
>
> The Department of Treasury and the Internal Revenue Service invite public comment on recommendations for items that should be included on the Guidance Priority List. Comments can be provided by mail, hand delivery, or e-mail. See for example Notice 2009-43, 2009-1 C.B. 1037.
>
> The Guidance Priority List can be obtained from the IRS website, www.irs.gov.

6. Where Can the Guidance Be Found?

Revenue Rulings are published in the Internal Revenue Bulletin, and subsequently in the Cumulative Bulletin, with the exception of revenue rulings involving:

- Issues answered by statute, treaty, or regulations;
- Issues answered by rulings, opinions, or court opinions previously published in the Bulletin;
- Issues that are of insufficient importance or interest to warrant publication;
- Determinations of fact rather than interpretations of law;
- Informers and informers' rewards; and
- Disclosure of secret formulas, processes, business practices, and similar information.

A revenue ruling is identified by two numbers. The first number is the year in which the revenue ruling was issued. The second number represents, sequentially, the order in which the revenue rulings were issued that year.

Revenue rulings can be found first in the Internal Revenue Bulletin and then subsequently in the Cumulative Bulletin. The Internal Revenue Bulletin is published weekly and numbered first with the year and second sequentially by week. A citation to the Internal Revenue Bulletin is considered a temporary citation. The Cumulative Bulletin is published twice a year. The first volume will be identified by the year followed by a "-1" and the

second volume will be identified by the year followed by a "-2." A citation to the Cumulative Bulletin is considered a permanent citation.

Example:

In Revenue Ruling 89-24, 1989-1 C.B. 24:

➤ "89" reflects the fact that the revenue ruling was issued in 1989.

➤ "24" reflects the fact that the revenue ruling is the 24th issued in 1989.

➤ "1989-1" reflects the fact that the ruling is contained in the first volume of the Cumulative Bulletin for 1989.

➤ "24" reflects the fact that the ruling can be found on page 24.

Revenue procedures affecting a taxpayer's rights or duties that relate to matters under the jurisdiction of the IRS are published in the Internal Revenue Bulletin and subsequently in the Cumulative Bulleting. They also are identified by two numbers. The first number is the year in which the revenue procedure was issued. The second number represents, sequentially, the order in which the revenue procedures were issued that year. As with revenue rulings, revenue procedures can be found first in the Internal Revenue Bulletin, and then in the Cumulative Bulletin.

Example:

In Revenue Procedure 89-24, 1989-1 C.B. 845:

➤ "89" reflects the fact that the revenue procedure was issued in 1989.

➤ "24" reflects the fact that the revenue procedure is the 24th issued in 1989.

➤ "1989-1" reflects the fact that the ruling is contained in the first volume of the Cumulative Bulletin for 1989.

➤ "845" reflects the fact that the revenue procedure can be found on page 845.

The same numbering system is used for Notices and Announcements.

Example:

In Notice 89-24, 1989-1 C.B. 660

➤ "89" reflects the fact that the Notice was issued in 1989,

➤ "24" reflects the fact that the Notice is the 24th issued in 1989.

➤ "1989-1" reflects the fact that the notice is contained in the first volume of the Cumulative Bulletin for 1989.

➤ "660" reflects the fact that the ruling can be found on page 660.

Prior to 1991, the IRS published in the Internal Revenue Bulletin acquiescences or nonacquiescences only in certain regular Tax Court opinions. In 1991, it expanded those it published to include other civil tax cases including Tax Court memorandum, district court, Claims Court (and subsequently the Court of Federal Claims), and circuit courts of appeals opinions.

The lists published during January through June each year are consolidated in a list published in the first weekly Bulletin in July and in the Cumulative Bulletin for January

through June. A consolidated list for each calendar year is published in the first weekly Bulletin for the following January and in the Cumulative Bulletin for the last half of the year in which the various lists were published.

C. Main Points ~~Int.~~   *Great summary*

Revenue Ruling:

- Gives guidance on how the IRS will treat a particular transaction by applying the Code, regulations, and any related statutes or tax treaties to a specific factual situation.
- Does not have the force and effect of regulations, but may be relied upon by a taxpayer if his facts and circumstances are substantially the same.
- Reflects the position of the IRS on a particular issue, but is not binding on the court. *no deference*

Revenue Procedure:

- Addresses procedural, rather than substantive, issues.
- Does not have the force and effect of a regulation, but may be relied upon by a taxpayer if his facts and circumstances are substantially the same.
- Sets forth directory, not mandatory, procedures.

Notice and Announcement:

- Public pronouncements containing guidance on matters of general importance.

Actions on Decisions:

- An *acquiescence* and *acquiescence in result only* indicates the IRS accepts the holding of the court in a case with the same controlling facts.
- An *acquiescence in result only* indicates the IRS disagrees or is concerned with the court's rational.
- A *nonacquiescence* signifies that, although no further review was sought, the IRS does not agree with the holding of the court and, generally, will not follow the decision in disposing of cases involving other taxpayers.
- With respect to a circuit court opinion, a *nonacquiescence* indicates that the IRS will recognize the precedential impact of the opinion on cases arising within the venue of the deciding circuit, but not follow the holding on a nationwide basis.

Publications:

- Pamphlets prepared to assist taxpayers in understanding the Internal Revenue Code.
- Explain the Code in the simplest terms possible.

Internal Revenue Bulletin and Cumulative Bulletin:

- The Internal Revenue Bulletin is published weekly.
- The Cumulative Bulletin is issued twice a year and is a compilation of the Internal Revenue Bulletins. The first volume contains the first half of the year, and the second volume contains the last half of the year.
- The third (and subsequent) volume(s) of the Cumulative Bulletin generally contains public laws.

Where can guidance be found?

Guidance	Location
Revenue Ruling	• Internal Revenue Bulletin (temporary) • Cumulative Bulletin (permanent) • Commercial publishers such as CCH, RIA, and Mertens • On-line on IRS website, www.irs.gov • Electronic services
Revenue Procedure	• Internal Revenue Bulletin (temporary) • Cumulative Bulletin (permanent) • Federal Register • Commercial publishers such as CCH, RIA and Mertens • On-line on IRS website, www.irs.gov • Electronic services
Notice	• Internal Revenue Bulletin (temporary) • Cumulative Bulletin (permanent) • Commercial publishers such as CCH, RIA and Mertens • On-line on IRS website, www.irs.gov • Electronic services
Announcement	• Internal Revenue Bulletin (temporary) • Cumulative Bulletin (permanent) • Commercial publishers such as CCH, RIA and Mertens • On-line on IRS website, www.irs.gov • Electronic services
Publications	• On-line on IRS website, www.irs.gov • Most public libraries, post offices, and some local IRS offices • Electronic services

D. Related Articles for Further Reading

• Kristin E. Hickman, *IRB Guidance: The No Man's Land of Tax Code Interpretation*, 2009 MICH. ST. L. REV. 239 (2009).

• Mitchell Rogovin, *The Four R's Revisited: Regulations, Rulings, Reliance, and Retroactivity in the 21st Century: A View From Within*, 46 DUQ. L. REV. 323 (2008).

• Ryan C. Morris, *Substantially Deferring to Revenue Rulings After Mead*, 2005 B.Y.U.L. REV. 999 (2005).

E. Problems

1. All of the following are divisions of the IRS, except:
    a. Wage and Investment Division.
    b. Small Business/Self-Employed Division.
    c. Criminal Investigation Division.
    d. Legislative Division.

2. The public guidance projects the IRS is working on are listed on:

    a. The Regulatory List.
    b. The Guidance Priority List, or Business Plan.
    c. The Project List.
    d. None of the above.

3. Revenue Rulings:

    a. Give guidance to a specific taxpayer as to how the IRS will treat the transaction.
    b. Give the public procedural advice.
    c. Give the public guidance as to how the IRS will treat a non-taxpayer specific transaction.
    d. Make general announcements.

4. Internal Revenue Bulletins:

    a. Are the authoritative instrument for the publication of official rulings and procedures issued by the IRS as well as other tax documents of interest to taxpayers and tax practitioners.
    b. Are published weekly.
    c. Are compiled twice a year into the Cumulative Bulletin.
    d. All of the above.

5. All of the following is true about Revenue Rulings, except:

    a. Have the force and effect of law.
    b. May be relied upon by a taxpayer if his facts and circumstances are substantially the same.
    c. Represents the IRS's position on a particular issue.
    d. Are not binding on the court.

6. Revenue Procedures:

    a. Give guidance to a specific taxpayer as to how the IRS will treat the transaction.
    b. Give the public procedural advice.
    c. Give the public guidance as to how the IRS will treat a non-taxpayer specific transaction.
    d. Make general announcements.

7. Publications:

    a. Are pamphlets that assist taxpayers in understanding the Code.
    b. Give guidance to a specific taxpayer as to how the IRS will treat the transaction.
    c. Give the public procedural advice.
    d. Give the public guidance as to how the IRS will treat a non-taxpayer specific transaction.

8. Notice and Announcements:

    a. Give guidance to a specific taxpayer as to how the IRS will treat the transaction.
    b. Give the public procedural advice.
    c. Give the public guidance as to how the IRS will treat a non-taxpayer specific transaction.
    d. Make general announcements.

9. An action on decision may be any of the following, except:
    a. Acquiescence.
    b. Acquiescence in result only.
    c. Nonacquiescence.
    d. Appeal pending.

10. On the IRS website, locate:
    a. The Priority Guidance List (Business Plan).
    b. The AOD on *Cox v. Commissioner* (514 F.3d 1119 (10th Cir. 2008)).
    c. IRB 2010-15.

11. Your client entered into a transaction that is identical to the facts of *McNamara v. Commissioner*, 236 F3d 410 (8th Cir. 2003). The IRS issued an action on decision, CC 2003-003, recommending nonacquiescence. In *McNamara* the Eighth Circuit ruled in favor of the taxpayer. Your client is currently under audit and the IRS is asking questions with respect to the transaction mentioned above. When you bring the *McNamara* decision to the attention of the IRS auditors, will they likely drop the issue and not seek a tax adjustment? Why or why not?

12. Locate IRS Publication 515. What topic does it discuss? *not authority at all.*

13. As you will learn when reading the next chapter, the IRS annually issues a statement that describes the steps for seeking a written opinion from the IRS on a particular set of facts. Do you think such statement is issued in the form of a Revenue Ruling or a Revenue Procedure? Why?

14. Consider *FPL Group, Inc. v. Commissioner*, T.C. Memo. 2005-210.
    a. What revenue ruling was at issue?
    b. Why was the revenue ruling relevant?
    c. Did the court follow the revenue ruling?

15. Consider Revenue Procedure 2005-15, 2003-1 C.B. 447.
    a. What issues does the procedure address?
    b. Under what circumstances would the information be helpful when assisting a client?
    c. Did the court follow the revenue procedure in *McGee v. Commissioner*, 123 T.C. 314 (2004)?
    d. Did the court follow the revenue procedure in *Haltom v. Commissioner*, T.C. Memo. 2005-209?

16. Consider Revenue Procedure 2003-11, 2003-1 C.B. 311.
    a. What information is contained in the notice?
    b. When would that information have been important in advising your clients?

17. Who is the current Commissioner of the Internal Revenue Service?

18. Who is the current Chief Counsel of the Office of Chief Counsel?

Individual taxpayer going to IRS and asking for guidance.

Chapter 7

Taxpayer-Specific Guidance from the Office of Chief Counsel

Taxpayer-Specific Guidance

- *What types of taxpayer-specific guidance are issued?*

- *In what areas will the IRS issue such guidance?*

- *To what extent is such guidance disclosed to the public?*

- *Where can the various types of guidance be found?*

The senior partner concluded his presentation to the client with, "Well, Mr. Rose, I think that that is the best tax advice we can give you based on how you want to structure the transaction."

Mr. Rose slowly nodded his head and said, "That was very comprehensive. I understand that we are possibly breaking some new ground here with what I want to do. I also understand that you have done all you could to anticipate the outcome based on what guidance is out there. But, wouldn't it be nice if we knew what the IRS thought of the transaction *before* I went ahead with it."

"Funny you should say that," the senior partner began slowly. "Because there was one more thing I was going to talk to you about. There is, in fact, a way to find out what the IRS thinks of a transaction before you enter into it. It is called a private letter ruling."

"Interesting. Please, tell me more."

Contents

A. Key Terms

After completing this chapter, you should be familiar with the following key terms:

➤   Private Letter Ruling

➤   Determination Letter

➤   Information Letter

➤   Technical Advice Memorandum

B. Discussion

In planning a particular transaction, a taxpayer may be interested in knowing how the IRS will treat the proposed transaction. Depending on the subject matter at issue, the taxpayer may have the opportunity to ask the Office of Chief Counsel. If provided to the taxpayer, the guidance will be in the form of a private letter ruling, determination letter, or information letter.

If the transaction has already been planned and carried out, and the proper tax consequences are being challenged by the IRS, resolution of a difference of opinion on the proper tax treatment may be through a technical advice memorandum.

1. Private Letter Ruling   *write before transaction not after*

If a taxpayer is interested in learning how the IRS would treat a particular transaction the taxpayer is contemplating or has yet to report on his income tax return, he can submit a private letter ruling request. Upon submission of the necessary information to the

appropriate Office of Associate Chief Counsel, the Associate office will give a **private letter ruling** as to how it believes the transaction should be treated. However, a ruling request cannot be used as a "second opinion" if the issue is under examination, in appeals, or in litigation.

Practice Note:

The first revenue procedure issued each year sets forth the procedures for requesting a private letter ruling.

The first revenue procedure issued each year provides extensive information on how to prepare a private letter ruling request, including a list of necessary information, a checklist of items to include, and a sample ruling request.

Practice Note:

A list of areas in which an Associate office will not issue a letter ruling or determination letter is set forth in the third revenue procedure issued each year.

The fees charged for a letter ruling vary according to categories or subcategories and must be paid in advance. Exhibit A of the first revenue procedure contains a schedule of the fees.

When issued, the taxpayer receiving the ruling generally is entitled to rely upon it. However, a taxpayer may not rely on a letter ruling issued to another taxpayer.

Section 6110(k)(3) provides:

Unless the Secretary otherwise establishes by regulations, a written determination may not be used or cited as precedent.

Case on Point:

Willamette Industries v. Commissioner
118 T.C. 126, 134 n10 (2002)

n.10. Petitioner also relies on the published revenue rulings and on a number of private letter rulings (PLRs), which it contends permitted sec. 1033 deferral in factual circumstances substantially similar to those we consider here. On brief, the parties devoted a relatively large portion of their arguments to discussing the PLRs. Although we have considered the rationale used by the parties in discussing the rulings, the parties and the Court are statutorily proscribed from citing the PLRs as precedent. See sec. 6110(k)(3).

Example:

The following is an example of a private letter ruling:

PRIVATE RULING 200510036

LEGEND:

Bank A = * * *
Amount D = * * *
Amount E = * * *

Amount F = * * *
IRA X = * * *
IRA Z = * * *

Dear * * *

This is in response to your letter dated April 15, 2003, in which you requested a ruling asking for a waiver of the 60-day rollover requirement. Letters dated July 9, 2004 and November 12, 2004, supplemented the request.

You have submitted the following facts and representations:

On * * * Amount F was distributed to you from IRA X. Amount F represents Amount D (the total amount in the IRA) minus Amount E which was withheld for federal income tax. On * * * you invested the money at bank A with the intent of eventually rolling over Amount D into an IRA at Bank A. The 60 day period for rolling over the distribution expired on * * *. On * * * you deposited, by means of a transfer, the funds into IRA Z.

During the period referred to in the above paragraph, you were suffering from leukemia and undergoing chemotherapy treatment. You developed an infection because of the treatment. Such infection lasted until the end of * * * Furthermore, during that period your daughter was pregnant.

During the last three weeks of your daughter's pregnancy, your daughter was suffering from toxemia and gallstones, and was in severe pain. You and your husband were caring for your daughter at this time, and also taking care of your daughter's 18 month-old child. Your daughter had her baby on * * * two days before the 60-day period expired.

Thus, in short, a combination of your illness, your daughter's complicated pregnancy, your daughter's illness, and your having to care for your grandchild, resulted in your failing to satisfy the 60-day rollover requirement by a minimal period of time.

Based on the facts and representations, you request that the Internal Revenue Service waive the 60-day rollover requirement with respect to the distribution of Amount D, because the failure to waive such requirement would be against equity or good conscience.

Section 408(d)(1) of the Code provides that, except as otherwise provided in section 408(d), any amount paid or distributed out of an IRA shall be included in gross income by the payee or distributee, as the case may be, in the manner provided under section 72 of the Code.

Section 408(d)(3) of the Code defines, and provides the rules applicable to IRA rollovers.

Section 408(d)(3)(A) of the Code provides that section 408(d)(1) of the Code does not apply to any amount paid or distributed out of an IRA to the individual for whose benefit the IRA is maintained if (i) the entire amount received (including money and any other property) is paid into an IRA for the benefit of such individual not later than the 60th day after the day on which the individual receives the payment or distribution; or (ii) the entire amount received (including money and any other property) is paid into an eligible retirement plan (other than an IRA) for the benefit of such individual not later than the 60th day after the date on which the payment or distribution is received, except that the maximum amount which may be paid into such plan may not exceed the portion of the amount received which is includible in gross income (determined without regard to section 408(d)(3)).

Section 408(d)(3)(B) of the Code provides that section 408(d)(3) does not apply to any amount described in section 408(d)(3)(A)(i) received by an individual from an IRA if at any time during the 1-year period ending on the day of such receipt such individual received any other amount described in section 408(d)(3)(A)(I) from an IRA which was not includible in gross income because of the application of section 408(d)(3).

Section 408(d)(3)(D) of the Code provides a similar 60-day rollover period for partial rollovers.

Section 408(d)(3)(I) of the Code provides that the Secretary may waive the 60-day requirement under sections 408(d)(3)(A) and 408(d)(3)(D) of the Code where the failure to waive such requirement would be against equity or good conscience, including casualty, disaster, or other events beyond the reasonable control of the individual subject to such requirement. Only distributions that occurred after December 31, 2001, are eligible for the waiver under section 408(d)(3)(I) of the Code.

Rev. Proc. 2003-16, 2003-4 I.R.B. 359, provides that in determining whether to grant a waiver of the 60-day rollover requirement pursuant to section 408(d)(3)(I), the Service will consider all relevant facts and circumstances, including: (1) errors committed by a financial institution; (2) inability to complete a rollover due to death, disability, hospitalization, incarceration, restrictions imposed by a foreign country or postal error, (3) the use of the amount distributed (for example, in the case of payment by check, whether the check was cashed); and (4) the time elapsed since the distribution occurred.

The information presented by you demonstrates that you were unable to complete the transaction because of serious medical conditions existing in your family.

Therefore, pursuant to section 408(d)(3)(I) of the Code, the Service hereby waives the 60-day rollover requirement with respect to the distribution of the amount from IRA X. Provided all other requirements of section 408(d)(3) of the Code, except the 60-day requirement, are met with respect to such distribution, the deposit into IRA Z, made by means of a transfer will be considered a rollover contribution within the meaning of section 408(d)(3) of the Code.

This ruling does not authorize the rollover of amounts that are required to be distributed by section 401(a)(9) of the Code, if any.

No opinion is expressed as to the tax treatment of the transaction described herein under the provisions of any other section of either the Code or regulations that may be applicable thereto.

This letter is directed only to the taxpayer who requested it. Section 6110(k)(3) of the Code provides that it may not be used or cited as precedent.

If you wish to inquire about this ruling, please contact * * * (ID * * * at (* * *) * * *- * * *. Please address all correspondence to SE:T:EP:RA:T3.

Sincerely yours,

Frances V. Sloan, Manager,
Employee Plans Technical Group 3

Enclosures:
Deleted copy of ruling letter
Notice of Intention to Disclose

2. Determination Letters *issued by Area director*

A **determination letter** is a written statement issued by an Area Director that applies tax law principles and precedents previously announced by the IRS to a specific set of facts. It is issued only when a determination can be made based on clearly established rules in the statute, a tax treaty, the regulations, a conclusion in a revenue ruling, or an opinion or court decision that represents the position of the IRS. The authority to issue determination letters is discretionary.

> **Practice Note:**
>
> Determination letters are primarily requested for a determination that:
>
> - A pension plan is a qualified plan; or
> - An organization has tax exempt status.

> **Practice Note:**
>
> The first revenue procedure issued each year sets forth the procedures for requesting a determination letter.
>
> The sixth revenue procedure sets forth procedures for issuing determination letters on the qualified status of pension, profit sharing, stock bonus, annuity, and employee stock ownership plans.

Selected Area Directors issue determination letters as to the qualification of certain organizations for exemption from income tax under Section 521 to the extent provided in the Exempt Organizations Handbook. After issuance, such letters are reviewed by the National Office to ensure uniformity in the application of the principles and precedents of the IRS.

The requesting taxpayer may rely on the determination letter. A taxpayer may not rely on a determination letter issued to another taxpayer.

3. Information Letters *issued by Area director or Associate office*

An **information letter** is a statement issued either by an Associate office or by an Area Director. It calls attention to a well-established interpretation or principle of tax law without applying it to a specific set of facts. An information letter may be issued if the taxpayer's inquiry indicates a need for general information or if the taxpayer's request does not meet the requirements of a private letter ruling and the IRS thinks general information will help the taxpayer.

> **Practice Note:**
>
> The first revenue procedure issued each year sets forth the procedures for requesting an information letter.

Example:

The following is an example of an information letter:

DEPARTMENT OF THE TREASURY
INTERNAL REVENUE SERVICE
WASHINGTON, D.C. 20224

OFFICE OF
CHIEF COUNSEL

3/25/2005

Number: **INFO 2005-0118**
Release Date: 6/30/05
UIL: 170.12-07

GENIN-135700-04
CC:ITA:B1

Dear   :

Thank you for your inquiry dated May 10, 2004, in which you ask whether you are entitled to claim a charitable contribution deduction under § 170 of the Internal Revenue Code for payments made to a   at which your children attend   school tuition-free. This letter is not a ruling, but rather provides information in response to the general question of what is deductible as a charitable contribution.

To be deductible under § 170, a payment must be a gift. A gift is a voluntary transfer of money or property that is made with no expectation of procuring a financial benefit commensurate with the amount of the transfer. *United States v. American Bar Endowment*, 477 U.S. 105, 118 (1986). No charitable contribution deduction is allowed for payments that are, in fact, tuition. Whether a payment is non-deductible tuition, or is a gift, is determined on a case by case basis, and is based on all the facts and circumstances. Rev. Rul. 83-104, 1983-2 C.B. 46.

If you believe that you need to report criminal activity, the Internal Revenue Service Criminal Investigation Informant Hotline can be reached by calling 1-800-829-0433.

For your convenience, I have enclosed Publication 526, "Charitable Contributions." If you have any questions, please call   , ID. No.   , at

Sincerely,

Karin G. Gross
Senior Technician Reviewer, Branch 1
Office of Associate Chief Counsel
(Income Tax & Accounting)

Enclosure

Information letters that are issued by an Associate office to members of the public are made available to the public. Information letters issued by the field office are not made available to the public. Information letters are advisory only and have no binding effect on the IRS.

Director request [handwritten]

4. Technical Advice Memorandum   *TAM* [handwritten]

issued by National office [handwritten]

A **technical advice memorandum** is advice or guidance furnished by the National Office upon request of a director in a case under examination, but not yet in litigation.[1] The advice assists the IRS in resolving the particular case. It also assists in establishing and maintaining consistent holdings on issues throughout the IRS. It addresses novel or complex legal issues where the IRS's position has not been previously established and sets forth what the IRS understands to be the proper interpretation and application of the tax laws to the facts of the specific case. Generally, when rendered, it represents a final determination of the position of the IRS with respect to a specific issue in a specific case.

A director will request technical advice when there is a lack of uniformity regarding how the issue should be resolved or when an issue is unusual or complex. Advice may be requested related to a technical or procedural question on the interpretation and proper application of the tax law, tax treaties, regulations, revenue rulings, notices, or other precedents to a specific set of facts.

Because the IRS is requesting the application of law to a specific set of facts, the IRS is required to make every effort to reach an agreement with the taxpayer as to the facts before requesting assistance. The field office will prepare the statement with the assistance of field counsel. The memorandum must include a statement of all the facts and the issues.

> **Practice Note:**
>
> The second revenue procedure issued each year sets forth the procedures for requesting a technical advice memorandum.

The technical advice memorandum provided by the Associate office will contain:

- A statement of the issues;
- Conclusions of the Associate office;
- Statement of the pertinent facts;
- Statement of the pertinent law, tax treaties, regulations, revenue rulings, and other precedents published in the Internal Revenue Bulletin, and court opinions; and
- Discussion of the rationale supporting the conclusions reached by the Associate office.

In general, the taxpayer's case will be processed on the basis of the conclusions in the technical advice memorandum. The field office will provide the taxpayer with a copy of the technical advice memorandum.

> **Practice Note:**
>
> Technical advice memoranda can be found on the IRS website at www.irs.gov, in the Electronic Reading Room.

Technical advice memoranda are released to the public, with taxpayer-specific and certain other types of information redacted. Under the procedures, the taxpayer has an op-

---

1. A technical advice memorandum can also be requested by an Area Director for Appeals, as long as the case is not in litigation.

portunity to participate in the redaction process. A taxpayer may not rely on a technical advice memorandum issued by the IRS to another taxpayer.

Case on Point:

Anderson v. Commissioner
123 T.C. 219, 222 n.6 (2004)

n.6 The technical advice memorandum generally reflected respondent's position in this case. Technical advice memoranda are a type of private letter ruling that is not to be cited as precedent unless regulations so provide. Sec. 6110(k)(3). No regulations so provide here.

Example:

The following is an example of a technical advice memorandum:

PRIVATE RULING 200327002

DATE: February 28, 2003

REFER REPLY TO: CASE MIS No.: TAM-145856-02/CC:ITA:B5

Release Date: 7/03/2003

Director, Appeals (Area 6)
Taxpayer Name: * * *
Taxpayer Address: * * *
Taxpayers' Identification No: * * *
Years Involved: * * *
Date of Conference: * * *

LEGEND:

ISSUE

Whether payments received by a U.S. resident alien, pursuant to interests in three foreign business enterprises created in her favor under foreign law by her father, should be included in her gross income under I.R.C. section 61.

CONCLUSION

The purported transfers to taxpayer do not effectively convey dominion and control of the income-producing assets involved; thus, "ownership" has not been effectively transferred to the taxpayer and she does not have income under section 61 as a result of the payments made to her pursuant to those purported transfers.

FACTS

In Contract Year A, when taxpayer was a minor resident in and a national of Foreign Nation, her appointed guardian and her father executed certain documents creating "gift" and "sub-interests" in three foreign business enterprises in favor of taxpayer. The documents created binding rights and obligations on the businesses and the parties under the law of Foreign Nation. We assume for purposes of this advice that the created sub-interests are neither trusts, partnerships, nor corporations for U.S. income tax purposes. It has been represented, and we expressly assume, that under U.S. income tax principles the enterprises are properly treated as partnerships.

Translations of the relevant documents state that the father may demand at any time during his life the return of the "gifted" sub-interest and/or determine how the income

derived from or the proceeds from disposal of such interest are used for the benefit of taxpayer. Moreover, father retains the right to receive and/or manage any proceeds from the disposal of the interests. Upon the father's death, the retained rights would devolve to his wife.

In Tax Year 1, Taxpayer and her husband (hereinafter, taxpayers) became U.S. resident aliens and commenced filing joint U.S. income tax returns. Taxpayers reported AmountA as income on their U.S. income tax return for that year attributable to the sub-interests. Subsequently, taxpayers filed an amended return (before expiration of the relevant statute of limitations period) for Tax Year 1 excluding the income from the foreign businesses. This position, together with certain collateral adjustments, would result in a refund for Tax Year 1. On later years' U.S. returns, taxpayers did not include the sub-interest payments in income. Taxpayers attached Form 8275 (Disclosure Statement) to their Tax Year 3 return, noting that the income from the three foreign enterprises was being excluded because the father retained sufficient ownership interests such that, for U.S. income tax purposes, the assignment of income doctrine prevented the "transfers" from being effective.

Consistent with their position as stated on Form 8275, taxpayers now argue that the transfers of the sub-interests are essentially without substance for purposes of establishing ownership under the Internal Revenue Code. They contend that under U.S. tax principles, the transfers are properly treated as anticipatory assignments of income which have no effect in shifting the responsibility for income taxation.

The Service, relying on section 61, has included in taxpayer's income the payments made to her for Tax Years 1, 3, 4, and 5. (Tax Year 2 is closed.) This treatment gives rise to the following deficiencies: Tax Year 3, AmountC; Tax Year 4, AmountD; Tax Year 5, AmountE.

LAW AND ANALYSIS

Under section 61(a) of the Internal Revenue Code, except where otherwise provided, gross income means all income from whatever sources derived, including, but not limited to, certain categories thereunder enumerated. Because the parties agree that the payments in issue here from the foreign business enterprises would be the functional equivalent of distributive shares of domestic partnership income (see section 61(a)(13)), it is assumed that specific characterization is appropriate. See Rev. Rul. 93-4, 1993-1 C.B. 225. That characterization would be appropriate, however, only in so far as the initial source payout from the business enterprise is concerned. See Rev. Rul. 73-254, 1973-1 C.B. 613.

The judicially-created assignment of income doctrine applies in determining which taxpayer must include an item of income. Under the doctrine, income from personal services (e.g., wages) must be included in the gross income of the person who rendered the services. Lucas v. Earl, 281 U.S. 111 (1930). Similarly, income from property (e.g., rents) must be included in the gross income of the person who owns the property. Blair v. Commissioner, 300 U.S. 5 (1937). Mere legal title is not dispositive of ownership; the significant factual inquiry goes to the actual beneficial interest and who controls the economic benefits (or shoulders the burdens) of that property. See, e.g., Serianni v. Commissioner, 80 T.C. 1090 (1983), aff'd, 765 F.2d 1051 (11th Cir. 1985); Hang v. Commissioner, 95 T.C. 74 (1990); Hook v. Commissioner, 58 T.C. 267 (1972). Taxpayer maintains that if there were two U.S. taxpayers involved, her father would still be liable for U.S. income taxes on any income generated by the assets "legally" transferred. If the degree and manner of control over the income-producing property is not significantly altered by the purported transfer, then the incidence of taxation does not shift. See P.R. Farms, Inc. v. Commissioner, T.C. Memo. 1984-549.

Under section 102, gifts are specifically excluded from gross income. Once the payments passed to taxpayer through her father's control, even if merely his constructive control, the nature of the payment must necessarily be reexamined. The actual nature of the payments to the daughter—as received in her hands—determines whether she has gross income under the Code, i.e., a distributive share of partnership income or a gift from her father (or mother, in the event of his death). While this determination might involve a factual inquiry, the ultimate characterization is a legal determination. Whether the doctrine prohibiting the anticipatory assignment of income is invoked or the payments are ruled gifts under section 102 from the father to the taxpayer, the relevant inquiry is the same: did the father retain dominion and control—and, hence, ownership—of the foreign assets?

Purported sale transactions and alleged gifts must meet the same test to be effective transfers of ownership and, thus, effective transfers of the incidence of income taxation. See, e.g., National Lead Co. v. Commissioner, 40 T.C. 282 (1963), aff'd, 336 F.2d 134 (2d Cir. 1964), cert. denied, 380 U.S. 908 (1965) (purported sale); Urbanovsky v. Commissioner, T.C. Memo. 1965-276 (purported gift). There must be a significant change in the economic relationship of the transferor to the property involved to effect a valid transfer of that property for income tax purposes. See Zmuda v. Commissioner, 731 F.2d 1417 (9th Cir. 1984), aff'g 79 T.C. 714 (1982). If the transferor retains dominion and control, then ownership and the incidence of income taxation thereon has not been shifted. See, e.g., Chase v. Commissioner, T.C. Memo. 1990-164, aff'd, 926 F.2d 737 (8th Cir. 1991); Estate of Applestein v. Commissioner, 80 T.C. 331 (1983).

The facts presented support the finding that taxpayer's father retained the essential right to receive the income generated by the enterprise. He retains the right to "call back" this income throughout his life and has passed that right in the event of his death to his wife. Any payouts from the enterprises appear to be subject to his decision to do with what he wishes-including those payments due to his daughter on her subinterests. The fact of the father's control of the payments is insurmountable, irrespective of whether he has ultimately gifted those amounts to the daughter.

On the basis of the specific language of the ineffectual "transferring" documents cited above, the legal conclusion based upon the facts presented is that for U.S. income tax purposes beneficial ownership never really changed. The taxpayer has not received effective ownership of the "sub-interests" and, thus, has no gross income with respect to the "sub-interests" in question.

Accordingly, the taxpayer's U.S. taxable income does not include any amounts attributable to the sub-interests.

CAVEAT

We express no opinion as to U.S. gift tax implications, if any, of these transactions under sections 2501 and 2511 of the Code.

A copy of this technical advice memorandum is to be given to the taxpayer(s). Section 6110(k)(3) of the Code provides that it may not be used or cited as precedent.

5. Where Can Taxpayer-Specific Guidance Be Found?

Private letter rulings and technical advice memoranda are not officially published by the IRS. However, commercial services do publish them. Private letter rulings, determi-

nation letters, information letters, and technical advice memoranda issued after 1996 can also be found on the IRS website, www.irs.gov, in the Electronic Reading Room.

When issued, private letter rulings and technical advice memoranda are given a number. The first four digits of the number is the year the advice was issued. The second two digits are the week the advice was issued, and the final number is, sequentially, the order in which the advice was issued that week. Before 2000, the year the advice was issued was reflected by only the last two digits of the year (rather than 4 digits).

Example:

In Private Letter Ruling 200113012:

➤ "2001" reflects the fact that the private letter ruling was issued in 2001

➤ "13" reflects the fact that the ruling was issued in the 13th week of 2001

➤ "012" reflects the fact that the ruling was the twelfth issued during that week.

C. Main Points

Private Letter Ruling:

- Provides advice on how a particular transaction will be treated by the IRS.
- Available only if the issue is not currently under examination or in a docketed case.
- Procedures for submitting a request are set forth in the first revenue procedure issued each year.
- In general, the requesting taxpayer may rely on the private letter ruling.
- A taxpayer may not rely on a letter ruling issued to another taxpayer.

Determination Letter:

- A written statement issued by an Area Director that applies tax law principles and precedents previously announced by the National Office to a specific set of facts.
- Issued only when a determination can be made based on clearly established rules.
- Procedures for submitting a request are set forth in the first revenue procedure issued each year.
- The requesting taxpayer may rely on the determination letter.
- A taxpayer may not rely on a determination letter issued to another taxpayer.

Information Letter:

- A statement issued either by the National Office or by an Area Director.
- Calls attention to a well-established interpretation or principle of tax law without applying it to a specific set of facts.
- Procedures for submitting a request are set forth in the first revenue procedure issued each year.
- Is advisory only and has no binding effect on the IRS.

Technical Advice Memorandum:

- Advice or guidance furnished by the National Office upon request by the field in a case under examination but not yet in litigation.

- The advice assists the IRS in resolving the particular case and in establishing and maintaining consistent holdings on issues throughout the IRS.

- It addresses novel or complex legal issues where the IRS's position has not been previously established and sets forth what the IRS understands to be the proper interpretation and application of the tax laws to the facts of the specific case.

- Represents a final determination of the position of the IRS with respect to a specific issue in a specific case.

- Procedures for submitting a request are set forth in the second revenue procedure issued each year.

- A taxpayer may not rely on a technical advice memorandum issued by the IRS to another taxpayer.

Where can the guidance be found?

Guidance	Publisher
Private Letter Ruling	• Commercial publishers, such as CCH, RIA, and Mertens • IRS website, www.irs.gov • Electronic services
Determination Letter	Not included in any official IRS publication, but are open for public inspection on the IRS website.
Information Letter	Not included in any official IRS publication, but are open for public inspection on IRS website.
Technical Advice Memorandum	• Commercial publishers, such as CCH, RIA, and Mertens. • IRS website, www.irs.gov • Electronic services

D. Related Articles for Further Reading

- Mitchell Rogovin, *The Four R's Revisited: Regulations, Rulings, Reliance, and Retroactivity in the 21st Century: A View From Within*, 46 Duq. L. Rev. 323 (2008).

- Judy S. Kwok, *The Perils of Bright Lines: Section 6110(k)(3) and the Ambiguous Precedential Status of Written Determinations*, 24 Va. Tax Rev. 863 (Spring, 2005).

- Joseph L. Wyatt, Jr., *Scouting for Settlements With IRS Help: Using the PLR Compass*, 12 Probate and Property 6 (March/April 1998).

- Lawrence Zelenak, *Should Courts Require the Internal Revenue Service to be Consistent?*, 40 Tax L. Rev. 411 (1985).

E. Problems

1. Private letter ruling 200417079 was issued in:

   a. 2004.
   b. 1917.
   c. 1979.
   d. 2000.

2. The IRS indicates how it would treat a proposed transaction through:

   a. A private letter ruling.
   b. A technical advice memorandum.
   c. An information letter.
   d. A determination letter.

3. The procedure for preparing a request for a private letter ruling can be found:

   a. In an IRS publication.
   b. In a technical advice memorandum.
   c. In the first revenue procedure issued each year.
   d. In a determination letter.

4. Who is entitled to rely on a private letter ruling?

   a. Any taxpayer with similar facts.
   b. All taxpayers.
   c. Any taxpayer who can establish he detrimentally relied upon the ruling.
   d. Only the taxpayer to whom it was issued.

5. The document that applies tax law principles and precedents previously announced by the National Office to a specific set of facts is a:

   a. Private letter ruling.
   b. Technical advice memorandum.
   c. Determination letter.
   d. Revenue procedure.

6. Who is entitled to rely on a technical advice memorandum?

   a. Any taxpayer with similar facts.
   b. All taxpayers.
   c. Any taxpayer who can establish he detrimentally relied upon the ruling.
   d. Only the taxpayer to whom it was issued.

7. The procedure for preparing a request for a technical advice memorandum can be found:

   a. In an IRS publication.
   b. In a technical advice memorandum.
   c. In the second revenue procedure issued each year.
   d. In a determination letter.

8. A letter from the IRS that indicates a pension plan is a qualified plan is most likely a:

   a. Private letter ruling.
   b. Technical advice memorandum.
   c. Information letter.
   d. Determination letter.

9. A technical advice memorandum is requested:

   a. When there is a lack of uniformity regarding how the issue should be resolved.
   b. When an issue is unusual.
   c. When an issue is complex.
   d. Any of the above.

10. The statement that calls attention to a well-established interpretation or principle of law without applying it to a specific set of facts is a:

    a. Private letter ruling.
    b. Technical advice memorandum.
    c. Information letter.
    d. Publication.

11. Advice from the National Office to the field on the tax treatment of a case under examination is a:

    a. Private letter ruling.
    b. Technical advice memorandum.
    c. Information letter.
    d. Determination letter.

12. Locate TAM 200224004.

    a. What issue is addressed in the advice?
    b. Could you cite the advice as authority for your position on a similar issue?
    c. If not, what use could you make of the advice?

13. Locate PLR 200513011.

    a. What issue is addressed in the ruling?
    b. Could you cite the ruling as authority for your position on a similar issue?
    c. If not, what use could you make of the ruling?

14. Locate information letter INFO 2005-0117.

    a. What issue is addressed in the letter?
    b. What use could you make of the information?

15. Your client, Mr. Dahl, is interested in reorganizing his corporation. Currently, one corporation runs both a baseball manufacturing business and a glove manufacturing business. Mr. Dahl would like each separate business to be conducted by a separate corporation; specifically, he would like the baseball manufacturing business to be conducted by one corporation and the glove manufacturing business to be conducted by a second corporation. He is adamant that the reorganization be tax free. You have done a substantial amount of research and believe you can structure the transaction as a divisive section 355 transaction and accomplish what Mr. Dahl wants. Mr. Dahl has asked whether it would be prudent to request a private letter ruling on the proposed transaction to assure that the IRS agrees that it would be tax free. What do you tell Mr. Dahl?

16. Please explain the difference between a private letter ruling and a revenue ruling (discussed in Chapter 6).

17. You represent Sam. Sam is contemplating entering into a large transaction in the near future. Based on your research, you have concluded that the tax consequences of such transaction are somewhat uncertain. As a result, you inform Sam that you would like to submit a private letter ruling request on his behalf. Sam wants to know

whether there is a filing fee for the request and the type of personal information that he will have to provide in such a request. What are the answers to Sam's questions?

18. Are there areas in which the IRS will not issue private letter rulings or determination letters? Examine Revenue Procedure 2010-3, 2010-1 I.R.B. 110, which is updated annually.

19. You have researched the applicability of the research credit and found several relevant private letter rulings. In what way could you utilize the private letter rulings in preparing a letter to the client? A memorandum to a partner? A brief?

Chapter 8

Documents Generated by the Office of Chief Counsel for Internal Use

[handwritten: Not so important but we should be aware of it.]

Internal-Use Documents

* *What types of documents are created?*

* *To what extent are such documents disclosed to the public?*

* *Where can the various types of guidance be found?*

Tammi rubbed her eyes then glanced at the clock. She had only two hours before her client was due in her office. She understood the basic tax issues related to her client's car wash business. Given that it was a cash intensive operation, the biggest issue would be establishing that all the income had been reported. There might also be some questions about whether all the deductions should be allowed. But, Tammi wanted to anticipate more specifically what documents or information the IRS might be looking for, how it would frame the issues, and what issues or documents it would find most relevant. Certainly, she thought, the IRS must have some guidelines its agents use to move forward on an issue. If she had that information, she could level the playing field and be in the best position possible to represent her client. As she turned to her computer, she wondered what kinds of documents the IRS generated internally for its revenue agents and which ones she could access.

Contents

Field Service advice :— Advice from National office related to the factual development of a case.

A. Key Terms

After completing this chapter, you should be familiar with the following key terms:

➤ Field Service Advice

➤ Technical Assistance

➤ Service Center Advice

➤ Litigation Guideline Memorandum

➤ Collection, Bankruptcy, and Summonses Bulletins

➤ Criminal Tax Bulletins

➤ Disclosure Bulletins

➤ General Counsel Memorandum

➤ Technical Memorandum

➤ Legal Memorandum

➤ Market Segment Specialization Program

➤ Audit Technique Guide

B. Discussion

In carrying out its obligation of enforcing the Code and providing guidance to its employees to assist them in enforcement, the Office of Chief Counsel generates a number of documents for internal use. Some of these documents may provide insight into the IRS's interpretation of issues and intended application of the Code. In recent years, these documents have become increasingly available to the public.

1. Field Service Advice *issued by office of Chief Counsel.*

Refer to diagram of page = 147

A goal of the National Office is to make certain that the Code is interpreted and applied uniformly by the field offices, the National Office, and the IRS. Because the attorneys in the National Office are considered the subject matter experts, if an issue arises that is difficult or significant, the field (or, less often an appeals officer or IRS agent) can request assistance from the National Office on how to proceed.[1] The request can be made when the issue is still undergoing factual development and the advice is intended to assist with the development of the case.

Issues covered in FSA are substantive tax issues.

no deference given by court.

> **Field Service Advice** is advice from the National Office related to the factual development of a case.

does not count for authority.

> **Practice Note:**
>
> Field service advice is requested when an issue is still undergoing factual development and the advice assists in the factual development of the case.
>
> A technical advice memorandum[2] is requested when the facts are fully developed and the advice assists in addressing unsettled areas of law.

The Associate Chief Counsel Office with subject matter jurisdiction over the issue will respond with written, legal advice to the requesting Associate Area Counsel (field) office. When issued, the response will contain the following:

- Statement of each issue;
- Conclusion for each issue, including any limitations or conditions to which the conclusion may be subject;
- Statement of facts; and
- Legal analysis, developing the strengths and weaknesses of the case and discussing authorities for and against the conclusion.

The response of the National Office is called field service advice. Advice may also be requested and given on industry-wide issues, hypothetical questions, or procedural matters.

---

1. A taxpayer cannot request field service advice.
2. For a discussion of technical advice memoranda, *see* Chapter 7, *Taxpayer-Specific Guidance from the Office of Chief Counsel.*

Quick Find:

Field Service Advice can be found on the IRS website, www.irs.gov, in the Electronic Reading Room.

Generally, the field office is not required to disclose to the taxpayer that field service advice has been requested. However, the office may so advise the taxpayer and even allow him to participate to some degree in the process.

Because field service advice focuses on how the law applies to the particular facts of a case, it assists the field only in the specific case in which the advice was issued. It may not be used or cited as precedent in any other case. Even with respect to the case in which it was requested, it does not represent a final determination of IRS position. Given that the advice assists the requesting office with the factual development of the case, the final position taken must be determined through the independent judgment of the field office with jurisdiction over the case, taking into account any factual and legal research, the field service advice received, taxpayer input, and all other relevant information. That being said, field service advice is highly regarded and the advice is generally followed.

Example:

The following is an example of field service advice:

REFERENCE: CC:DOM:FS:FI&P, TL-N-8945-97, REWade

TEXT:

date: MAY 13 1998

to: District Counsel, Kentucky-Tennessee CC:SER:KYT:NAS

Attention: Vallie C. Brooks, Special Litigation Assistant

from: Assistant Chief Counsel (Field Service) CC:DOM:FS

subject: [TEXT REDACTED]

This responds to your request for Field Service Advice in the above captioned case.

DISCLOSURE LIMITATIONS

Field Service Advice constitutes return information subject to I.R.C. §6103. Field Service Advice contains confidential information subject to attorney-client and deliberative process privileges and if prepared in contemplation of litigation, subject to the attorney work product privilege. Accordingly, the Examination, Appeals, or Counsel recipient of this document may provide it only to those persons whose official tax administration duties with respect to this case require such disclosure. In no event may this document be provided to Examination, Appeals, Counsel, or other persons beyond those specifically indicated in this statement. Field Service Advice may not be disclosed to taxpayers or their representatives.

Field Service Advice is not binding on Examination or Appeals and is not a final case determination. Such advice is advisory and does not resolve Service position on an issue or provide the basis for closing a case. The determination of the Service in the case is to be made through the exercise of the independent judgment of the Field office with jurisdiction over the case.

ISSUES

1. Whether the target corporation, or the taxpayer (as successor to the target), is entitled to deductions under section 162 for payments made on a liability arising prior to the acquisition of the target by the taxpayer.

2. Whether the reimbursement for such payments by the selling stockholder of the target corporation under the stock sale agreement is includible in the gross income of the taxpayer.

CONCLUSIONS

1. The target corporation, or the taxpayer (as successor to the target), is entitled to deductions under sections 162 and 381(c)(4) for payments made on a liability arising prior to the acquisition of the target by the taxpayer.

2. The reimbursement for such payments by the seller is not includible in the gross income of the taxpayer, except to the extent of the interest received on the reimbursed expenses (which amount is includible in the income of the taxpayer for its [TEXT REDACTED] year). The tax benefit rule does not apply.

FACTS

The facts, taken from your Field Service Advice ("FSA") request and the materials submitted therewith, are as follows. In [TEXT REDACTED], [TEXT REDACTED] (the "taxpayer") purchased all of the outstanding stock of [TEXT REDACTED] (the "target") from [TEXT REDACTED] (the "seller"). No election was made under section 338. Consequently, both parties treated the transaction as a taxable sale of stock. The target was later liquidated tax-free under section 332 and currently operates as a division of the taxpayer....

DISCUSSION

In this case, as noted above, the taxpayer and the seller agreed, at the time of the sale of target, that the seller would reimburse the taxpayer, on behalf of target, for the expenses incurred by either corporation in defending certain described lawsuits that had been filed at the time of the sale of the target to the taxpayer. Thus, under the relation-back principle of Arrowsmith v. Commissioner, 344 U.S. 6 (1952), rehearing denied, 344 U.S. 900 (1952), the seller is treated as if it had contributed to the target, prior to the sale, the amount that the seller ultimately paid to the taxpayer under its reimbursement guarantee.

* * *

In your FSA request, you ask that we provide our comments on whether the taxpayer should be requested to submit more specific facts regarding the nature of the litigation beyond that explained in the Form 10-K report referred to in your memorandum, or whether for purposes of litigation, you should proceed to issue the statutory notice without allowance of the claim, thereby leaving the merits of the claim to be resolved by Appeals along with the other nondesignated adjustments. Absent any reason to believe that the putative facts recited are, indeed, untrue — and you offer no suggestion as to why that should be suspected at all — it is our view that those facts are adequate upon which to base the conclusions set forth herein.

For further information concerning the Corporate issues discussed above, please call Grid Glyer at (202) 622-7930. For further information concerning the Income Tax and Accounting issues discussed above, other than the tax benefit rule, please call Oreste

Russ Pirfo at (202) 622-7900. For further information concerning the tax benefit rule, please call Michael Nixon at (202) 622-7920.

For further information generally, or for specific information concerning the lease stripping issue in this case that has been designated for litigation, please call Roger E. Wade at (202) 622-7870.

DEBORAH A. BUTLER

By: JOEL E. HELKE, Chief, Financial Institutions & Products Branch, Field Service Division

Attachment: Nondocketed Case File
cc: District Counsel, Connecticut-Rhode Island, Attention: Attorney Carmino J. Santaniello

2. Technical Assistance

If a field office, Office in the National Office other than the one having subject-matter jurisdiction, or the Department of Treasury need advice on a technical issue, the request is submitted to the Office in the National Office with the subject matter expertise. In response to such a request, the Office will issue **Technical Assistance**. In general, technical assistance is legal advice that addresses the interpretation or application of the internal revenue laws generally but is not advice intended to assist in the resolution of a specific case.

> **Practice Note:**
>
> Examples of when Technical Assistance may be requested include the following:
>
> - To assist other Associate Chief Counsel offices on requests for rulings and technical advice and other matters involving issues of concern to more than one other Associate office;
> - To review for technical accuracy booklets, pamphlets, tax return forms, instructions, etc.;
> - To assist with cases in litigation;
> - To prepare position papers on issues together with the underlying rationale or historical development.

Technical assistance is advisory only and does not represent an expression of the views of the IRS as to the application of law, regulations, and precedents to the facts of a specific case. If the request involves a specific taxpayer, the response is advisory only, is not binding on the recipient, and cannot serve as the basis for closing the case.

3. Service Center Advice

Service Center Advice is written legal advice on significant issues in the form of a memorandum furnished by the National Office upon the request of an IRS Submission Processing or Customer Service Center with respect to their tax administration responsibilities. In general, it will address the interpretation or application of the internal rev-

No defence
No authority

enue laws generally; it is not legal advice that is intended to assist in the resolution of a specific taxpayer's case.

Service Center Advice is legal advice on a significant issue from the National Office to a Service Center.

Quick Find:

Service Center Advice memoranda can be found on the IRS website, www.irs.gov, in the Electronic Reading Room.

Example:

The following is an example of service center advice:

IRS CCA 200441030; RS

REFERENCE: CC:INTL:B03:TBHughes, SCAF-165417-03, UILC: 861.08-00, 904.00-00, 904.02-00

date: August 20, 2004
to: Associate Area Counsel (Washington, D.C., Group 2)
(Small Business/Self-Employed)
from: Branch Chief, Branch 3
(Associate Chief Counsel (International))
subject: Request for Assistance — Service Center Advice

This Chief Counsel Advice responds to your request for assistance dated April 8, 2004. This advice may not be used or cited as precedent.

ISSUES

1. How should foreign source income be calculated for purposes of the foreign tax credit limitation when a self-employed taxpayer makes deductible contributions to a U.S. retirement plan?

2. How is a U.S. retirement plan distribution, derived (in whole or in part) from foreign-sourced income, taxed?

CONCLUSIONS

1. Retirement plan contributions should be allocated to all of a self-employed taxpayer's earned income and ratably apportioned between earned income from U.S. and foreign sources.

2. Retirement plan distributions are taxable in their entirety when the contributions to the plan were deductible in the year of the contribution. The portion of the distribution that is attributable to contributions in respect of foreign source earned income is treated as foreign source income, and the remainder is U.S. source income.

FACTS

Your inquiry concerns an example involving a hypothetical single taxpayer, T, who lives in the United States and works both inside and outside the United States. T does not qualify for the foreign earned income exclusion under section 911(a) but is eligible to claim the foreign tax credit. Over a period of years, T makes contributions to a money purchase Keogh retirement plan, with the contributions made in whole or in part from foreign source earned income. The plan provides for a fixed formula for contributions and does not provide for after-tax elective employee contributions or

matching contributions. The foreign source income earned by T is subject to foreign taxes, for which T claims foreign tax credits subject to the limitations of section 904. T has the following deductible expenses: expenses related to the production of his income, the self-employment tax, and retirement plan contributions. T also claims the standard deduction and personal exemption on his tax return.

LEGAL AUTHORITY

Sections 904(a) and (d) provide that the amount of the allowable foreign tax credit in any taxable year may not exceed the tentative U.S. income tax (i.e., determined prior to application of the foreign tax credit) multiplied by a fraction, the numerator of which is the taxable income from sources without the United States in a particular category of income described in section 904(d) and the denominator of which is the taxpayer's entire taxable income. In other words, the foreign tax credit is limited to the lower of the foreign tax paid with respect to income in the separate category or the U.S. tax attributable to foreign source income in that category. This limitation prevents the foreign tax credit from offsetting U.S. tax on U.S. source income, which would otherwise occur where the tax rate imposed by a foreign country on income earned in that country is in excess of the U.S. rate. Section 904(b) provides rules for determining taxable income for the purpose of computing the foreign tax credit limitation, including a provision concerning personal exemptions, which is discussed below. Income from personal services and other income not described in section 904(d)(1)(A) through (H) is generally described in section 904(d)(1)(I), referred to as "general limitation income." ...

ANALYSIS

In determining the foreign tax credit limitation fraction, section 904(b)(1) and § 1.861-8(e)(11) provide that neither the numerator (foreign source taxable income) nor the denominator (worldwide taxable income) is reduced by the deduction for personal exemptions. The taxpayer's other deductions must be allocated to a class consisting of all or a portion of the taxpayer's gross income, and then apportioned between U.S. and foreign source gross income in the class on the basis of the factual relationship between the deduction and the grouping of gross income, or in the absence of any such relationship, ratably among such groupings on the basis of gross income. [TEXT REDACTED]

* * *

Under the Code and regulations the foreign tax credit limitation operates properly to limit the allowable credit to the pre-credit U.S. tax imposed on the taxpayer's foreign source taxable income as computed under U.S. tax rules, within the carryover periods established in section 904(c). Taxable income (and the foreign source portion of U.S. taxable income) must be computed in accordance with U.S. rules, which may differ from the foreign tax law rules used to compute the amount of foreign tax owed. See, e.g., United States v. Goodyear, 493 U.S. 132 (1989). Income tax treaties may modify U.S. and foreign law to reduce the incidence of double taxation. See, e.g., Article 18(2) of the 2001 U.S.-U.K. Income Tax Treaty, in which the U.S. and U.K. agreed to allow deductions for contributions to qualified pension plans maintained in the other state. In addition, where income is subject to double taxation because of timing differences in how taxable income is computed under U.S. and foreign law, taxpayers may be able to apply for competent authority relief under the mutual agreement article of an applicable income tax treaty.

Please call (202) 622-3850 if you have any further questions.

Barbara A. Felker, Chief, Branch 3, Office of the Associate Chief Counsel (International)

4. Litigation Guideline Memoranda

Litigation Guideline Memoranda (LGM) provide information and instruction relating to litigating procedures and methods and standards and criteria on issues and matters of significant interest to litigating attorneys in the Office of Chief Counsel. The memoranda are not taxpayer specific, but rather set forth the IRS's position on a particular issue as of the time of issuance of the memorandum. Generally, they contain discussions of cases and precedents to be followed in the various circuit courts of appeals.

> **Litigation Guideline Memoranda** set forth the IRS's position on a particular issue.

LGMs are now available to the public. While providing a substantial amount of information and legal analysis, an LGM may not be cited as precedent.

5. Collection, Bankruptcy, and Summonses Bulletins, Criminal Tax Bulletins, and Disclosure Bulletins

The IRS prepares Collection, Bankruptcy, and Summonses Bulletins; Criminal Tax Bulletins; and Disclosure Bulletins. The **Collection, Bankruptcy and Summonses Bulletin** (previously titled the General Litigation Bulletin) is published monthly and contains summaries of recent court cases of interest to anyone handling general litigation issues, plus summaries of Chief Counsel Advice issued by the Collection, Bankruptcy, and Summonses Division of the Office of the Associate Chief Counsel (Procedure and Administration) and available for public inspection under section 6110. The Collection, Bankruptcy, and Summonses Bulletin was discontinued after June 2001.

The **Criminal Tax Bulletins** are compilations of recent cases pertaining to criminal tax matters as published by the Office of the Division Counsel/Associate Chief Counsel (Criminal Tax).

Disclosure Litigation Bulletins are published periodically by the Office of the Assistant Chief Counsel (Disclosure & Privacy Law). They provide litigation developments and discussion of other disclosure-related issues that arise primarily under Section 6103, the Freedom of Information Act, and the Privacy Act of 1974 as these issues relate to IRS and Chief Counsel operations.

The Bulletins are informational and are not considered directives. The information contained in the Bulletins may not be cited as authority.

> **Quick Find:**
> The Bulletins can be found on the IRS website, www.irs.gov, in the Electronic Reading Room.

> **Practice Note:**
> The Office of Chief Counsel previously issued a Tax Litigation Bulletin which contained summaries of recent court cases, certiorari recommendations, and large case/Industry Specialization Program news. The last Bulletin was issued in May 1996.

Example:

The following is an example of a Criminal Tax Bulletin:

Criminal Tax Bulletin

This bulletin is for informational purposes. It is not a directive.

Department of Treasury, Internal Revenue Service
Office of Chief Counsel, Criminal Tax Division

1997 IRS CTB LEXIS 5

June 1997

SUPREME COURT CASES

Parameters Of The Knock And Announce Rule

In *Richards v. Wisconsin*, 117 S. Ct. 1416 (1997), Wisconsin police officers obtained a warrant to search Richards' hotel room for drugs, but the magistrate rejected a provision in the warrant that would have given the officers authorization for a "no knock" entry.

An officer dressed as a maintenance man knocked on Richards' door and identified himself as a maintenance man. When Richards opened the door, he saw a uniformed officer standing behind the "maintenance man" and slammed the door shut. The officers kicked down the door, caught Richards trying to escape, and found cash and cocaine in the bathroom. In denying Richards' motion to suppress the evidence on the ground that the officers did not knock and announce their presence before forcing entry, the trial court found, based on Richards' strange behavior, it was reasonable to believe that he might try to destroy evidence or escape. Furthermore, the disposable nature of the drugs justified the decision not to knock and announce. Richards appealed the decision to the Wisconsin Supreme Court and that court affirmed.

The Wisconsin Supreme Court ruling was based on its conclusion that police officers are never required to knock and announce their presence when executing a search warrant in a felony drug case. The court found that it is reasonable to assume that all felony drug crimes will involve an extremely high risk of serious, if not deadly, injury to the police as well as the potential for the disposal of the drugs prior to police entry. Thus, a *per se* exception to the knock and announce rule in such cases is reasonable and justified....

TITLE 26 AND TITLE 26 RELATED CASES

Gaudin **In Regard To 26**

U.S.C. §7206(1) And (2)

In *United States v. Tandon*, 111 F.3d 482 (6th Cir. 1997), Tandon, a physician, was convicted on three counts of willfully filing false personal income tax returns for the years 1986, 1987 and 1988 in violation of 26 U.S.C. §7206(1) and one count of willfully aiding and assisting in the filing of a false corporate return for the year 1988 in violation of §7206(2). His convictions stemmed from his understatement of income derived from his medical practice and his overstatement of depreciation expense generated on a leased Rolls-Royce. At trial, the district court gave an instruction to the jury that the issue of materiality was a question solely for the court to decide. The court further instructed the jury that "the omitted income and additional deductions, if proven, constitute a material falsity [and] if you find that these amounts as reported were false, then

the return is false as to a material matter." Upon conviction, Tandon was sentenced to 18 months in prison, a year of supervised release and fined $10,000. During the pendency of Tandon's appeal, the Supreme Court decided *United States v. Gaudin*, 115 S. Ct. 2310 (1995) (holding where materiality is an element of the crime and raises a question of fact, it must be decided by a jury).

Based on the *Gaudin* reasoning, Tandon argued that the district court committed reversible error by failing to submit the question of materiality to the jury, even though Tandon himself had requested the instruction that was given on materiality. On review of this issue, the Sixth Circuit observed that the *Gaudin* decision has put the circuits in a quandary as to how to deal with the group of cases where the jury instructions, though correct at the time of trial, have been called into question at the time of review. Without stating whether there was *Gaudin* error in this case (although it seems that the court must have presumed as much), the Sixth Circuit distinguished this case from the other post-Gaudin cases on the basis that Tandon actually requested the instruction. The court ascribed such error as invited error—an error introduced by the complaining party which will cause reversal only in a most exceptional situation. The court then ruled this case did not present the exceptional case. Finding that the invited error did not seriously affect the fairness, integrity or public reputation of the proceedings and that there was overwhelming evidence against Tandon, the court concluded that the invited error did not amount to reversible error and upheld Tandon's convictions....

6. General Counsel Memoranda

[handwritten: issued along with revenue-rulings]

Under an old structure of the IRS, General Counsel Memoranda (GCM) were prepared as a mechanism for the National Office to communicate legal advice to what was then the Assistant Commissioner (Technical). In general, they were prepared in connection with the review of proposed private letter rulings, proposed technical advice memoranda, and proposed revenue rulings. After an internal reorganization, GCM became the formal legal opinion of Chief Counsel when responding to inquiries from a National Office function outside of Chief Counsel or when explaining the legal basis for a position taken in a technical advice memorandum, letter ruling, or revenue ruling.

[handwritten margin note: No deference by a court as authority after March 12, 1981]

Because each General Counsel Memorandum addresses a specific issue, each is numbered and indexed so that it can be used for research purposes and, if necessary, retrieved. When a conclusion in a letter ruling, technical advice memorandum, or other document is contrary to an existing General Counsel Memorandum, a new General Counsel Memorandum is prepared to revoke or modify the prior General Counsel Memorandum. In addition, if a General Counsel Memorandum is found to be incorrect for any other reason, it is modified or revoked.

While no particular format is required, most GCMs will follow the same format. Each will have an opening paragraph which sets forth the nature of the case (*i.e.*, submission of a proposed revenue ruling for concurrence or comment), issue, conclusion, facts, and analysis. It will set forth the issues presented, the conclusions reached, and a brief factual summary. The body of the GCM contains a lengthy legal analysis of the substantive issues and the recommendations and opinions of the Office of Chief Counsel. The GCM is often accompanied by a draft of the proposed determination that reflects the changes and modifications recommended in the GCM.

GCM are rarely issued any more. In fact, only one has been issued since 1997.

Quick Find:

General Counsel Memoranda can be found on the IRS website, www.irs.gov, in the Electronic Reading Room.

Example:

The following is an example of a General Counsel Memorandum:

G.C.M. 38977

"This document is not to be relied upon or otherwise cited as precedent by taxpayers."

Revenue Ruling 83-73

April 22, 1983

REFERENCE:

CC:I-142-79
Br3:RBCanter

TEXT:
***

GERALD G. PORTNEY
Associate Chief Counsel (Technical)

Attention: Director, Corporation Tax Division

In your memorandum dated May 25, 1979, you forwarded a proposed revenue ruling (Control No. 7808222811) for our concurrence or comment. References herein to the proposed revenue ruling refer to your proposed revenue ruling.

ISSUES

(1) Does I.R.C. § 381(c)(4) or (c)(16) permit an acquiring corporation to deduct a payment it makes to settle a contingent obligation of a corporation it acquired in a statutory merger when the merger agreement included an indemnity clause whereby the shareholders of the acquired corporation agreed to reimburse the acquiring corporation for payment of such obligation?

(2) Should the amount paid to the acquiring corporation by the former shareholders of the acquired corporation pursuant to the indemnity clause be recognized as income to the acquiring corporation?

CONCLUSIONS

(1) The proposed revenue ruling concludes that section 381(c)(16) does not apply because the contingent obligation was not reflected in the amount of consideration transferred by the acquiring corporation to the transferor but that the acquiring corporation is entitled under section 381(c)(4) to deduct its payment of the liability.

While we agree that section 381(c)(4) rather than section 381(c)(16) is applicable to allow the deduction, we are unable to concur in your statement that "the obligation was not reflected in the amount of consideration transferred, and [therefore] under section 381(c)(16), such section does not apply." Section 381(c)(16) is inapplicable only if the liability is reflected in the amount of consideration paid to the

transferor We believe that the effect of the reimbursement payments by the former shareholders of the transferor corporation is to adjust the amount of consideration transferred so that it does reflect the contingent obligation. Therefore, section 381(c)(16) does not govern whether the acquiring corporation can deduct its payment of the obligation.

We agree that the deduction is allowed under section 381(c)(4) even though section 381(c)(16) is inapplicable.

(2) The proposed revenue ruling concludes that the principles of the tax benefit rule dictate that the acquiring corporation recognize as income the amount of reimbursement it received to the extent that it receives a tax benefit by deducting its payment of the obligation for which it was reimbursed.

We disagree with this conclusion. The reimbursement payments should not be seen as additional income to the acquiring corporation. Rather, under the relation-back principle of Arrowsmith v. Commissioner, 344 U.S. 6 (1952), the former shareholders of the transferor corporation should be treated as having contributed the amount of these payments to the capital of the transferor corporation immediately before the merger. Because all that the acquiring corporation gave up in the merger was the stock of the acquiring corporation, under section 1032(a) the acquiring corporation recognizes no income.

FACTS

The taxpayer, M corporation, employing the calendar year as its accounting period, merged with R corporation on December 1, 1977, in a reorganization qualifying under I.R.C. § 368(a)(1)(A). Under the terms of the merger agreement and applicable state law, M obtained all the assets and assumed all the liabilities of R, including a contingent claim discussed below.

As a condition of the merger, A and B, the shareholders of R, agreed with M to reimburse M for any after-tax expenses that M might incur as the result of a specific contingent claim that E, an employee of R, had against R. M transferred stock to R equal to the fair market value of R's assets less R's liabilities. Contingent liabilities of R, including the contingent liability to E, did not enter into this computation.

On January 15, 1979, M settled E's claim for 700x dollars. A and B reimbursed M 500x dollars during 1979, which was M's after-tax cost of the settlement with E based upon the assumption that M could deduct the payment to E and would not have to report the reimbursement as income.

M and R used the accrual method of accounting prior to December 1, 1977, and M continued to use that method after the merger.

ANALYSIS

I.R.C. § 381(a)(2) provides that when a corporation acquires the assets of another corporation in an exchange to which I.R.C. § 361 applies, the acquiring corporation will succeed to and take into account certain specific items of the transferor corporation. Section 361 provides for the nonrecognition of gain or loss in a statutory merger under section 368(a)(1)(A).

Section 381(c)(16) provides that if the acquiring corporation

(A) assumes an obligation of the transferor corporation that, after the date of transfer, gives rise to a liability, and

(B) such liability, if paid or accrued by the transferor corporation, would have been deductible in computing its taxable income,

the acquiring corporation will be entitled to deduct such item when paid or accrued as if it were the transferor. But this subsection will not apply if the obligation is reflected in the amount of stock, securities or other property transferred by the acquiring corporation for the transferor's property. Such an obligation is subject to section 381(c)(4)....

A revised proposed revenue ruling consistent with the views expressed in this memorandum is attached.

GEORGE H. JELLY
Director
By: SIGMUND J. LIBERMAN
Assistant Director
Interpretative Division

7. Technical Memoranda

Once the decision has been made to issue a Treasury Decision, an attorney in the Office of Chief Counsel will be designated to prepare a draft. Once prepared, the draft will go through many levels of review, with each reviewer suggesting edits or re-writes, until the proposed Treasury Decision reaches its ultimate destination, the Office of the Assistant Secretary (Tax Policy) at the Department of Treasury.

Technical memoranda are prepared as an aid to those reviewing the draft Treasury Decision. There is no standard format, but the memorandum generally summarizes or explains the proposed rules, provides background information, states the issues involved, identifies any controversial legal or policy questions, discusses the approach taken by the draftsperson, and gives the reasons for the approach taken. In sum, it generally explains the IRS's reasons for adoption of a Treasury Decision or may provide a detailed explanation of the application of the regulation. Because a technical memorandum may summarize a position that was taken in the regulation, or point out where a position was taken and then give the options and explain why a particular route was chosen, the technical memorandum may give more information about the regulation than is in the Treasury Decision itself.

> Technical Memoranda are prepared to assist those reviewing a draft of a Treasury Decision.

8. Legal Memoranda

Once the decision has been made to issue a revenue ruling on a particular topic or issue, an attorney in the Office of Chief Counsel will be designated to prepare a draft of the revenue ruling. Once prepared, the draft will go through many levels of review, with each reviewer suggesting edits or re-writes, until the proposed revenue ruling reaches its ultimate destination, the Office of the Assistant Secretary (Tax Policy) at the Department of Treasury.

As an aid to those who are reviewing the proposal, the draft revenue ruling may be accompanied by a "publication package." Sometimes, but not always, the publication package will include a legal memorandum which operates as a briefing memorandum, providing a comprehensive summary of the drafter's legal research as well as the drafter's

evaluation of the proposed ruling's strengths and weaknesses. However, the legal memorandum is not altered from the time it was originally written to reflect any changes made to the revenue ruling during the review process. Thus, a legal memorandum will not always reflect the official position of the IRS on a given issue.

Legal Memoranda are prepared to assist those reviewing a draft of a revenue ruling.

9. Documents Generated to Assist with Examinations

The IRS's **Market Segment Specialization Program** (MSSP) or Examination Specialization focuses on assignment of limited segments to identified examiners who have specialized knowledge in a concentrated area. A market segment generally consists of an industry, such as the swine farm industry or commercial banking, or a profession, such as ministers and veterinarians. On occasion, an issue requiring specialized audit techniques, such as executive compensation or passive activity losses, may comprise a market segment. The examiners focus on the segment to which they are assigned.

The Market Segment Specialization Program allows certain examiners to specialize in a particular market segment.

Audit technique guides (ATG) are prepared to assist the specialized examiners in identifying facts and developing issues that commonly arise in the selected market segments. The guides contain examination techniques, business practices, industry terminology, and any other information that will assist examiners in performing examinations. They may also include such valuable items as issues the examiner should consider, questions the examiner should ask the taxpayer, a summary of the law, the position of the IRS, and sample interviews. However, ATGs are not intended to provide lengthy, detailed legal analysis or resolve controversial or unusual legal issues.

Audit Technique Guides are prepared to assist specialized examiners in identifying facts and developing issues that commonly arise in a selected market segment.

Quick Find:

ATGs

Audit Technique Guidelines are prepared and maintained by the Small Business/Self-Employed Division. They are publicly available and are located on the IRS website, www.irs.gov.

Practice Note:

Audit Technique Guides are available for the following industries, professions, and issues:

- Aerospace Industry
- Air Transportation
- Child Care Providers
- Coal Excise Tax

- Commercial Banking
- Construction Industry
- Cost Segregation
- Credit for Increasing Research Activities (i.e., Research Tax Credit)
- Executive Compensation — Fringe Benefits
- Factoring of Receivables
- Farmers
- Foreign Insurance Excise Tax
- Golden Parachutes
- Hardwood Timber Industry
- Inland Waterways
- IRC 162(m) Salary Deduction Limitation
- IRC 183: Activities Not Engaged in for Profit
- Laundromat Industry
- Lawsuit Awards and Settlements
- Ministers
- New Vehicle Dealership
- Non-Qualified Deferred Compensation
- Obligations Not in Registered Form
- Obligations Not in Registered Form D
- Oil and Gas Industry
- Ozone Depleting Chemicals (ODC) Excise Tax
- Partnerships
- Passive Activity Losses
- Placer Mining
- The Port Project
- Poultry Industry
- Reforestation Industry
- Rehabilitation Tax Credit
- Research Credit Claims
- Retail Industry
- Sections 48A and 48B — Advanced Coal and Gasification Project Credits
- Split Dollar Life Insurance
- Sports Franchises
- Stock Based Compensation
- Structured Settlement Factoring
- Swine Farm Industry
- Tobacco Industry
- Veterinary Medicine

10. Where Can Documents Generated Internally Be Found?

Some of the documents generated by the IRS and Office of Chief Counsel for internal use can be found on the IRS website at www.irs.gov. Some documents also can be found through various electronic tax services.

C. Main Points

Field Service Advice:

- Advice from the National Office to the field attorneys on an issue that is difficult or significant.

- Assists with factual development of the case.

- Advice given by the National Office on industry-wide issues, hypothetical questions, or procedural matters.

- Assists the field only in the specific case in which the advice was issued.

- May not be used or cited as precedent in any other case.

- Even with respect to the case in which it was requested, does not represent a final determination of IRS position.

Technical Assistance:

- Advice from an Associate Chief Counsel Office to a field office, Office in the National Office other than the one having subject-matter jurisdiction, or the Department of Treasury on a technical issue.

- Advice that addresses the interpretation or application of the internal revenue laws generally and not used to assist in the resolution of a specific case.

- Advisory only.

Service Center Advice:

- Written legal advice on significant issues issued to an IRS Submission Processing or Customer Service Center with respect to their tax administration responsibilities.

- Generally addresses the interpretation or application of the internal revenue laws generally.

- Not intended to assist specific taxpayers in resolution of their case.

Litigation Guideline Memoranda:

- Provide information and instruction relating to litigating procedures and methods and standards and criteria on issues and matters of significant interest to litigating attorneys in Chief Counsel.

- Are issue specific, setting forth the IRS's position on a particular issue.

Collection, Bankruptcy and Summonses Bulletins:

- The Collection, Bankruptcy and Summonses Bulletin (previously titled the General Litigation Bulletin) contains summaries of recent court cases of interest to anyone handling general litigation issues, plus summaries of Chief Counsel Advice issued by the Collection, Bankruptcy, and Summonses Division of the Office of the Associate Chief Counsel (Procedure and Administration).

- The Collection, Bankruptcy, and Summonses Bulletin was discontinued after June 2001.

Criminal Tax Bulletins:

- The Criminal Tax Bulletins contain compilations of recent cases pertaining to criminal tax matters as published by the Office of the Division Counsel/Associate Chief Counsel (Criminal Tax).

Disclosure Bulletins:

- Disclosure Litigation Bulletins are published periodically by the Office of the Assistant Chief Counsel (Disclosure & Privacy Law), providing litigation developments and discussion of other disclosure-related issues that arise primarily under Section 6103, the Freedom of Information Act, and the Privacy Act of 1974 as these issues relate to IRS and Chief Counsel operations.

General Counsel Memoranda:

- Legal advice prepared in connection with the review of proposed private letter rulings, proposed technical advice memoranda, and proposed revenue rulings.
- Indexed by issue.
- Available to the public.

Technical Memoranda:

- Legal advice prepared as an aid to those reviewing a draft Treasury Decision.
- May set forth the IRS's reasons for adoption of a Treasury Decision or may provide a detailed explanation of the application of the regulation.

Legal Memoranda:

- Legal memorandum which operates as a briefing memorandum, providing a comprehensive summary of the drafter's legal research as well as the drafter's evaluation of a proposed revenue ruling's strengths and weaknesses.
- Will not always reflect the official position of the IRS on a given issue.

Market Segment Specialization Program (MSSP):

- Focuses on assignment of limited segments to identified examiners who have specialized knowledge in a concentrated area.
- A market segment generally consists of an industry, a profession, or, on occasion, an issue requiring specialized audit techniques.
- Audit technique guides (ATG) are prepared to assist examiners in identifying facts and developing issues that commonly arise in the selected market segments.

Where can internal IRS documents be found?

Guidance	Location
Field Service Advice	• On the IRS website, www.irs.gov, in the Electron Reading Room • Electronic tax services
Service Center Advice	• On the IRS website, www.irs.gov, in the Electronic Reading Room • Electronic tax services
Litigation Guideline Memoranda	• Electronic tax services
Collection, Bankruptcy and Summonses Bulletins	• On the IRS website, www.irs.gov, in the Electronic Reading Room • Electronic tax services
Criminal Tax Bulletins	• On the IRS website, www.irs.gov, in the Electronic Reading Room • Electronic tax services
Disclosure Bulletins	• On the IRS website, www.irs.gov, in the Electronic Reading Room • Electronic tax services
General Counsel Memorandums	• On the IRS website, www.irs.gov, in the Electronic Reading Room • Electronic tax services
Technical Memoranda	• Electronic tax services
Legal Memoranda	• Electronic tax services
Audit Technique Guides	• On the IRS website, www.irs.gov, in the Electronic Reading Room • Electronic tax services

D. Related Article for Further Reading

• Judy S. Kwok, *Note: The Perils of Bright Lines: Section 6110(k)(3) and the Ambiguous Precedential Status of Written Determinations*, 24 Va. Tax Rev. 863 (2005).

E. Problems

1. The document prepared to assist revenue agents in auditing a particular industry is:
    a.   Technical memoranda.
    b.   Field service advice.
    c.   Audit technique guide.
    d.   Litigation guideline memorandum.

2. Field service advice provides the following:
    a.   Assistance on how to factually develop the case.
    b.   Assistance on settlement of the case.
    c.   Assistance on a novel or unsettled area of law.
    d.   Assistance on selection of the proper trial court.

3. The document prepared in conjunction with drafting a Revenue Ruling, and used by those reviewing the draft, is:

   a. Technical memorandum.
   b. Legal memorandum.
   c. Service center advice.
   d. Litigation guideline memorandum.

4. If the Associate Chief Counsel of Passthroughs and Special Industries requests advice from the Associate Chief Counsel Corporate, the response will take the form of:

   a. Field service advice.
   b. Settlement advice memorandum.
   c. Technical assistance.
   d. Litigation guideline memorandum.

5. The document prepared in conjunction with drafting a Treasury Decision, and used by those reviewing the draft, is:

   a. Technical memorandum.
   b. Legal memorandum.
   c. Service center advice.
   d. Litigation guideline memorandum.

6. Advice rendered by the National Office to an IRS Submission Processing Center (Service Center) is referred to as:

   a. Field service advice.
   b. Technical assistance.
   c. Litigation guideline memorandum.
   d. Service center advice.

7. Litigation Guideline Memoranda:

   a. Provide information and instruction relating to litigating procedures and methods and standards and criteria on issues and matters of significant interest to litigating attorneys in Chief Counsel.
   b. Are not taxpayer specific.
   c. Set forth the IRS's position on a particular issue.
   d. All of the above.

8. All of the following contain summaries of recent court cases of interest to attorneys litigating in the area, except:

   a. Collection, Bankruptcy, and Summonses Bulletins.
   b. Criminal Tax Bulletins.
   c. Disclosure Bulletins.
   d. Chief Counsel Bulletins.

9. Using an on-line resource, locate the following documents. Identify a situation when you would find the document helpful.

   a. A GCM that discusses the "educational purpose" standard of Section 501(k) and the requirements of Rev. Proc. 75-50.
   b. A LGM that discusses the deliberative process privilege.
   c. A Disclosure Litigation Bulletin that discusses the new organizational name.
   d. A Tax Litigation Bulletin that discusses foreign tax credits and the gasoline tax.

10. On the IRS website, locate the following documents. Identify a situation when you would find the document helpful.

    a. GCM 39892.

    b. Audit Technique Guide for Partnerships.

11. Your client, Mrs. Barns, walks into your office. She has operated a race horse breeding facility for many years. While she has experienced some success, she has never earned a profit. Mrs. Barns explains to you that she received a notice from the IRS that her business is being audited. She would like to know what kind of issues the IRS will be focusing on, what kind of documentation the revenue agent might request, and what kind of questions the agent might ask her.

    a. What IRS document would assist you in answering Mrs. Barns' questions?

    b. Can you locate the document?

    c. How would you respond to Mrs. Barns' questions?

12. Your client, Mr. Metz, operates a small pharmaceutical company that conducts a substantial amount of medical research. For many years it has claimed the research credit allowed under section 41. Mr. Metz has just informed you that the company is now being audited by the IRS. He is interested in knowing what factual information the IRS may be interested in obtaining to determine if the company is entitled to the research credit.

    a. Might the IRS have created any documents related to the factual development of a case involving the research credit?

    b. What kind of document?

    c. Can you find any such documents?

13. You have been asked by the senior partner to give a presentation on some of the most recent criminal tax cases. Your area of expertise is like-kind exchanges, so you don't have a working knowledge of criminal tax cases.

    a. What document might give you summaries of the most recent criminal tax cases?

    b. Can you find such a document?

    c. What cases would you plan on discussing?

14. Using an electronic source, can you locate a litigation guideline memorandum discussing the application of the *Danielson* rule?

15. Locate the Audit Technique Guide on Child Care Providers.

    a. What definitions does it provide?

    b. What questions does it suggest the revenue agent ask?

    c. What expenses are discussed?

Chapter 9

Gaining Access to Government Documents

Access to Documents

- *What documents can be accessed through section 6110?*

- *What documents can be accessed through the Freedom of Information Act?*

- *Which is the proper statute for obtaining documents?*

Jill laid the private letter ruling down on the conference table. "This ruling is very close to what the client wants to do."

"Yes, I agree. But, there are some differences. Or, I guess I should say that there might be some differences." Luke went through some of the facts not mentioned in the letter ruling that were relevant to the client's planned transaction. "And whether the transaction in the private letter ruling has the same facts or not will determine how much our client could use the ruling to anticipate the IRS's position on his proposed transaction."

"It would be nice to nail this down a bit. Any chance we could look at the underlying facts, facts not mentioned in the letter ruling?"

Luke thought about that for a minute before answering. "Well," he began slowly, "I am not sure. But, what I do know is that there are some statutory provisions that provide limited access to government documents. Of course, certain types of private taxpayer information must be redacted first. Let me do some research and see if one of those provisions will allow us to look at the documents that underlie this private letter ruling."

"Great. Let me know what you find out."

Contents

A. Key Terms

After completing this chapter, you should be familiar with the following key terms:

➤ Written determination
➤ Chief Counsel advice
➤ Background file document
➤ Reading Room
➤ Freedom of Information Act (FOIA)

B. Discussion

Some documents issued by the IRS and Office of Chief Counsel can be obtained by the public. The Code requires that the IRS allow inspection of any issued written determination and any background file document relating to the written determination. Before being made available for inspection, however, certain information is required to be removed from the document and other information may be removed under claimed privileges. The Code sets forth procedures for withholding such information, including participation in the redaction process by the taxpayer to whom the written determination was issued. If a taxpayer requesting the document believes too much information has been withheld from a released document, the Code sets forth procedures for obtaining withheld information. Finally, the Code sets forth specific time frames that determine when the IRS must make written determinations publicly available and provides remedies for unauthorized disclosure.

All written determinations and background file documents must be obtained through the procedures set forth in the Code. All remaining documents, if accessible, can be obtained through the Freedom of Information Act.

The Freedom of Information Act establishes a statutory right to access government information. It describes how to obtain access to agency documents and describes matter that is exempt from disclosure. A significant number of lawsuits have been filed by Tax Analysts under the Freedom of Information Act to obtain documents issued by the National Office.

1. Section 6110

The IRS must allow public inspection of any issued written determination and any background document file relating to the written determination. A **written determination** includes:[1]

- Rulings;
- Determination letters;
- Technical advice memoranda; and
- Chief Counsel advice.

Chief Counsel advice is written advice or instructions from the National Office that is issued to field or Campus (Service Center) employees of the IRS or Chief Counsel and conveys any legal interpretation of a revenue provision; any IRS or Chief Counsel position or policy concerning a revenue provision; or any legal interpretation of state law, foreign law, or other federal law relating to the assessment or collection of any liability under a revenue provision.[2] A "revenue provision" includes existing or former internal revenue laws, regulations, revenue rulings, revenue procedures, other administrative interpretations or guidance, tax treaties, and court opinions.[3]

Practice Note:

Currently, Chief Counsel advice is considered by the IRS as including:

- Field service advice
- Technical assistance to the field
- Service center advice
- Litigation guideline memoranda
- Tax Litigation Bulletins
- General Litigation Bulletins
- Collection, Summonses, and Bankruptcy Bulletins
- Disclosure Litigation Bulletins
- Criminal Tax Bulletins

A written determination does *not* include:

- Any matter to which Section 6104 applies, providing for public inspection of certain exempt organizations and trusts;

---

1. I.R.C. §6110(b)(1)(A).
2. I.R.C. §6110(i)(1)(A).
3. I.R.C. §6110(i)(1)(B).

- Tax convention information;
- Advanced pricing agreements and related background information; and
- Closing agreements entered into under section 7121 or any similar agreement.

A background file document related to a written determination includes:[4]

- The request for the written determination;
- Any written material submitted in support of the request;
- Any communication (written or otherwise) between the IRS and persons outside the IRS in connection with the written determination received before issuance of the written determination; and
- Any subsequent communication between the National Office and a district director concerning the factual circumstances underlying a request for a technical advice memorandum or concerning a request by the Area director for reconsideration by the National Office of a proposed technical advice memorandum.

A background file document does *not* include:

- Communication between the Department of Justice and the IRS or Chief Counsel relating to any pending civil or criminal case or investigation;
- Communication between IRS employees and Chief Counsel employees;
- Internal memorandum or attorney work product prepared by the IRS or Chief Counsel which relates to the development of the conclusion of the IRS in a written determination;
- Correspondence between the IRS and any person relating solely to the making of or extent of deletions or a request for postponement of the time a written determination is made available to the public;
- Material relating to a request for a ruling or determination letter that is withdrawn or the IRS declines to answer, a request for technical advice the IRS declines to answer, or appeal of a taxpayer from the Area director's decision to not seek technical advice; or
- Response to a request for technical advice that the Area director declines to adopt and the Area director's request for reconsideration thereof.[5]

Timing of Release. Whether or not a request to access the document has been made, the IRS has 60 days after issuance to make any necessary deletions and release a nontaxpayer specific Chief Counsel advice for public inspection.[6] Similarly, unless the subject of a judicial action to restrain disclosure, the IRS generally must make any taxpayer-specific written determination and background file document available for public inspection no earlier than 75 days, and no later than 90 days, after the notice of intention to disclose is mailed to the specific taxpayer.[7] In satisfaction of its disclosure requirement, the IRS releases newly issued Chief Counsel advice on a weekly basis on the IRS website, www.irs.gov.[8] Technical advice memoranda and rulings are also available on the IRS web-

---

4. I.R.C. § 6110(b)(2).
5. Treas. Reg. § 301.6110-2(g)(2).
6. I.R.C. § 6110(i)(4)(A).
7. I.R.C. § 6110(g)(1)(A).
8. In addition to being made subject to public inspection, issued Chief Counsel Advice must be made available electronically within one year after issuance. Section 3509(d)(4), Pub. L. No. 106-554.

site in the electronic reading room. Finally, issued technical advice memoranda, rulings, and Chief Counsel advice are available for public inspection in the National Office **Reading Room.**

Practice Note:

Because technical advice memoranda, private letter rulings, and Chief Counsel advice are available through the IRS website, there is little reason to make a request to the Reading Room or physically visit the Reading Room to access such documents.

Request for Access. For the rare occasion when a written determination is available for public inspection only upon request, or a person wants to access a background file document, a request must be made to the National Office Reading Room or proper Disclosure Office.[9] A background file document related to a written determination is available for public inspection only after the related written determination is publicly available.

Practice Note:

The telephone number of the National Office Reading Room is 202-622-5164. It is located in room 1621 of the IRS Headquarters building at 1111 Constitution Avenue, N.W. in Washington, D.C. It is open from 9 a.m. to 4 p.m. Mondays through Fridays, except holidays.

Example:

Below is a sample request for documents from a technical advice memorandum background file.

Internal Revenue Service
Attn:
[proper office; see IRS Disclosure Offices for address list]

Dear Sir or Madam:

This is a request under Section 6110 for the background file documents relating to (identify the documents or information as specifically as possible). I am requesting a copy of all of the documents in the file. I do not wish to inspect the documents first. I am willing to pay fees for this request up to a maximum of $XX. If you estimate that the fees will exceed this limit, please inform me before processing the documents.

I understand that I will be notified of the fees before the documents are scheduled for release and that payment must be made before the documents are released to me.

Sincerely,

Name
Address
Telephone Number

When visiting the Reading Room, an IRS employee will always be present. The document requester cannot take the documents out of the room, but may make copies (and pay a copying fee) or take notes about the documents.

---

9. *See* Treas. Reg. § 301.6110-1(c)(1).

Practice Note:

For additional information on access to government documents, go to the IRS website, www.irs.gov. Click on Freedom of Information Act. There is a substantial amount of information located on that page; several headings listed under "Guidance Accessing Info" provide very helpful information.

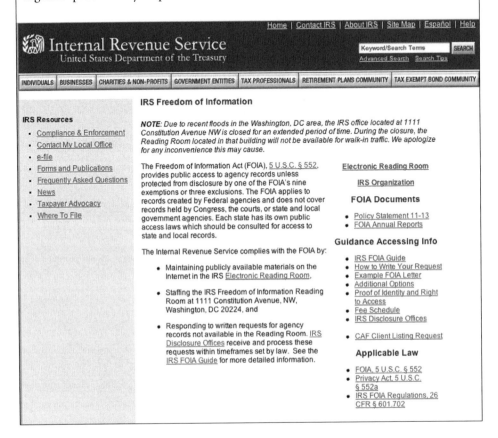

Fees and Cost. If a request is made for a written determination or for background file documents, the IRS can assess actual costs incurred in searching for and making required deletions from any documents made available based on the request. However, if the IRS believes furnishing the document benefits the general public, it may furnish the documents without charge or at a reduced charge. It can also waive the copying and other fees if the search was made pursuant to a previous inspection request. The person making the request will be notified of the total cost of processing the documents, and the fees must be paid before the documents will be released.[10]

Redaction Process. Before any documents are made available for public inspection (whether released voluntarily by the government or pursuant to a request), certain information must be deleted from the documents. For written determinations other than Chief Counsel advice, the IRS must delete names, addresses, and other identifying details of the person to whom the written determination pertains and of any other person iden-

---

10. *See* Rev. Proc. 95-15, 1995-1 C.B. 523.

tified in the written determination or any background file document. Identifying numbers include:

- Telephone number;
- License number;
- Social security number;
- Employee identification number;
- Credit card number; and
- Selective service numbers.

Identifying details include any information that would permit a person generally knowledgeable in the appropriate community to identify the person. The determination of whether information would identify a person is made based on information publicly available at the time the written determination or background file document is made available to the public and on information that will subsequently become available. The appropriate community is the group of persons who would be able to associate a particular person with a category of transactions, such as the one in the written determination or background file document.

Practice Note:

The following are examples of items that would be deleted in all events:

➤ Taxpayer's name;
➤ Taxpayer's address;
➤ Taxpayer's identification number;
➤ Court docket number;
➤ Policy numbers;
➤ Outside consultants (names of individuals, but not necessarily firms);
➤ Authorized representatives (names of individuals, but not necessarily firms);
➤ "Brand name" product lines;
➤ References to another case involving the same taxpayer;
➤ Beneficiaries;
➤ Patents and trademarks;
➤ Trade secrets;
➤ Any quotation from an opinion or searchable database (*i.e.*, SEC filings), if they are associated with the taxpayer.

Practice Note:

The following might be deleted, given the particular facts of the document and the timing of the release:

➤ Dollar figures;
➤ Dates, including tax years;
➤ Percentages;
➤ Type of business, if unique or small industry;
➤ Shareholder information;
➤ Taxpayer location, including State of incorporation;
➤ Countries of operation;
➤ Region, district, city, circuit court;
➤ References to state law;

> ➤ References to unique federal law that impacts few individuals or industries;
> ➤ Name of local IRS officers and employees;
> ➤ "Generic" product lines;
> ➤ Taxpayer-hired consultants (firm names);
> ➤ Firm authorized to represent the taxpayer;
> ➤ Any other information that could be cross-referenced in other publicly available sets of information including electronic databases, such as LEXIS.

For written determinations that are Chief Counsel advice, as with other written determinations, the IRS must delete names, addresses, and other identifying details of the person to whom a written determination pertains and of any other person identified in the written determination or related background file documents. In addition, the IRS must make the same deletions as provided for under the Freedom of Information Act (as discussed below).

2. Freedom of Information Act

The **Freedom of Information Act (FOIA)**[11] establishes a statutory right to access government information. It is designed to provide citizens information about the inner workings of the government. To achieve this purpose, FOIA creates a judicially enforceable public right to disclosure of agency material.

In general, IRS information is divided into three categories:

1.   Information required to be published in the Federal Register;

2.   Information required to be made available for public inspection and copying or, in the alternative, to be published and offered for sale; and

3.   Information required to be made available to any member of the public upon specific request.

a. Items Required to Be Disclosed

In general, under the first category the IRS is required to publish the following information in the Federal Register:[12]

- Descriptions of its central and field organization and the established places at which, the persons from whom, and the methods whereby the public may obtain information, make submittals or requests, or obtain decisions from the IRS;

- Statement of the general course and method by which its functions are channeled and determined, including the nature and requirements of all formal and informal procedures that are available;

- Rules of procedure, descriptions of forms available or the places at which forms may be obtained, and instructions as to the scope and contents of all papers, reports, or examinations;

- Substantive rules of general applicability adopted as authorized by law and statements of general policy or interpretations of general applicability formulated and adopted by the IRS; and

---

11. 5 U.S.C. §552, *et seq.*
12. Treas. Reg. §601.702(a)(1).

- Each amendment, revision, or repeal of matters referred to above.

Under the second category the IRS is required to make available to the public:[13]

- Final opinions, including concurring and dissenting opinions, and orders, if such opinions and orders are made in the adjudication of cases;

- Statements of policy and interpretations which have been adopted by the IRS but not published in the Federal Register;

- Administrative staff manuals and instructions to staff that affect a member of the public; and

- Agency records that have been, or the agency expects to be, the subject of repetitive requests.

For records created after October 31, 1996, the IRS must make the material available on its website, www.irs.gov. In addition, the documents can be made available through the Reading Room.

> **Practice Note:**
> With the elimination of Regional Offices under the Restructuring and Reform Act of 1998, the sole remaining Reading Room is located in Washington, D.C.

Under the third category the IRS must make reasonably described records available to a person who submits a proper request.[14]

A request for records must:

- Be in writing;

- Be signed by the requester;

- State that it is made pursuant to the Freedom of Information Act, 5 U.S.C. § 552, or regulations thereunder;

- Be mailed to the office of the IRS official who is responsible for the control of the requested records;

- Reasonably describe the records;

- In the case of a request for records the disclosure of which is limited by statute or regulations, establish the identity and the right of the person making the request to the disclosure of the records;

- Set forth the address where the requester desires to be notified of the determination as to whether the request will be granted;

- State whether the requester wishes to inspect the records or desires to have a copy made and furnished without prior inspection;

- State the firm agreement of the requester to pay the fees for search and duplication or request that such fees be reduced or waived and state the justification for such reduction or waiver; and

- Identify the category of the requester and state how the records will be used.

Only requests that comply with the above will be processed. The IRS will notify a requester, in writing, of any requirements that have not been met. Noteworthy, requests

---

13. 5 U.S.C. § 552(a)(2); Treas. Reg. § 601.702(b)(1)(I).
14. 5 U.S.C. § 552(a)(3)(A); Treas. Reg. § 601.702(c)(4).

for opinions or to answer questions or that require the IRS to perform legal research or create documents are not proper FIOA requests.

Upon receiving a request for records, the IRS is required to search its files for any documents responsive to the individual's request and make the documents promptly available to the individual, subject to applicable exemptions. The adequacy of the IRS's search is judged by a standard of reasonableness.

If the request will be granted and the requester wants a copy of the requested records, the IRS will mail to the requester a statement of fees and request for payment. When the payment is received, the IRS will mail the copies to the requester with an explanation of any necessary deletions or withholding. If no fees are due, the copies will be promptly mailed to the requester.

If the request will be granted and the requester wants to inspect the documents, he will be notified of the place and time the requested records can be inspected and of the fees involved in complying with the request.

If the request is denied, in whole or in part, the IRS will notify the requestor by mail and include a brief statement of the grounds for not granting the request. The IRS will also make a reasonable effort to estimate the volume of requested matter denied. The requester can appeal the denial of the request.[15]

b. Items Exempt from Disclosure

The following matters are exempt from FOIA's disclosure requirements:

Exemption 1.   Matters specifically authorized under criteria established by an Executive order to be kept secret in the interest of national defense or foreign policy and that are in fact properly classified pursuant to such Executive order.[16]

Generally, the IRS will utilize this exemption to withhold treaty-related matters.

Exemption 2.   Matters related solely to the internal personnel rules and practices of the IRS which communicate to IRS personnel information or instructions relating to:

- Enforcement tolerances and criteria with respect to the allocation of resources;

- Criteria for determining whether or not a case merits further enforcement action;

- Enforcement tactics, including but not limited to investigative techniques, internal security information, protection of identities of confidential sources of information used by the IRS, and techniques for evaluating, litigation, and negotiating cases of possible violations of civil or criminal laws; or

- Use of parking facilities, regulation of lunch hours, statements of policy as to sick leave and the like.[17]

The purpose of the exemption is to relieve an agency from the burden of assembling and maintaining for public inspection matter in which the public could not reasonably be expected to have an interest. To come within this exemption, first the IRS must establish that the document is predominantly internal. Second, the IRS must establish ei-

---

15. The requester can file an administrative appeal. *See* Treas. Reg. §601.702(c)(10). If a proper request is denied upon appeal or if no determination is made within the regulatory time frame, the requestor may file a complaint in district court. *See* 5 U.S.C. §552(a)(4); Treas. Reg. §601.702(c)(11).

16. 5 U.S.C. §552(b)(1).

17. 5 U.S.C. §552(b)(2).

ther that disclosure may risk circumvention of IRS regulations or that the document relates to trivial administrative matters of no genuine public interest.

In *Church of Scientology of Texas v. IRS*, information related to allocation of IRS resources satisfied the first part of the test to the extent it was predominantly internal. However, there was no evidence that disclosure of the information would risk circumvention of IRS regulations and the information was of genuine interest to the public. Specifically, it was information as to how the taxpayers' money was allocated. Thus, the information did not fall within the exemption.[18] In contrast, a routing slip containing information about a proposed meeting was predominantly internal and related to trivial administrative matters of no genuine public interest. The routing slip came within the exemption and could be withheld.[19]

Exemption 3. Matters specifically exempted from disclosure by statute, provided the statute requires that the matters be withheld from the public in such a manner as to leave no discretion on the issue or establishes particular criteria for withholding or refers to particular types of matters to be withheld.[20]

Section 6103 qualifies as a statute referred to in the exemption. The anti-disclosure provisions of Section 6103 take precedence over FOIA, and the provisions of Section 6103 cannot be avoided be resorting to FOIA. Pursuant to Section 6103, in general, returns and return information are confidential; an IRS employee is prohibited from disclosing a return or return information.[21]

Practice Note:

Under section 6103(b)(2)(A) return information is:

> A taxpayer's identity, the nature, source, or amount of his income, payments, receipts, deductions, exemptions, credits, assets, liabilities, net worth, tax liability, tax withheld, deficiencies, over assessments, or tax payments, whether the taxpayer's return was, is being, or will be examined or subject to other investigation or processing, or any other data, received by, recorded by, prepared by, furnished to, or collected by the Secretary with respect to a return or with respect to the determination of the existence, or possible existence, of liability (or the amount thereof) of any person under this title for any tax, penalty, interest, fine, forfeiture, or other imposition, or offense.

Return information does not include data in a form that cannot be associated with, or otherwise identify, directly or indirectly, a particular taxpayer. Such "form" means more than simply removing taxpayer identifying information. Rather, it refers to statistical studies, compilations, and other similar reformulation of return information. For example, under this exception, discriminant function scores[22] and tax return information related to the person other than the person making the request[23] have been held to be exempt from disclosure.

---

18. *Church of Scientology of Tex v. IRS*, 816 F. Supp. 1138, 1149 (W.D. Tex. 1993).

19. *Id.*

20. 5 U.S.C. §552(b)(3).

21. I.R.C. §6103(a). Exceptions to the general rule are set forth in I.R.C. §6103(c)-(o).

22. *Yon v. IRS*, 671 F. Supp. 1344 (S.D. Fla. 1987). A DIF score has been used by the IRS as a method to select tax returns for examination.

23. *Yon v. IRS*, 671 F. Supp. 1344 (S.D. Fla. 1987).

Rule 6(e) of the Federal Rules of Criminal Procedure also qualifies as a statute referred to in the exemption.[24] Rule 6(e)(2) prohibits disclosure of matters occurring before a grand jury. Rules generally do not qualify as statutes for purposes of the exemption. However the applicability of Rule 6(e) was specifically adopted by an Act of Congress.[25] To come within the exemption, the agency must establish a nexus between the record and the operation of the grand jury. The touchstone is whether disclosure would tend to reveal some secret aspect of the grand jury's investigation. Thus, information and records presented to a grand jury, the names of individuals subpoenaed, identities of jurors, substance of grand jury testimony, and information indicating the focus of the grand jury is protected.

Exemption 4.   Trade secrets and commercial or financial information obtained from a person and privileged or confidential.[26]

The purpose of the exemption is to encourage individuals to provide certain kinds of confidential information to the government. If a person was obliged to furnish financial or commercial information to the government, the information will be treated as confidential if disclosure is likely to impair the government's ability to obtain necessary information in the future or to cause substantial harm to the competitive position of the person from whom the information was obtained. Any financial or commercial information provided to the government on a voluntary basis is protected if it is of a kind that the provider would not customarily release to the public.

Exemption 5.   Inter-agency or intra-agency memorandums or letters which would not routinely be available by law to a party other than an agency in litigation with the agency.[27]

This exemption includes communications:

- That the IRS has received from another agency;
- That the IRS generates in the process of issuing an order, decision, ruling or regulation, drafting proposed legislation, or otherwise carrying out its functions and responsibilities; or
- That is the attorney work product of Chief Counsel or is generated by the Office as attorney for the IRS.

This exemption applies to documents normally privileged in the civil discovery context. Thus, documents subject to the attorney-client, work-product, and governmental deliberative privilege are generally exempted.[28] However, the privilege as applied in FOIA cases is not in every case consistent with the privilege as applied between private parties. It protects the decision-making process of government agencies. As such, it does not apply to final agency actions that constitute statements of policy or final opinions or that implement established policy.

In *Taxation with Representation Fund v. IRS*, the taxpayer filed suit seeking General Counsel Memoranda (GCM), Technical Memoranda (TM), and Actions on Decisions (AODs).[29] The IRS claimed they were exempt from disclosure under the deliberative

---

24. *Fund for Constitutional Gov't v. Nat'l Archives and Records Serv.*, 656 F.2d 856, 870 (D.C. Cir. 1981).

25. *See* 18 U.S.C. §§ 1771, 3772.

26. 5 U.S.C. § 552(b)(4).

27. 5 U.S.C. § 552(b)(5).

28. *See, e.g., Tax Analysts v. IRS*, 391 F. Supp. 2d 122 (D.C. Cir. 2005).

29. *Taxation With Representation Fund v. IRS*, 646 F.2d 666 (D.C. Cir. 1981), *aff'g in part and remanding in part* 485 F. Supp. 263 (D.D.C. 1980).

process privilege. The Court of Appeals for the District of Columbia found that GCMs that are revised to reflect the final position of the National Office and are widely distributed were not pre-decision and not protected by the deliberative process privilege.[30] Similarly, TMs issued in connection with decisions and regulations approved by Treasury were not pre-decisional.[31] Finally, AODs that opted for no appeal (including cases of acquiescence or nonacquiescence) constituted explanations of the IRS's final legal position on an issue and were not pre-decisional.[32] To the extent the documents were not protected by the privilege, they were required to be disclosed.[33]

Practice Note:

The following have been held to fall under the exemption and, thus, were *not* required to be disclosed:

- Drafts of a revenue ruling and accompanying background notes;
- GCM that addressed whether a proposed revenue procedure should be pursued, and that did not address the substantive contents of the proposal;
- Documents prepared in connection with a tax investigation with which a special agent was involved and later compiled for the investigation of the special agent that reflected the deliberative process of the agency in deciding whether to discipline the agent; and
- Draft technical memorandum that was to assist agency decision-makers in deciding whether to issue an agency explanation of a regulation.

Practice Note:

The following have been held to fall outside the exemption and, thus, were required to be disclosed:

- A GCM that set forth current agency interpretations;
- A memorandum from District Counsel (field office) that provided instruction and legal interpretation of provisions of the Code to the agents conducting an examination; and
- Field service advice memoranda.

Exemption 6.   Personnel and medical files and similar files the disclosure of which would constitute a clearly unwarranted invasion of personal privacy.[34]

The purpose of the exemption is to protect individuals from the injury and embarrassment that can result from the unnecessary disclosure of personal information. To come within the exemption, first, the file at issue must be protected; the file must contain personal information about an individual. Second, the disclosure must constitute a clearly unwarranted invasion of the individual's personal privacy. This invasion requires a balancing of the individual's right of privacy against the public interest in disclosure of the information at issue. However, the exemption does not protect nonconfidential information, even if contained in a protected file.

---

30. *Id.* at 682–83.
31. *Id.* at 683.
32. *Id.* at 684. *See also Tax Analysts v. IRS*, 81-2 USTC (CCH) ¶ 9784, 48 AFTR2d (RIA) 6175 (D.D.C. 1981).
33. *Id.*
34. 5 U.S.C. § 552(b)(6).

In *Wine Hobby USA, Inc. v. IRS*, the taxpayer brought suit to obtain the names and addresses of all persons who registered to produce wine for family use in the Mid-Atlantic region. At the time, all persons who produced wine were subject to certain taxes. An exemption was allowed for a head of household who produced wine for family use and not for sale. The taxpayer sold amateur winemaking equipment and supplies. Its purpose in obtaining the names of those exempt from the tax was to forward to them its catalogues for equipment and supplies.

In determining whether Exemption 6 applied, the court first found that the list of names and addresses constituted a protected "file" because it contained information of a personal quality.[35] The court then found that disclosure of the list was an invasion of personal privacy and went on to balance the seriousness of the release of the names and addresses with the purpose asserted for the release. Because the list was sought for private commercial exploitation, no direct or indirect public interest in disclosure of the list existed. The court concluded that the invasion of privacy would be clearly unwarranted and held that the list of names and addresses was exempt from disclosure.[36]

Exemption 7.   Investigatory records compiled for law enforcement purposes, including records prepared in connection with civil, criminal or administrative Government litigation and adjudicative proceedings, but only to the extent that the production of such records:

(A) Could reasonably be expected to interfere with enforcement proceedings;

(B) Would deprive a person of a right to a fair trial or an impartial adjudication;

(C) Could reasonably be expected to constitute an unwarranted invasion of personal privacy;

(D) Could reasonably be expected to disclose the identity of a confidential source and in the case of a record compiled by a criminal law investigation, or by an agency conducting a lawful national security intelligence investigation, confidential information furnished only by a confidential source;

(E) Would disclose techniques and procedures for law enforcement investigations or prosecutions, or would disclose guidelines for law enforcement investigations or prosecutions if such disclosure could reasonably be expected to risk circumvention of the law; or

(F) Could reasonably be expected to endanger the life or physical safety of law enforcement personnel.[37]

Exemption 7 is intended to permit the IRS to keep certain records confidential, lest it be hindered in its investigations or placed at a disadvantage when presenting its case. To come within the exemption, the IRS must first show that a law enforcement proceeding is pending or prospective. "Law enforcement" applies to civil, criminal, and regulatory proceedings. The records must arise during the course of an investigation and must involve the detection or punishment of violations of law. Criminal tax investigations, audits, collection activities, consideration of tax exempt applications, church examinations, conduct investigations, and litigation come within law enforcement purposes.

The records must have been compiled for law enforcement purposes. Compiled means that it is composed of materials collected and assembled from various sources or other

---

35. *Wine Hobby USA, Inc. v. IRS*, 502 F.2d 133, 135 (3d Cir. 1974), *rev'g* 363 F. Supp. 231 (E.D.Pa. 1973).
36. *Wine Hobby USA, Inc.*, 502 F.2d at 135–37.
37. 5 U.S.C. §552(b)(7).

documents and can include documents originally compiled for non-law enforcement purposes.

The courts will also consider the law enforcement powers of the agency. In the District of Columbia District Court, the court distinguished between agencies supporting criminal law enforcement and agencies having a mixture of law enforcement and administrative functions.[38] For agencies whose principal function is not law enforcement, a more exacting scrutiny is applied. The IRS is considered a mixed-function agency.[39] Under the stricter scrutiny, the exemption applies only to investigations that focus directly on specifically alleged illegal acts, illegal acts of particular identified officials, acts that could, if proved, result in civil or criminal sanctions. Under this test, the purpose of the document must include information gathered in the course of an inquiry as to an identifiable possible violation of the law, whether the individual were a private citizen or a government employee. The determining factor, however, is the purpose for which the IRS compiled the document. Second, the agency must show that the records or information fall with one of the above six categories.

Exemption 8.   Information contained in or related to examination, operating, or condition reports prepared by, on behalf of, or for the use of an agency responsible for the regulation or supervision of financial institutions.[40]

Generally, the IRS has not claimed this exemption as a basis for withholding materials.

Exemption 9.   Geological and geophysical information, data, including maps, concerning wells.[41]

Generally, the IRS has not claimed this exemption as a basis for withholding materials.

3. Tax Analyst Law Suits

Prior to the amendment of Section 6110 to include Chief Counsel advice, Tax Analyst, which publishes Tax Notes, Tax Notes Today, and Highlights & Documents, brought a lawsuit under the FOIA seeking disclosure of 1,300 written field service advices (FSAs). The IRS denied the request, claiming the documents were exempt from disclosure as tax return information under Exemption 3 (matters specifically exempted from disclosure by statute) and the attorney-client privilege, work product privilege, and deliberative process privilege pursuant to Exemption 5 (intra-agency memorandums not routinely available by law to a party other than an agency in litigation with the agency).

In evaluating the IRS's claim that the documents were protected by Section 6103, the district court noted that the FSAs contained some return information but did not *themselves* constitute return information. Exemption 3 would allow the IRS to withhold return information contained in the FSA, but not the FSAs in their entirety.

---

38. *Pratt v. Webster*, 673 F.2d 408, 417–19 (D.C. Cir. 1982), *rev'g and remanding* 508 F. Supp. 751 (D.D.C. 1981).

39. *Rural Hous. Alliance v. Dep't of Agriculture*, 498 F.2d 73, 81–82 (D.C. Cir. 1974); *Tax Analysts v. IRS*, 152 F. Supp. 2d 1 (D.C. Cir. 2001), *aff'd in part and rem'd in part*, 294 F.3d 71 (D.C. Cir. 2002).

40. 5 U.S.C. §552(b)(8).

41. 5 U.S.C. §552(b)(9).

The district court next considered whether the FSAs could be withheld under Exemption 5. It concluded that the FSAs were post-decisional documents which set forth working law of the IRS and that statements of policy and interpretation adopted by the IRS were not protected by the attorney-client privilege. As such, they could not be withheld pursuant to Exemption 5. The parties agreed that, to the extent the text set forth the mental impressions, conclusions, opinions, or legal theories of the attorney concerning litigation, it could be withheld under the work-product privilege.[42]

On appeal, the Circuit Court of Appeals for the District of Columbia conducted its own analysis and agreed the legal analysis contained in the FSAs did not constitute return information under Section 6103.[43] In considering whether the FSAs were protected under Exemption 5, the circuit court agreed that the FSAs were post-decisional and constituted agency law, even if the conclusions were not formally binding. Thus, they did not come within the deliberative privilege exemption.[44] In analyzing withholding the documents under the attorney-client privilege, the court held that the communication had to contain confidential information concerning the IRS. When an official transmitted facts to the National Office, no new or confidential information concerning the IRS was imported. Thus, to the extent the legal conclusions were based on information obtained from a taxpayer, it was not protected. However, information conveying the scope, direction, or emphasis of audit activity was protected by the attorney-client privilege.[45] Finally, in applying the work product privilege, the circuit court noted that the doctrine protected not only the mental impressions, conclusions, opinions, or legal theories of an attorney, but also factual materials prepared in anticipation of litigation. To the extent any part of an FSA was prepared in anticipation of litigation, it was protected.[46]

In a separate lawsuit, Tax Analysts sought disclosure of six categories of documents produced by the National Office: legal memoranda (LM), Litigation Guideline Memoranda, Tax Litigation Bulletins, technical assistances, Field Service Advice Monthly Reports, and Pending Issue Reports. Subsequent to filing of the lawsuit, Section 6110 was enacted. To the extent the documents requested could be obtained under Section 6110, they were dismissed from the taxpayer's FOIA request. Such documents included technical assistances to the field, Tax Litigation Bulletins, and post-1985 Litigation Guideline Memoranda, leaving the court with jurisdiction over LM, pre-1986 Litigation Guideline Memoranda, other technical assistances, Field Service Advice Monthly Reports (FSA Report), and Pending Issue Reports (PIR).[47]

The IRS had withheld those portions of the LM that reflected the opinions and analysis of the author and did not ultimately form the basis of the final revenue ruling. Because the withheld portions were predecisional, the court agreed with the redactions.[48]

---

42. *Tax Analysts v. IRS*, 96-1 USTC (CCH) ¶ 50,205, 77 AFTR2d (RIA) 1386 (D.D.C. 1996).

43. *Tax Analysts*, 117 F.3d 607, 611–16 (D.C. Cir. 1997). On remand, the district court held that tax return information that could be redacted pursuant to I.R.C. § 6103 was return information that would be redacted from technical advice memoranda under I.R.C. § 6110(c)(i). *Tax Analysts v. IRS*, 98-1 USTC (CCH) ¶ 50,407, 81 AFTR2d (RIA) 1784 (D.D.C. 1998).

44. *Tax Analysts*, 117 F.3d at 616–18.

45. *Tax Analysts*, 117 F.3d at 618–20.

46. *Tax Analysts*, 117 F.3d at 620.

47. *Tax Analysts v. IRS*, 2000-1 USTC (CCH) ¶ 50,370 (D.D.C. 2000).

48. *Tax Analysts v. IRS*, 97 F. Supp. 2d 13, 15–18 (D.C.C. 2000).

The IRS released the FSA Reports[49] and PIR[50] with taxpayer return information withheld. In nondocketed cases, the taxpayer's name and the requesting office was withheld. In all docketed cases, the issue statement was withheld. The court agreed the information withheld was proper.[51] The IRS eventually released pre-1986 LGMs to Tax Analysts, rendering the issue of their disclosure moot.[52]

The court was left to consider four categories of technical assistances: technical assistance to program managers in the National Office, technical assistance to component offices of the National Office, technical assistances to specific taxpayers, and technical assistance to federal and state government agencies.[53]

The IRS claimed one technical assistance could be withheld under Exemption 3 (matters specifically exempted from disclosure by statute). The technical assistance contained tax treaty information, specifically the identity of a treaty partner. As a statute included under Exemption 3, Section 6105(a) provides that tax convention information cannot be disclosed. The information at issue was received pursuant to a tax convention and pertained to a specific taxpayer.[54] Therefore, the entire document was properly withheld under Exemption 3.[55]

The IRS claimed that some of the technical assistances were exempt from disclosure under Exemption 7(E). Exemption 7(E) exempts information compiled for law enforcement purposes to the extent that the production of the records or information would disclose techniques and procedures for law enforcement investigations, prosecutions, or would disclose guidelines for law enforcement investigations or prosecutions if such disclosure could reasonably be expected to risk circumvention of the law.[56] As a threshold inquiry, the IRS was required to establish that the technical assistance included information gathered for law enforcement purposes or, specifically, in the course of an inquiry as to an identifiable possible violation of the law. The IRS made such a showing with respect to only some of the technical assistances. Examples of technical assistances that did not meet the threshold requirement included those giving advice concerning an issue arising with respect to the filing of documents by taxpayers in general, assessment of proposed changes to an identified income tax form, and an evaluation of a proposed draft of an Appeals Settlement Guideline.[57]

For those technical assistances for which the IRS had met the threshold inquiry, the IRS established the information came within Exemption 7(E) in that its disclosure could reasonably be expected to risk circumvention of the law. The portions withheld summarized how a tax avoidance scheme was carried out, including identification of vulnerabilities in

---

49. The FSA Report was generated monthly to assist in monitoring the progress of FSAs, coordinate with the various components of the office, and alert recipients to emerging issues. *Tax Analysts,* 97 F. Supp. 2d at 18.

50. A PIR assists in tracking the assignment of technical advice memoranda, private letter rulings, congressional correspondence, technical assistance, and revenue ruling projects. *Tax Analysts, supra.*

51. *Tax Analysts,* 97 F. Supp. 2d at 18–19.

52. *Tax Analysts v. IRS,* 152 F. Supp. 2d 1, 4 (D.D.C. 2001), *aff'd in part and remanded in part,* 294 F.3d 71 (D.C. Cir. 2002).

53. *Id.*

54. *See* I.R.C. §6105(c)(1)(E).

55. *Tax Analysts v. IRS,* 152 F. Supp. 2d 1, 10–14 (D.C.C. 2001), *aff'd in part and remanded in part,* 294 F.3d 71 (D.C. Cir. 2002).

56. 5 U.S.C. §552(b)(7)(E).

57. *Tax Analysts,* 152 F. Supp. 2d at 15.

the IRS operations that allowed the scheme to be successful. The court agreed that such information in the technical assistance could be withheld.[58]

Finally, the IRS claimed that some of the technical assistance were exempt under Exemption 5 (intra-agency memorandums not routinely available by law to a party other than an agency in litigation with the agency) based on the work product privilege or deliberative process privilege. To the extent the IRS could establish that the documents were prepared in anticipation of litigation or for trial (even to the extent it included agency working law), such portions of the documents were exempt.[59] Technical assistances discussing recommendations on whether to settle rather than litigate, whether to designate a case for litigation, and whether to appeal an adverse decision of the Tax Court were properly withheld.[60]

In considering the IRS's argument that some technical assistances were exempt under the deliberative process privilege, the court noted the similarity between technical assistances to program managers that addressed the interpretation or application of the internal revenue laws generally and taxpayer specific technical assistances and FSAs. Similar to FSAs, they included reviews of the proper interpretation of sources of tax law and were treated as final documents when issued. Accordingly, they were not covered by the deliberative privilege exemption.[61]

With respect to the remaining technical assistances to program managers, they reflected a give-and-take discussion regarding proposed tax forms, possible administrative or legislative changes, and proposed amendments. Thus, they were pre-decisional and not required to be disclosed.[62]

Finally, technical assistances to other divisions in the National Office were subject to modification or rejection prior to finalization into the final work product. The National Office expected internal debate to follow such technical assistances written between divisions. Thus, the court agreed they constituted a give-and-take discussion between components, were pre-decisional, and were not required to be disclosed.[63]

In 2005, Tax Analysts filed suit for the disclosure of some National Office e-mails. Chief Counsel attorneys provide advice to field attorneys. Chief Counsel Notice 2004-012 stated that legal advice that could be rendered in less than two hours need not be released to the public as chief counsel advice. Tax Analysts filed a lawsuit under the Freedom of Information Act seeking disclosure of such e-mails.

Having lost in the district court, in the appellate court the IRS argued that, because the advice was not formally reviewed, it was not legal advice "prepared by any national office component" as provided under Section 6110 and, therefore, was not required to be disclosed. The appellate court found that chief counsel advice is broadly defined. Furthermore, it did not distinguish between advice rendered in less than two hours and advice that took longer. The court held that the e-mails must be disclosed.[64]

Subsequent to the First Circuit's holding, the IRS issued Chief Counsel Notice CC-2008-002 addressing the affect of the litigation. It provides that emailed legal advice is chief counsel advice if it conveys:

---

58. *Tax Analysts v. IRS*, 152 F. Supp. 2d 1, 14–17 (D.C.C. 2001), *aff'g in part and remanding in part*, 294 F.3d 71 (D.C. Cir. 2002).
   59. *Id.* at 19.
   60. *Id.*
   61. *Id.* at 21–23.
   62. *Id.* at 23–24.
   63. *Id.* at 24–25.
   64. *Tax Analysts v. IRS*, 495 F.3d 676 (D.C. Cir. 2007), aff'g 416 F. Supp. 2d 119 (D.D.C. 2006).

- An interpretation of a revenue provision;

- An IRS or Counsel position or policy concerning a revenue provision; or

- A legal interpretation of any law relating to the assessment or collection of a liability under a revenue provision.

It also provides that e-mail should not be used to issue formal legal advice and should be used to communicate responses to relatively routine and simple questions.

4. Proper Statute for Obtaining Disclosure of Information

FOIA is limited by the Internal Revenue Service Reform and Restructuring Act of 1998. The legislative history of Section 6110 makes it clear that Congress intended Section 6110 to replace FOIA with respect to written determinations and related background file documents.[65] Specifically, public inspection of Chief Counsel advice can be accomplished only through section 6110 and not pursuant to FOIA. Documents other than written determinations and related background file documents can still be obtained through FOIA. *See* Figure 9.1.

Figure 9.1

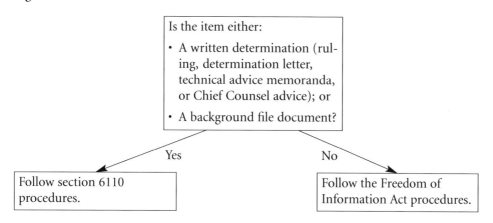

---

65. H.R. CONF. REPT. NO. 105-599 at 126.

The following is a summary of documents and the provision under which they are required to be disclosed, subject to any applicable exemption or right to withhold:

Item	Authority for Disclosure
Private Letter Ruling	Section 6110
Determination Letter	Section 6110
Technical Advice Memoranda	Section 6110
Field Service Advice	Section 6110 (*see also* Ann. 99-4, 1999-1 C.B. 324)
Technical Assistance to Field	Section 6110
Technical Assistance to Others	FOIA
Service Center Advice	Section 6110
Post-1985 Litigation Guideline Memoranda	Section 6110; Ann. 99-81, 1999-2 C.B. 244
Tax Litigation Bulletins	Section 6110
General Litigation Bulletins	Section 6110
Criminal Tax Bulletins	Section 6110
Field Service Advice Monthly Reports	FOIA
Pending Issue Reports	FOIA
AODs	FOIA; Ann. 82-17, 1982-5 I.R.B. 18
General Counsel Memoranda	FOIA; Ann. 82-17, 1982-5 I.R.B. 18
Information Letters	FOIA; Ann. 2000-2, 2001 C.B. 295
Technical Memoranda	FOIA; Ann. 82-17, 1982-5 I.R.B. 18
Written Determinations denying or revoking tax exempt status	Section 6110; Action on Decision 2004-02
Legal advice conveyed by e-mail from Chief Counsel's National Office attorneys to IRS and Counsel field personnel	Section 6110

C. Main Points

Section 6110:

- The IRS must allow public inspection of any issued written determination and any background document file relating to the written determination.

- A written determination includes rulings, determination letters, technical advice memoranda, and Chief Counsel advice.

- The IRS has 60 days from issuance to make any necessary deletions and release a nontaxpayer specific Chief Counsel advice for public inspection.

- The IRS generally must make any taxpayer-specific written determination and background file document available for public inspection no earlier than 75 days, and no later than 90 days, after the notice of intention to disclose is mailed to the specific taxpayer.

- Issued Chief Counsel Advice must be made available electronically within one year after issuance.

- If the written determination is available for public inspection only upon request, or a person wants to access a background file document, a request must be made to the National Office Reading Room.

- If a request is made for a written determination or for background file documents, the IRS can assess actual costs incurred in searching for and making required deletions from any documents made available based on the request.

- Before any documents are made available for public inspection (whether released voluntarily by the government or pursuant to a request), certain information must be deleted from the documents.

- Section 6110 must be used to obtain access to written determinations and related background file documents.

Freedom of Information Act:

- The Freedom of Information Act (FOIA) establishes a statutory right to access government information.

- The IRS must publish certain types of information in the Federal Register.

- The IRS must make certain types of information available to the public.

- The IRS must make some types of information available to the public upon specific request.

- Certain items are statutorily exempt from FOIA's disclosure requirements.

- Documents other than written determinations and related background file documents can be obtained through FOIA.

D. Related Articles for Further Reading

- John L. Abramic, *Advance Pricing Agreements: Confidential Return Information or Written Determinations Subject to Release?*, 76 CHI.-KENT 1823 (2001).

- Lisa A. Reilly, *The Freedom of Information Act and the Withholding of Documents Under Section 6103 of the Internal Revenue Code*, 55 GEO. WASH. L. REV. 937 (1987).

- Vivian M. Raby, *The Freedom of Information Act and the IRS Confidentiality Statute: A Proper Analysis*, 54 U. CIN. L. REV. 605 (1985).

- Patricia L. Agliano, Long v. Internal Revenue Service: *A Miscalculation of the Freedom of Information Act's Applicability to Section 6103(b) of the Internal Revenue Code*, 5 VA. TAX REV. 441 (1985).

- Edward A. Tomlinson, *Use of the Freedom of Information Act for Discovery Purposes*, 43 MD. L. REV. 119 (1984).

- Mark A. Segal, *Tax Data Disclosure Under the Freedom of Information Act: Evolution, Issues and Analysis*, 9 AKRON TAX J. 79 (1992).

E. Problems

1. Upon receiving a request for records under the FOIA, the IRS must:
    a. Search its files for any documents responsive to the individual's request and make the documents available to the individual.
    b. Place all requested documents in the National Office Reading Room.
    c. Deny the request unless the IRS deems the request reasonable.
    d. Respond to the request within one year.

2. Section 6110 allows pubic inspection of all of the following, except:
    a. Rulings.
    b. Determination letters.
    c. Technical advice memoranda.
    d. Internally prepared documents.

3. Chief Counsel advice includes all of the following, except:
    a. Litigation guideline memoranda.
    b. Advanced pricing agreements.
    c. Criminal Tax Bulletins.
    d. Field service advice.

4. Under the FOIA, the IRS must make all of the following available to the public, except:
    a. Judicial opinions.
    b. Statements of policy adopted by the IRS but not published in the Federal Register.
    c. Administrative staff manuals.
    d. All documents prepared by Chief Counsel attorneys.

5. A background file document includes all of the following, except:
    a. Communication between the Department of Justice and the IRS related to a pending criminal investigation.
    b. Request for written determination.
    c. All written material submitted in support of the request.
    d. Any communication between the National Office and a district director concerning the factual circumstances underlying a request for technical advice.

6. Under the FOIA, the IRS is required to publish all of the following in the Federal Register, except:
    a. Descriptions of its field organization.
    b. Statements of its formal procedures.
    c. Background file documents.
    d. Substantive rules of general applicability.

7. If a person would like to inspect background file documents, the person must:
    a. Locate the attorney in the National Office who drafted the related written determination and make a request of that attorney.
    b. Make a request to the National Office Reading Room.
    c. Make a request of the Chief Counsel.
    d. None of the above, as the document is not available for inspection.

8. The Freedom of Information Act:

    a. Establishes a statutory right to access government information.
    b. Requires that all documents issued by the government be made available to the public upon request.
    c. Requires that all documents issued by the government be placed in the National Office Reading Room.
    d. Requires that all documents be published in the Federal Register.

9. When visiting the IRS Reading Room:

    a   An IRS employee will always be present.
    b. No documents may be removed from the room.
    c. Copies may be made of documents.
    d. All of the above.

10. All of the following are identifying details that must be deleted from a written determination before the document is released, except:

    a. Taxpayer's name.
    b. Case citations.
    c. Trade secrets.
    d. Court document number.

11. If a request is made to inspect a written determination or related background file documents, which of the following is true?

    a. The IRS can assess actual costs incurred in searching for and making required deletions from any documents made available based on the request.
    b. There is never any cost associated with an inspection.
    c. The fee for inspecting the documents can be paid after the person requesting them determines if the documents have any value.
    d. None of the above is true.

12. Before any document is released to the public or made available for inspection, which of the following is true?

    a. The person to whom the determination was issued must consent to the disclosure.
    b. The attorney who prepared the written determination must consent to the disclosure.
    c. Certain identifying details must be deleted from the documents.
    d. A year must have passed since issuance of the written determination.

13. Visit the FOIA room on the IRS website.

    a. Locate 5 U.S.C. §552.
    b. Locate the regulations under FOIA.
    c. Locate information on how to write a FOIA request.
    d. Locate information on the fees charged for a FOIA request.
    e. Link into the electronic reading room.

14. Under what circumstances might you make a request under section 6110? Under what circumstances might you make a FOIA request? What kind of information would you need to make a request?

Chapter 10

Researching the Issue

[handwritten note: Use secondary authority to locate and understand the primary authority]

Research

[handwritten note: related to research project]

- *Which treatises are organized by code section?*
- *Which treatises are organized by topic?*
- *Are there treatises that address specific subject matter areas?*
- *Can research be conducted using electronic media?*

"Well, that is it for this morning's session," the presenter said. "I'll see most of you after the lunch break."

Lisa looked down at her notes. The presenter had spent the entire morning covering many different types of authority in the tax area. There were so many to consider. The various trial, circuit court, and Supreme Court opinions were just the beginning. Statutes; legislative history; final, temporary, and proposed regulations; and preambles also could be helpful. All that, and government-issued documents hadn't even been addressed yet. Lisa sighed, wondering how she could ever get a handle on all these sources when researching an issue. She rose from her table and moved up to the front of the room to stand in line with the others who had questions for the presenter.

When it was finally her turn, Lisa laid out her problem. "There is so much information out there on any one topic. How could I possible locate all the documents relevant to my issue? And locate the information in a timely manner!"

"Ah, I see you have been paying very close attention to the information so far. Not to worry, though. Commercial publishers long ago recognized the need for some way to organize the information, whether based on a specific issue or Code section. So, they prepared treatises that organize court cases, regulations, government documents, and sometimes other documents. This afternoon we will talk about the different types of treatises and what information each contains. I think you will see that, for the most part, they are an excellent source for starting your research."

Contents

A. Key Terms

After completing this chapter, you should be familiar with the following key terms:

- ➤ CCH's Standard Federal Tax Reporter
- ➤ RIA's United States Tax Reporter
- ➤ RIA's Federal Tax Coordinator 2d
- ➤ BNA's Tax Management Portfolio Series
- ➤ Mertens Law of Federal Income Taxation
- ➤ LexisNexis
- ➤ WestLaw
- ➤ RIA's Checkpoint
- ➤ CCH's Tax Research Network

B. Discussion

Various commercial publishers have prepared treatises that contain a substantial amount of information about the internal revenue code and how it has been interpreted. These treatises can be invaluable as research tools. Depending on the service, a researcher might find the Code, regulations, legislative history, and references to case law and various documents published by the government within the treatise. Key, however, is knowing how to access this information.

1. Research through Treatises Organized by Code Section

Commerce Clearing House (CCH) and the Research Institute of America (RIA) offer treatises that are organized by Code section. Quite simply, to begin researching in CCH or RIA, the researcher could turn to the Code section of interest.

CCH's Standard Federal Tax Reporter. CCH publishes the Standard Federal Tax Reporter series. The series is composed of 25 loose-leaf volumes and is devoted exclusively to income tax. CCH also publishes the Federal Estate and Gift Tax Reporter and the Federal Excise Tax Reporter. In its volumes, the Standard Federal Tax Reporter includes a substantial amount of information including:

- Internal Revenue Code, with changes and amendments and references to Public Law numbers

- Treasury regulations, with amendments

- Summaries of judicial opinions on income tax issues

- Revenue Rulings, Revenue Procedures, and other items published in the Cumulative Bulletin

- CCH's explanations of various rules

Specifically, the series includes two volumes that contain the current Internal Revenue Code and amendment notes beginning in 1954. Tables in the front of the first volume allow the researcher to cross-reference sections to the 1939 and 1954 Codes. The first volume contains current income tax provisions from section 1 to section 1000. The second volume contains section 1001 to the end of the Code, including estate and gift, employment and excise, and procedural provisions and related statutes. It also contains non-codified provisions.

Eighteen of the volumes contain a discussion of the tax law. This portion of the series is referred to as "Compilations." Within these volumes, the Code is arranged in numerical order. For each Code section, first the Code section is presented, followed by portions of relevant Committee Reports, applicable regulations, CCH's explanation of the Code provision, and summaries of court opinions and rulings issued after 1912. Of course, the researcher should locate and read any court opinions or rulings cited in the materials before relying on them.

Most tax research will begin in the relevant volume of the Compilations. The spine of each volume indicates which Code section and CCH paragraph reference numbers are contained in the volume. Thus, the researcher could simply turn to the Code section of interest. However, if the researcher is unsure which Code section to consider, he could use the topical index to locate paragraph references to places in the Compilations that discuss the matter of interest. The topical index lists topics alphabetically. Each topic is followed by a reference to one or more paragraph numbers.

Example:

The following is an example of information found in the Topical Index:

Topical Index   **10,581**
References are to paragraph (¶) numbers.

GROSS INCOME—continued
. nonresident aliens 27,345; 27,348.01
. notes . . . . 5504.01—5504.022; 5706.594;
. . . . 21,009.04
. . cancelled 21,412.204
. . cost of goods sold, inclusion 5600.36
. . in lieu of cash 21,005.476
. . in payment of interest 5704.29
. . year taxable 21,005.7005
. nuclear decommissioning costs . . . . . 6450—
. . . . 6452.01
. nuisance claim in litigation 21,005.6875
. Nurse Cadet Corps 5504.765
. nutrition program, cash benefits . 33,506.292
. oil and gas properties, lifting costs . . 5600.36
. oil leases 5706.585
. oil well interests 5504.138
. oil well operation 5504.392
. omission from returns, limitations on
    assessment and collection . 38,970; 42,940
. . personal holding companies 38,972
. option proceeds 5504.394; 21,005.873;
    30,614.01—30,614.525
. options received as payment of income
. . . . 5902
. original issue discount . . . 31,260—31,262.40
. . doubtful collectibility 31,262.30
. . election to treat all interest as OID
. . . . 31,261E; 31,262.073
. . short-term obligations . . 31,420—31,421.35
. . treatment of debt instruments purchased
    at a premium 31,261B; 31,262.03
. overceiling prices 5901.55
. overcharges 21,005.7015
. own bonds purchased at discount . . 5804.51
. owner-consumed goods 5600.75
. ownership. 2150.55
. ownership of income . . . 5504.195—5504.203
. . admission of error 5504.195
. . . allocation—see Allocation: income
. . burden of proof 5504.196
. . distributive share determined . . . 5504.197
. . evidence, sufficiency of . . . . 5504.198—
. . . . 5504.192
. . exempt organization 5504.199
. . income taxable to another 5504.20
. . Mankind United, income from . . . 5504.201
. . money or goods received 5504.201
. . real estate transactions 5504.202
. . stock transactions 5504.203
. . stockholders v. corporation . . . . 2300.01—
. . . . 2300.78
. paper patronage dividends . . . 5603; 5604.01
. pari-mutuel fund payments 5504.140
. partly within and partly without U.S.,
    personal property manufactured or
    produced within U.S., sale outside
. . . . 27,161—27,165
. . manufactured inventory property
. . . . 27,161.002
. partners 5805
. . taxes paid by another 5504.6726
. partners and partnerships 25,081
. . computation of 25,101
. patent rights sold
. . nonresident alien 27,348.153
. patronage dividends—see also Patronage
    dividends . . . . 5604.01—5604.30; 32,362.01
. patronage refund credit 21,005.7022
. payment for release of wife's dower
. . . . 2250.59
. payment for use of property 5706.01
. payment in gold 5700.25
. payment received as recompense for
    counsel's error 5900.19
. pension funds recovered by employer
. . . . 7062.73
. pensions 6140.14; 18,207.015

GROSS INCOME—continued
. per diem allowances . . . 5507.114; 5507.3613
. percentage of profit of another . 21,005.7028
. personal expenses paid by third party
. . . . 5504.036
. personal holding company 23,190
. personal injuries 6662.04
. personal property sold abroad . . . 28,049.70
. physical personal injuries or sickness
. . . . 6662.04
. poison pill plan 5707B.35; 29,226.308
. political contributions 5504.406
. political contributions misappropriated
. . . . 5901.56
. political organizations, compensation
    donated to 2200.29
. political payoffs 2150.80
. pool profits 5504.658
. possession, reduced to 21,009.01
. possessions of U.S., source
. . citizens 28,240
. . corporations 28,380; 28,394.031
. post-dated checks 21,005.8765
. premiums, banks 5704.023
. prepaid income—see Prepaid income
. price ceiling violations 5901.55
. price reduction v. commission 5507.156
. prizes and awards . . 6201; 6204.01—6204.85;
. . . . 6553.03
. professional service corporation . . . 2300.65
. profits before incorporation 2300.53
. prospective employee, reimbursed expenses
. . . . 5507.396
. prostitution 5901.564
. protection payment received by union
    official 5901.35
. publishers, magazines, paperbacks, and
    records returned after close of tax year
. . . . 21,540—21,543.40
. purchase and leaseback 5706.599
. purchase price adjustment, indebtedness
    gratuitously forgiven 5802.26
. purchase price adjustments 5600.43
. purchase requirement 5504.139
. purchaser's assignees paying tax of
    purchaser 5504.674
. qualified state tuition programs . . . 5504.022
. railroad retirement benefits . . 6420—6421.20
. railroad termination allowances . . . 5504.188
. railroads . . . . 5504.43—5504.4425
. reacquisition of real property 5504.042
. real property sold in lots 5605; 5701.01;
. . . . 5701.021
. . cost basis 5701.01
. rebates 5504.449; 5504.492
. reconstruction of—see Reconstruction of
    income
. recovery of capital . . . . 5704.313—5704.3148
. . rents and royalties distinguished . 5706.606
. reduction of purchase price 5504.494
. refunds
. . interest on 5704.023; 5704.363
. . taxes 5504.041; 5504.4485; 21,005.726
. refusal to accept payment 21,009.202
. reimbursement for loss
. . delayed acceptance 5900.21
. reimbursement of expenses—see also
    Reimbursement . . . . 5504.037; 5504.4863—
. . . . 5504.505
. . contributions to retirement plan . 5504.487
. . entertainment expenses 5507.3975
. . estimated amounts 5504.4875
. . meals, payments in cash 5507.3967
. . tenant allowances 5504.5002
. related activities of family members
. . . . 5600.79
. rentals and royalties—see Rentals and
    royalties

2005(Index) CCH—Standard Federal Tax Reports   **GRO**

Or, if the researcher is basing his research on a case or ruling, the researcher could locate the case or ruling in the finding lists located in the Citator Volumes and find paragraph references to the Compilations where the case or ruling is discussed.

Example:

The following is an example of information found in the Citator volume:

PER   **95,548**   ————CCH————

Perry, Carey J.—continued
Serbousek, TC, Dec. 34,353(M), 36 TCM 479, TC Memo. 1977-105
● DC-NC—74-1 USTC ¶9244; 376 FSupp 15
Perry, Carl C. . . . . ¶42,827.65
● DC-La—79-2 USTC ¶9441
Perry, Carlton H. . . . . ¶8523.2748, 8590.1268, 11,007.464, 14,417.30, 14,854.42
● CA-9—Taxpayer on appeal, 11/19/96
● TC—Dec. 51,308(M); 71 TCM 2840; TC Memo. 1996-194
Perry, Carolyn . . . . . ¶3507.10, 3507.18, 10,650.11
● SCt—Cert. denied, 111 SCt 1418
● CA-5—(aff'g TC in unpublished opinion), 8/15/90, 912 F2d 1466
● TC—Dec. 45,533; 92 TC 470
Rev. Rul. 93-27
Bragg, TC, Dec. 49,341(M), 66 TCM 1047, TC Memo. 1993-479
Bowman, TC, Dec. 50,691(M), 69 TCM 2886, TC Memo. 1995-259
Clanton, TC, Dec. 50,863(M), 70 TCM 534, TC Memo. 1995-416
Lerma, TC, Dec. 51,048(M), 70 TCM 1540, TC Memo. 1995-586
Wise, TC, Dec. 50,968(M), 70 TCM 1095, TC Memo. 1995-513
Adams, TC, Dec. 51,866(M), TC Memo. 1997-63, 73 TCM 1913
Vinikoor, TC, Dec. 52,674(M), 75 TCM 2185, TC Memo. 1998-152
Barr, TC, Dec. 53,244(M), 77 TCM 1370, TC Memo. 1999-40
Kidder, TC, Dec. 53,587(M), TC Memo. 1999-345, 78 TCM 602
Tonn, TC, Dec. 54,349(M), 81 TCM 1670, TC Memo. 2001-123
Concordia Est., TC, Dec. 54,856(M), 84 TCM 254, TC Memo. 2002-216
Flood, TC, Dec. 54,247(M), 81 TCM 1175, TC Memo. 2001-39
Perry, Carolyn P. . . . . ¶2250.12, 39,651G.305
● TC—Dec. 44,864(M); 55 TCM 1164; TC Memo. 1988-280
Perry, Cedric R. . . . . ¶38,184.52
● DC-NC—2004-2 USTC ¶50,385
Perry, Charlys G. . . . . ¶35,192.43
● TC—Dec. 48,195(M); 63 TCM 2924; TC Memo. 1992-258
Friedman, CA-2, 95-1 USTC ¶50,235, 53 F3d 523
Laird, Jr., TC, Dec. 50,236(M), 68 TCM 1191, TC Memo. 1994-564
Gill, TC, Dec. 49,112(M), 65 TCM 2993, TC Memo. 1993-274
Kelly, TC, Dec. 51,673(M), 72 TCM 1389, TC Memo. 1996-529
Silverman, CA-6, 97-2 USTC ¶50,499, 116 F3d 172
Perry Co., Inc., Claude R. . . . . (Excise Tax)
● DC-Tex—65-2 USTC ¶15,662; 352 F2d 339
Perry & Co., Inc., J. M. . . . . . . ¶8638.2935, 23,074.35
● CA-9—(aff'g BTA), 41-2 USTC ¶9492; 120 F2d 123
Smith, CA-5, 61-1 USTC ¶9122, 285 F2d 91
O'Dwyer, CA-4, 59-1 USTC ¶9441, 266 F2d 575
Kerr-Cochran, Inc., CA-8, 58-1 USTC ¶9352, 253 F2d 121
Maroosis, CA-9, 51-1 USTC ¶9182, 187 F2d 228
Gillette Est., CA-9, 50-1 USTC ¶10,774, 182 F2d 1010
San Joaquin Brick Co., CA-9, 42-2 USTC ¶9629, 130 F2d 220
Essick, DC-Calif, 52-2 USTC ¶10,872
World Publishing Co., DC-Okla, 47-1 USTC ¶9280, 72 FSupp 886
Allen, TC, Dec. 44,718(M), 55 TCM 641, TC Memo. 1988-166
Turner, TC, Dec. 27,344(M), 24 TCM 544, TC Memo. 1965-101
Sandy Estate Co., TC, Dec. 27,195, 43 TC 361
Van Hummell, TC, Dec. 27,034(M), 23 TCM 1765, TC Memo. 1964-290
Turnbull, TC, Dec. 26,428, 41 TC 358
Southland Industries, Inc., TC, Dec. 15,467(M), 5 TCM 950
Boyle Co., TC, Dec. 14,313(M), 3 TCM 1335
California Motor Transport Co., Ltd., TC, Dec. 13,154(M), 1 TCM 974
● BTA—Dec. 11,030-F; March 5, 1940
Perry & Co., R. H. . . . . . . (Expired Excess Profits Tax)
● BTA—Dec. 4036; 12 BTA 328
Friedlaender, TC, Dec. 21,920, 26 TC 1005
Perry Corp. . . . . (Expired Excess Profits Tax)
● BTA—Dec. 290; 1 BTA 788
Perry, Curtis B. . . . . ¶15,108.20, 39,651G.65
● CA-9—(aff'g TC), 96-2 USTC ¶50,405; 91 F3d 82

Perry, Curtis B.—continued
Goldberg, TC, Dec. 51,878(M), 73 TCM 1988, TC Memo. 1997-74
Beall, CA-9, 2000-2 USTC ¶50,577, 229 F3d 1156
Parker, TC, Dec. 53,591(M), TC Memo. 1999-347, 78 TCM 621
Asher, TC, Dec. 52,749(M), 75 TCM 2516, TC Memo. 1998-219
Corrigan, TC, Dec. 56,034(M), TC Memo. 2005-119, 89 TCM 1313
● TC—Dec. 49,879(M); 67 TCM 3035; TC Memo. 1994-247
Edmondson, TC, Dec. 51,523(M), 72 TCM 482, TC Memo. 1996-393
Perry, Donald M. . . . . ¶10,800.342, 32,053.36, 32,084.245
● TC—Dec. 28,853; 49 TC 508; A. 1968-2 CB 2
Franco, TC, Dec. 48,544(M), 64 TCM 928, TC Memo. 1992-577
Reed, TC, Dec. 52,376(M), 74 TCM 1300, TC Memo. 1997-533
Lackey, E. Gerald, TC, Dec. 34,500(M), 36 TCM 890, TC Memo. 1977-213
Rubnitz, Alan A., TC, Dec. 34,202, 67 TC 621
Kolb, Sr., TC, Dec. 33,400(M), 34 TCM 1171, TC Memo. 1975-272
Burton, TC, Dec. 33,294(M), 34 TCM 898, TC Memo. 1975-208
Shrout, TC, Dec. 31,933(M), 32 TCM 398, TC Memo. 1973-89
Reed, TC, Dec. 30,736(M), 30 TCM 321, TC Memo. 1971-77
Blue Flame Gas Co., TC, Dec. 30,020, 54 TC 584
Perry & Dorminey. . . . . ¶22,204.30
● BTA—Dec. 369; 1 BTA 995; A. IV-1 CB 3
Perry, E. G. . . . . ¶16,004.2195
● BTA—Dec. 3229; 9 BTA 796; A. VII-2 CB 31
Rosenbloom Finance Corp., BTA, Dec. 7270, 24 BTA 763
Gossett, BTA, Dec. 6893, 22 BTA 1279
Tootle, BTA, Dec. 6331, 20 BTA 892
Kennedy, BTA, Dec. 5338, 16 BTA 1372
Blumenthal, BTA, Dec. 4214, 12 BTA 1205
Perry, E. Gordon . . . . ¶21,009.1235, 21,817.577
● BTA—Dec. 8128; 28 BTA 497
Rife, CA-5, 66-1 USTC ¶9239, 356 F2d 883
Heyman, Richard S., TC, Dec. 35,230, 70 TC 482
Wilkerson,, TC, Dec. 35,156, 70 TC 240
Goldwyn, TC, Dec. 16,031, 9 TC 510
Perry, Earl V. . . . ¶10,650.152, 10,650.31, 12,543.131
● TC—Dec. 20,473; 22 TC 968
Sutherland, TC, Dec. 47,808(M), 62 TCM 1533, TC Memo. 1991-619
Dritz, Max, TC, Dec. 29,718(M), 28 TCM 874, TC Memo. 1969-175
Hotel Continental, Inc., TC, Dec. 50,806(M), 70 TCM 295, TC Memo. 1995-364
Wise, TC, Dec. 50,968(M), 70 TCM 1095, TC Memo. 1995-513
Hobbs, TC, Dec. 26,910(M), 23 TCM 1258, TC Memo. 1964-208
Factor, TC, Dec. 22,992(M), 17 TCM 459, TC Memo. 1958-94
Schultz, TC, Dec. 22,971, 30 TC 256
Friedlaender, TC, Dec. 21,920, 26 TC 1005
Rope, TC, Dec. 21,790(M), 15 TCM 707, TC Memo. 1956-140
McBride, TC, Dec. 20,884, 23 TC 926
Perry Est., Emily B. (See Planters Nat'l Bank and Tr. Co.)
Perry, Frank L. ¶39,658.115, 42,283.71, 42,302.81, 42,309.67
● TC—Dec. 42,924(M); 51 TCM 597; TC Memo. 1986-100
Perry, Sr., Est., Frank M. . . . . ¶41,743.80
● CA-5—91-1 USTC ¶50,283; 91-1 USTC ¶60,073; 931 F2d 1044
Allbritton, CA-5, 94-2 USTC ¶50,550, 37 F3d 183
Johnson Est., CA-5, 93-1 USTC ¶50,251, 985 F2d 1315
Hanson, CA-5, 92-2 USTC ¶50,554, 975 F2d 1150
Taylor, DC-Ala, 94-1 USTC ¶60,165
Williams, ClsCt, 93-1 USTC ¶50,036, 26 ClsCt 1031
Nalle III, TC, Dec. 49,809(M), 67 TCM 2747, TC Memo. 1994-182
Williford, TC, Dec. 49,753(M), 67 TCM 2542, TC Memo. 1994-135
Powers, TC, Dec. 49,059, 100 TC 457
Price, TC, Dec. 49,804, 102 TC 660
Ripley, Jr., TC, Dec. 49,802, 102 TC 654
Mills, Jr., TC, Dec. 53,267(M), 77 TCM 1471, TC Memo. 1999-60
Comtec Systems, Inc., TC, Dec. 50,747(M), TC Memo. 1995-310, 70 TCM 52

When using the Standard Federal Tax Reporter, research is not complete before checking Volume 19, New Matters, for current developments as the majority of updates to the compilation volumes are accomplished through this volume. The Cumulative Index in Volume 19 coordinates the Compilations with the new matters by direct reference from paragraph number in the Compilations to the related "New Matter" paragraph number.

Example:

The following is information found in the New Matters volume:

| 26 ‖ 6-16-2005 | Cumulative Index to 2005 Developments
(For Reports 1-26)
See also Cumulative Index at page 75,251. | **75,375** |

From Compilation Paragraph No.		To New Development Paragraph No.
	Code Sec. 6304—Fair tax collection practices	
38,079	.60	Isley, DC N.J. —Notice and demand were proper 50,115
	.60	Lehmann, TCM —Notices of balance due qualified as notice and demand for payment 48,017
	.60	Tilley aff'd, CA-4 (unpub. op.) (¶50,125)—On another issue. Cert. denied 10/04/2004.
	Code Sec. 6311—Payment of tax by commercially acceptable means	
38,089	.01	TeleFile program to terminate August 16—Ann. 46,429
	.101	E-payment options detailed—Fact Sheet 46,267
	Code Sec. 6320—Notice and opportunity for hearing upon filing of notice of lien	
38,134	.028	Prevo, TC —No jurisdiction over petition filed in violation of automatic stay 47,906
	.20	Burke, TC —IRS could pursue tax collection where individual raised invalid arguments, delayed proceedings 48,010
	.20	Fishbach, TCM —Taxpayer's petition for lien reconsideration rejected 47,959
	.20	Perry, DC N.C. —Jurisdiction lacking over late-filed complaint 49,821
	.20	Winters, Jr., TCM —Tax liability could not be offset by alleged Schedule C losses 47,930
	.20	Jackling, DC N.H. —Individual could not challenge liability for penalty at CDP hearing 50,159
	.89	Parker, Jr., TCM —CDP hearing must be held at IRS office closest to taxpayer 47,735
	Code Sec. 6321—Lien for taxes	
38,136	.101	Choate, DC Tenn. —Federal tax liens attached upon issuance of assessment 49,820
	.101	McCorkle, TC —Collection not prevented by IRS's forfeiture of prior payment 47,953
	.32	Ruggerio, DC Md. —Tax liens did not attach to real property purchased by third party 50,328
	.36	Old Natl. Bank, DC Ind. — (¶50,639)—District court had jurisdiction to reduce to judgment outstanding taxes. IRS tax lien on accounts receivables attached at creation of receivables 50,331
	.535	Gallivan, BC-DC Mo. —Tax lien attached to 50 percent of property 49,822
	.56	Sequoia Property Equipment, LP aff'd, CA-9 (unpub. op.) (¶50,182)—Limitations period in Federal Debt Collection Procedures Act did not bar fraudulent conveyance claim. Cert. denied 3/21/2005.
	.64	Johnson, Jr. Est., DC Mich. —Tax lien trumped ex-wife's interest in marital home 50,339
	.65	Novotny aff'd, CA-10 (unpub. op.) (¶50,639)—District court had jurisdiction to reduce judgment on outstanding taxes. Cert. denied 10/04/2004.
	.66	Cody, DC Va. —Relatives were nominee owners of delinquent taxpayers' property 50,213
	Code Sec. 6323—Validity and priority against certain persons	
38,160	.032	The IRS has issued inflation-adjusted tax rate tables for tax years beginning in 2005—Rev. Proc. 46,093
	.038	The IRS has issued inflation-adjusted tax rate tables for tax years beginning in 2005—Rev. Proc. 46,093
	.109	Bank of America, N.A., DC Okla. —Tax lien had priority over security interest as to money disbursed after expiration of 45-day grace period 50,105
	.109	Old Natl. Bank, DC nd. —IRS tax lien on accounts receivable had priority over simultaneous bank security interest 50,331
	.115	NuMed Home Health Care Inc., BC-DC Fla. —Damages from tortious conversion arose only while tax lien had first priority status 50,364
	.124	Greene, FedCl —State guaranty fund superior to federal tax claims against insolvent life insurer 49,846

In addition to the updates, the Standard Federal Tax Reporter is kept up to date with the "CCH Tax Focus and Features" division in Volume 19, which analyzes important income tax problems of current interest and describes their significance for purposes of tax planning. They also spotlight diverse Code and regulation provisions bearing on one particular subject and discuss controversial tax issues over which two or more courts have disagreed or upon which there is limited authority. In addition, the "CCH Comments" division discusses significant rulings and decisions interpreting the law and regulations, with special emphasis given to intricate new problems not yet settled by the courts and to avenues of possible tax savings.

Example:

The following is an example of CCH Comments:

CCH COMMENTS   May 12, 2005

¶ 48,701   Tax Court Backs IRS's Tough "Hardship" Standards for
                        Accepting Offers in Compromises

The IRS did not abuse its discretion by rejecting two offers in compromise and proceeding to file a Federal Tax Lien on a taxpayer's property. The Tax Court held that the taxpayer had significant equity in a house to be able to pay off his outstanding tax liability in full. Both offers in compromise were not supported by "an inability to pay."[1]

Recent Trend

Especially with the run up in real estate prices in many areas over the past several years, it is clear that the IRS intends to fully value those assets in deciding whether an offer in compromise (OIC) should be accepted, even if the taxpayer is forced to disrupt family life by either moving or refinancing to the hilt.

Ability to pay

Both of the taxpayer's OICs were based on doubt as to collectability. The IRS rejected both OICs because a calculation of the taxpayer's disposable income and assets showed he had the ability to pay off his tax liability in full. The determination of the taxpayer's reasonable basic living expenses did not include the maintenance of an affluent or luxurious standard of living.

The taxpayer submitted his own list of expenses and claimed he paid all of the household expenses for him and his wife. However, the IRS adjusted his monthly expenses according to its own national and local living expense standards. The Tax Court held that the IRS did not abuse its discretion by relying on its own national and local expense averages.

The IRS also prorated the taxpayer's expenses. The taxpayer's monthly expenses were reduced because his wife was receiving passive income. Thus, the taxpayer's monthly household expenses were reduced to reflect her ability to contribute toward household expenses as well.

After calculating the taxpayer's disposable income and examining his assets, the IRS found both of the offers to be well short of what the taxpayer could actually pay. The Tax Court agreed. The taxpayer's second offer of $2,200 toward his tax liability of approximately $38,000 was also inadequate. The reasonable collection potential (RCP) of the liability exceeded both the amount of the offer and the full amount of the tax liability. The taxpayer's 25 percent equity in a house valued at over $600,000 that he shared with his wife was more than enough to cover the tax liability.

Economic hardship

The taxpayer also claimed that he was suffering from economic hardship when he submitted his second OIC and thus it must be accepted. The first hardship factor claimed by the taxpayer was the financial impact of his wife's permanent disability. The taxpayer made bald assertions in his offer that his wife became disabled in 1999 and was unemployable. However, the taxpayer presented no evidence of the financial impact of her disability. Thus, the Tax Court held that the IRS did not have an adequate basis to find that a hardship actually existed and properly refused to consider the disability.

The taxpayer also claimed that his inability to borrow from financial institutions constituted an economic hardship as well. However, the Tax Court was unimpressed with his evidentiary showing. The taxpayer merely claimed that the existence of the tax lien would make it impossible to borrow against his home. The taxpayer neither attempted to borrow nor did he show that the lien affected his ability to secure financing.

Comment. The case reflects the high bar set by the IRS in reviewing OICs by taxpayers. Several members of Congress have publicly called for changes to be made to the OIC program to give taxpayers a better chance of having an OIC accepted by the IRS.

Back references: ¶41,130.025 and ¶41,130.035.

---

[1] Hawkins, T.C. Memo 2005-88, Dec. 55,99(M).

2005(19) CCH—Standard Federal Tax Reports   ¶48,701

In addition to updates, Volume 19 includes other valuable information such as a Legislative Status Table that sets forth the income or related tax bills introduced and reported out by either the House Ways and Means Committee or the Senate Finance Committee and a brief description of the bill provisions and the latest actions taken. It also includes a listing and description of laws passed by the current Congress. The text of some bills and committee reports may be included. Finally, the volume includes Treasury Decision preambles, digests of Tax Court decisions, rulings, and the Supreme Court docket.

CCH also publishes Taxes on Parade, a weekly review of the tax news. It covers new developments and tax news of current interest. Periodically, the service includes special issues that cover revenue bills, explanatory Committee Reports, and new tax laws with explanations.

Practice Note:

The CCH Index contains the following information about "Other Aids for Tax Work":[1]

Extras ...

Special issues speed news of the progress of major revenue bills through Congress and include the final text and explanation. Timely booklets and special releases are also sent to subscribers.

2010 Tax Calendar—Rate Tables ...

A tax calendar in this special division in the Index Volume indicates the final dates for filing various returns and meeting other requirements imposed by the Internal Revenue Code and Regulations. Rate tables list the present rates for income, estate, gift, and excise taxes. Also included are the income tax rates for past years. Withholding tables for all payroll periods are also reproduced.

Checklists ...

This division in the Index Volume lists various deductibles by type—personal, business, tax, etc. Also listed is a wide variety of income items. All lists provide paragraph references to the Compilations for full details. A Tax Election checklist assembles the numerous tax elections available under the Internal Revenue Code and Regulations into one location.

Special Tables ...

In this division in the Index Volume are special tables that apply in special areas of the income tax law. Included are annuity computation tables that apply in connection with the computation of annuities under Code Sec. 72, redemption value tables for U.S. savings bonds and tables for computing the interest due on overpayments and underpayments of tax. Also included in this division are credit rates and bond factor amounts related to the low-income housing credit, the AFR per diem rate tables, and various depreciation tables, including the current MACRS tables and prior depreciation rate tables, such as the ADR system tables.

Tax Terms ...

In this division in the Index Volume, commonly used words and phrases are defined, with references to the Compilations for additional information.

---

1. Standard Federal Tax Reporter (CCH), Index, ¶ 7.

Tax Planning ...

Major income tax factors to be considered in tax planning are discussed in separate divisions in Volume 1. Individual and business tax planning considerations are addressed in a Frequently Asked Questions format. In addition, the inflation adjustment guide provides a handy reference to items affected by inflation adjustments. This special planning information can be adapted to test in advance the tax results of various plans. The tax consequences of alternatives and elections are pointed out, all for assistance in helping keep taxes at legal lows.

Tax Return Preparers ...

A special division of Volume 1 is devoted to the responsibilities that the Internal Revenue Code places on persons who prepare income tax returns for compensation. Not only do the Code and Regulations spell out the details of those responsibilities, the Code also imposes sanctions against preparers who willfully avoid or attempt to avoid the statutory requirements.

Tax Treaties ...

As an aid to the determination of income exempt under treaty, the full text of the Canadian tax treaty and protocols and summaries of other tax conventions are reproduced in the Tax Treaties division in Volume 11.

Administration-Procedure ...

Administrative and procedural matters occupy the major portions of Volume 17 and 18. These Compilations are also based on the Code and Regulations, with editorial comments and annotations. Special features include a listing of official forms by number and subject, lists of IRS personnel, the Tax Court Rules, and the procedure for appeal to the Courts of Appeals.

Expired Income Tax and Excess Profits Tax Laws ...

Summaries of expired or repealed Code provisions is presented in two divisions in Volume 18 at ¶ 44,351 and ¶ 44,651. Also included are citations of cases and rulings handed down under these provisions.

How to Cite the Reports ...

The STANDARD FEDERAL TAX REPORTER is cited by year, volume and paragraph number. These numbers are combined with the letters "CCH" and the paragraph number (¶) of the matter to which reference is made for citation purposes. Thus, "2010(1) CCH ¶ 4350" refers to the 2010 STANDARD FEDERAL TAX REPORTER, Volume 1, ¶ 4350. Prior to the year 2000, only two digits were used to indicate the year. Thus, a reference to "86(10) CCH ¶ 6672" directs you to Volume 10 of the 1986 edition, ¶ 6672.

Chart 10.1 Summary of Information Contained in CCH's Federal Standard Tax Reporter

Volume	Contents
1	• Inflation Adjustment Guide • Tax Planning Information • Who is the Taxpayer? • Tax Return Preparers • Constitutionality, Tax Protest, Tax Schemes • Tax Tables: Rate Schedules • Tax Credits • Minimum Tax, Tax Preferences, Environmental Tax
1–18 (Compilations)	For each income tax Code section: • Code section, with amendments • Select Committee Reports • Treasury regulations, including final, temporary, and proposed regulations • CCH's explanation • Digest of related court opinions, revenue rulings, revenue procedures, and other government documents
11 (Foreign Income, Nonresident Aliens, Foreign Tax Credit)	In addition to foreign tax coverage, includes Tax Treaty information
18 (IRS Procedural Rules, Practice Rules, Definitions)	In addition to coverage of administrative and procedural matters, includes: • Listing of official forms and publications by number and subject • List of IRS personnel • Tax Court Rules • Summaries of expired or repealed Code provisions, including citations of cases and rulings handed down under those provisions
19 (New Matters)	Current developments: • Legislative Status Table • CCH Tax Focus and Features • CCH Comments • Topic Index to 2005 Developments • Cumulative Index to 2005 Developments • 2005 Finding Lists • 2005 Case Table • Recent IRBs • Treasury Decision Preambles • Select PLR and TAM digests • Select Tax Court decision digests
Code Volume 1	• Complete, official text of income tax provisions of the Internal Revenue Code of 1986, §1–§1000 • Source Notes—Finding Lists (current Code sections can be traced back to the 1939 Code)
Code Volume 2	• Complete, official text of the remainder of the income tax provisions (§1001 to the end of the Code); including the estate, gift, and generation-skipping transfer tax provisions; employment and excise tax provisions; and procedure provisions

	• Related statutes—texts of laws that affect federal taxation but do not appear in the Code and non-codified provisions • 1939 Code Amendments—shows amendments to the 1939 Code made since enactment of the 1954 Code
Index	• Main Topical Index—Index for the Compilations • Tax Calendars • Tax Rate Tables • Withholding Tables • Special Tables (*e.g.*, Depreciation Rate Tables, Annuity Tables, Savings Bond Tables, Per Diem Rate Tables) • Checklists (*e.g.*, Form 1040 Checklist, Checklist for Medical Expenses, Checklist for Tax Elections) • Definitions of Tax Terms
Citator Volume A–M	Lists the cases in which the taxpayers' surnames or business or organization names begin with the letters A through M and cross-references them to the Compilations based on paragraph number

Citator Volume N–Z	• Lists the cases in which the taxpayers' surnames or business or organization names begin with the letters N through Z and cross-references them to the Compilations based on paragraph number
	• Finding Lists with cross-references to the Compilations based on paragraph number for;
	  ◦ Revenue Rulings
	  ◦ Revenue Procedures
	  ◦ Treasury Decisions
	  ◦ Other IRS and Treasury Department Documents
	  ◦ Committee Reports

USTC Advance Sheets	• Preambles to proposed regulations • Opinions issued by courts other than the Tax Court

RIA's United States Tax Reporter. The Research Institute of America (RIA) publishes the United States Tax Reporter. The series is composed of 21 loose-leaf volumes and devoted exclusively to income tax. In its volumes, the United States Tax Reporter includes a substantial amount of information including:

- Internal Revenue Code, with changes and amendments
- Treasury regulations, with amendments
- Summaries of judicial opinions on income tax issues
- Revenue rulings, revenue procedures, and other items published in the Cumulative Bulletin
- RIA's explanations of various rules

Specifically, the series includes two volumes that contain the current Internal Revenue Code and amendment notes beginning in 1954. Twenty-one of the volumes contain a discussion of the tax law (compilations). Within these volumes, the Code is arranged in numerical order. First, the Code section is presented, followed by portions of relevant Committee Reports, applicable regulations, RIA's explanation of the Code provision, and annotations of decisions and rulings. Preambles to proposed amendments to the regulations are located in Volume 18.

The spine of each volume indicates which Code section and RIA paragraph reference numbers and keyword topics are contained in the volume. Within the volumes, paragraph numbers are keyed to the Code section. To find the Code section of interest, the paragraph number is determined by adding a zero to the end of the Code section. To find a related committee report, add a "1" to the Code section. For final and temporary regulations, add a "2"; for proposed regulations, add a "3". For editorial explanations, add a "4" and for annotations, add a "5".

Example:

The following is an example of the lead paragraphs for section 102:

Code section	¶ 1020
Committee Reports	¶ 1021
Final and Temporary Regulations	¶ 1022
Proposed Regulations	¶ 1023
Explanation	¶ 1024
Annotations	¶ 1025

Practice Note:

Explanations in the text include:[2]

Caution: A caution is used to notify subscribers of tax consequences that may not be apparent, and where appropriate, to indicate what should be done.

Observation: Observations provide helpful insight and analysis beyond reporting cited material. Observations are used specifically in order to:

- Expand a court's holding beyond a particular case's facts (i.e., derive a principle of law from the court decision);

- Point out the interrelationship between legal rules (e.g., indicating the consequences under the code section (if any) that will result if a taxpayer follows the procedures being explained under the current code section);

- Point out the practical effects of a decision or ruling, if the effect is not obvious from the rule or the explanation;

- Point out uncertainty or ambiguity of a rule of law or scope of a decision; and

- Critique a case holding (by explaining why the decision isn't supported by or is in conflict with existing legal authority).

Tax Tip: Tax Tips are used to provide taxpayers with the means to achieve a desired tax result, to obtain a tax refund, to comply with a legal rule, or avoid a potential problem.

Example: Examples are used to show the actual operation of a rule discussed in an explanation.

Information that is not directly related to a Code section, but related to the subject matter, is found in paragraphs ending with a "6" or "7". To find information on a repealed Code section, add an "8" to the end of the Code section. If RIA provides an explanation that addresses a number of related Code sections, it will be located immediately before the first Code section of the related group and be followed by a "9".

---

2. UNITED STATES REPORTER (RIA), How to Use United States Reporter, Vol. 1, p. 2.

Example:

- Information on tax claims in bankruptcy proceedings is located after the material on section 6872 (suspension of limitations on making assessments in bankruptcy proceedings) and is given the paragraph number ¶ 68,726.
- Information on repealed section 453C is found at ¶ 453C8.

Most tax research will begin in the volume containing the relevant Code section.

For example, the researcher could simply turn to the Code section of interest. However, if the researcher is unsure which Code section to consider, he could use the main topical index to locate paragraph references to places in the compilation volumes that discuss the matter of interest. The main index lists topics alphabetically. Each topic is followed by a reference to one or more paragraph numbers. The Supplemental Index covers matter added to the Reporter, but not yet included in the Main Index.

Or, if the researcher is basing his research on a case or ruling, the researcher could locate the case or ruling in the finding lists located in the Main and Supplementary Tables of Cases or Main and Supplementary Table of Rulings, respectively, and find paragraph references to the compilation volumes where the case or ruling is discussed. If research is based on a case, the Current Table of Cases should be consulted first, then the Supplementary Table of Cases. The Current Table and the Supplementary Table list cases that have been added to the service since the last revision of the Main Table of Cases, as well as cases and court proceedings not yet reflected in the body of the service. If the case is not listed in the Current Table or Supplementary Table, the Main Table should be consulted.

The Supplementary Table of Rulings also carries a reference to the paragraph in the IRS Rulings section of Volume 16 where the full text of the current year's rulings, procedures, notices and announcements can be found.

Research is not complete before checking Volume 16, where weekly updates of current developments are located. The updates contain cross-references to the most recent cases and ruling digests during the few weeks after initial reporting but before annotation of the compilation volumes. It also contains cross-references to Bulletin articles and full-text rulings.

Volume 16 also includes a New Legislation Status Table that lists the progress of reported and introduced tax bills authored by Committee Chairman as they go through the legislative process.

The "Weekly Alert" is maintained in a separate volume. It provides reporting and analysis articles and digests on recent court cases and rulings, new and proposed legislation, regulations, and other tax-related developments. It includes a "Practice Alert" column featuring planning articles and practice aids prepared by experts in their field and a "Washington Alert" column written by the Washington Bureau Director, providing an insider's view and analysis of what's happening in Washington, D.C.

Chart 10.2 Summary of Information Contained in RIA's United States Tax Reporter

Volume	Contents
1 (Index)	• Supplementary Index • Main Index • Glossary

2 (Tables)	• Tax-related tables, including:
	  ○ Withholding Tables
	  ○ Tax Tables for Individuals
	  ○ Tax Tables for Estates and Trusts
	  ○ Tax Tables for Corporations
	  ○ Estate & Gift Tax Rates
	  ○ Excise Tax Rates
	  ○ Tables Reflecting the Factors Used by the IRS to Compute Interest on Tax Deficiencies
	  ○ Daily Compounding Interest Tables
	  ○ Applicable Federal Rates
	  ○ Per Diem Allowance Tables
	• It also includes the following finding list tables:
	  ○ Current Table of Cases
	  ○ Supplementary Table of Cases
	  ○ Main Table of Cases
	  ○ Supplementary Table of Rulings
	  ○ Main Table of Rulings

3–15A (Compilations)	• For each income tax Code section:
	  ○ Code section
	  ○ Select Committee Reports
	  ○ Treasury regulations, including final, temporary, and proposed regulations
	  ○ RIA's explanation
	  ○ Digest of related court opinions, revenue rulings, revenue procedures, and other court documents

16 (Recent Developments)	• Cross-Reference Table • Current Rulings of Internal Revenue Service • Cross-Reference Table New Legislation Status Table • Cross-Reference Table List of IRS Publications • List of Irregularly Numbered Regulations • List of Regulations Under Redesignated Code Sections • Numerical List of Forms • Alphabetical List of Forms
17 and 17A (AFTR2d Decisions Advance Sheets)	Advance Sheets — full text of court opinions, except the Tax Court, relating to federal income taxes for the current year
18 (Federal Tax Regulations)	• Finding list of preambles to proposed amendments to tax regulations • Preamble to proposed regulations
Code Volume 1	• Code Topic Index • Table of Code Sections • Code sections 1 through 1000
Code Volume 2	• Table of Code Sections • Code sections 1001 through the end of the Code

2. Research through Treatises Organized by Topic

RIA, Mertens, and Bureau of National Research (BNA) offer treatises that are organized by topic. To begin researching in RIA, Mertens, or BNA, the researcher could simply locate the volume that contains the topic of interest.

RIA Federal Tax Coordinator 2d. In addition to the United States Tax Reporter, RIA also publishes a treatise organized by topic. The treatise divides tax into the areas of income, gift, estate, and excise tax and organizes them into separate chapters identified by tabs. Each chapter discusses a particular subject matter or transaction. The analysis may include a discussion of the Code, regulations, legislative history, or important cases. If there has been a change in the law, the analysis will discuss the law prior to and after the change. Also included in the analysis are practice notes, such as the following:

Observations: For professional analysis or commentary that is not part of cited authorities.

Caution: To warn of dangers that arise in particular tax situations and, where appropriate, to indicate what should be done.

Recommendation: To provide specific, carefully studied guides to action which will keep taxes at a legal minimum.

Illustrations: To clarify the tax rules and problems discussed, with simple easy-to-follow illustrations.

Illustration: For examples derived from official sources, with footnote citations to the authorities.

All relevant Code and regulations considered in the Volume are included after the analysis section, behind the blue tab marked *Code & Regs*.

The coordinator has 39 volumes (some Volumes are labeled with a number and an "A" or "B"). Volumes 4 through 26 address substantive provisions, while the remaining volumes contain indexes:

- Topic Index
- Findings Tables
  - Code
  - Regulations
- Findings Tables (cont.)
  - Cases
  - Rulings & Releases

To begin research, the researcher could simply locate the volume that contains the topic of interest. The spine of each volume indicates the topics covered in the volume. Each volume is further subdivided by a tab card. After each tab card is a table of topics, the Broad Reference Table, that divides the subject matter covered by the chapter into major topics and provides a cross-reference to paragraph numbers. The Broad Reference Table is followed by the Detailed Reference Table, which further subdivides the topics listed in the Broad Reference Table and also contains a cross-reference to paragraph numbers in the analysis section that discusses that topic. After the Detailed Reference Table, the Topics

Treated Elsewhere section provides a cross-reference to topics that are treated at a different location in the Tax Coordinator.

If the researcher is unsure which volume includes the relevant topic, the correct volume could be located by using the Topic Index. The Topic Index provides a topical listing of topics covered in the volumes. In the Topic Index Volume is both a Current Topic Index and a Main Topic Index. The Current Topic Index includes material issued after the publication of the Main Topic Index.

Alternatively, if the researcher knows the relevant Code or regulation provision, ruling, or court decision, he could locate the relevant topic through the Finding tables. It includes the following:

- Internal Revenue Code Finding Table (Volume 1)
- Regulations and Treasury Decisions Finding Tables (Volume 2)
- Rulings and Releases Finding Table (Volume 2)
- Cases and Decisions Finding Table (Volume 2)

The Finding tables provide a cross-reference to the volume and paragraph numbers that discuss the Code section, regulation, ruling, or case.

RIA Tax Coordinator 2d also provides a method to enter the volumes based on the problem under consideration. Volume 3 contains a Tax-Savings Opportunities Checklist. The Checklist contains a number of transactions intended to be used as planning tools. Under the paragraph number, RIA gives an overview of applicable rules relevant to the transaction. It also sets forth planning advice and tax tips for taking advantage of the rules while avoiding pitfalls. Through a series of questions, it points out the aspects that the researcher should know about the transaction, describes the action to be taken, and cross-references to the paragraph that provides an explanation of the transaction.

The Current Legislation Table (in Volume 3) lists each tax bill that has been reported to Congress in the current session. It includes a brief description of the bill, its status, and a cross-reference to paragraph number.

The treatise is kept up to date weekly with new or replacement pages, eliminating the need for a new development section. In addition, the "Federal Taxes Weekly Alert" sets forth the important tax developments for the week covered and special analyses and recommendations for tax-wise action in handling specific tax problems. It also provides a cross-reference to relevant discussions in the Federal Tax Coordinator 2d. The Alerts are maintained in a separate volume.

Chart 10.3 Summary of Information Contained in RIA's Federal Tax Coordinator 2d

Volume	Contents
Topic Index	Topic Index: • Current Topic Index • Main Topic Index
1	Finding Tables: • Code Index • Regulations Index
2	Finding Tables (cont.): • Cases Index • Rulings and Releases Index

3	Practice Aids: • Sample Client Letters • Tax Saving Opportunities Checklists • Tax Calendars • Rates and Tax Tables • Daily Compound Interest Tables • Tax Return Form Tables and Features Current Legislation Table
4–26 (Compilations)	• Subject matter volumes
20	All income, gift, and estate tax treaties currently in effect between the U.S. and foreign countries
27 and 27A	Proposed Regulations
28	Current Internal Revenue Bulletins (older IRBs are kept in "transfer binders")

BNA Tax Management Portfolio Series. BNA has prepared over 300 portfolios, authored by prominent attorneys or accountants. They are organized into three series:

- U.S. Income Series

- Estates, Gifts and Trusts Series

- Foreign Income Series

Within each Series are portfolios covering a myriad of topics. Each portfolio is divided into three sections. The first section, Detailed Analysis, offers a detailed analysis of the topic; the pages are indexed with an "A". The Detailed Analysis might include any of the following: planning opportunities, alternative approaches, probable IRS positions, pertinent Code provisions, IRS rulings and procedures, tax cases on point and conflicting cases, and pitfalls to avoid.

The second section, Working Papers, includes relevant forms, documents, and other background tools; the pages are indexed with a "B". The Working Papers might include any of the following: procedural checklists, IRS forms and documents, suggested resolutions and forms of contract, forms for state and local use, sample plans and clauses, and related IRS information.

The last section, the Bibliography and Reference section, includes a comprehensive list of documents useful to practitioners in conducting research; the pages are indexed with a "C". The Bibliography and Reference section might include: statutes and regulations; Congressional committee reports; cases cited in the Detailed Analysis section; IRS rulings and procedures; tax articles in professional journals; and agreements, conventions and treaties.

Practice Note:

BNA Portfolios are often a favored research source of practitioners due to the substantial number of Working Papers included in each portfolio.

To begin research, the researcher could simply locate the portfolio that contains the topic of interest. If the researcher is unsure which portfolio includes the relevant topic, the correct portfolio could be located by using the Portfolio Index Binder. The Binder provides a topical and numerical listing of all the portfolios.

Example:

The following is an example of the Numerical Finding List:

NUMERICAL FINDING LIST

66-4th	Real Estate Mortgages
184-4th	Transactions in Stock, Securities and Other Financial Instruments
186	Financial Instruments: Special Rules
188	Taxation of Equity Derivatives
290-2nd	Charitable Contributions by Corporations
320-2nd	International Pension Planning
350	Plan Selection—Pension and Profit-Sharing Plans
351-4th	Plan Qualification—Pension and Profit-Sharing Plans
352-3rd	Specialized Qualified Plans—Cash Balance, Target, Age-Weighted and Hybrids
353-3rd	Employee Benefits for Small and Mid-Sized Employers
354-7th	ESOPs
355-5th	IRAs, SEPs and SIMPLEs
356-3rd	Nondiscrimination Testing and Permitted Disparity in Qualified Retirement Plans
357-3rd	Pension Plan Terminations—Single Employer Plans
358-3rd	Cash or Deferred Arrangements
359-4th	Multiemployer Plans—Special Rules
360-3rd	Qualified Plans—IRS Determination Letter Procedures
361-4th	Reporting and Disclosure Under ERISA
362-2nd	Securities Law Aspects of Employee Benefit Plans
363-3rd	Age, Sex and Disability Discrimination in Employee Benefit Plans
365-2nd	ERISA — Fiduciary Responsibility and Prohibited Transactions
366	State Taxation of Compensation and Benefits
370-3rd	Qualified Plans—Taxation of Distributions
371-4th	Employee Plans—Deductions, Contributions and Funding
372-2nd	Church and Governmental Plans
373-2nd	Employee Benefits for Tax-Exempt Organizations
374-2nd	Plan Disqualification and ERISA Litigation
375	EPCRS — Plan Correction and Disqualification
378-2nd	Estate and Gift Tax Issues for Employee Benefit Plans
381-2nd	Statutory Stock Options
383-3rd	Nonstatutory Stock Options
384-3rd	Restricted Property—Section 83
385-4th	Deferred Compensation Arrangements
386-3rd	Compensating Employees with Insurance
388-5th	Tax-Deferred Annuities—Section 403(b)
389-4th	Medical Plans: COBRA, HIPAA, HRAs, HSAs and Disability
390-3rd	Reasonable Compensation
391-3rd	Employment Status—Employee v. Independent Contractor
392-5th	Withholding, Social Security and Unemployment Taxes on Compensation
393-2nd	Accounting for Pensions and Deferred Compensation
394-4th	Employee Fringe Benefits
395-2nd	VEBAs and Other Self-Insured Arrangements
396	Golden Parachutes
397-3rd	Cafeteria Plans
398	Reductions in Force
399	Employee Benefits for the Contingent Workforce
501-2nd	Gross Income: Overview and Conceptual Aspects
502-2nd	Gross Income: Tax Benefit, Claim of Right and Assignment of Income
503-2nd	Deductions: Overview and Conceptual Aspects
504-2nd	Deduction Limitations: General
505-2nd	Trade or Business Expenses and For-Profit Activity Deductions
506-2nd	Tax Credits: Concepts and Calculation
507-2nd	Income Tax Liability: Concepts and Calculation
515-2nd	Divorce and Separation
517-2nd	Scholarships and Educational Expenses
519-2nd	Travel and Transportation Expenses — Deduction and Recordkeeping Requirements
520	Entertainment, Meals, Gifts and Lodging — Deduction and Recordkeeping Requirements
521-2nd	Charitable Contributions: Income Tax Aspects
522-2nd	Tax Aspects of Settlements and Judgments
523-2nd	Deductibility of Legal and Accounting Fees, Bribes and Illegal Payments
525-2nd	State, Local, and Federal Taxes
527-2nd	Loss Deductions
530-3rd	Depreciation: General Concepts; Non-ACRS Rules
531-2nd	Depreciation: MACRS and ACRS
533-2nd	Amortization of Intangibles
534-2nd	Start-Up Expenditures
535	Time Value of Money: OID and Imputed Interest
536-2nd	Interest Expense Deductions
538-2nd	Bad Debts
539-2nd	Net Operating Losses—Concepts and Computations
540-2nd	Discharge of Indebtedness, Bankruptcy and Insolvency
541-3rd	Tax Aspects of Restructuring Financially Troubled Businesses
543	The Mark-to-Market Rules of Section 475
545	Equipment Lease Characterization
546	Annuities, Life Insurance, and Long-Term Care Insurance Products
547-2nd	Home Office, Vacation Home, and Home Rental Deductions
549-2nd	Passive Loss Rules
550-2nd	At-Risk Rules
554-3rd	The Attribution Rules
556	Research and Development Expenditures
557	Tax Planning for the Development and Licensing of Patents and Know-How
558	Tax Planning for the Development and Licensing of Copyrights, Computer Software, Trademarks and Franchises
559-2nd	**Tax Aspects of Franchising**
560	Income Tax Basis: Overview and Conceptual Aspects
561-2nd	Capital Assets
563-2nd	Depreciation Recapture—Sections 1245 and 1250
564	Related Party Transactions
565-2nd	Installment Sales
567-3rd	Taxfree Exchanges Under Section 1031
568-3rd	Involuntary Conversions
570-2nd	Accounting Methods—General Principles
572-2nd	Accounting Methods—Adoption and Changes
574	Accounting Periods
575	Accounting for Long-Term Contracts
576-2nd	Uniform Capitalization Rules: Inventory; Self-Constructed Assets; Real Estate
577-2nd	Uniform Capitalization Rules: Special Topics; Method Change Rules
578-2nd	Inventories: General Principles; LIFO Method
581	Estimated Tax
583	Income Tax Credits: The Investment Credit
584	Rehabilitation Tax Credit and Low-Income Housing Tax Credit
587	Noncorporate Alternative Minimum Tax
590-2nd	**Taxation of Real Estate Transactions—An Overview**
591	Real Estate Transactions by Tax-Exempt Entities

8-29-05

The researcher could also access the correct portfolio by using the Key Word Index. Each Series has its own index, with an alphabetical key word listing that cross-references the key words to a specific page in a specific portfolio. Page numbers after the colon starting with "A" refer to the Detailed Analysis sections. Those numbers after the colon beginning with "C&A" refer to the Changes & Analysis of New Developments Sections. A number appearing to the right of a bold-faced heading indicates the main portfolio on point.

Example:

The following is an example of the Key Word Index:

MAILING OF RETURNS
See FILING REQUIREMENTS; TIMELY MAILED/TIMELY FILED RULE
Registered or certified mail. *See* REGISTERED OR CERTIFIED MAIL

MAINTENANCE EXPENSES
See REPAIRS

MALPRACTICE
ERISA preemption, 374:A-63, C&A:A-64

MANAGEMENT FEES
Private equity funds, 735:A-23
Production of income expense deduction, 523:A-9, A-22

MANDATORY RETIREMENT
Age discrimination, 363:A-14, A-19 et seq.
Sex discrimination, 363:A-29

MANUFACTURED HOMES
See HOMES

MANUFACTURERS
Inventory valuation, 578:A-23
LIFO inventory. *See* LAST-IN, FIRST-OUT (LIFO) INVENTORY METHOD
Long term contracts. *See* LONG TERM CONTRACTS
Percentage of completion method of accounting, 576:A-42
Start-up expenditures, 534:A-12
Uniform capitalization rules. *See* UNIFORM CAPITALIZATION RULES

MARITAL DEDUCTION (ESTATE TAX)
See also TAX MANAGEMENT EGT PORTFOLIOS INDEX
Family partnership interests, 722:A-20(4)
Franchise transfers, 559:A-48
IRA distributions, 378:A-28
QTIP, repeal of §2056(b)(7) upon repeal of estate tax, 700:C&A:A-59
Qualified plan distributions, 378:A-28

MARITAL DEDUCTION TRUSTS
Credit shelter trusts, coordination with, 378:A-30, A-61
Pre-retirement estate planning, 378:A-59, C&A:A-60

MARK-TO-MARKET RULES
Main discussion, 543
Affiliated groups of corporations. *See* Consolidated group members, *this heading*
Amortizable bond premium, 543:A-8
Application of §475, 543:A-7
Bad debts, 543:A-9
Change of accounting method, 543:A-23
—Automatic change, 543:A-24; 572:A-60
—Enactment of §475, at time of, 543:A-23
—§481 adjustments, 543:A-12, C&A:A-13
—Request for consent
——Mandatory change, 543:A-24
——Nondealer, becoming, 543:A-24, C&A:A-53
—Statutorily mandated change, 543:A-24; 572:A-66
—Voluntary election allowed, 543:A-24
Character of gain or loss, 543:A-39
—Capital asset treatment, 543:A-39
—Commodities dealers, 543:A-51
—Net earnings from self-employment, 543:A-4
—Ordinary income treatment, 543:A-39, A-51
Commodities dealers and traders, 543:A-51
—"Commodity," 543:A-51
—Dealer election to be treated as securities dealer, 543:A-14, A-51; 561:A-101
—Derivatives dealers, 543:A-52; 561:A-101
—Election procedure, 543:A-52, C&A:A-53
—Ordinary income treatment, 543:A-51
—Traders' election, 543:A-14, A-52
Consolidated group members, 756:A-39
—Hedging transactions, 543:A-36, A-47
—Notional principal contract transfers, 543:A-46

—Related parties, dealer status, 543:A-15
—Returns, 543:A-45
—State taxes, 543:A-65
—Transfers of securities among, 543:A-45
Constructive ownership transactions. *See* CONSTRUCTIVE OWNERSHIP TRANSACTIONS, §1260
Constructive sales treatment, §1259, 186:A-35; 543:A-5
Coordination of §475 with other IRC provisions, 543:A-7
Dealers. *See* Securities dealers, *this heading*
Debt instruments, 543:A-8
—Exception of instruments issued by taxpayer, 543:A-29
—Integrated hedges of, 543:A-37
Derivatives
—Commodities derivative financial instrument held by commodities derivatives dealer, 543:A-52; 561:A-101
—Definition of derivative securities, 543:A-27
—Securities not held for investment status, 543:A-34
Exceptions from §475, 543:A-33 et seq.
Extension of time to make election, 543:C&A:A-13
Foreign securities dealers, 543:A-63
§481 accounting adjustment, 543:A-12, C&A:A-13
Global dealing regs., 543:A-59 et seq.
Hedging transactions
—Consolidated group members, 543:A-36, A-47
—Exceptions from §475, 184:A-38(8); 543:A-39
—"Hedge," 543:A-4, A-28, A-35
—Integration of debt instruments, 543:A-37
—Items not marked-to-market, securities hedging, 543:A-39
"Held for investment" securities. *See* Securities "held for investment," *this heading*
Identification of exempt securities, 543:A-43
—Improper identification, 543:A-44
Legislative history, 543:A-1, A-3
Market discount bonds, 543:A-8
Nondealer, becoming, 543:A-24, C&A:A-25
Nonfinancial customer paper exception, 543:A-4, A-19
—"Nonfinancial customer paper," 543:A-20
—Prior law, 543:A-18
Notional principal contracts, 570:A-28
—Consolidated group members, transfers among, 543:A-46
—Securities not deemed held for investment, 543:A-34
OID, 543:A-8
Passive activities, 549:C&A:A-73; 590:C&A:A-101
PFICs, 700:A-15
Pre-§475 rules, 543:A-3
Recognition before realization rules, 543:A-7
Regulated futures contracts, 184:A-8
REMICs
—Exceptions to securities definition, 543:A-30
—Resulting interests, 543:A-35
RICs, PFIC-related transactions, 740:A-64
Securities
—"Core" securities, 543:A-27
—Customer paper exception. *See* Nonfinancial customer paper exception, *this heading*
—Definition, 543:A-3, A-27
—Derivatives. *See* Derivatives, *this heading*
—Exceptions, 543:A-29
—FASITs, 741:A-66(2)
—Hedging transactions. *See* Hedging transactions, *this heading*
—"Held for investment" securities. *See* Securities "held for investment," *this heading*
—Not held for investment securities, 543:A-34
—Notional principal contracts. *See* Notional principal contracts, *this heading*
—*Per se* rule, securities deemed "held for investment," 543:A-33
—REMIC residual interest exceptions, 543:A-30
—§1032 securities exception, 543:A-30
—§1256 contract exception, 543:A-29

Securities dealers, 570:A-27; 578:A-35
—Accounting method change. *See* Change of accounting method, *this heading*
—Consolidated groups. *See* Consolidated group members, *this heading*
—"Customer paper" exception, prior law. *See* Nonfinancial customer paper exception, *this heading*
—Dealer-customer relationship, 543:A-11
—"Dealer in securities," 543:A-11
—Disposition of securities, 543:A-10
—Foreign dealers, 543:A-63
—Life insurance companies and products exception, 543:A-20
—Negligible sales exception, 543:A-16
—"Once a dealer, always a dealer," 543:A-20
—Opting out of exception to dealer status, 543:A-24
—Related parties, 543:A-15
—Voluntary election allowed, 543:A-14
Securities held for investment
—Capital loss treatment for securities identified by dealer as, 543:A-39
—Definition, 543:A-33
—Identification requirements, 543:A-43
——§1236 and §475 interplay, 543:A-44
Securities traders, 535:A-12, A-14
Securitization transactions, 543:A-35
State taxes, 543:A-65
Straddles, 184:A-38(6)
Substituted basis, 543:A-7
Traders, 535:A-12, A-14
§1256 contracts, 543:A-29
—Hedging transactions exception, 184:A-38(7)
Valuation rules, 543:A-55

MARKET DISCOUNT BONDS
See also ORIGINAL ISSUE DISCOUNT (OID)
Main discussion, 535
In general, 535:A-132(6); 536:A-112
Accrual of, 535:A-136 et seq.
Amount of discount, 535:A-134
Basis
—Adjustments to, 560:A-75
—Gain on disposition of, 560:A-75
Change of accounting method, 572:A-61
Current inclusion of interest income, 536:A-112
Deductibility of interest, 535:A-142; 536:A-112
Deferral of interest deduction, 535:A-142
Definition, 536:A-112
Dispositions of, 535:A-141
Elections, 535:A-140
—Revocation of, 535:C&A:A-140
Excluded debt instruments, 535:A-135
Mark-to-market rules, 543:A-8
"Market discount," 535:A-134
Mortgage-backed security certificate holders, 741:A-120
Nonrecognition transactions, 535:A-141; 772:A-59
Options, 535:A-135
Partnerships, contributions to, 711:A-32
REITs, 742:A-27
RICs, 740:A-12, A-73
Transfers to controlled corporations, 758:A-11; 759:A-37
Unrealized receivables of partnerships, §751 property, 720:A-60, A-66

MARKET SEGMENT SPECIALIZATION PROGRAM AUDITS
See now EXAMINATION SPECIALIZATION (ES) PROGRAM

MARKING TO MARKET
See MARK-TO-MARKET RULES

MARRIAGE PENALTY
2001 EGTRRA changes, 503:A-25
2003 JGTRRA changes, 503:C&A:A-25; 507:A-9
2004 WFTRA changes, 507:A-9

For latest developments, always check the Changes and Analysis of New Developments and the Table of Contents in front of each portfolio.

Alternatively, the Code Section Index could be used; it cross-references Code provisions to all portfolios by portfolio number and topic in which that Code section is discussed. Entries below the Code section are arranged alphabetically according to the titles of the portfolio. Each portfolio title is followed by an indicator of the Service (*e.g.*, U.S. Income (US), Foreign Income (F), or Estates, Gifts, and Trusts (EGT)) and the portfolio's number. An asterisk (*) preceding a portfolio title refers to the main portfolio(s) on point.

Example:

The following is an example of the Code section Index:

§995
63

INTERNAL REVENUE CODE SECTION — MASTER INDEX

§961 - ADJUSTMENTS TO BASIS OF STOCK IN CONTROLLED FOREIGN CORPORATIONS AND OF OTHER PROPERTY
Aliens Who Invest in the United States Through a Low-Cost Jurisdiction (F), 944
Controlled Foreign Corporations – Section 956 (F), 929
Foreign Corporation Earnings and Profits (F), 932
Income Tax Basis: Overview and Conceptual Aspects (US), 560
Subpart F – General (F), 926
* Subpart F – Sections 959-964, 1248 and Related Provisions (F), 930

§962 - ELECTION BY INDIVIDUALS TO BE SUBJECT TO TAX AT CORPORATE RATES
* Indirect Foreign Tax Credit (F), 902
Subpart F – General (F), 926
* Subpart F – Sections 959-964, 1248 and Related Provisions (F), 930

§963 - RECEIPT OF MINIMUM DISTRIBUTIONS BY DOMESTIC CORPORATIONS *(REPEALED)*
Subpart F – General (F), 926

§964 - MISCELLANEOUS PROVISIONS
CFCs -- Foreign Personal Holding Company Income (F), 927
Controlled Foreign Corporations – Section 956 (F), 929
* Foreign Corporation Earnings and Profits (F), 932
Other Transfers Under Section 367 (F), 920
Subpart F – General (F), 926
* Subpart F – Sections 959-964, 1248 and Related Provisions (F), 930
Tax Aspects of Foreign Currency (F), 921

§965 - TEMPORARY DIVIDENDS RECEIVED DEDUCTION
Foundations of U.S. International Taxation (F), 900
Subpart F -- General (F), 926
Taxation of Regulated Investment Companies (US), 740

§970 - REDUCTION OF SUBPART F INCOME OF EXPORT TRADE CORPORATIONS
Subpart F – Sections 959-964, 1248 and Related Provisions (F), 930
U.S. Income Taxation of Foreign Corporations (F), 908

§971(c) - EXPORT TRADE ASSETS
Controlled Foreign Corporations – Section 956 (F), 929

§982 - ADMISSIBILITY OF DOCUMENTATION MAINTAINED IN FOREIGN COUNTRIES
* Compelled Production of Documents and Testimony in Tax Examinations (US), 633
Foreign Corporation Earnings and Profits (F), 932
Income Tax Treaties – Administrative and Competent Authority Aspects (F), 940
Tax Crimes (US), 636
Transfer Pricing: Judicial Strategy and Outcomes (F), 888
* Transfer Pricing: Records and Information (F), 891
U.S. Income Taxation of Foreign Corporations (F), 908
U.S. Income Taxation of Nonresident Alien Individuals (F), 907

§985 - FUNCTIONAL CURRENCY
Capital Assets (US), 561
CFCs – Foreign Base Company Income (Other Than FPHCI) (F), 928
CFCs -- Foreign Personal Holding Company Income (F), 927
* Foreign Corporation Earnings and Profits (F), 932
Foreign Tax Credit Limitation – Section 904 (F), 904
Foundations of U.S. International Taxation (F), 900
Other Transfers Under Section 367 (F), 920
Outbound Transfers Under Section 367(a) (F), 919
Subpart F – Sections 959-964, 1248 and Related Provisions (F), 930
* Tax Aspects of Foreign Currency (F), 921
U.S. Income Taxation of Foreign Corporations (F), 908

§986 - DETERMINATION OF FOREIGN TAXES AND FOREIGN CORPORATION'S EARNINGS AND PROFITS
* Foreign Corporation Earnings and Profits (F), 932
Indirect Foreign Tax Credit (F), 902
Other Transfers Under Section 367 (F), 920
Subpart F – Sections 959-964, 1248 and Related Provisions (F), 930
* Tax Aspects of Foreign Currency (F), 921
U.S. Income Taxation of Citizens and Residents Abroad (F), 918
U.S. Income Taxation of Foreign Corporations (F), 908

§987 - BRANCH TRANSACTIONS
Foundations of U.S. International Taxation (F), 900
Outbound Transfers Under Section 367(a) (F), 919
* Tax Aspects of Foreign Currency (F), 921
U.S. Income Taxation of Foreign Corporations (F), 908

§988 - TREATMENT OF CERTAIN FOREIGN CURRENCY TRANSACTIONS
Capital Assets (US), 561
CFCs – Foreign Base Company Income (Other Than FPHCI) (F), 928
CFCs – Foreign Personal Holding Company Income (F), 927
Foreign Corporation Earnings and Profits (F), 932
Foreign Tax Credit Limitation – Section 904 (F), 904
Foundations of U.S. International Taxation (F), 900
Interest Expense Deductions (US), 536
* Tax Aspects of Foreign Currency (F), 921
Transactions in Stock, Securities and Other Financial Instruments (US), 184
U.S. Income Taxation of Foreign Corporations (F), 908
U.S. Tax-Related Accounting Issues of Multinational Corporations (F), 948

§989 - OTHER DEFINITIONS AND SPECIAL RULES
CFCs – Foreign Base Company Income (Other Than FPHCI) (F), 928
Foreign Corporation Earnings and Profits (F), 932
Passive Foreign Investment Companies – Sections 1291-1297 (F), 923
Subpart F – Sections 959-964, 1248 and Related Provisions (F), 930
* Tax Aspects of Foreign Currency (F), 921
U.S. Income Taxation of Foreign Corporations (F), 908

§991 - TAXATION OF A DOMESTIC INTERNATIONAL SALES CORPORATION
Deductions: Overview and Conceptual Aspects (US), 503
Foreign Sales Corporations (F), 934
Gross Income: Overview and Conceptual Aspects (US), 501
S Corporations: Operations (US), 731
U.S. Income Taxation of Foreign Corporations (F), 908

§992 - REQUIREMENTS OF A DOMESTIC INTERNATIONAL SALES CORPORATION
Deduction Limitations: General (US), 504
Foreign Sales Corporations (F), 934
U.S. Income Taxation of Foreign Corporations (F), 908

§993 - DEFINITIONS
Allocation and Apportionment of Expenses – Regs. §1.861-8 (F), 906
Mineral Properties Other Than Gas and Oil – Operation (US), 603
Tax Credits: Concepts and Calculation (US), 506
U.S. Income Taxation of Foreign Corporations (F), 908

§995 - TAXATION OF DISC INCOME TO SHAREHOLDERS
Foreign Sales Corporations (F), 934
S Corporations: Operations (US), 731
Source of Income Rules (F), 905
U.S. Income Taxation of Foreign Corporations (F), 908

For latest developments, always check the **Changes and Analysis of New Developments** and the **Table of Contents** in front of each portfolio.

Finally, the IRS Forms Index gives a numerical listing (form number, then title) of all IRS forms in the portfolios and an alphabetical listing (by title and publication number) of all IRS publications in the portfolios.

The portfolios are kept up to date with Changes and Analysis of New Developments sheets. The updates are inserted directly into the front of the Detailed Analysis section.

Practice Note:

The BNA Tax Management Portfolio Index offers the following "Ten Tips for Thorough, Effective Tax Research":[3]

1. To Find Topics or Code Sections discussed, look in your Portfolio Index Binder under the Portfolio Classification Guide, Code Section Index or Key Word Index.

2. For a Summary of a Portfolio, read the Portfolio Description Sheet at the front of the Portfolio.

3. For an Outline of Discussion in a Portfolio and page references to topics, check the Table of Contents at the front of the Portfolio.

4. For a List of the Working Papers in a Portfolio, look at the Item Description Sheet at the beginning of the Working Papers section.

5. For a Summary of Problems and Solutions in a Portfolio, read the Portfolio Description Sheet at the front of the Portfolio.

6. For Rulings and Other Sources, check the Bibliography and References section at the back of the Portfolio.

7. For the Latest Developments in an area covered by a Portfolio, look at the Changes and Analyses pages inserted in the front of the Portfolio, and also the indexes of the Weekly Reports.

8. For a Specific IRS Form or publication, look in the IRS Forms Index, located in the Portfolio Index Binder.

9. For Further Research or Comment on an issue, look in the Memorandum Index in the Master Binder. It will point you to discussions in the biweekly Memorandum.

10. To Find Any Unofficial Comment, check the Memorandum's "Washington Items" Index in the Master Binder.

Mertens Law of Federal Income Taxation. Mertens has a 24 Volume series covering income tax provisions. Volumes 1 through 15 address income tax issues, while the remaining volumes contain the following:

- Index Volume
- Tables Volumes
- Tables of Cases Volume
- Current Developments and Status Table
- Regulation Preambles (1986–1995)
- Regulation Preambles
- Proposed Regulation Preambles (1986–1995)
- Proposed Regulation Preambles
- Current Material

Mertens also provides a volume containing the revenue rulings and revenue procedures.

---

3. BNA Tax Management Portfolio Index, What Is It—How to Use The Portfolio Index, p. 9.

Practice Note:

Mertens has a reputation for providing thorough and in-depth coverage of tax topics.

To begin research, the researcher could simply locate the volume that contains the topic of interest. If the researcher is unsure which volume includes the relevant topic, the correct volume could be located by using the Index Volume. The Index Volume provides a topical listing of topics covered in the volumes.

Example:

The following is an example of the Topical Index:

INDEX

CORPORATIONS—Cont'd
Bonds—Cont'd
   original issue discount—Cont'd
      example, **38:61, 38:66**
   premiums
      generally, **38:62, 38:67**
      election, **38:65, 38:70, 38:71**
      example, **38:63, 38:68**
      reorganizations, **38:75, 38:80**
      repurchase, **38:71, 38:76, 38:77**
   property exchanges, **38:74, 38:79**
   refinancing, cancellation of debt,
      11:13
   reorganizations, **38:75, 38:80**
   repurchase
      generally, **38:70, 38:75**
      cancellation of debt, **11:12**
      premium deductions, **38:71,**
         38:76, 38:77
   retirement, **38:70, 38:75**
   sale of business, **38:76, 38:81**
   serial maturity, **38:69, 38:74**
Books and records
   attorney's possession, **55A:36**
   production of, **55A:37**
Building and loan associations,
   38:105
Business activity, separate entity
   treatment
   generally, **38:12**
   factors determining, **38:13**
Buy/sell agreements
   generally, **38B:45**
   obligations of corporation, **38B:48**
   shareholders as conduit for,
      38B:49
Callable bonds, **38:67, 38:72**
Cancellation of debt, gifts, **7:18**
Cancelled debt, capital contributions,
   38:38, 38:40
Capital contributions
   after incorporation, **38:35, 38:36**
   basis of property received
      generally, **38:36, 38:37**
      nonshareholders, prior law,
         38:39
   benefits exchanged for, **38:25**

CORPORATIONS—Cont'd
Capital contributions—Cont'd
   cancelled debt, **11:27, 38:38,**
      38:40
   cash, nonshareholders, **38:37,**
      38:38
   construction funds
      generally, **38:33**
      prior law, **38:34, 38:35**
   debt cancellations, **11:27, 38:38,**
      38:40
   donative intent, **38:29**
   equity increased by, **38:26**
   examples, **38:30**
   government subsidies as
      generally, **38:31**
      income treatment, **38:32, 38:33**
   initiation fees as, **38:25**
   membership fees as, **38:25**
   money, nonshareholders, **38:37,**
      38:38
   nonshareholders
      basis, prior law, **38:39**
      cash, **38:37, 38:38**
      prior law, **38:31**
   paying installments with, **15:11**
   postincorporation, **38:35, 38:36**
   profit rights, effect of, **38:27**
   property for stock, **38:23**
   restrictions on, **38:28**
   Section 118, **38:22**
   Section 1032, **38:23**
   voluntary, **38:29**
   what are, **38:24**
Capital gains, **38:53, 38:56**
Carrybacks, capital gain rules, **22:83**
Carryovers
   NOLs
      generally, **38:52, 38:55**
      prior law, **38:102**
   tax attributes, **38:48, 38:50**
Cash contributions, nonshareholders,
   38:37, 38:38
Cash method accounting, **12A:04**
Charitable contributions
   accrual method, **31:119**
   appraisal requirement, **31:53**

Alternatively, if the researcher knows the relevant Code or regulation provision, he could locate the relevant topic through the Code or regulations references. These references are located in the Tables Volume.

Example:

The following is an example of the Code section Index:

INTERNAL REVENUE CODE

IRC	Section	IRC	Section
46(c)(6)(B)	7:219	47(d)(2)(B)	32B:27
46(c)(7)	23A:187, 32A:02, 32A:105	47(d)(3)(A)	32B:27
46(c)(8)	32A:02	47(d)(3)(B)	32B:27
46(c)(8)(A)	24B:03, 32A:02, 32A:121	47(d)(3)(C)(i)	32B:27
		47(d)(3)(C)(ii)	32B:27
46(c)(8)(C)	32A:02	47(d)(3)(D)	32B:27
46(c)(8)(D)(iv)	24B:23	47(d)(3)(E)	32B:27
46(c)(8)(D)(v)	24B:23	47(d)(3)(F)	32B:27
46(d)(1)	32A:120	47(d)(4)	32B:27
46(e)(3)(B)	25:68	47(d)(5)	32B:27
46(f)(5)	23A:99	48	24C:41, 32A:121, 40:23
47	32A:17, 32A:81.50, 32B:04, 35:144.30, 41B:162, 41B:201, 42:07, 47A:68	48(a)	23A:128, 32A:25, 32A:26, 32A:47
47(a)	32B:04, 32B:05, 32B:22, 47A:68	48(a)(1)	23A:99, 25:107, 32A:25, 32A:26
47(a)(1)	38B:84	48(a)(1)(A)	32A:104
47(b)	41B:254	48(a)(1)(B)	32A:104
47(b)(1)	32B:27	48(a)(1)(B)(ii)	32A:104
47(b)(2)	43:147	48(a)(1)(B)(iii)	32A:104
47(c)(1)(A)	32B:04, 32B:09, 32B:17	48(a)(1)(C)	32A:104
47(c)(1)(A)(i)	32B:09	48(a)(1)(E)	32B:29
47(c)(1)(A)(ii)	32B:09	48(a)(2)	32A:26
47(c)(1)(A)(iii)	32B:09, 32B:16	48(a)(2)(B)	32A:25
47(c)(1)(A)(iv)	32B:09	48(a)(2)(B)(v)	23:83
47(c)(1)(B)	32B:04, 32B:09, 32B:19	48(a)(2)(B)(x)	45E:165
47(c)(1)(C)(i)	32B:10, 32B:11	48(a)(2)(C)	32A:27
47(c)(1)(C)(ii)	32B:10, 32B:13	48(a)(3)	32A:25, 32A:28
47(c)(2)(A)	32B:04, 32B:09, 32B:23	48(a)(4)(A)	32A:25, 32A:27
47(c)(2)(A)(i)	32B:22	48(a)(4)(C)	32A:27
47(c)(2)(A)(ii)	32B:22	48(a)(8)	23A:183, 23A:187, 23A:188, 23A:198, 32A:110
47(c)(2)(B)	32B:04, 32B:35	48(a)(9)	23A:79, 32A:107
47(c)(2)(B)(i)	32B:35	48(a)(10)	23A:99
47(c)(2)(B)(iv)	32B:29	48(a)(10)(A)	23A:99
47(c)(2)(B)(v)	32B:33, 32B:39	48(a)(10)(B)	23A:99
47(c)(2)(B)(vi)	32B:33, 32B:38	48(a)(10)(B)(i)	23A:99
47(c)(2)(C)	32B:29	48(a)(10)(B)(ii)	23A:99
47(c)(3)(A)	28:140	48(a)(10)(B)(iii)	23A:99
47(d)(1)	32B:27	48(a)(10)(B)(iv)(I) – (V)	23A:99
47(d)(2)(A)	32B:27	48(a)(10)(B)(iv)(V)	23A:99
		48(a)(10)(B)(v)	23A:99
		48(a)(10)(B)(vi)	23A:99
		48(b)	23:135

© West, a Thomson business Pub. 8/2003 (MTR)   IRC-13

Similarly, if the researcher knows a relevant case, he could locate the discussion of the case through the Table of Cases in the Table of Cases Volume. The researcher should first check the main Table of Contents listing, then the Supplement.

Example:

The following is an example of the Table of Cases:

LAW OF FEDERAL INCOME TAXATION

v. Swent, 155 F2d 513 (CA4 1946) — § 45:23

v. Swift, 54 F2d 746 — §§ 15:19, 15:36

v. Swift & Co. Employees' Benefit Ass'n, 151 F2d 625 (CA7 1945) — § 44A:38

v. Tax-Penn Oil Co., 300 US 481, 81 L Ed 755, 57 S Ct 569 (1937) — § 28:148

v. Tellier, 383 US 687, 16 L Ed 2d 185, 86 S Ct 1118 (1966) — §§ 24A:26, 24A:38, 25:16, 25:78, 25A:08, 25A:14, 25A:18, 25H:68, 28:143

v. Tennessee Co., 111 F2d 678 (CA3 1940) — § 40:44

v. Tenney, 120 F2d 421 (CCA1 1941) — §§ 5:43, 5:47, 17:27

v. Terre Haute, Indianapolis & Eastern Traction Co., 24 BTA 197 — § 23A:116

v. Terry, 69 F2d 969 (CA5 1934) — § 19:06

v. Tew, 108 F2d 570 (CCA6, 1940) — §§ 20:02, 20:05

v. Texas Pipe Line Co., 87 F2d 662 (CCA3, 1937) — §§ 25E:02, 25E:04

v. Thatcher & Son, 76 F2d 900 (CA2 1935) — § 25:15

v. Thomas, 261 F2d 643 (CA1, 1958) — §§ 55B:16, 55B:43

v. Thompson, 222 F2d 893 (CA3, 1955) — §§ 55B:02, 55B:14

v. Thomson, 311 US 527, 85 L Ed 319, 61 S Ct 373 (1941) — § 22:70

v. Tillotson Mfg. Co., 76 F2d 189 (CCA6 1935) — § 5:24

v. Timken, 141 F2d 625 (CA6 1944) — §§ 10:02, 10:13, 10:24, 12:53

v. Timken, Estate of, 141 F2d 625 (CCA6 1944) — § 5:18

v. Timmer, 78 F2d 599 (CCA6 1935) — §§ 42A:02, 60:16

v. Titus Oil & Inv. Co., 132 F2d 969 (CCA10 1943) — § 24:133

v. Tower, 327 US 280, 90 L Ed 670, 66 S Ct 532 (1946) — §§ 5:39, 5:49, 35A:07, 38A:19.50

v. T.R. Miller Mill Co., 102 F2d 599 (CCA5 1939) — §§ 26:15, 26:16, 26:28, 26:29

v. Transport M&E Co., 478 F2d 831 (CA8 1983) — § 50:235

v. Transport Manufacturing & Equipment Co., 478 F2d 731 (CA8 1973) — §§ 45I:06, 50:244

v. Transport Trading & Terminal Corp., 176 F2d 570, 49–2 USTC ¶ 9337 (CA2 1949) — §§ 38B:02, 38B:70

v. Treganowan, 183 F2d 288 (CA2 1950) — §§ 25:121, 25H:38, 25H:40, 38A:27

v. Trust of Neustadt, 131 F2d 528 (CCA2 1942) — §§ 43:27, 43:104, 43:113

v. Tufts, 461 US 300, 75 L Ed 2d 863, 103 S Ct 1826 (1983) — §§ 11:10, 20:10, 22A:68, 28:130, 31:94, 31A:71, 35:93, 35:261, 35A:32, 35A:37, 35A:67, 43:154, 54:06, 54:11, 54:55, 54:56, 54:59, 54:64

v. Tufts, 651 F2d 1058 (CA5 1981) — § 22:58

v. Turner, 410 F2d 752 (CA6 1969) — § 22:109

v. Turney, 82 F2d 661 (CCA5 1936) — § 12A:119

v. Tuttle, 89 F2d 112 (CCA6 1937) — § 37:27

v. Tyler, 72 F2d 950 (CA3 1934) — § 10:29

v. Tyng, 106 F2d 55 (CCA2 1939) — §§ 22:90, 22:102, 43:12

v. Ullman, 30 BTA 764 — § 12A:153

v. Ullmann, 77 F2d 827 (CCA2 1935) — § 5:15

v. Union County Trust Co., 22 AFTR 1242 (D NJ 1938) — § 53:16

v. Union P. R. Co., 86 F2d 637 (CCA2 1936) — § 12:50

Table of Cases-204

Finally, if the researcher knows the relevant ruling, he could locate the relevant topic through the Rulings Table in the Tables Volume.

On a rotating basis, some chapters are rewritten. For those that are not, supplements with updated information are provided monthly and cumulative supplements are provided semiannually and located at the beginning of the relevant chapter. Mertens also publishes monthly a Developments and Highlights newsletter; the newsletters are contained in the Current Materials volume.

3. Research through Topic-Specific Treatises

Some publishers offer treatises that cover specific topics within the realm of tax. For example, the treatises may cover only corporate tax or the taxation of employee benefits. These treatises are extremely helpful for more in-depth research into the covered subject matter area. Often times, they may offer planning opportunities, information about completing relevant forms, and alerts to traps for the unwary.

The following is a summary of some of the subject matter treatises offered:

Treatise	Author(s)	Publisher
Charitable Gifts	Colliton, Gingiss	Thomson Reuters RIA (WGL)
Estate Planning and Wealth Preservation: Strategies & Solutions	Henkel	Thomson Reuters RIA (WGL)
Federal & State Taxation of Limited Liability Companies	Cartano	CCH, Inc.
Federal Estate and Gift Taxation	Stephens, Maxfield, Lind, Calfee, Smith	Thomson Reuters RIA (WGL)
Federal Income Taxation of Corporations & Shareholders	Bittker, Eustice	Thomson Reuters RIA (WGL)
Federal Income Taxation of Corporations Filing Consolidated Returns	Dubroff, Blanchard, Broadbent, Duvall	LexisNexis (Matthew Bender)
Federal Income Taxation of Individuals	Bittker, McMahon, Zelenak	Thomson Reuters RIA (WGL)
Federal Income Taxation of Intellectual Properties & Intangible Assets	Kittle-Kamp, Postlewaite, Cameron	Thomson Reuters RIA (WGL)
Federal Income Taxation of Inventories	Schneider	LexisNexis (Matthew Bender)
Federal Income Taxation of Passive Activities	Carnevale, Harrington, Sutton	Thomson Reuters RIA (WGL)
Federal Income Taxation of Real Estate	Robinson	Thomson Reuters RIA (WGL)
Federal Income Taxation of S Corporations	Eustice, Kuntz	Thomson Reuters RIA (WGL)
Federal Tax Collections, Liens & Levies	Elliott	Thomson Reuters RIA (WGL)

Federal Taxation of Financial Instruments & Transactions	Keyes	Thomson Reuters RIA (WGL)
Federal Taxation of Income, Estates & Gifts	Bittker, Lokken	Thomson Reuters RIA (WGL)
Federal Taxation of Partnerships & Partners	McKee, Nelson, Whitmire, Whitmire, Huffman	Thomson Reuters RIA (WGL)
Federal Taxes Affecting Real Estate	Glynn	LexisNexis (Matthew Bender)
IRS Practice & Procedure	Saltzman, Book	Thomson Reuters RIA (WGL)
Limited Liability Companies: Tax and Business Law	Bishop, Kleinberger	Thomson Reuters RIA (WGL)
Litigation of Federal Civil Tax Controversies	Kafka, Cavanagh	Thomson Reuters RIA (WGL)
Partnership Taxation	Postlewaite, Pennel, Willis	Thomson Reuters (WGL)
State Taxation	Hellerstein, Hellerstein	Thomson Reuters RIA (WGL)
Subchapter S Taxation	Christian, Grant	Thomson Reuters RIA (WGL)
Tax Planning for Corporations and Shareholders	Cavitch, Cavitch	LexisNexis (Matthew Bender)
Taxation of Exempt Organizations	Hill, Mancino	Thomas Reuters RIA (WGL)
Taxation of Regulated Investment Companies & Their Shareholders	Johnston, Brown	Thomson Retuers (WGL)
U.S. International Taxation	Kuntz, Peroni	Thomson Reuters RIA (WGL)

4. Research through Electronic Media

LexisNexis. Research can be conducted through **LexisNexis**'s subscription service.

Practice Note:

The LexisNexis electronic research website can be found at www.lexis.com.

The LexisNexis database can be utilized in three distinct ways. First, the database can be searched based on a word search. From the tabs on the top of the screen, click on "Search." Then, select the appropriate folder, either the appropriate court or area of law (usually "Taxation") or other appropriate folder.

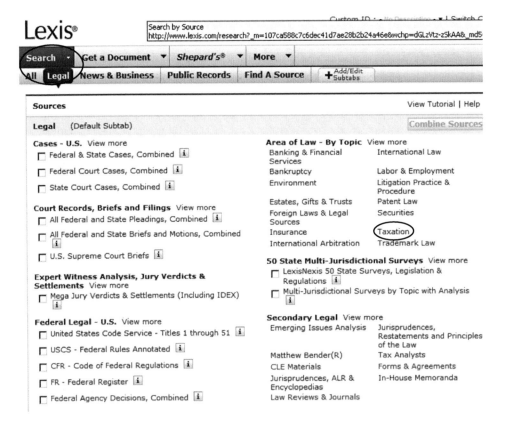

Copyright 2006 LexisNexis, a division of Reed Elsevier Inc. All Rights Reserved. LexisNexis and the Knowledge Burst logo are registered trademarks of Reed Elsevier Properties Inc. and are used with the permission of LexisNexis.

If the folder "Taxation" is selected, a new screen appears, giving additional options to further refine the folder in which the researcher can conduct the research.

Copyright 2006 LexisNexis, a division of Reed Elsevier Inc. All Rights Reserved. LexisNexis and the Knowledge Burst logo are registered trademarks of Reed Elsevier Properties Inc. and are used with the permission of LexisNexis.

Further selection can be made, further refining the search, until the correct file is located. Finally, a search can be conducted based on a word search.

The following is a list of common tax documents and the file in which they are located in LexisNexis:

To Find:	Select the Area of Law as: Taxation, then
Tax Court Memorandum Opinions	US Tax Court Memorandum Decisions
Tax Court Opinions	US Tax Court Cases
Tax Court Summary Opinions	US Tax Court Summary Opinions
District Court Opinions	US District Court Tax Cases
Revenue Rulings	Administrative Materials & Regulations IRS Cumulative Bulletin and Internal Revenue Bulletin

Revenue Procedures	ᐧᐧ Administrative Materials & Regulations ᐧᐧ IRS Cumulative Bulletin and Internal Revenue Bulletin
Private Letter Rulings	ᐧᐧ Administrative Materials & Regulations ᐧᐧ IRS Private Letter Rulings and Technical Advice Memoranda
Technical Advice Memoranda	ᐧᐧ Administrative Materials & Regulations ᐧᐧ IRS Private Letter Rulings and Technical Advice Memoranda
Service Center Advice	ᐧᐧ Administrative Materials & Regulations ᐧᐧ Federal ᐧᐧ Agency Decisions ᐧᐧ Service Center Advice
Actions on Decision	ᐧᐧ Administrative Materials & Regulations ᐧᐧ IRS General Counsel Memos, Actions on Decisions & Technical Memos
Litigation Guideline Memoranda	ᐧᐧ Administrative Materials & Regulation ᐧᐧ Federal ᐧᐧ Agency Decisions ᐧᐧ Litigation Guideline Memoranda
General Counsel Memoranda	ᐧᐧ Administrative Materials & Regulations ᐧᐧ IRS General Counsel Memos, Actions on Decisions & Technical Memos
Technical Memoranda	ᐧᐧ Administrative Materials & Regulations ᐧᐧ IRS General Counsel Memos, Actions on Decisions & Technical Memoranda
Field Service Advice	ᐧᐧ Administrative Materials & Regulations ᐧᐧ Federal ᐧᐧ Agency Decisions ᐧᐧ IRS Field Service Advice Memorandums
Criminal Tax Bulletins	ᐧᐧ Administrative Materials & Regulations ᐧᐧ Federal ᐧᐧ Agency Publications ᐧᐧ Criminal Tax Bulletin
General Litigation Bulletins	ᐧᐧ Administrative Materials & Regulations ᐧᐧ Federal ᐧᐧ Agency Publications ᐧᐧ General Litigation Bulletin
Tax Litigation Bulletins	ᐧᐧ Administrative Materials & Regulations ᐧᐧ Federal ᐧᐧ Agency Publications ᐧᐧ Tax Litigation Bulletin
IRS Disclosure Litigation	ᐧᐧ Administrative Materials & Regulations Bulletins ᐧᐧ Federal ᐧᐧ Agency Publications ᐧᐧ IRS Disclosure Litigation Bulletin

Second, if the researcher has the citation of a relevant document, he can retrieve the full text of that document through the "Get a Document" function. Any of the following types of documents could be retrieved this way:

- Announcement
- General Counsel Memorandum
- Notice
- Private Letter Ruling
- Revenue Procedure
- Revenue Ruling
- Technical Advice Memo
- Technical Memo

Once the document is located, documents containing similar language patterns to the selected document can be found by using the "More Like Selected Text" button. Cases containing the same headnote as the selected case can be found by using the "More Like Headnote" button. Other cases or law review articles that discuss the selected case can be located by clicking on the Shepard's Signal indicator.

WestLaw. Research can be conducted through West's **WestLaw** subscription service.

> **Practice Note:**
>
> The WestLaw electronic research website can be found at www.westlaw.com.

Tax research can be conducted in a variety of fashions in WestLaw. The most common means is through a word search in one of WestLaw's many databases. If the researcher knows the name of the database in which he wishes to search, he can simply type the database identifier in the "Search for a databases" text box and click "go." If the researcher is unsure of the name of the database, he can click on "View Westlaw Directory."

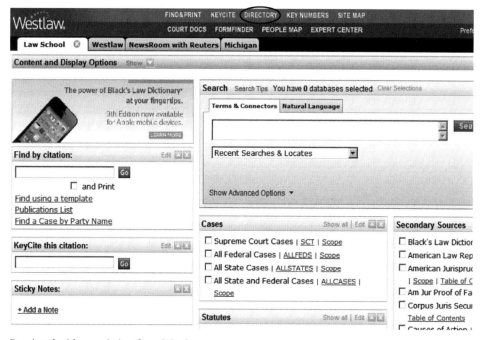

Reprinted with permission from WestLaw.

For convenience, the researcher may want to add the Tax Tab. Once added, simply clicking on the tab bill take the researcher to WestLaw's tax database. Within the Taxation database there are several tax topics to select from. Once the appropriate folder is chosen, a word search can be conducted using one of two word search methods—Natural Language or Terms and Connectors.

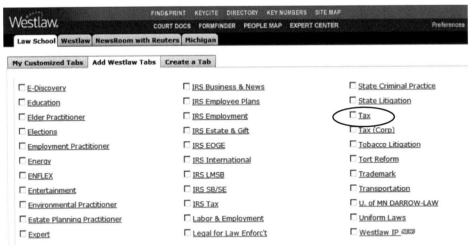

Reprinted with permission from WestLaw.

If the researcher knows the citation to the document that he is searching for, the document can be accessed directly through the "Find" function. Documents can be accessed through the "Find" function without entering a database. The researcher can simply type the citation in the "Find this document by citation" textbox in the left hand corner of the screen and click "go."

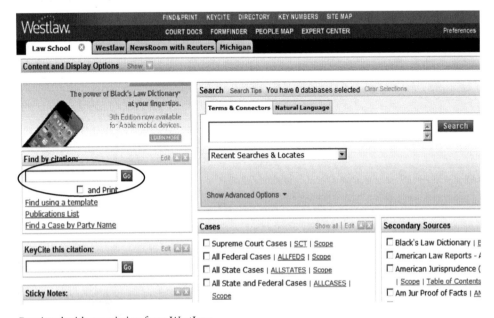

Reprinted with permission from WestLaw.

The following is a list of common tax documents and the file in which they are located in WestLaw:

To Find:	Select the Area of Law as: Taxation, then
Tax Court Memorandum Opinions	✲ Federal Tax Materials—Cases, IRC, Regs, IRS Materials-complete list ✲ Federal Taxation—Tax Court Cases
Tax Court Opinions	✲ Federal Tax Materials—Cases, IRC, Regs, IRS Materials-complete list ✲ Federal Taxation—Tax Court Cases
Tax Court Summary Opinions	✲ Federal Tax Materials—Cases, IRC, Regs, IRS Materials-complete list ✲ Federal Taxation—Tax Court Cases
District Court Opinions	✲ Federal Tax Materials—Cases, IRC, Regs, IRS Materials-complete list ✲ Federal Tax Cases—Other Databases ✲ District Courts
Revenue Rulings	✲ Federal Tax Materials—Cases, IRC, Regs, IRS Materials-complete list ✲ Revenue Rulings
Revenue Procedures	✲ Federal Tax Materials—Cases, IRC, Regs, IRS Materials-complete list ✲ Revenue Procedures
Private Letter Rulings	✲ Federal Tax Materials—Cases, IRC, Regs, IRS Materials-complete list ✲ IRS Releases—Other Databases ✲ IRS Private Letter Rulings and Technical Advice Memoranda
Technical Advice Memoranda	✲ Federal Tax Materials—Cases, IRC, Regs, IRS Materials-complete list ✲ IRS Releases—Other Databases ✲ IRS Private Letter Rulings and Technical Advice Memoranda
Service Center Advice	✲ Federal Tax Materials—Cases, IRC, Regs, IRS Materials-complete list ✲ IRS Releases—Other Databases ✲ IRS Service Center Advice
Actions on Decision	✲ Federal Tax Materials—Cases, IRC, Regs, IRS Materials-complete list ✲ IRS Releases—Other Databases ✲ Actions on Decisions & Technical Memos
Litigation Guideline Memoranda	✲ Federal Tax Materials—Cases, IRC, Regs, IRS Materials-complete list ✲ IRS Releases—Other Databases ✲ IRS Litigation Guideline Memoranda
General Counsel Memoranda	✲ Federal Tax Materials—Cases, IRC, Regs, IRS Materials-complete list ✲ IRS Releases—Other Databases ✲ General Counsel Memoranda

Technical Memoranda	✧ Federal Tax Materials—Cases, IRC, Regs, IRS Materials-complete list ✧ IRS Releases—Other Databases ✧ Technical Memoranda
Field Service Advice	✧ Federal Tax Materials—Cases, IRC, Regs, IRS Materials-complete list ✧ IRS Releases—Other Databases ✧ IRS Field Service Advice
Criminal Tax Bulletins	✧ Federal Tax Materials—Cases, IRC, Regs, IRS Materials-complete list ✧ IRS Releases—Other Databases ✧ IRS Litigation Bulletins
General Litigation Bulletins	✧ Federal Tax Materials—Cases, IRC, Regs, IRS Materials-complete list ✧ IRS Releases—Other Databases ✧ IRS Litigation Bulletins
Tax Litigation Bulletins	✧ Federal Tax Materials—Cases, IRC, Regs, IRS Materials-complete list ✧ IRS Releases—Other Databases ✧ IRS Litigation Bulletins
IRS Disclosure Litigation Bulletins	✧ Federal Tax Materials—Cases, IRC, Regs, IRS Materials-complete list ✧ IRS Releases—Other Databases ✧ IRS Litigation Bulletins

RIA's Checkpoint. Research can be conducted through **RIA's Checkpoint** subscription service. The database can be searched with a key word search. Select a Practice Area, then enter a key word search. RIA has pre-designed search templates to search for specific types of tax information.

RIA Checkpoint also has a Table of Contents feature. The researcher can browse through Checkpoint's contents in the same way he would scan the headings in a book's table of contents. The Table of Contents can be expanded by opening folders and subfolders. The Table of Contents can also be searched. RIA Checkpoint also allows the researcher to view alphabetized indexes for some source sets.

Specific documents can be found through a citation search. Under the "Find by Citation" selection, the citation for the desired document can be inserted.

CCH's Tax Research NetWork. Research can be conducted through **CCH's Tax Research Network** subscription service. From the toolbar, research can be conducted by using the search function or by selecting a specific library. The service offers the following libraries:

- Accounting/Auditing
- Federal
- State
- Financial & Estate
- Special Entities
- Pension & Payroll
- International

- Perform Plus II
- ClientRelate
- Tools
- Training & Support

Research could also be conducted from the toolbar by locating a particular case by citation.

Other Sources. There are a number of other electronic sources, some through the internet and some by CD.

Many internet sites offer tax information free of charge. The following is a listing of some of those cites:

Information	Website
Code of Federal Regulations	www.gpoaccess.gov/cfr/index.html
Congressional Record	www.gpoaccess.gov/crecord.html
Constitution	• www.gpoaccess.gov/constitution/index.html
	• loc.gov/law/help/usconlaw/index.php
	• www.archives.gov/exhibits/charters/ constitution.html
Department of Justice, Tax Division	www.usdoj.gov/tax/
Federal Register	• www.gpoaccess.gov/fr/index.html
Federal Tax Code	• www.gpoaccess.gov/uscode/index.html
	• www.law.cornell.edu/uscode/26
Financial Accounting Standards Board	www.fasb.org
Government documents	www.irs.gov
House Ways and Means Committee Reports	www.waysandmeans.house.gov
Internal Revenue Bulletins	www.irs.gov
Internal Revenue Service	www.irs.gov
Joint Committee on Taxation	www.house.gov/jct
Legislation on Internet	thomas.loc.gov
Senate Finance Committee	www.finance.senate.gov
Social Security Administration	www.ssa.gov
Tax Court Opinions	www.ustaxcourt.gov
Tax Forms	www.irs.gov
Tax Regulations	www.irs.gov
U.S. House of Representatives	www.house.gov
U.S. Senate	www.senate.gov
U.S. Treasury Department	www.ustreas.gov
White House	www.whitehouse.gov

C. Main Points

Treatises:

- Commercial publishers publish treaties that can be used as research tools to locate authority or information regarding a topic or Code section.

- Treatises are organized either by Code section or by topic.

- Treatises can contain a substantial amount of information, including legislative history, treasury regulations, preambles, annotations, status of pending bills, etc.

Topic-Specific Treaties:

- Commercial publishers publish treaties on specific topics.

- Treatises on specific topics are excellent resources for more intricate or in-depth tax research.

Electronic Media:

- Commercial publishers provide electronic research tools.

- Some electronic research is through the internet.

- Some electronic research is through compact disk or CD-ROM.

D. Related Articles for Further Reading

- Thomas R. Keefe, *The Invisible Web: What You Can't See Might Hurt You*, Res. Advisor, May 2002, at 1.

- Mary Rumsey, *Runaway Train: Problems of Permanence, Accessibility, and Stability in the Use of Web Sources in Law Review Citations*, 94 Law Libr. J. 27 (2002).

- Gary W. White, *Internet Resources for Taxation: A Selective, Annotated Guide*, Legal Reference Services Q., Vol. 18(4), at 49 (2001).

- Gail Levin Richmond, *Federal Tax Locator: Basic Tax Library*, Community Tax L. Rep., Fall/Winter 2001, at 11.

- Robert C. Berring, *Legal Information and the Search for Cognitive Authority*, 88 Cal. L. Rev. 1673 (2000).

- Lisa Smith-Butler, *Cost Effective Legal Research*, Legal Reference Services Q., Vol. 18(2), at 61 (2000).

- Katherine T. Pratt, *Federal Tax Sources Recommended for Law School Libraries*, 8 Law Libr. J. 387 (1995).

- Carol A. Roehrenbeck & Gail Levin Richmond, *Three Researchers in Search of an Alcove: A Play in Six Acts*, 84 Law Libr. J. 13 (1992).

- Louis F. Lobenhofer, *Tax Law Libraries for Small and Medium-Sized Firms*, Prac. Tax Law., Fall 1988, at 17 and Winter 1989, at 31.

- Gail Levin Richmond, *Research Tools for Federal Taxation*, 2 Legal Reference Services Q., Spring 1982, at 25.

E. Problems

1. Treatises are organized by the following:

   a. Date the Code section was enacted or date the regulation was enacted.
   b. Court to issue the opinion or date opinion was issued.
   c. Code section or topic.
   d. Public law number or date Code section was enacted.

2. Which treatises are organized by topic?

   a. BNA's Tax Management Portfolios and CCH's Federal Standard Tax Reporter.
   b. CCH's Federal Standard Tax Reporter and Mertens.
   c. RIA's Federal Tax Coordinator and RIA's United States Reporter.
   d. RIA's Federal Tax Coordinator, BNA's Tax Management Portfolio and Mertens.

3. Which treatises are organized by Code section?

   a. BNA's Tax Management Portfolios and CCH's Federal Standard Tax Reporter.
   b. CCH's Federal Standard Tax Reporter and RIA's United States Reporter.
   c. RIA's Federal Tax Coordinator and RIA's United States Reporter.
   d. RIA's Federal Tax Coordinator, BNA's Tax Management Portfolio and Mertens.

4. Mr. James, your client, is interested in completing a section 355 tax-free spin off. He has come to you for advice on how to structure the transaction so that it will be tax free. He also wants you to advise him with respect to the preparation of all necessary documents. Of all the available treatises, which one would provide the most information in your quest to adequately advise Mr. James?

5. Mr. Sunnan has come to you with a proposed transaction. After listening to how he intends to structure the transaction, you have some concerns that it might be challenged by the government under one of the "substance over form" arguments. You tell Mr. Sunnan that you need to do some additional research before you can give him any advice. Which type of treatise would you use, one organized by Code section or one organized by topic? Look in one organized by Code section and one organized by topic. How do the results you found compare? Which one was easier to search?

6. Ms. White has come to you with a statutory notice of deficiency. She has asked you to prepare a petition to be filed in the Tax Court. Unfortunately, in your practice you have not yet had an opportunity to prepare a petition, but believe you could do so after some research. To understand what is required to be included in a petition, which type of research would you prefer, written sources or on-line? Conduct research using one written source and one on-line source. Which source was easier to search?

7. Mrs. Witherspoon is interested in investing in property that will generate the low income housing credit. She has asked you to advise her about what kind of property will qualify and what other requirements must be met to qualify for the credit. You tell Mrs. Witherspoon that you need to do some additional research before you can give her any advice.

   a. Which type of research would you prefer, written sources or on-line?
   b. Of the written sources, which type of treatise would you use, one organized by Code section or one organized by topic?

    c.   Conduct research using one on-line source and two written sources, one organized by Code section and one organized by topic. Of the three, which source was the easiest to use?

8. The managing partner in your law firm asks you for a brief description of each tax bill that has been reported to Congress during the current session. What treatise discussed in this chapter would be of the most assistance?

9. Your client plans to enter into a transaction that is identical to the facts described in PLR 9608006. You have read Chapter 7 of this book and realize that a taxpayer may not rely on a letter ruling issued to another taxpayer. As result you need to perform further research. How can PLR 9608006 assist you in finding more information on the transaction? Please take such steps and describe some of the information that you find.

10. You are researching a tax issue for a client and find a discussion in Mertens that is directly on point. The discussion in Mertens answers all of the tax issues you had identified. Are there any other steps that you should take before providing advice to your client?

Chapter 11

International Tax Research

International Tax Research

- *What resources are available on foreign tax law?*

- *What is the role of tax treaties in the U.S. tax system?*

- *Where can U.S. tax treaties be found?*

- *Where can U.S. international tax law be found?*

"Well Mr. Willenberg, what can we help you with today? You mentioned on the phone that you needed some tax advice," said Mr. Pittman, the senior tax partner, as he sat down behind his large mahogany desk.

"My family and I are vacationing in the United States and my wife and I thought it might be a good idea to get some tax advice from a U.S. tax attorney. I am going to receive a very large dividend from a U.S. company in May and I wanted to confirm that it will not be subject to taxation in the United States. I live in Germany and the dividend will be taxed in my home country. Since the dividend will be taxed in Germany it should not be subject to income tax in the U.S., right?" asked Mr. Willenberg in a powerful German accent.

"I'm sorry, but that is not the case. Normally there is a 30 percent U.S. withholding tax on dividends paid from a U.S. corporation to a nonresident." explained Mr. Pittman.

"What, that can't be right. Am I going to be taxed on that same dividend in Germany at a tax rate of well over 30 percent?" questioned Mr. Willenberg as he shifted nervously in his chair.

"It may not be as bad as it sounds," said Mr. Pittman in a calming voice. "I am pretty certain that the United States and Germany have entered into a tax treaty that should greatly reduce or potentially even eliminate the 30-percent U.S. withholding tax. We can confirm that the United States and Germany do have an income tax treaty and we can also check to see what rate of tax applies to dividends under the treaty."

Mr. Willenberg now looked a little more at ease. "Please do check into the treaty," he stated calmly.

Mr. Pittman stood up as he talked and started to examine the collection of books in his office. "We will get right on that. Also, Germany may have a foreign tax credit mechanism that allows you to take a tax credit on your German tax return for any income taxes incurred in a foreign country. We can do a quick check to see if Germany has a foreign tax credit mechanism; however, you are going to have to talk to a German attorney to get a detailed explanation."

"I am glad I stopped. I just assumed since the dividend was taxable in Germany that it would not be taxable in the United States," said Mr. Willenberg.

Contents

A. Key Terms

After completing this chapter, you should be familiar with the following key terms:

- ➤ Inbound Taxation
- ➤ Outbound Taxation
- ➤ Treaty
- ➤ U.S. Model Income Tax Treaty
- ➤ OECD Model Income Tax Treaty
- ➤ Treasury Technical Explanation

➤ Instruments of Ratification

➤ Competent Authority

➤ Last-in-time

B. Discussion

1. Overview of International Tax

The phrase "international tax" generally refers to the tax dilemma created when the owner of income and the source of such income reside in different countries. Every international tax matter potentially involves the taxing jurisdiction of at least two independent countries and requires a thorough analysis of the tax consequences in the country in which the taxpayer resides and the country where the income is generated. The obvious question is in which jurisdiction is the income taxable—in the country of the taxpayer's domicile, the country where the income was generated, or both. The answer may vary depending on the type of income and the countries involved.

The tax consequences in each country will depend on whether the two countries involved have a controlling tax treaty in place and the method by which each country exercises its income tax jurisdiction. Typically countries exercise income tax jurisdiction based either on the connection the taxpayer has to the country or the connection the income has to the country or both. The United States exercises its taxing jurisdiction based on both the connection the taxpayer has to the United States and the connection the income has to the United States. The United States taxes its citizens, residents, and domestic corporations based on their connection to the United States. United States citizens, residents, and domestic corporations are taxed in the United States on their worldwide income—whether derived from the United States or abroad. The United States tax system is commonly referred to as a worldwide income tax system. The United States taxes non-residents and foreign corporations based on connections between the non-resident's or foreign corporation's income and the United States. As a general matter, the United States taxes non-residents and foreign corporations only on their income from U.S. sources.

2. Specific Internal Revenue Code Provisions Dealing with International Taxation

The United States has enacted comprehensive Internal Revenue Code provisions that implement and elaborate on the U.S. international tax system. U.S. international tax law is generally contained in Subtitle A, Chapter 1, Subchapter N of the Code. The U.S. international Code provisions can be divided into two major subtopics, inbound international tax provisions and outbound international tax provisions. Inbound international tax provisions address the taxation by the United States of foreign persons and foreign corporations. Outbound international Code provisions address the taxation of U.S. citizens, residents, and domestic corporations on their income generated outside of the United States.

Someone is coming in from foreign country.

Inbound Taxation. The inbound Code provisions are covered in Subtitle A, Chapter 1, Subchapter N, Part II ("Nonresident Aliens and Foreign Corporations") of the Code (sections 871–898). The inbound provisions cover a broad range of topics, such as expatriation to avoid taxation (section 877), the imposition of tax on gross transportation income of nonresident aliens and foreign corporations (section 877) and the taxation of compensation of employees of foreign governments or international organizations (section 893). (A detailed discussion of all of the inbound international provisions is beyond the scope of this chapter and book.) Some of the major principles of U.S. inbound taxation are covered in sections 871–873 and 881–883. Generally, under such provisions foreign individuals and foreign corporations are only subject to taxation in the United States on U.S. source income. A 30-percent withholding tax is imposed on the U.S. source income of nonresident aliens that is derived from fixed or determinable annual or periodical gains, profits, or income (FDAP).

Practice Note:

The following types of income are examples of FDAP income:

➤ Interest
➤ Dividends
➤ Rents
➤ Salaries
➤ Wages
➤ Annuities
➤ Remunerations
➤ Premiums
➤ Scholarship and fellowship grants
➤ Other grants, prizes and awards
➤ Alimony

The 30-percent rate applies to the gross U.S. FDAP income (no deductions are allowed); however, the 30-percent flat withholding rate only applies to U.S. source income that is not effectively connected with a trade or business in the United States (effectively connected income or ECI). Effectively connected income is taxed, after allowable deductions, under the U.S. graduated tax rate system. Generally, income generated from a trade or business in the United States is considered effectively connected income.

Practice Note:

The following types of income are examples of income effectively connected with a trade or business in the United States:

➤ Income from a partnership that is engaged in a trade or business in the United States is usually considered to ECI.
➤ Income from personal services conducted in the United States is generally considered ECI.
➤ Business profits from the sale of products, services, or merchandise in the United States is normally considered ECI.
➤ Gains and losses from the sale or exchange of U.S. real property are taxed as if they were ECI.

Someone is doing business outside the USA.

Outbound Taxation. The outbound Code provisions are covered in Subtitle A, Chapter 1, Subchapter N, Part III ("Income from Sources Without the United States") (sections 871–898) U.S. citizens, residents, and domestic corporations are taxed in the United States on their worldwide income. Like the inbound Code provisions, the provisions addressing the foreign earned income of U.S. citizens and residents are complex and lengthy, covering a variety of international tax issues. (A detailed discussion of the outbound Code provisions are also beyond the scope of this chapter and book.) As a result, only a couple of the outbound tax issues will be touched on. Two of the main topics covered within the outbound provisions are the Foreign Tax Credit and "Subpart F."

Foreign Tax Credit (Sections 901–908). In order to mitigate the potential for double taxation on foreign source income, U.S. taxpayers are allowed a tax credit for income taxes paid in foreign countries ("direct foreign tax credit"). Domestic corporations may also receive additional foreign tax credits for taxes paid by a foreign subsidiary ("indirect foreign tax credit"). Domestic corporations receive indirect foreign taxes credits upon the receipt of dividends from a foreign subsidiary. Effectively, domestic corporations are treated as having paid the subsidiary's foreign income taxes related to the distributed earnings. The indirect foreign tax credit was implemented in order to reduce the risk of triple taxation (the foreign corporate level, the U.S corporate level, and the individual shareholder level). There is generally no threat of triple taxation to individuals that own foreign subsidiaries either directly or through non-taxable entities. Therefore, individuals are not eligible for indirect foreign tax credits.

Both the indirect and direct foreign tax credits are limited to the U.S. tax that would otherwise be imposed on the taxpayer's foreign source income. The limitation was put in place in order to prevent U.S. taxpayers from crediting foreign taxes in an amount in excess of the U.S. tax rate. However, the foreign tax credit limitation is applied on the aggregate of all of a taxpayer's foreign source income.

Subpart F. The separate legal existence of a foreign subsidiary corporation is respected for U.S. tax purposes. As a result, U.S. shareholders of foreign corporations are not generally taxed on such entity's income or earnings until such earnings are distributed to the U.S. shareholders as a dividend. However, under Subpart F of Subtitle A, Chapter 1, Subchapter N, Part III (commonly referred to as "subpart F") "U.S. shareholders" of "controlled foreign corporations" (CFC) are taxed on their share of passive-type income of the CFC at the time in which the income is earned by the CFC. Subpart F contains detailed explanations with respect to what type of income is subject to subpart F and also the definitions of CFC and U.S. shareholder.

Source rules. Subchapter N also contains detailed rules for determining whether income is generated from U.S. sources or foreign sources. Such determination is essential in assessing whether a non-resident alien is subject to U.S. taxation and also in determining the foreign tax credit implications to U.S. citizens, residents, and domestic corporations. The sourcing rules are contained in sections 861–865.

Within the IRS, the Office of Associate Chief Counsel (International) has jurisdiction over virtually all issues relating to the international provisions of the Code. The Office of Associate Chief Counsel (International) is divided into branches, with each branch assigned responsibility for specific international Code provisions.

**Chart 11.1 The Office of Associate Chief Counsel Organizational Chart
(excluding APA branches) Including Examples of Branch Responsibility**

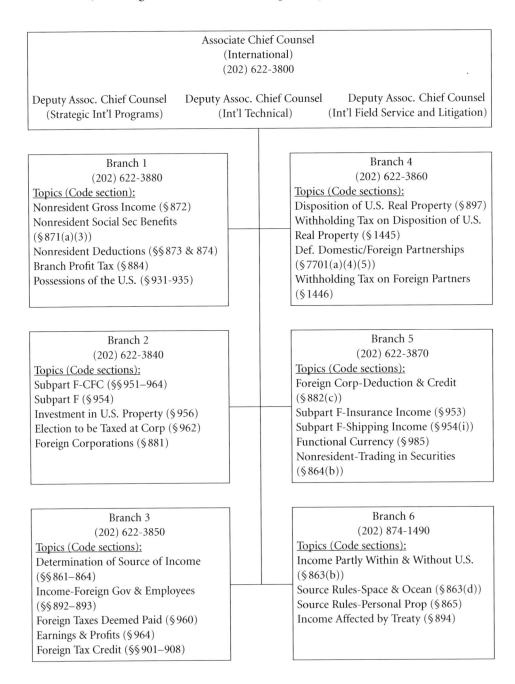

In addition to enacting comprehensive Code provisions covering international taxation, the United States has also entered into several tax treaties that may impact the U.S.
tax consequences of international income.

3. Treaties *or Conventions*
(Amendment to a treaty is called protocol)

A treaty is an international agreement or compact between two or more independent nations and governed by international law. Treaties come in two basic forms, bilateral and multilateral. Treaties between two countries are referred to as bilateral treaties, while treaties between more than two countries are referred to as multilateral treaties. Treaties are commonly referred to as "conventions" and may be supplemented or amended by a subsequent treaty, referred to as a "protocol."

Who makes the treaties from USA :–) The office of Tax Policy who also assists IRS and the most powerful authority in USA

a. Model Income Tax Treaties

No two U.S. income tax treaties are exactly identical. Variations among U.S. treaties "are necessary to address ... particular aspects of [a] treaty partner's tax law."[1] In some cases variations among U.S. treaties result from substantive concessions by either the United States or the treaty partner during treaty negotiations.

Notwithstanding the fact that no two U.S. treaties are exactly identical, there is a fairly high level of uniformity among all U.S. treaties. Such uniformity results from the fact that the United States and treaty partners generally base all of their treaties and treaty negotiations on a model treaty. The two key model treaties for U.S. international tax purposes are the **U.S. Model Income Tax Treaty** and the **Organisation for Economic Co-operation and Development ("OECD") Model Income Treaty**.

U.S. Model Income Tax Treaty. The Treasury Department published the first "United States Model Income Tax Convention" ("U.S. Model Treaty") in 1971. The second version of the United States Model treaty was published in 1996. The latest and third version was issued in 2006. The U.S. Model Treaty and its Technical Explanation are the starting point for all U.S treaties and treaty negotiations. However, the U.S. Model Treaty is not intended to serve as the ideal U.S. tax treaty. Instead it was adopted to assist in the negotiation process by helping negotiators identify differences in the treaty policy between the United States and the potential treaty partner.[2]

Research Tip:

The 1996 and 2006 U.S. Model Treatys and corresponding Technical explanations can be found on-line on both the Treasury Department website at www.treas.gov. and the IRS website at www.irs.gov.

OECD Model Income Tax Treaty. The OECD is an international organization of 30 member countries, including the United States, committed to democratic government and the market economy. One of the OECD's overriding goals is for its member countries to work together "to address the economic, social, environmental and governance challenges of the globalizing world economy[....]"[3] The OECD regularly produces publications, internationally agreed instruments, and recommendations to assist member and non-member countries in a global society.

---

1. Preamble to Treas. Technical Explanation, U.S. Model Income Tax Convention, (Sept. 20, 1996).
2. Id.
3. Organisation for Economic Co-operation and Development, Tax Treaties, available at http://www.oecd.org/topic/0,2686,en_2649_33747_1_1_1_1_37427,00.html.

Treaties do not impose or create tax. They only serve to limit the amount of tax that member countries

276   11 · INTERNATIONAL TAX RESEARCH

or taxpayers in member countries.

As mentioned above, the OECD has produced a model income tax treaty ("OECD Model Treaty"). The purpose of the OECD Model Treaty is the avoidance of double taxation. It accomplishes this goal by allocating taxing rights between the country in which the taxpayer resides ("resident country") and country where the income is generated ("source country"). Generally, under the OECD Model Treaty the burden is on the source country to eliminate double taxation in situations "where there are competing taxing rights."[4] The OECD has produced a detailed commentary to the OECD Model treaty that provides a thorough explanation of each provision of the OECD Model Tax Treaty.

The OECD Model Treaty and its commentary are considered the benchmark for treaty negotiations by most developed countries, including non-member countries. It is estimated that over 1,500 treaties world-wide are based on the OECD Model Treaty provisions and/or its principles.[5] The OECD Model Treaty is an ambulatory document in that it is regularly being updated as the global economy changes.

The U.S. Model Treaty is in part based on the OECD Model Treaty and its commentary. The Technical Explanation of the U.S. Model Treaty provides:

> [T]he publication of a U.S. Model does not represent a lack of support for the work of the OECD in developing and refining its Model treaty. To the contrary, the strong identity between the provisions of the OECD and U.S. Models reflects the fact that the United States drew heavily on the work of the OECD in the development of the U.S. Model.[6]

United Nations Model Tax Treaty. The United Nations has also published its own model income tax treaty titled "United Nations Model Double Taxation Convention Between Developed and Developing Countries". The United Nations model treaty is similar to the U.S. Model treaty and the OECD model treaty. However, it generally grants more taxation rights to the country that is the source of the income than either the OECD or U.S. Model treaties.

b. Specific Income Tax Treaties

Model treaties, such as the OECD and the U.S. Model treaties, are crafted to assist in the negotiation and development of specific bilateral tax treaties. A model treaty and its commentary may be helpful in interpreting a particular treaty; however, it is the specific treaty between the contracting parties that is binding and not a model treaty.

The United States currently has over 50 bilateral income tax treaties. Each individual U.S. income tax treaty will contain provisions negotiated and tailored to the particular issues and needs of the United States and the treaty partner. However, as mentioned earlier, U.S. income tax treaties generally have a great deal of similarities.

All U.S. income tax treaties attempt to mitigate the risk of double taxation. Generally the mitigation of double taxation is accomplished through specific articles that assign the primary right to tax income to the recipient's country of domicile rather than the country where the income was generated. Each treaty generally has articles covering the taxation of specific income items such as dividends, interest, and royalties.

---

4. Commentary to OECD Model Income Tax Convention, pmbl. (updated as of Sept. 8 2005).
5. Organisation for Economic Co-operation and Development, Tax Treaties, available at http://www.oecd.org/topic/0,2686,en_2649_33747_1_1_1_1_37427,00.html.
6. Preamble to Treas. Technical Explanation, U.S. Model Income Tax Convention, (Sept. 20, 1996).

Example:

> CONVENTION BETWEEN THE GOVERNMENT OF THE UNITED
> STATES OF AMERICA AND THE GOVERNMENT OF JAPAN FOR THE
> AVOIDANCE OF DOUBLE TAXATION AND THE PREVENTION OF
> FISCAL EVASION WITH RESPECT TO TAXES ON INCOME
>
> ARTICLE 10 [Dividends]
>
> 1. Dividends paid by a company which is a resident of a Contracting State to a resident of the other Contracting State may be taxed in that other Contracting State.
> 2. However, such dividends may also be taxed in the Contracting State of which the company paying the dividends is a resident and according to the laws of that Contracting State, but if the dividends are beneficially owned by a resident of the other Contracting State, except as provided in paragraphs 4 and 5, the tax so charged shall not exceed:
> (a) 5 percent of the gross amount of the dividends if the beneficial owner is a company that owns directly or indirectly, on the date on which entitlement to the dividends is determined, at least 10 percent of the voting stock of the company paying the dividends;
> (b) 10 percent of the gross amount of the dividends in all other cases. This paragraph shall not affect the taxation of the company in respect of the profits out of which the dividends are paid....

Example:

> ARTICLE 11 [Interest]
>
> 1. Interest arising in a Contracting State and paid to a resident of the other Contracting State may be taxed in that other Contracting State.
> 2. However, such interest may also be taxed in the Contracting State in which it arises and according to the laws of that Contracting State, but if the beneficial owner of the interest is a resident of the other Contracting State, the tax so charged shall not exceed 10 percent of the gross amount of the interest....
>
> ARTICLE 12 [Royalties]
>
> 1. Royalties arising in a Contracting State and beneficially owned by a resident of the other Contracting State may be taxed only in that other Contracting State.

U.S. income tax treaties also generally cover income items such as rents, gains, business profits, personal service income, and other income items.

Example:

> CONVENTION BETWEEN THE GOVERNMENT OF THE UNITED
> STATES OF AMERICA AND THE GOVERNMENT OF JAPAN FOR THE
> AVOIDANCE OF DOUBLE TAXATION AND THE PREVENTION OF
> FISCAL EVASION WITH RESPECT TO TAXES ON INCOME
>
> ARTICLE 14 [Personal Services]
>
> 1. Subject to the provisions of Articles 15, 17 and 18, salaries, wages and other similar remuneration derived by a resident of a Contracting State in respect of an employment shall be taxable only in that Contracting State unless the employment is exercised in the other Contracting State. If the employment is so exercised, such remuneration as is derived therefrom may be taxed in that other Contracting State.

2. Notwithstanding the provisions of paragraph 1, remuneration derived by a resident of a Contracting State in respect of an employment exercised in the other Contracting State shall be taxable only in the first-mentioned Contracting State if:
(a) the recipient is present in that other Contracting State for a period or periods not exceeding in the aggregate 183 days in any twelve month period commencing or ending in the taxable year concerned;
(b) the remuneration

All modern U.S. income tax treaties also specifically define the persons that are eligible for the benefits provided by the particular treaty.

Example:

CONVENTION BETWEEN THE GOVERNMENT OF THE UNITED STATES OF AMERICA AND THE GOVERNMENT OF JAPAN FOR THE AVOIDANCE OF DOUBLE TAXATION AND THE PREVENTION OF FISCAL EVASION WITH RESPECT TO TAXES ON INCOME

ARTICLE 1 [General Scope]

1. This Convention shall apply only to persons who are residents of one or both of the Contracting States, except as otherwise provided in the Convention....

ARTICLE 4 [Residence]

1. For the purposes of this Convention, the term "resident of a Contracting State" means any person who, under the laws of that Contracting State, is liable to tax therein by reason of his domicile, residence, citizenship, place of head or main office, place of incorporation, or any other criterion of a similar nature, ...

The discussion of specific articles and examples provided above just touches on some of the main provisions of U.S. income tax treaties. Each treaty may contain over thirty articles covering such matters as termination, exchange of information, and the taxation of students and teachers, among other things.

c. Other Tax Treaties

So far, the focus has been on fully developed income tax treaties; however, on occasion, the United States has entered into agreements with various countries for the exchange of information with respect to taxes ("exchange of information agreement"). Generally under an exchange of information agreement the treaty partners agree to provide each other assistance and exchange information in the prevention of tax fraud and the evasion of taxes. Such assistance generally comes in the form of tax related information, which is provided at the request of one of the treaty partners.

The United States has also entered into several estate tax treaties. More recent estate tax treaties also include gift tax and generation-skipping tax provisions. The main purpose of estate, gift, and generation-skipping tax treaties is the elimination or mitigation of multiple transfer taxes on gifts and inheritances.

In somewhat rare situations, other types of treaties influence or directly impact U.S. tax consequences. For example, the Tax Court in *Amaral v. Commissioner*[7] held that the

---

7. 90 T.C. 802 (1988).

taxation of NATO employees was governed by the Ottawa Agreement and London Agreement. The Court found that, under such agreements, the salaries of employees hired directly by NATO were exempt from taxation in the member countries. As a result, the NATO salary of a U.S. citizen was exempt from U.S. taxation.

4. How Do Treaties Come into Force?

Not dissimilar to other agreements, treaties are formed through negotiations. In the United States, the authority to enter into treaties is vested in the president under the U.S. Constitution. As a result, the negotiation of treaties on behalf of the U.S. is performed by the executive branch. Generally, U.S. treaties are negotiated by the State Department; however, tax treaties are negotiated by the Treasury Department. Responsibility for tax treaty negotiations within the Treasury Department lies with the Assist Secretary for Tax Policy and the International Tax Counsel. The Office of International Tax Counsel initiates treaty negotiations on behalf of the United States. Once treaty negotiations commence the Treasury Department announces such fact and invites comment from interested parties.

Example:
The following is an example of an invitation for comments regarding a treaty negotiation:

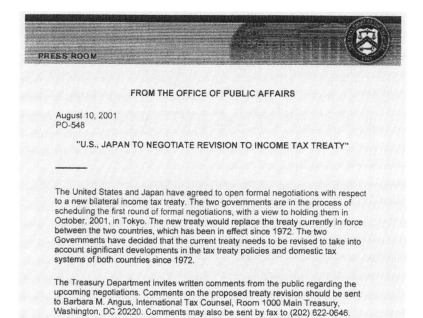

PRESS ROOM

FROM THE OFFICE OF PUBLIC AFFAIRS

August 10, 2001
PO-548

"U.S., JAPAN TO NEGOTIATE REVISION TO INCOME TAX TREATY"

The United States and Japan have agreed to open formal negotiations with respect to a new bilateral income tax treaty. The two governments are in the process of scheduling the first round of formal negotiations, with a view to holding them in October, 2001, in Tokyo. The new treaty would replace the treaty currently in force between the two countries, which has been in effect since 1972. The two Governments have decided that the current treaty needs to be revised to take into account significant developments in the tax treaty policies and domestic tax systems of both countries since 1972.

The Treasury Department invites written comments from the public regarding the upcoming negotiations. Comments on the proposed treaty revision should be sent to Barbara M. Angus, International Tax Counsel, Room 1000 Main Treasury, Washington, DC 20220. Comments may also be sent by fax to (202) 622-0646.

Negotiations are conducted through written and oral communications. These written and oral communications can be helpful in interpreting the treaty after it comes into force. In some circumstances, the delegations exchange diplomatic notes at the time the treaty is signed. Diplomatic notes generally set forth common or agreed understanding, with respect to treaty provisions, reached during negotiations.

Example:

2003 Diplomatic Note, signed November 6, 2003, to the 2003 U.S.-JAPAN income tax treaty, signed November 6, 2003.

November 6, 2003

Excellency:

I have the honor to acknowledge receipt of Your Excellency's note of today's date which reads as follows:

"Excellency:

I have the honor to refer to the Convention between the Government of Japan and the Government of the United States of America for the Avoidance of Double Taxation and the Prevention of Fiscal Evasion with respect to Taxes on Income which was signed today (hereinafter referred to as "the Convention") and to the Protocol also signed today which forms an integral part of the Convention, and to confirm, on behalf of the Government of Japan the following understanding reached between the Government of Japan and the Government of the United States of America:

His Excellency, Ryozo Kato, Ambassador of Japan.

1. In order to avoid application of the local inhabitant taxes or the enterprise tax as provided for in paragraph 3 of Article 8 of the Convention, if a political subdivision or local authority of the United States seeks to levy a tax similar to the local inhabitant taxes or the enterprise tax in Japan on the profits of any enterprise of Japan from the operation of ships or aircraft in international traffic in circumstances where the Convention would preclude the imposition of a Federal income tax on those profits, the Government of the United States will use its best endeavors to persuade that political subdivision or local authority to refrain from imposing such tax.

2. It is understood that the principle as set out in paragraph 1 of Article 9 of the Convention may apply for the purposes of determining the profits to be attributed to a permanent establishment. It is understood that the provisions of Article 7 of the Convention shall not prevent the Contracting States from treating the permanent establishment as having the same amount of capital that it would need to support its activities if it were a distinct and separate enterprise engaged in the same or similar activities. With respect to financial institutions other than insurance companies, a Contracting State may determine the amount of capital to be attributed to a permanent establishment by allocating the institution's total equity between its various offices on the basis of the proportion of the financial institution's risk-weighted assets attributable to each of them.

3. With reference to Article 9 of the Convention, it is understood that double taxation can be avoided only if tax authorities share a common understanding of the principles to be applied in resolving transfer pricing cases. Therefore, the Contracting States shall undertake to conduct transfer pricing examinations of enterprises and evaluate applications for advance pricing arrangements in accordance with the Transfer Pricing Guidelines for Multinational Enterprises and Tax Administrations of the Organisation for Economic Cooperation and Development (hereinafter referred to as "the OECD Transfer Pricing Guidelines"), which reflect the international consensus with respect to these issues. The domestic transfer pricing rules, including the transfer pricing methods, of each Contracting State may be applied in resolving transfer pricing cases under the Convention only to the extent that they are consistent with the OECD Transfer Pricing Guidelines....

If the foregoing understanding is acceptable to the Government of the United States of America, I have the honor to suggest that the present note and Your Excellency's reply to that effect should be regarded as constituting an agreement between the two Governments in this matter, which shall enter into force at the same time as the Convention."

I avail myself of this opportunity to extend to Your Excellency the assurance of my highest consideration.

I have further the honor to confirm on behalf of the Government of the United States of America that the foregoing understanding is acceptable and to agree that Your Excellency's note and this note shall be regarded as constituting an agreement between the two Governments which shall enter into force at the same time as the Convention.

I avail myself of this opportunity to renew to Your Excellency the assurance of my highest consideration.

For the Secretary of State:

The United States traditionally starts the negotiation process by sending a copy of the most current U.S. Model Treaty to the prospective treaty partner. The United States views the U.S. Model Treaty as a negotiation tool and does not expect potential treaty partners to accept the document without variation.[8] In essence, the Model Treaty serves as the United States' opening offer in treaty negotiations.

If negotiations result in an agreed upon treaty, the heads of the delegations initial the treaty, signifying that an agreement has been reached subject to approval through the appropriate legal procedures of each country. In the United States the treaty is first reviewed by the Treasury Department. Once the Treasury Department has completed its review, the draft treaty is submitted by the Secretary of Treasury to the Secretary of State. At such time the Secretary of Treasury formally requests that the Secretary of State approve the draft treaty for signature. The power to sign treaties on behalf of the United States has been delegated to the Secretary of State.

Once the State Department has completed its review of the draft treaty, the Secretary of State forwards the draft treaty to the president along with a "Letter of Submittal." The Letter of Submittal generally provides that the treaty is being forwarded to the president with the view that it be formally ratified.

Example:

LETTER OF SUBMITTAL

Department of State,
Washington, August 26, 2003.

The President,
The White House.

The President: I have the honor to submit to you, with a view to its transmission to the Senate for advice and consent to ratification, the Protocol Amending the Con-

---

8. Preamble to Treas. Technical Explanation, U.S. Model Income Tax Convention, (Sept. 20, 1996).

vention Between the Government of the United States of America and the Government of the Democratic Socialist Republic of Sri Lanka for the Avoidance of Double Taxation and the Prevention of Fiscal Evasion with Respect to Taxes on Income Signed at Colombo on March 14, 1985, together with an exchange of notes, signed at Washington on September 20, 2002 (the "Protocol").

The proposed Protocol updates the Income Tax Convention signed with Sri Lanka on March 14, 1985, which was transmitted to the Senate on October 2, 1985 (S. Treaty Doc. 99-10), to conform with the U.S. Model Income Tax Convention, as modified by certain provisions applicable to developing countries.

Many provisions of the proposed Protocol relate to amendments to the U.S. Internal Revenue Code that have occurred since the Convention was signed in 1985. For example, Article 1 of the proposed Protocol extends to former long-term residents the tax regime now applicable to former U.S. citizens who renounce their citizenship for tax-avoidance reasons. Most other provisions of the proposed Protocol update the language of the Convention to account for changes in U.S. treaty policy that have occurred since the Convention was signed. For example, Article 6 of the proposed Protocol provides a source-country exemption for income from the use, maintenance, or rental of shipping containers.

The exchange of notes resolves two important issues regarding interpretation of the Convention. First, Article 8 of the Convention, as amended by Article 6 of the Protocol, states that Sri Lanka will provide to the United States most-favored-nation treatment with respect to shipping income. Sri Lanka has provided an exemption to the United Kingdom and Poland in Sri Lanka's existing income tax conventions with those countries. Sri Lanka has agreed in the notes to extend this exemption to the United States on a most-favored-nation basis.

Second, Sri Lanka has agreed in the notes to exchange information from Sri Lankan financial institutions. The issue of information exchange was responsible for a ten-year delay in our concluding the Protocol. The repeal of Sri Lanka's bank secrecy legislation and Sri Lanka's agreement last year to provide tax information from financial institutions was critical to our ability to reach agreement on the Protocol.

The proposed Protocol, like the 1985 Convention, is subject to ratification. It will enter into force upon the exchange of instruments of ratification. The 1985 Convention and the Protocol are expected to be brought into force at the same time. The Protocol will have effect in accordance with Article 29 of the 1985 Convention. Thus, it will have effect with respect to taxes withheld at source on the first day of the second month next on which the Convention enters into force. The effective date for other types of taxes is for taxable periods beginning on or after the first day of January of the year in which the Convention enters into force.

The Department of the Treasury and the Department of State cooperated in the negotiation of the Protocol and the exchange of notes. They have the full approval of both Departments.

Respectfully submitted.

Colin L. Powell.

Under the Constitution, the president has the power to enter into a treaty only with the advice and consent of the Senate by a two-thirds vote. As a result, the president submits the signed treaty to the Senate with a "Letter of Transmittal" requesting Senate ratification.

Example:

LETTER OF TRANSMITTAL

The White House, October 28, 2003.

To the Senate of the United States:

I transmit herewith, for Senate advice and consent to ratification, the Protocol Amending the Convention Between the Government of the United States of America and the Government of the Democratic Socialist Republic of Sri Lanka for the Avoidance of Double Taxation and the Prevention of Fiscal Evasion with Respect to Taxes on Income signed at Colombo on March 14, 1985, together with an exchange of notes, signed at Washington on September 20, 2002 (the "Protocol"). I also transmit, for the information of the Senate, the report of the Department of State concerning the Protocol.

The Protocol would amend the Convention to make it similar to tax treaties between the United States and other developing nations. The convention would provide maximum rates of tax to be applied to various types of income and protection from double taxation of income. The Convention, as amended by the Protocol, also provides for resolution of disputes and sets forth rules making its benefits unavailable to residents that are engaged in treaty shopping.

I recommend that the Senate give early and favorable consideration to this Protocol in conjunction with the Convention, and that the Senate give its advice and consent to ratification.

George W. Bush.

Quick Find:

Treaty documents, such as Letters of Submittal and Letters of Transmittal, can be found on the Library of Congress "Thomas" website at http://www.thomas.loc.gov. Click on "Treaties" and a search can be conducted by "Congress" (i.e., 108th Congress), "Words and Phrases," "Treaty Number," or "Type of Treaty." Coverage starts in 1975.

Once the "Letter of Transmittal" is received, the Senate submits the treaty to the Senate Foreign Relations Committee for review and comment prior to the Senate conducting full hearings on the treaty. The Senate Foreign Relations Committee conducts public hearings on the treaty in order to provide interested parties the opportunity to comment on the treaty. Prior to the hearings the Treasury Department and the Joint Committee on Taxation prepare explanations of the treaty and submit such explanations to the Senate Foreign Relations Committee. The Treasury Department's explanation is referred to as the Treasury Technical Explanation.

Example:

Treasury Technical Explanation, dated February 25, 2004, of the 2003 U.S.-Japan income tax treaty, signed Nov. 6, 2003.

DEPARTMENT OF THE TREASURY TECHNICAL EXPLANATION OF THE CONVENTION BETWEEN THE GOVERNMENT OF THE UNITED STATES OF AMERICA AND THE GOVERNMENT OF JAPAN FOR THE AVOIDANCE OF DOUBLE TAXATION AND THE PREVENTION OF FISCAL EVASION WITH RESPECT TO TAXES ON INCOME AND ON CAPITAL GAINS,

SIGNED AT WASHINGTON ON NOVEMBER 6, 2003

Document Date: February 25, 2004

This is a technical explanation of the Convention between the Government of the United States of America and the Government of Japan for the Avoidance of Double Taxation and the Prevention of Fiscal Evasion with respect to Taxes on Income, signed at Washington on November 6, 2003 (the "Convention"), and the Protocol also signed at Washington on November 6, 2003, which forms an integral part thereto (the "Protocol"). In connection with the negotiation of the Convention, the delegations of the United States and Japan developed and agreed upon an exchange of Diplomatic Notes (the "Notes"). The Notes constitute an agreement between the two governments that shall enter into force at the same time as the entry into force of the Convention. The Notes are intended to give guidance both to the taxpayers and to the tax authorities of the Contracting States in interpreting the Convention. The Notes and Protocol are discussed below in connection with relevant provisions of the Convention.

References are made to the Convention between the Government of the United States of America and the Government of Japan for the Avoidance of Double Taxation and the Prevention of Fiscal Evasion with respect to Taxes on Income, signed at Tokyo on March 8, 1971 (the "prior Convention"). The Convention and Protocol replace the prior Convention.

Negotiations took into account the U.S. Treasury Department's current tax treaty policy and the Treasury Department's Model Income Tax Convention, published on September 20, 1996 (the "U.S. Model"). Negotiations also took into account the Model Tax Convention on Income and on Capital, published by the Organization for Economic Cooperation and Development, as updated in January 2003 (the "OECD Model"), and recent tax treaties concluded by both countries.

The Technical Explanation is the Treasury Department's analysis of each section of the treaty. It is intended to provide guidance as to the policy behind particular treaty provisions, as well as understandings reached between the treaty partners with respect to the application and meaning of treaty terms and provisions. The Treasury Technical Explanation is unilaterally prepared by the Treasury Department without the assistance of the treaty partner. However, copies of the Treasury Technical Explanation are generally sent for review to the treaty partner before the document is finalized. In rare cases the proposed treaty partner has affirmatively expressed its general agreement with the Treasury Technical Explanation. Often the treaty partner unilaterally prepares a similar document as part of the legal process of the partner country.

As discussed above, the Joint Committee on Taxation also prepares an independent explanation of the treaty for the Senate Finance Committee. The Joint Committee's explanation is called the "Explanation of Proposed Treaty Between the United States and _____" ("Joint Committee Explanation"). The Joint Committee generally has access to the Treasury Technical Explanation when drafting the Joint Committee Explanation. The Joint Committee Explanation provides an overview of the U.S. and treaty partner's international tax rules, an article-by-article explanation of the treaty, and a discussion of issues relating to the treaty.[9]

---

9. See e.g., Joint Committee on Taxation, Explanation of Proposed Protocol to the Income Tax Treaty Between the United Stated and Netherlands JCX-54-04, 108th Cong., 2nd Sess. (September 16, 2004). An example of the issue perceived by the Joint Committee and discussed in the Joint Committee Ex-

Example:

Joint Committee on Taxation Report, dated February 19, 2004,
to the 2003 U.S.-JAPAN income tax treaty.

EXPLANATION OF PROPOSED INCOME TAX TREATY
BETWEEN THE UNITED STATES AND JAPAN

Scheduled for a Hearing before the

COMMITTEE ON FOREIGN RELATIONS

UNITED STATES SENATE

ON FEBRUARY 25, 2004

Prepared by the Staff of the JOINT COMMITTEE ON TAXATION

FEBRUARY 19, 2004

INTRODUCTION

This pamphlet,[1] prepared by the staff of the Japan Committee on Taxation, describes the proposed income tax treaty between the United States and Japan as supplemented by a protocol (the "proposed protocol") and an exchange of diplomatic notes (the "notes"). The proposed treaty, proposed protocol, and notes were signed on November 6, 2003. Unless otherwise specified, the proposed treaty, the proposed protocol, and the notes are hereinafter referred to collectively as the "proposed treaty." The Senate Committee on Foreign Relations has scheduled a public hearing on the proposed treaty for February 25, 2004.[2]

Part I of the pamphlet provides a summary of the proposed treaty. Part II provides a brief overview of U.S. tax laws relating to international trade and investment and of U.S. income tax treaties in general. Part III contains a brief overview of Japanese tax laws. Part IV provides a discussion of investment and trade flows between the United States and Japan. Part V contains an article-by-article explanation of the proposed treaty. Part VI contains a discussion of issues raised by the proposed treaty.

I. SUMMARY

The principal purposes of the proposed treaty are to reduce or eliminate double taxation of income earned by residents of either country from sources within the other country and to prevent avoidance or evasion of the taxes of the two countries. The proposed treaty also is intended to promote close economic cooperation between the two countries and to eliminate possible barriers to trade and investment caused by overlapping taxing jurisdictions of the two countries....

The Joint Committee Explanation and the Treasury Technical Explanation are generally released to the public shortly before the Joint Committee conducts a public hearing with respect to the treaty. Officials from the Treasury Department and generally the Joint Committee on Taxation testify at the proposed treaty hearings. Other interested parties are generally allowed to submit written comments to the Senate Foreign Relations Committee prior to the committee conducting hearings on the proposed treaty.

---

planation of Proposed Protocol to the Income Tax Treaty between the United States and Netherlands was whether the zero dividend withholding tax contained in the proposed treaty created a perception or signaled a shift in U.S. tax treaty policy away from the model treaty.

> **Quick Find:**
> The text of the testimony of Treasury officials before the Senate Foreign Relations Committee can be found at www.treas.gov.

After the hearings are concluded, the Senate Foreign Relations Committee votes to recommend to the U.S. Senate that it give its advice and consent to ratification or not to consent to ratification. In rare situations, the Senate Foreign Relations Committee has voted to recommend to the U.S. Senate that it consent to ratification subject to a condition or reservation.

Once the Senate Foreign Relations Committee makes its recommendation, the treaty is reported to the entire Senate. Senate advice and consent requires a two-thirds vote of the members present. Senators can offer amendments or reservations to the treaty that must be acted on prior to approval. Generally, the Senate approves treaties that have been submitted by the president without amendments or reservations. In the event the Senate does approve the treaty with reservation or an amendment, it may be necessary to renegotiate the treaty in order to get ratification by the treaty partner.

> **Example:**
> The U.S. Senate consented to ratification of the 1981 Malta-U.S. Tax Treaty subject to an amendment regarding dividends. The amendment was accepted by the Malta government.

Once the Senate has provided its advice and consent, the final step is the exchange of instruments of ratification. The instruments of ratification are a certification by each of the treaty partners that the treaty has been approved through the appropriate legal channels of the particular country. In the United States the president or his delegate certifies that constitutional requirements have been met. Once the constitutional requirements have been meet, the Treasury Department issues a press release announcing the treaty entering into force.

Example:

The following is an example of a notice of entering into a treaty with Japan:

PRESS ROOM

FROM THE OFFICE OF PUBLIC AFFAIRS

March 29, 2004
JS-1275

Treasury Celebrates Entry into Force of New
U.S.-Japan Tax Treaty

Every year the blossoming of Washington's cherry trees, a gift to the United States from Japan, herald the arrival of spring. This year the cherry blossoms also herald the entry into force of the new income tax treaty between the United States and Japan. The new tax treaty entered into force upon the exchange of instruments of ratification between Howard H. Baker, Jr., Ambassador of the United States to Japan, and Ichiro Aisawa, Senior Vice-Minister for Foreign Affairs of Japan, at a ceremony on March 30th in Tokyo.

"The accelerated timeline on which the governments of both countries have acted to bring the new tax treaty into force reflects the strong mutual commitment to cross-border trade and investment between the United States and Japan. The new U.S.-Japan treaty will significantly reduce existing tax barriers to investment and trade in both directions," said Treasury Secretary Snow. "This enhanced tax treaty relationship will foster still closer economic ties between the world's two largest economies, enhancing the global competitiveness of our businesses and creating new opportunities for international trade and investment, which will mean more growth and jobs. Because of the swift action taken by both governments, key benefits of the new tax treaty will be available to our businesses right away this summer."

The new tax treaty replaces the existing income tax treaty between the United States and Japan, which dates back to 1971. The new agreement is a complete modernization of the treaty relationship to reflect the changes in economic relations between the two countries that have taken place over the last thirty years.

The provisions of the new tax treaty related to source-country withholding taxes are applicable beginning on July 1, 2004. The provisions related to other taxes generally are applicable for taxable years beginning on or after January 1, 2005.

The most dramatic advances in the new tax treaty are reflected in the reciprocal reductions in source-country withholding taxes on income from cross-border investments. The new tax treaty provides for the complete elimination of withholding taxes on all royalty income. Given the importance of the cross-border use of intangibles between the United States and Japan, this is a key provision. The new tax treaty also provides for the complete elimination of withholding taxes on certain interest income, including interest income earned by financial institutions, and on dividend income paid to parent companies with a controlling interest in the paying company. Because the new tax treaty entered into force before April 1st, the reductions in withholding taxes will be applicable as of July 1st.

The new tax treaty also ensures treaty benefits in appropriate circumstances for investments made through partnerships, allowing flexibility in business form. In addition, the new tax treaty includes important provisions regarding the application of international standards for transfer pricing between affiliated companies operating in both countries.

The new tax treaty was signed by Secretary Snow and Ambassador Ryozo Kato, Ambassador of Japan to the United States, in Washington on November 6, 2003.

The United States and Japan announced on August 10, 2001, that they had agreed to open formal negotiations with respect to a new tax treaty.

A treaty will generally go into force on the day in which the instruments of ratification have been exchanged. In some situations the treaty does not require instruments of ratification and instead requires that the contracting states notify each other when their respective constitutional and statutory requirements have been met. Under such circumstances, the treaty goes into force when both parties have provided notice. The effective date of the treaty is generally a specific day and month following the treaty going into force. Treaties may specify different effective dates for different types of taxes covered under the treaty.

Example:

CONVENTION BETWEEN THE GOVERNMENT OF THE UNITED STATES OF AMERICA AND THE GOVERNMENT OF JAPAN FOR THE AVOIDANCE OF DOUBLE TAXATION AND THE PREVENTION OF FISCAL EVASION WITH RESPECT TO TAXES ON INCOME

ARTICLE 30

1. This Convention shall be subject to ratification, and the instruments of ratification shall be exchanged as soon as possible. It shall enter into force on the date of the exchange of instruments of ratification.

2. This Convention shall be applicable: ...
(b) in the United States:
(i) with respect to taxes withheld at source:
(aa) for amounts paid or credited on or after July 1 of the calendar year in which the Convention enters into force, if the Convention enters into force before April 1 of a calendar year; or
(bb) for amounts paid or credited on or after January 1 of the calendar year next following the date on which the Convention enters into force, if the Convention enters into force after March 31 of a calendar year; and
(ii) with respect to other taxes, for taxable periods beginning on or after January 1 of the calendar year next following the date on which the Convention enters into force.

Protocols go through the same negotiation and ratification procedures as an original treaty.

5. Relationship of Treaties with the Internal Revenue Code

The United States has entered into over 50 bilateral income tax conventions with a variety of countries. The conventions are intended to mitigate incidents of double taxation and provide uniform tax treatment between the treaty countries on income items, such as dividends and royalties. The U.S. international Code provisions and bilateral tax treaties often supplement each other. "[I]f there is no conflict between the two, then the code and the treaty should be read harmoniously, to give effect to each."[10]

---

10. *Pekar v. Commissioner*, 113 T.C. 158 (1995).

However, conflicts can arise between the two authorities. In resolving conflicts between a Code provision and a treaty provision, the provision that was adopted "last-in-time" will control. The courts have reached this conclusion through interpretation of the Supremacy Clause of the Constitution, Article VI, section 2, which provides, "This Constitution, and the Laws of the U.S. which shall be made in Pursuance thereof; and all Treaties made, or which shall be made, under the authority of the U.S., shall be the supreme law of the land."[11] The Supreme Court has interpreted the Supremacy Clause to mean that acts of Congress, such as the Code, and treaties are of equal weight, both of which being subject to repeal or modification "by an act of a later date."[12]

Section 7852 reiterates the fact that revenue statutes and treaties are legal equals. It states, "For purposes of determining the relationship between a provision of a treaty and any law of the U.S. affecting revenue, neither the treaty nor the law shall have preferential status by reason of its being a treaty or law." The "last-in-time" rule can be a potential pitfall when conducting international tax research. A researcher must first come to a conclusion under the Code. Once such conclusion is reached, it must then be examined on a country-by-country basis in order to determine whether the relevant Code provision has been modified with respect to a particular country by a treaty between the United States and the particular country. If there is a conflict between the treaty and Code it must be determined which of the two is last-in-time and, therefore, controlling.

The "last-in-time" rule and congressional willingness to enact legislation that overrides a treaty provision has not gone unnoticed by our treaty partners. Several partners to recently enacted treaties have requested some level of protection in the event Congress enacts legislation that overrides a treaty provision. Such protection has come in the form of specific treaty provisions that provide a review mechanism in the event of a change in the domestic law of one of the treaty partners that substantially impacts the treaty. For example the recently enacted income tax treaty between the United States and Japan provides:

> If a Contracting State considers that a substantial change in the laws relevant to this Convention has been or will be made in the other Contracting State, the first-mentioned Contracting State may make a request to that other Contracting State in writing for consultations with a view to determining the possible effect of such change on the balance of benefits. The requested Contracting State shall enter into consultations with the requesting Contracting State within three months from the date on which the request is received by the requested Contracting State.[13]

The OECD has also responded to the enactment of treaty overrides under domestic law. The OECD has issued a report denouncing the unilateral enactment of treaty overrides as a violation of international law and the Vienna Convention.

The United States is at least in theory subject to the same risk that a treaty partner might enact domestic legislation that overrides a provision of a U.S. bilateral tax treaty. However, as discussed in the OECD report on treaty overrides, in many situations the treaty partner is unable to take such steps under its domestic law.

---

11. U.S. Const. art. VI, § 2.
12. *Edye v. Robertson*, 112 U.S. 580 (1884).
13. Convention for the Avoidance of Double Taxation and the Prevention of Fiscal Evasion with Respect to Taxes on Income, Nov. 6, 2003, U.S.-Japan, art. 29, TIAS.

Example:

Excerpt from the OECD Report on Treaty Overrides:

For example, Article 55 of the French Constitution of 1958 provides that treaties regularly ratified or accepted shall possess, from the moment of publication, superiority over ordinary laws. A similar principle is embodied in Article 94 of the Dutch Constitution. Here, the treaty obligations prevail, also under domestic law, over any conflicting provisions or prior and posterior laws. On the other hand, the United States has chosen, in accordance with Article VI, paragraph 2, of its Constitution, to give treaty obligations equal rank with domestic law and thus to make such obligations subject to the "lex posterior" rule in the case of irreconcilable conflicts. In the Federal Republic of Germany Article 59, paragraph 2, of the Fundamental Law provides for the transformation of the treaty into domestic law and treaties so transformed normally have precedence over national law. In the United Kingdom domestic legislation implementing treaty obligations is subject to amendment or repeal by later legislation. Under the Constitution of Finland, treaties which may conflict with prior domestic law require approval by Act of Parliament and after such approval will have the same rank as that Act.

almost identical to Code.

6. How Do Courts Interpret Treaties?

The United States has adopted a contract approach to interpreting treaties. A treaty is to be viewed as a contract between the independent nations.[14] Under such approach, "[t]he basic aim of treaty interpretation is to ascertain the intent of the parties who have entered into agreement, in order to construe the document in a manner consistent with that intent."[15] Specific words contained within the treaty are to be interpreted in a fashion that is consistent with the genuine shared expectations of the treaty partners. The starting point for determining the shared expectations or intent of the contracting parties is the treaty language itself. The clear language of the treaty is controlling unless the "application of the words of the treaty according to their obvious meaning effects a result that is inconsistent with the intent or expectations of the signatories."[16] All modern U.S. tax treaties contain an Article that defines key terms. If a treaty defines a term, the treaty definition is controlling. The U.S. Model treaty and most modern U.S. bilateral treaties also provide guidance in interpreting undefined terms. When a term is left undefined by a treaty, Article III(2) of the U.S. Model Treaty provides that the domestic law of the country applying the treaty shall determine the meaning of the term, unless the "context requires the Competent Authorities agree to a common meaning." Most modern U.S. income tax treaties contain a provision similar to Article III(2) of the Model Treaty.

Similar to interpreting a contract, when the language of a treaty is ambiguous courts will look to extrinsic materials in determining the shared expectations of the contracting parties. However, in the case of treaties, courts "have been more willing to resort to extra-textual, preparatory material to determine meaning, and also to allow for more liberal in-

---

14. *Snap-on Tools, Inc. v. United States*, 26 Cl. Ct. 1045 (1992), aff'd, 26 F.3d 137 (Fed. Cir. 1994).
15. *Maximov v. United States*, 299 F.2d 565 (2nd Cir. 1962).
16. *Sumitomo Shoji America v. Avagliano*, 457 U.S. 176, 180, (1982), quoting Maximov v. United States, 373 U.S. 49, 54 (1963).

terpretation of the words of a treaty."[17] Courts may look to numerous extrinsic materials in arriving at the contracting parties' shared expectations.

Negotiating History. Treaty negotiations are conducted through written and oral communications, which create a negotiating history. On several occasions U.S. courts have examined materials generated as part of the treaty negotiation process in order to determine the shared expectations of the contracting parties. In one such case, the Court of Claims relied on an affidavit prepared by the leader of the U.S. negotiating team in interpreting a provision of the United States-United Kingdom Convention.[18] The affidavit provided that there were no discussions between the United States and United Kingdom negotiating teams with respect to the impact of a particular Code provision on the application of the treaty.[19]

Ratification History. United States courts also routinely examine documents created as part of the treaty ratification process. Typically ratification documents, such as the Treasury Technical Explanation, are unilaterally created without the assistance or affirmative approval of the treaty partners. Despite the unilateral nature of Treasury Technical Explanations, they are entitled to a great deal of deference in U.S. treaty interpretation. "The Technical Explanation reveals the intent of the Treasury with respect to the Convention and, as numerous federal courts have stated 'the meaning attributed to treaty provisions by the Government agency charged with their negotiation and enforcement is entitled to great weight.'" In Xerox Corp. v. United States[20] the Court of Claims concluded that the United Kingdom had at least tacitly accepted the Treasury Department interpretation of a particular treaty provision. Such conclusion was based on the fact that the Treasury interpretation was contained in the Treasury Technical Explanation, which had been sent to the U.K. negotiators. However, the U.K. delegation never affirmatively communicated their approval of the Treasury Technical Explanation. On appeal, the Federal Circuit Court strongly disagreed with the conclusion reached by the Claims Court.[21]

Competent Authority Agreements. When the Competent Authorities (discussed later in this chapter) of the contracting parties reach an agreement with respect to a disputed treaty interpretation, U.S. courts will generally defer to such interpretation. Courts are generally reluctant to impinge on Competent Authorities agreements. "As the Supreme Court stated in Sumitomo … 'Our role is limited to giving effect to the intent of the Treaty parties. When the parties to a treaty both agree as to the meaning of a treaty provision, and that interpretation follows from the clear treaty language, we must, absent extraordinary strong contrary evidence, defer to that interpretation.'"[22]

Model Tax Treaties. Most bilateral income tax treaties are modeled on or heavily influenced by the OECD Model Treaty. As a result, courts find the OECD Model Treaty and its official commentary useful in interpreting provisions of U.S. income tax treaties that are based on such materials.

---

17. Snap-on Tools, Inc., 26 Cl. Ct. at 1065.

18. Id. at 1063.

19. Id.

20. Xerox Corp. v. United States, 14 Cl. Ct. 455, 463 (1988), rev'd, 41 F.3d 647, 656 (Fed. Cir. 1995).

21. Xerox Corp. v. United States, 41 F.3d 647, 656 (Fed. Cir. 1995).

22. Xerox Corp. v. United States, 14 Cl. Ct. 455, 467 (1988) rev'd, 41 F.3d 647, 656 (Fed. Cir. 1995).

Case on Point:

Taisei Fire & Marine Ins. Co. v. Commissioner
104 T.C. 535 (1995)

Our examination shows that the relevant provisions of the Convention are not only based upon, but are duplicative of, article 5, comments 4 and 5, of the 1963 O.E.C.D. Draft [Model] Convention (hereinafter referred to as the 1963 Model). See letter of transmittal from President Nixon to the Senate requesting ratification of the Convention, dated May 11, 1971, 2 Tax Treaties (CCH) par. 5222, p. 34,021-3; Senate Committee on Foreign Relations, Report on Tax Convention with Japan and Tax Protocol with France (Nov. 22, 1971), 1973-1 C.B. 642, 643. While the 1963 Model itself provides no more definition than the Convention, the model is explained in part by a commentary, which states in pertinent part:

15. Persons who may be deemed to be permanent establishments must be strictly limited to those who are dependent, both from the legal and economic points of view, upon the enterprise for which they carry on business dealings (Report of the Fiscal Committee of the League of Nations, 1928, page 12). Where an enterprise has business dealings with an independent agent, this cannot be held to mean that the enterprise itself carries on a business in the other State. In such a case, there are two separate enterprises. Given the absence of any provision dealing with insurance or reinsurance in the U.S.-Japan Convention, our holding herein that Fortress is not a permanent establishment of petitioners is consistent with the approach suggested by the O.E.C.D. Model and the application thereof in the U.S.-Belgium Convention.

In view of our holding, we do not reach the further issue in respect of the inclusion in petitioners' 1988 taxable income of certain reductions in pre-1988 estimates of unpaid losses.

The U.S. Model Treaty and its Technical Explanation also serve as a tool for treaty interpretation. The Model Treaty is the starting point for U.S. negotiations and can provide insight into the intent of U.S. negotiators with respect to the meaning of particular terms or provisions.

Treasury Interpretations. In some cases, the Treasury Department issues a revenue ruling or regulations that provides its treaty interpretation.[23] Treasury regulations under tax conventions can be found in part 500–599 of the Code of Federal Regulations.

7. Competent Authority a way to resolve dispute between treaties.

Most U.S. income tax treaties provide a mechanism for residents of the contracting states to bring issues and problems regarding the application of the convention to the attention of a respective country's competent authority. The mechanism is generally referred to as the "mutual agreement procedure." The mutual agreement procedure article in U.S. income tax treaties is generally based on article 25 of the U.S. model treaty which states, "Where a person considers that the actions of one or both of the Con-

---

23. As discussed in Chapter 6, Public Guidance from the Office of Chief Counsel, a revenue ruling is treated by the U.S. courts as the position of the U.S. government.

tracting States result or will result for him in taxation not in accordance with the provisions of this Convention, he may ... present his case to competent authority of either Contracting State."[24]

If the competent authority of the contracting state in which the case is presented determines that the taxpayer's case has merit, and is unable to reach a unilateral solution, it presents the matter to its foreign counterpart. The competent authorities of both contracting states then meet and attempt to reach an agreement that is consistent with the spirit of the treaty and the objective of avoiding double taxation.

U.S. income tax treaties generally designate the Secretary of Treasury as the U.S. Competent Authority. Such authority has been delegated to the Deputy Commissioner (International), Large and Mid-Size Business Division. The Deputy Commissioner (International), Large and Mid-Size Business Division, acts as the U.S. competent authority in administering the operating provisions of tax treaties, including reaching mutual agreements in specific cases, and in interpreting and applying tax treaties. In interpreting and applying tax treaties, the Deputy Commissioner (International), Large and Mid-Size Business Division, acts only with the concurrence of the Associate Chief Counsel (International). In such role, the Deputy Commissioner, is responsible for treaty administration, including entering into competent authority settlements and treaty interpretation and application.

Competent authority negotiations are a government-to-government activity, conducted by the U.S. and foreign competent authorities; the taxpayer does not participate in such negotiations. If the U.S. and foreign competent authorities reach an agreement, the U.S. Competent Authority will notify the taxpayer. The taxpayer then has the option of either accepting or rejecting the agreement. If the taxpayer accepts the agreement, it is final and is not subject to further administrative or judicial review. In the event the agreement is rejected, the taxpayer can withdraw the request for competent authority assistance and seek any available judicial or administrative review of the issue in either the United States or the treaty partner country.

When the competent authorities reach an agreement that is acceptable to the taxpayer, generally such agreement will not be disclosed to the public. Section 6105(a) provides that tax convention information shall not be disclosed. Included in the definition of "tax convention information" is any agreement entered into with the competent authority of one or more foreign governments under a tax treaty. However, the general rule that competent authority agreements are not subject to disclosure does not apply under section 6105(b):

(1) to the disclosure of tax convention information to persons or authorities (including courts and administrative bodies) entitled to such information under a tax treaty,

(2) to any generally applicable procedural rules regarding application for relief under a tax convention,

(3) to the disclosure of tax convention information on the same terms as return information may be disclosed under paragraph (3)(C) or (7) of section 6103(i), or

(4) in any case not described in paragraph (1), (2), or (3), to the disclosure of any tax convention information not relating to a particular taxpayer if the Secretary determines, after consultation with each other party to the tax convention, that such disclosure would not impair tax administration.

---

24. U.S. Model Income Tax Convention, art. 25 (Sept. 20, 1996).

Disclosure of competent authority agreements to the public most commonly takes place under section 6105(b)(2), when the agreement generates "generally applicable rules." Such disclosure by the IRS first comes in the form of a News Release. A copy of the News Release is then generally issued in the form of either a Notice or an Announcement.

Example:

The following is an example of an IRS News Release, announcing the results of negotiations between Competent Authorities:

INTERNAL REVENUE SERVICE

IRS 🏛News Release

| Media Relations Office | Washington, D.C. | Media Contact: 202.622.4000 |
| www.IRS.gov/newsroom | | Public Contact: 800.829.1040 |

U.S. and Austria Agree on Tax Treatment of Certain Scholarships

IR-2005-20, March 1, 2005

WASHINGTON — The Competent Authorities of Austria and the United States have reached a mutual agreement on the taxation of certain scholarships under Article 20 (Students and Trainees) and Article 21 (Other Income) of the U.S.-Austria income tax treaty.

The agreement constitutes a Mutual Agreement in accordance with the Income Tax Treaty Between Austria and the United States. The Treaty entered into force on Feb. 1, 1998.

The agreement can be found on the IRS Web site.

Links:

- U.S.-Austria Competent Authority Agreement (PDF 10K) --
  http://www.irs.gov/pub/irs-utl/AustriaAgreement.pdf
- Agreement attached.

— 30 —

Example:

The following is an example of an agreement entered into by competent authority:

COMPETENT AUTHORITY AGREEMENT

The Competent Authorities of Austria and the United States enter into the following agreement ("Agreement") concerning the interpretation of Articles 20, 21 and 23 of the Convention Between the Republic of Austria and the United States of America for the Avoidance of Double Taxation and the Prevention of Fiscal Evasion with Respect to Income Taxes, signed May 31, 1996. The Agreement is entered into under Article 24 (Mutual Agreement Procedure). For the purposes of this Agreement, "Article" refers to an Article of the Treaty.

It is agreed that the exemption described in Article 20 (Students and Trainees) does not apply to payments for maintenance, education or training received by a student who is, or was immediately before visiting the United States, a resident of Austria, and who is present in the United States for the purpose of full-time education at a recognized education institution, if such scholarship is paid out of U.S. sources, e.g. in the case where the payer of income is a U.S. foundation. Accordingly, such a scholarship payment is taxable according to the domestic tax laws of the United States and Austria.

In any case, pursuant to Article 23 (Non-Discrimination), Austrian students shall not be subjected in the United States to any taxation or any requirement connected therewith, which is other or more burdensome than the taxation and connected requirements to which U.S. nationals in the same circumstances are or may be subjected. This principle would *mutatis mutandis* apply in the reciprocal situation of a U.S. student subject to tax in Austria according to the general rules of Articles 20 and 23.

Furthermore it is understood that a scholarship granted for the purposes of postgraduate research derived by a student, who is present in the other Contracting State only for research purposes, and not for the purposes of full-time education at a recognized educational institution nor for full-time training, is not covered by Article 20 (Students and Trainees). The taxable treatment of such payments would be governed by the rules of Article 21 (Other Income) and thus taxable solely by the State of residence.

_____
Robert H. Green
Director, International (LMSB)
Internal Revenue Service
U.S. Department of the Treasury

_____
Dr. Heinz Jirousek
Deputy Head, International Tax Affairs
Division
Federal Ministry of Finance

_____
Date

_____
Date

Quick Find:

Recent IRS Competent Authority disclosures, and in some cases the actual text of the competent authority agreements, can be found on the IRS website at www.irs.gov.

U.S. treaties set forth the procedures for invoking the competent authority mechanism in a very general fashion. However, the IRS has issued Revenue Procedure 2006-54 which sets forth detailed procedures for requesting the assistance of the U.S. Competent Authority. Revenue Procedure 2006-54 outlines the conditions under which the procedure applies and also sets forth detailed steps for requesting competent authority assistance. Revenue Procedure 2006-54 does not expand or limit competent authority assistance granted under any treaty. As a result, taxpayers are urged to examine the specific treaty under which relief is being sought in order to determine if competent authority relief is available under the particular circumstances. Competent Authority relief is only available when there is a treaty between the United States and another country granting such relief. A request for competent authority assistance is to be in the form of a letter that is dated and signed. The letter must include a statement that competent authority assistance is being requested and must include all the information required under Revenue Procedure 2006-54.

Revenue Procedure 2006-54 provides simplified procedures for requesting competent authority relief for small case taxpayers. Individuals are considered small case taxpayers and eligible for an abbreviated request if the total proposed adjustment involved in the matter is not greater than $200,000. Corporations and partnerships are eligible if the proposed adjustment is $1,000,000 or less. Other taxpayers will be considered small case taxpayers if the proposed adjustment is not greater than $200,000.

Practice Note:

A comparison of the information required for small case taxpayers and the information required for all other taxpayers under Revenue Procedure 2006-54 can be found in the table below:

Required Information Under Rev. Proc. 2006-54	Required Information Under Rev. Proc. 2006-54 for Small Case Taxpayers
• a reference to the specific treaty and the provisions therein pursuant to which the request is made;	• a statement indicating that this is a matter subject to the small case procedure;
• the names, addresses, U.S. taxpayer identification number and foreign taxpayer identification number (if any) of the taxpayer and, if applicable, all related persons involved in the matter;	• the name, address, U.S. taxpayer identification number and foreign taxpayer identification number (if any) of the taxpayer and, if applicable, all related persons involved in the matter;
• a brief description of the issues for which competent authority assistance is requested, including a description of the relevant transactions, activities or other circumstances involved in the issues raised and the basis for the adjustment, if any;	• a description of the issue and the nature of the relief sought;

• if applicable, a description of the control and business relationships between the taxpayer and any relevant related person for the years in issue, including any changes in such relationship to the date of filing the request;	• the years and amounts involved with dollars respect to the issues in both U.S. and foreign currency;
• the taxable years and amounts involved with respect to the issues in both U.S. and foreign currency;	• the name of the treaty country;
• the IRS office that has made or is proposing to make the adjustment or, if known, the IRS office with examination jurisdiction over the taxpayer;	• if applicable, powers of attorney with respect to the taxpayer;
• an explanation of the nature of the relief sought or the action requested in the United States or in the treaty country with respect to the issues raised, including a statement as to whether the taxpayer wishes to apply for treatment similar to that provided under Rev. Proc. 99-32, 1999-2 C.B. 296;	• on a separate document, a statement that the taxpayer consents to the disclosure to the competent authority of the treaty country (with the name of the treaty country specifically stated) and that competent authority's staff, of any or all of the items of information set forth or enclosed in the request for U.S. competent authority assistance within the limits contained in the tax treaty under which the taxpayer is seeking relief. The taxpayer may request, as part of this statement, that its trade secrets not be disclosed to a foreign competent authority. This statement must be dated and signed by a person having authority to sign the taxpayer's federal tax returns and is required to facilitate the administrative handling of the request by the U.S. competent authority for purposes of the recordkeeping requirements of section 6103(p) of the Code. Failure to provide such a statement will not prevent the U.S. competent authority from disclosing information under the terms of a treaty; and
• a statement whether the period of limitations for the years for which relief is sought has expired in the United States or in the treaty country;	• a penalties of perjury statement in the following form: Under penalties of perjury, I declare that I have examined this request, including accompanying documents, and, to the best of my knowledge and belief, the facts presented in support of the request for competent authority assistance are true, correct and complete.
• a statement of relevant domestic and foreign judicial or administrative proceedings that involve the taxpayer and related persons, including all information related to notification of the treaty country;	

• to the extent known by the taxpayer, a statement of relevant foreign judicial or public administrative proceedings that do not involve the taxpayer or related persons but involve the same issue for which competent authority assistance is requested;	
• a statement whether the request for competent authority assistance involves issues that are currently, or were previously, considered part of an Advance Pricing Agreement ("APA") proceeding or other proceeding relevant to the issue under consideration in the United States or part of a similar proceeding in the foreign country;	
• if applicable, powers of attorney with respect to the taxpayer, and the request should identify the individual to serve as the taxpayer's initial point of contact for the competent authority;	
• if the jurisdiction of an issue is with an IRS Appeals office, a summary of prior discussions of the issue with that office and contact information regarding the IRS Appeals officer handling the issue; also, if appropriate, a statement whether the taxpayer is requesting the Simultaneous Appeals procedure as provided in section 8 of revenue procedure 2006-54;	
• in a separate section, the statement and information required by section 9.02 of revenue procedure 2006-54 if the request is to serve as a protective claim;	
• on a separate document, a statement that the taxpayer consents to the disclosure to the competent authority of the treaty country (with the name of the treaty country specifically stated) and that competent authority's staff, of any or all of the items of information set forth or enclosed in the request for U.S. competent authority assistance within the limits contained in the tax treaty under which the taxpayer is seeking relief. The taxpayer may request, as part of this statement, that its trade secrets not be disclosed to a foreign competent authority. This statement must be dated and signed by a person having authority to sign the taxpayer's federal tax returns and is required to facilitate the	

administrative handling of the request by the U.S. competent authority for purposes of the recordkeeping requirements of section 6103(p) of the Code. Failure to provide such a statement will not prevent the U.S. competent authority from disclosing information under the terms of a treaty.	
• a penalties of perjury statement in the following form: Under penalties of perjury, I declare that I have examined this request, including accompanying documents, and, to the best of my knowledge and belief, the facts presented in support of the request for competent authority assistance are true, correct and complete. The declaration must be dated and signed by the person or persons on whose behalf the request is being made and not by the taxpayer's representative. The person signing for a corporate taxpayer must be an authorized officer of the taxpayer who has personal knowledge of the facts. The person signing for a trust, an estate or a partnership must be respectively, a trustee, an executor or a partner who has personal knowledge of the facts; and	
• any other information required or requested under revenue procedure 2006-54, as applicable. *See, e.g.,* section 7.06 of revenue procedure 2006-54, which requires the provision of certain information in the case of a request for the accelerated competent authority procedure, and section 10 of such procedure, which requires the provision of certain information in the case of a request for Rev. Proc. 99-32 treatment. Requests for supplemental information may include items such as detailed financial information, comparability analysis, or other material relevant to a transfer pricing analysis.	

Revenue Procedure 2006-54 also delineates those circumstances in which the U.S. Competent Authority will not accept a request for assistance. For example, Revenue Procedure 2006-54 provides that competent authority assistance generally will not be granted when the taxpayer has rejected a competent authority resolution of the same of similar facts or when the taxpayer is not entitled to the treaty benefit requested.

8. How to Find U.S. Tax Treaties and Their Legislative History

All U.S. treaties, whether bilateral or multilateral, are listed in Treaties in Force (TIF). The publication lists all treaties and international agreements on record with the U.S. Department of State. It is arranged in two parts. Part 1 lists bilateral treaties by country. For each country, Part I lists all treaties in force alphabetically by subject matter. Part 2 lists multilateral treaties and international agreements to which the United States is a party. U.S. income tax treaties are listed in Part 1. TIF is updated annually. TIF includes the date the treaty entered into force, the parties, and citations to the treaty.

Quick Find:

The State Department maintains an on-line version of TIF at www.state.gov.

TIF citations are to the official State Department Source of treaty text, Treaties and Other International Agreements (TIAS). TIAS is printed in slip form. The series of individual pamphlets are consecutively numbered starting at 1501. The individual pamphlets overtime are issued as part of bound volumes of United States Treaties and Other International Agreements (UST). There is currently a long delay between a treaty entering into force and TIAS publication. A treaty citation to TIAS without a number indicates that the treaty has yet to be published in TIAS.

TIF, TIAS and UST are focused on all U.S. treaties, not just U.S. income tax treaties. Further, all three are subject to delays; in the case of TIAS and UST, it can take several years for publication. There are several sources for U.S. tax treaties that are more timely and dedicated solely to U.S. income tax treaties and tax treaty related documents.

The text of most U.S. tax treaties can be found on-line on the IRS website at www.irs.gov. The website has the complete texts of over 60 U.S. income tax treaties and their corresponding technical explanations. The website is updated periodically. As a result it may not contain the most current treaty for a particular country. The text of U.S. tax treaties and their legislative history can also be obtained from the following address:

> Department of Treasury
> Office of Public Correspondence
> 1500 Pennsylvania Ave. NW RM 3419
> Washington, DC 20220

U.S. tax treaties are also published in the Internal Revenue Bulletin along with the Treasury Technical Explanation and Senate Reports. The documents are then reprinted as part of the Cumulative Bulletin.

IRS Publication 901, titled "U.S. Tax Treaties," is also a helpful treaty research tool. The publication gives a country-by-country summary of all U.S. tax treaties, including the reduced rates of U.S. income tax for residents of the particular treaty country. At the back of the publication are helpful tables that list the countries that have income tax treaties with the United States, the effective date of the treaties, and the tax rates under a treaty for different kinds of income. The publication also contains a "What's New" section that discusses recently negotiated U.S. tax treaties and the effective date of the new treaties.

The Treasury Department website also contains the full text of treaties entered into after 1995. However, the treaties are in their proposed form, prior to ratification by the Senate. In some cases the final version ratified by the Senate may differ from the proposed version.

Quick Find:

The Treasury website can be found at www.treas.gov. To find the draft tax treaties use the search terms "tax treaty documents" in the websites internal search engine.

The site also contains the full text of each corresponding Treasury Technical Explanation and Joint Committee on Taxation Explanation. The text of the testimony of Treasury officials before the Senate Committee on Foreign Relations can also be found on the Treasury Department website.

U.S. tax treaties are also available through a number of commercial publishers in a variety of different formats. LexisNexis, WestLaw, RIA, CCH, and Tax Analysts all make U.S. tax treaties available through their on-line subscription services.

U.S. tax treaties are also reproduced by several publishers in a loose-leaf format.

Chart 11.2 Examples of Commercial U.S. Tax Treaty Resources

Commercial U.S. Tax Treaty Resources

Source/Publisher	Format	Comments
Rhoades & Langer, U.S. International Taxation and Tax Treaties (Mathew Bender).	Loose-leaf, also available through LexisNexis.	This six volume loose-leaf treatise serves as an international tax treatise and also includes the annotated text of all U.S. tax treaties currently in force. Also, contains the text of U.S. estate and gift tax treaties. The treaties are arranged alphabetically by treaty partner.
Federal Tax Coordinator, 2d (RIA).	Loose-leaf, also available through RIA's on-line subscription service, RIA Checkpoint.	Volume 20 contains all income, gift, and estate tax treaties currently in effect between the U.S. and foreign countries.
Tax Treaties (CCH).	Loose-leaf, also available trough CCH's on-line subscription service, CCH Tax Research Network.	Contains text of Model Treaties and U.S. income tax treaties. It is arranged alphabetically by treaty partner and includes Treasury Department Technical Explanation and relevant regulations, rulings, and court decisions.
Tax Management Portfolios (BNA).	Portfolio.	The Tax Management Foreign Income Portfolios called "Business Operations

		in _____ " generally contain the U.S. tax treaty with the country discussed in the portfolio. Treaties are located in the "Worksheets" section of the particular country's portfolio. Treaties can also be located by the classification index.
Worldwide Tax Treaties (Tax Analysts).	CD and on-line.	Contains tax treaties, treaty-related news, the OECD model income tax treaty, the complete U.S. tax treaty legislative histories, and analysis of cross-border transactions.
IBFD Worldwide Tax Treaties.	On-line, available through RIA's subscription service.	Contains treaties concerning the avoidance of double taxation of income and capital; estates, inheritance, and gifts; and the OECD Model Treaty.
Tax Treaties (Warren Gorham & Lamont).	Loose-leaf.	Contains text of U.S. income and estate and gift tax treaties. Also includes negotiation and ratification documents such as diplomatic notes, Treasury Technical Explanation, Joint Committee on Taxation Explanation, and Assistant Treasury Secretary statements. The treaties are arranged alphabetically by treaty partner.

9. Foreign Tax Law

Every international tax issue potentially involves the taxing jurisdiction of two independent countries. The focus up to this point has been on researching U.S. international tax rules. However, in many cases it may be helpful or even necessary to have a basic understanding of the tax laws of another country. There are several sources of country-specific tax information.

Tax Management publishes Foreign Income Portfolios called "Business Operations in _____" (for example, Business Operations in Hong Kong) for most developed countries (Business Operations Portfolios). Each Business Operations Portfolio provides a description of the business regulatory structure in the particular country, a discussion of the choice of entity options, and a relatively detailed description of the general tax scheme for corporate and individual income taxation in such country. The tax discussion focuses on taxation of residents and nonresidents. Each portfolio also contains a "Working Pa-

pers" section that contains such things as sample tax forms and, if applicable, any tax treaties entered into with the United States.

The larger accounting firms also often publish guides to doing business in most foreign jurisdictions. The guides generally include a description of the regulatory and tax system in the particular country for residents and nonresidents. They also contain practical information on the country's history, public holidays, and transportation options.

A great deal of information on the tax systems of various countries can also be found electronically on the web. Like all information on the web, one must question the reliability and timeliness of such information. However, most countries have official websites that contain up-to-date information on the country's tax system. Such websites generally contain practical information, such as forms and publications, that guide nonresidents through the country's tax system. In most cases, the website is sponsored by the agency within the country responsible for enforcing the country's revenue laws. However, not all of the websites are in English and the amount of information provided varies by country.

RIA's electronic subscription service, Checkpoint, has a wealth of information on the tax laws of foreign countries. The electronic service contains English translations of the tax and commercial laws of most countries in "RIA Worldwide Tax and Commercial Law". The service also contains "IBFD Regional Analysis" which provides summaries of the tax laws of almost every country.

The Tax and Accounting Sites Directory website can be of great assistance in locating the official website of most countries' taxing authority. The site has a comprehensive index and links to the official tax authority websites of most countries.

Quick Find:

The Tax and Accounting Sites Directory can be found at www.taxsites.com. To access the website of a particular country, click on "international tax websites." Once on the page, just choose the country of interest.

Example:

The excerpt below is from Brochure -003, "Income from Salary" issued by the Central Board of Revenue Government of Pakistan. Brochure -003 was located by going to www.taxsites.com and clicking "international," "@Country-Specific Tax Sites," "Pakistan," and "Central Board of Pakistan." The Central Board of Pakistan website contains a vast amount of information, including brochures such as -003, income tax forms, and contact information.

Revenue Division
CENTRAL BOARD OF REVENUE
GOVERNMENT OF PAKISTAN

Brochure -003
July 2003

Revenue Division
Central Board of Revenue
Government of Pakistan
Brochure -003
July 2003

Introduction

This brochure gives basic information for the benefit and use of persons deriving income from salary to understand their obligations and compute the chargeable income from "salary" under the Income Tax Ordinance, 2001. It is equally informative and useful from the employers' perspective.

In this brochure some terms that are not familiar to taxpayers used for the first time are in *italic bold* and explained appropriately.

This brochure is to assist the taxpayers and reflects the legal position at the time of printing. In case of any conflict the legal provisions of the law shall always prevail over the contents of this brochure.

Comments and suggestions

We welcome your comments about this brochure and your suggestions for future editions.

You can e-mail us at membertpef@cbr.gov.pk

or

You can write to us at the following address:

Taxpayer Education and Facilitation,
Central Board of Revenue,
Constitution Avenue, Islamabad

General Concepts of Taxation

The Federal levy on income (Income Tax), with effect from July 01, 2002, is governed by the Income Tax Ordinance, 2001 and Income Tax Rules, 2002. It is an annual charge on the *taxable income* for a *tax year*, if it exceeds the *maximum amount that is not chargeable to tax.*

"Taxable Income" means *total income* as reduced by deductible allowance on account of Zakat paid under the Zakat and Usher Ordinance, 1980 other than Zakat paid on a debt, the profit of which is chargeable to tax under the head "Income from Other Sources" and the deduction is admissible against such profit on debt.

"Total Income" is the sum of income under the following heads: Salary, Income from property; Income from business; Capital gains; and Income from other sources [like dividend, royalty, profit on debt, ground rent, rent from sub-lease of land or building, income from lease of any building together with plant or machinery, prize on prize bond, winnings from a raffle, lottery or crossword puzzle, or a *loan, advance, deposit or gift* (subject to certain conditions)].

Income under a specific head for a tax year is the total of the amounts derived under that head, which are chargeable to tax, as reduced by the deductions, if any, admissible under the Income Tax Ordinance, 2001....

The scope of total income under the Income Tax Ordinance, 2001 is determined with reference to residential status of a taxpayer. In case of *resident individual* it is both *Pakistan source income and foreign source income*, while in case of *non-resident individual* it is restricted to Pakistan source income only.

An individual is **"resident individual"** if: he is present in Pakistan for 182 days or more in a tax year; or he is present in Pakistan for 90 days or more in a tax year and for 365 days or more in the four years preceding the tax year; or *he is an employee or official of the Federal or Provincial Government posted abroad in a tax year*....

An individual is **"non-resident"** if he is not a resident individual.

"Pakistan source income" is defined in section 101 of the Income Tax Ordinance, 2001, which caters for incomes under different heads and situations. Some of the relevant Pakistani source incomes are as under:

Salary received from any *employment* exercised in Pakistan wherever paid;

Salary paid by, or on behalf of, the Federal Government, a Provincial Government, or a local authority in Pakistan, wherever the employment is exercised;

Dividend paid by resident company;

Profit on debt paid by a resident person;

Property or rental income from the lease of immovable property in Pakistan;

Pension or annuity paid by a resident person or permanent establishment of a non-resident person;

"Foreign source income" is all such incomes, which are not Pakistan source income.

The Tax and Accounting Sites Directory website also contains links to country-specific websites that are privately sponsored, such as www.worldwide-tax.com. Worldwide-tax.com gives basic tax information for various countries. For each country listed the site contains tax information such as tax rates, types of legal entities, filing dates, a brief description of the country's individual and corporate tax systems and a description of the country's social security tax system.

The OECD also maintains country-specific tax information on its website. Such information generally relates to tax policy rather than the practical application of a country's tax laws.

Quick Find:

The OECD website can be found at www.oecd.org.

The discussion above just touches on some of the foreign tax information contained on the web. A search of the internet will produce volumes of information relating to country-specific tax law; however, the reliability of such information must be confirmed.

---

10. Specific Treatises Dealing with International Taxation

As discussed in Chapter 10, Researching the Issue, various commercial publishers have prepared treatises that contain a substantial amount of information on U.S. income tax law. Several of the treatises discussed in length in Chapter 10 contain a vast amount of information on U.S. international tax law. Treatises arranged by Code section, CCH's Standard Federal Tax Reporter and RIA's United States Tax Reporter, cover the international provisions of the Code. Treatises arranged by topic, RIA's Federal Tax Coordinator 2d and Mertens Law of Federal Income Taxation, cover international issues.

BNA's Tax Management Portfolio Series contains "Foreign Income Portfolios" covering U.S. international issues and foreign business and tax matters. International tax issues can be researched through several methods in the Foreign Income Portfolios. Issues can be examined by topic, Code section, or keyword by using the appropriate index in the index volume. BNA has over 70 spiral portfolios in its Foreign Income Tax Portfolios series.

There are also several tax treatises dedicated solely to international taxation or international tax issues.

Chart 11.3 Examples of Treatises Dedicated to International Taxation

Treatise	Author(s)	Publisher
Foreign Tax Credits	Andersen	Thomson RIA (WGL)
Analysis of United States Income Tax Treaties	Andersen	Thomson RIA (WGL)
U.S. Taxation of International Mergers, Acquisitions and Joint Ventures	Dolan	Thomson RIA (WGL)
International Transfer Pricing: OECD Guidelines	Lowell, Burge & Levey	Thomson RIA (WGL)
U.S. Taxation of Foreign Controlled Businesses	Levey	Thomson RIA (WGL)
International Tax & Estate Planning	Lawrence	Practicing Law Institute
U.S. International Taxation: Practice and Procedure	Lowell & Governale	Thomson RIA (WGL)
U.S. International Transfer Pricing	Lowell, Burge, & Briger	Thomson RIA (WGL)
International Income Tax Rules of the United States	McIntyre	LexisNexis
U.S. International Taxation: Agreements, Checklists & Commentary	Lowell, Tilton, Sheldrick & Donohue	Thomson RIA (WGL)
Principles of Financial Derivatives: US & International Taxation	Colon & Aquilino	Thomson RIA (WGL)
U.S. International Estate Planning	Streng	Thomson RIA (WGL)
Foundations of International Tax	Braetz	Foundation Press
Fundamentals of International Taxation: U.S. Taxation of Foreign Income and Foreign Taxpayers	Bittker, Looken, Culverhouse	Thomson RIA
International Taxation	Isenbergh	Foundation Press
U.S. International Taxation	Kuntz, Peroni	Thomson RIA
International Taxation in a Nutshell	Doernberg	West

11. On-Line Resources for International Taxation

All of the on-line subscription services (LexisNexis, WestLaw, RIA, and CCH), discussed in Chapter 10, Researching the Issue, maintain materials on international taxation. The on-line subscription services generally provide all of the U.S. Code provisions, regulations, and

IRS publications dedicated to U.S. international taxation. In addition, they generally contain treaties, journals, and U.S. tax treaties dedicated to international taxation.

A vast amount of information on international taxation can also be found on-line through free sites. The IRS website, www.irs.gov, contains several pages, publications, tax forms, and links dedicated to international taxation. For example, the site contains descriptions of key U.S. international tax concepts, information on U.S. Competent Authority assistance, and international tax news and events. Most U.S. tax treaties and their ratification history can also be found on the IRS website.

Quick Find:

The international tax section of the IRS website can be located by going to www.irs.gov. Once at the IRS website, click on "businesses" and "international businesses." International tax forms and publications can be found on the website through either a word search or by examining the list of forms and publications.

Practice Note:

Examples of the IRS Publications covering international tax topics include:

➤ Publication 686, Certification for Reduced Tax Rates in Tax Treaty Countries

➤ Publication 514, Foreign Tax Credit for Individuals

➤ Publication 597, Information on the United States-Canada Income Tax Treaty

➤ Publication 570, Tax Guide for Individuals With Income From U.S. Possessions

➤ Publication 54, Tax Guide for U.S. Citizens and Resident Aliens Abroad

➤ Publication 593, Tax Highlights for U.S. Citizens and Residents Going Abroad

➤ Publication 513, Tax Information for Visitors to the United States

➤ Publication 516, U.S. Government Civilian Employees Stationed Abroad

➤ Publication 519, U.S. Tax Guide for Aliens

➤ Publication 901, U.S. Tax Treaties

➤ Publication 515, Withholding of Tax on Nonresident Aliens and Foreign Corporations

---

Several other free websites contain international tax information, such as the OECD website and the Windstar Publishing Inc. website. Also, there are several international tax associations, such as International Tax Planning Association, that maintain websites containing some international tax information. The Tax and Accounting Sites Directory website (www.taxsites.com) maintains an index and links to a vast number of websites containing international tax information, including all of the ones referenced above.

C. Main Points

• International tax issues involve the taxing jurisdiction of two or more countries.

• U.S. international tax law is generally contained in Subtitle A. Chapter 1, Subchapter N of the Code.

The U.S. international tax Code provisions can be divided into two major subtopics, inbound international tax provisions and outbound international tax provisions.

- The U.S. has entered into more than 50 bilateral income tax treaties, which may impact the U.S. tax consequences of international income.

- Most U.S. income tax treaties contain a "mutual agreement procedure" article that allows a resident of the contracting states to seek relief from a "competent authority" when the resident believes that the actions of one or both of the contracting parties is not in accordance with the convention.

- Under the U.S. Constitution the president has the power to enter into treaties with advice and consent of the Senate by a two-thirds vote.

- U.S. tax treaties can be found through various sources including the IRS website.

- In the process of negotiating and ratifying a treaty, several pieces of documentation are created such as Diplomatic Notes and the Treasury Department Technical Explanation.

- Courts may look to numerous extrinsic materials, such as the Treasury Technical Explanation and competent authority agreements, when interpreting tax treaties.

- The Code and treaties are legal equals. When there is a conflict between a Code provision and a treaty provision the last-in-time will control.

- Information on foreign tax law can be obtained through various sources such as Tax Management's Foreign Income Portfolios and on internet sites operated by a particular country's taxing authority.

- A great deal of information on U.S. international tax law can be found on-line. The IRS website has an extensive collection of international tax materials.

D. Related Articles for Further Reading

- Tracey Bridgman, *Federal Tax Research*, E.B. Williams Library Research Guides, Georgetown University Law Center, updated Oct. 14, 2009 http://www.ll.georgetown.edu/guides/federal_tax.cfm (updated July 28, 2004).

- Warren Crowdus, *The Interaction of Treaty and Code Source Rules*, J. INT'L TAX'N (April 2002).

- John A. Townsend, *Tax Treaty Interpretation*, 55 TAX LAW. 221 (2001).

- Philip F. Postlewaite & Dave S. Makarski, *The A.L.I Tax Treaty Study — A Critique and a Proposal*, 49 TAX LAW. 731 (1999).

- David L. Raish & N. Susan Stone, *Issues Paper on the Tax Treaty Making Process*, 46 TAX LAW. 477 (1993).

E. Problems

1. The Treasury Department Technical Explanations is:
   a. Prepared with the assistance of the treaty partner.
   b. Prepared during the treaty negotiation process.
   c. Not made available to the public.
   d. Entitled to a great deal of deference when interpreting U.S. tax treaties.

2. The U.S. Model Income Tax Treaty:
   a. Is the starting point for U.S. treaty negotiations.
   b. Is used as a "take it or leave it" offer in treaty negotiations.
   c. Represents a lack of support for the OECD Model Treaty.
   d. Is not used to assist in U.S. treaty interpretation.

3. What materials are used by U.S. courts in interpreting U.S. tax treaties?
   a. The U.S. Model Treaty and its technical explanation.
   b. The Treasury Technical Explanation.
   d. Competent Authority agreements.
   e. The OECD Model Treaty and its commentary.
   f. All of the above.

4. Inbound taxation refers to:
   a. The taxation of U.S. citizens and residents on their income generated abroad.
   b. The taxation of non-resident aliens in the United States.
   c. Taxation under the London agreement.
   d. The taxation of U.S. citizens by foreign governments.

5. Describe the inter-relationship between the international provisions of the Code and U.S. bilateral income tax treaties.

6. The Tax Court has held there is a conflict between section 842(b) and Article VII of the U.S.-Canada Tax Treaty. Please examine both provisions. Which is controlling for U.S. tax purposes?

7. The Treasury Explanation and other treaty ratification documents are often used to assist courts in interpreting treaties. Should ratification documents be used as a tool to interpret U.S. treaties? Why or why not?

8. Examine Article 24 of the U.S.-Austria Income Tax Convention. What is the purpose of such article?

9. Does the United Kingdom have a foreign tax credit mechanism? What resource did you use to arrive at your answer?

10. Can a trust qualify for treaty relief under the U.S.-Japan Treaty?

11. Eastern Oil Corporation, a domestic corporation, has a Saudi Arabian subsidiary, Saudi Oil Ltd. Saudi Oil Ltd. was established under Saudi law and pays taxes in Saudi Arabia. Saudi Oil Ltd. is currently under tax audit in Saudi Arabia. The Saudi tax officials are not asserting that Saudi Oil Ltd. has underpaid its taxes. However, they are asserting that Eastern Oil Corporation has a taxable presence in Saudi Arabia. As a result, the tax officials have asserted that Eastern Oil Corporation should be paying taxes in Saudi Arabia. Eastern Oil Corporation would like to seek the assistance of the U.S. Competent Authority. What steps should Eastern Oil Corporation take?

12. What is the definition of "U.S. Shareholder" for purposes of Subpart of F of Subtitle A, Chapter 1, Subchapter N, Part III of the Code?

13. Find IRS Publication 515. Describe how the publication could be of assistance.

14. Which branch of the Office of Associate Chief Counsel (International) is responsible for U.S. foreign tax credit issues? What is the phone number of such branch?

15. Examine the February 25, 2004, testimony of Barbra M. Angus, International Tax Counsel, United States Department of the Treasury, before the Senate Committee on Foreign Relations on pending income tax agreements. What two tax treaties does Barbra M. Angus urge the Committee and the Senate to take prompt and favorable action on?

16. Locate the website of the United Kingdom HM Revenue and Customs office. Find the following information:
    a. Form SA-100 — Individual Tax Return.
    b. The 2005 Tax Credits Update Newsletter.
    c. Notice 704/1 VAT Refunds for travelers departing from the European Community (EC).

17. When did the following treaties enter into force?

    a. 1998 U.S.-Estonia Income Tax Convention.
    b. 2003 U.S.-Japan Income Tax Convention.
    c. 2002 U.S.-Mexico Second Protocol amending the Convention between the United States and Mexico.

18. Is Code Section 901 an inbound or an outbound international Code provision?

Chapter 12

Cite Checking

[handwritten: Related to research project]

Cite Checking

[handwritten: Purpose of Cite Checking 1) To check if the case we are looking at still good law and then, 2) It helps us find other primary authorities.]

- *Why check your citations?*
- *In what other ways is cite checking beneficial?*
- *How is cite checking done?*

Elizabeth walked into Connie's office. "I thought you could use this," Elizabeth said as she set a cup of coffee down on Connie's desk.

"Oh, is it that obvious?"

"Well, you have been hunched over your computer all day. I don't know how you can see straight any more. What is it that you are working on so intently?" Elizabeth settled into a chair opposite Connie's desk.

"I have been doing some research for a client on hobby loss limitations. I found some excellent language dealing with horse breeding. It really supports the position my clients want to take."

"That doesn't seem to be such a problem." Elizabeth said.

"Well, it wouldn't be if my clients' hobby were horse breeding. It's not. They breed golden retrievers. What I am looking for is whether a court has used language similar to what I found in the horse breeding case when considering a different hobby. In other words, I want to make sure the law isn't limited to the facts before the court in the horse breeding case."

"What have you tried so far?"

"A lot of word searches that have gotten me no where."

"Have you tried cite checking the case?"

"Cite checking? How can that help me?"

Contents

A. Key Terms

After completing this chapter, you should be familiar with the following key terms:

➤ Cite Checking

➤ Citing Cases

➤ Shepard's Federal Tax Citator

➤ RIA's Citator Series

➤ CCH's Standard Federal Tax Reporter

➤ Shepard's Federal Statute Citations

➤ Shepard's Code of Federal Regulations Citations

B. Discussion

Trial court decisions can be overturned by circuit courts of appeals. In turn, circuit courts can be overturned by the Supreme Court. In addition, one circuit court may disagree with a position taken by another court. Thus, before a researcher relies on a court opinion, he should make sure that it has not been overruled, reversed, criticized, limited, or distinguished. This process is referred to as **cite checking**.

> Through **cite checking** a case, the researcher determines whether the case has been overruled, reversed, criticized, limited, or distinguished.

In evaluating the status of a case, some citation sources also provide a list of cases that cite to the case being checked. These cases are often referred to as **citing cases**. Because the citing case cites to the case under consideration, presumably addressing the same issue, the researcher can read the citing case and see if it contains an analysis or facts that are beneficial to the researcher.

> **Citing cases** are cases that cite to the case under consideration.

Some citation sources also contain references to annotations and law review articles that have cited the case at issue. These sources may provide additional valuable information.

1. Cite Checking Cases

Shepard's Federal Tax Citator. LexisNexis publishes **Shepard's Federal Tax Citator**. To cite check a case, first select the correct volume that contains the type of reporter of the case being considered (*i.e.*, Tax Court, American Federal Tax Reports 2d, etc.). The Federal Tax Citator shows citations to federal court tax cases reported in:

- United States Reports
- American Federal Tax Reports
- United States Tax Cases
- United States Supreme Court Reports, Lawyers' Edition
- Supreme Court Reporter
- Federal Reporter
- Federal Supplement
- Federal Rules Decisions
- Bankruptcy Reporter
- Federal Claims Reporter
- Claims Court Reporter
- United States Board of Tax Appeals Reports
- Tax Court of the United States Reports
- United States Tax Court Reports
- Tax Court Memorandum Decisions

Then locate the correct volume based on the year in which the opinion was issued. The cases are organized by reporter and then chronologically first by volume number, then page number. The citation and any parallel citations will be listed first. After that, any action taken on the case will be indicated. In addition to providing any subsequent action on a case, the Citator also indicates all cases that have cited the case under consideration. The citing cases are organized by jurisdiction and court. Where relevant, Shepard's includes a superscript numeral that corresponds to a headnote in the case being cite checked. Finally, consult all subsequent volumes and supplements for later developments in the case.

Example:

The following is an example of the information found in Shepard's Federal Tax Citator Case Edition Supplement 2002–2006 Part I, page 505:

UNITED STATES TAX CASES (CCH)   Vol. 68-2

Column 1

```
(391US83)
(20LE448)
(88SC1517)
FSAdv
  [#199946008
FSAdv
  [#199952041
FSAdv
  [#200103006
FSAdv
  [#200117020
FSAdv
  [#200135020
FSAdv
  [#200206010
IRCCA
  [#200224007
ReR#77-221
ClCt
2002-1UTC¶
  [ 50389
52FedCl 173
97TAXJ6
¶ 9390
s) 47TCt723
¶ 9391
ReR#71-120
¶ 9400
Cir. 11
392F3d1274
178ARF390n
¶ 9402
s) 47TCt723
ReR#69-466
¶ 9410
Cir. 3
300F3d323
Cir. 9
d) 91AF2d2613
d) 2003-2UTC¶
  [ 50555
d) 65Fed Appx
  [642
¶ 9423
74TCt446
74TCt#31
Cir. 9
2004-2UTC¶
  [ 50308
376F3d1023
¶ 9429
123TCt82
¶ 9431
f) 2005TCM LX
  [215
f) 2005TCM
  [#214
¶ 9432
(21AF2d1517)
(396F2d452)
s) 68-2UTC¶
  [ 12536
54TCt#162
```

Column 2

```
Cir. 8
71-1UTC¶
  [ 12740
¶ 12499
ReR#77-461
Cir. 2
f) 2002-2UTC¶
  [ 60443
f) 294F3d354
Cir. 5
2004-1UTC¶
  [ 60478
306FS2d673
Cir. 11
99-2UTC¶
  [ 60365
81FS2d1223
Tex
~) 157SW849
¶ 12500
Cir. 5
2003-1UTC¶
  [ 50418
256FS2d540
¶ 12502
ReR#71-507
¶ 12504
ReR#77-194
¶ 12509
ReR#78-399
¶ 12511
ReR#69-164
¶ 12515
Estate of
Goodall v
Commissioner
1968
s) 68-1UTC¶
  [ 9245
cc) 106FS699
¶ 12516
Ala
~) 837So2d856
¶ 12522
118TCt288
d) 118TCt297
118TCt419
d) 118TCt#14
118TCt#25
FSAdv
  [#200143004
80TAX(7)17
¶ 12526
f) ReR#74-556
¶ 15782
ReR#69-318
¶ 15784
ReR#77-391
¶ 15800
(21AF2d539)
(390US39)
(19LE889)
(88SC697)
ReR#77-51
```

Column 3

```
Cir. 2
334FS2d368
d) 334FS2d370
Cir. 3
f) 327FS2d529
Cir. 5
98Fed Appx
  [991
f) 98Fed Appx
  [992
Cir. 6
87AF2d901
2001-1UTC¶
  [ 50283
361F3d922
5Fed Appx350
f) 297FS2d962
368FS2d850
Cir. 7
250FS2d1043
Cir. 8
318F3d856
d) 405F3d716
Cir. 9
f) 2005USDist
  [LX22295
Cir. 11
2002-2UTC¶
  [ 50620
218FS2d1348
ClCt
57FedCl 55
Calif
#) 107CaR2d
  [759
#) 124CaR2d64
#) 127CaR2d
  [220
130CaR2d223
12CaR3d207
D C
831A2d912
Ill
j) 773NE218
Md
837A2d1050
N Y
742NYS2d921
Ore
f) 85P3d342
Pa
831A2d746
69ChL1191
69ChL1319
72ChL881
90Geo1690
99HLR640
104HLR178
113HLR501
84McL1544
101McL2557
104McL779
68MnL677
154PaL335
90VaL1
```

Column 4

```
¶ 15801
ReR#77-51
Cir. 3
386F3d542
173FS2d311
Cir. 6
368FS2d849
Cir. 7
250FS2d1043
Cir. 8
d) 405F3d717
ClCt
57FedCl 55
Calif
#) 127CaR2d
  [220
Pa
831A2d744
113HLR501
84McL1544
68MnL677
¶ 15802
124TCt283
Cir. 6
368FS2d850
Cir. 8
j) 430F3d918
Calif
#) 127CaR2d
  [220
12CaR3d207
Mich
q) 668NW395
Pa
831A2d746
Wyo
100P3d402
102CR2027
113HLR501
101McL2557
68MnL677
¶ 15809
ReR#91-27
¶ 15822
Cir. 9
182FS2d975
¶ 15838
Cir. 5
204FS2d983
215FS2d822
¶ 15847
Cir. 10
324FS2d1251

Vol. 68-2

¶ 9436
2002TCM#148
¶ 9437
FSAdv
  [#199933005
¶ 9438
2002TCM#119
FSAdv
  [#199907002
```

Column 5

```
FSAdv
  [#199909018
FSAdv
  [#199911003
FSAdv
  [#199913004
FSAdv
  [#199916005
d) FSAdv
  [#199921002
FSAdv
  [#199922012
FSAdv
  [#199929002
FSAdv
  [#199945013
FSAdv
  [#200004016
f) FSAdv
  [#200004016
FSAdv
  [#200010032
FSAdv
  [#200021005
FSAdv
  [#200024003
FSAdv
  [#200031007
FSAdv
  [#200034010
FSAdv
  [#200133013
FSAdv
  [#200148039
Ltr#200323014
Ltr#200336004
Ltr#200413010
Ltr#200512020
f) IRCCA
  [#200235004
Mass
764NE368
80TAX(3)91
100McL891
¶ 9439
IRCCA
  [#200235004
80TAX(3)91
¶ 9441
ReR#73-51
¶ 9447
FSAdv
  [#199926004
115YLJ680
¶ 9450
f) ReR#68-645
¶ 9455
s) 47TCt724
¶ 9460
ReR#74-166
Cir. 8
906FS528
CtCl
82-2UTC¶
  [ 13483
```

Column 6

```
¶ 9470
Cir. 3
74-2UTC¶
  [ 9557
74-2UTC¶
  [ 9640
379FS496
ClCt
2002-1UTC¶
  [ 50192
51FedCl 447
¶ 9473
ClCt
68FedCl 326
¶ 9474
FSAdv
  [#199922012
d) FSAdv
  [#199922012
FSAdv
  [#200133013
¶ 9479
97HLR1143
¶ 9480
2002TCM#128
¶ 9486
FSAdv
  [#199925016
¶ 9493
Cir. 2
91AF2d2322
2003-1UTC¶
  [ 50495
67Fed Appx23
¶ 9499
2006TCM LX
  [16
2002TCM#125
2006TCM#14
Cir. 9
2005-2UTC¶
  [ 50613
326BRW822
¶ 9500
96HLR886
¶ 9502
124TCt251
ReR#90-20
¶ 9516
118TCt244
82TCt#60
118TCt#13
¶ 9519
ReR#2002-69
¶ 9521
FSAdv
  [#199930005
La
f) 898So2d401
¶ 9528
ReR#98-15
¶ 9534
Ind
762NE745
```

RIA Citator Series. Cases can be cite checked by case name in **RIA's Citator Series**. Note that the Citator Series is not a part of RIA's United States Tax Reporter.

In the Citator Series, first locate the case based on the year it was issued.[1] The cases are organized alphabetically. The first entry will give you the location of the case, whether official or unofficial. It provides subsequent action taken on a case and a list of all citing cases. Next, consult all subsequent volumes and supplements for later developments in the case.

CCH's Standard Federal Tax Reporter. In **CCH's Standard Federal Tax Reporter**, cases can be cite checked through the Cases Finding List. First, locate the case in the Finding List. Following the case is a history of the case. Bullets (•) are used to indicate action taken by any court that considered the case. Some citing cases are listed under the bulleted citation. However, the citator list includes as citing cases only those cases CCH deems relevant; the list is not comprehensive.

---

1. RIA's Citator Series was previously owned and published by Prentice-Hall, then Maxwell Macmillan. The name "Prentice-Hall" had been used on the Series, but has not been used since Volume 3.

Example:

The following is an example of the information found in CCH's Standard Federal Tax Reporter:

PER 95,538 ————CCH————

Perdue, Franklin P. ...... ¶ 11,660.502, 39,455.68, 39,651G.165, 39,654.60
● TC—Dec. 47,648(M); 62 TCM 845; TC Memo. 1991-478
Scull Est., TC, Dec. 49,840(M), 67 TCM 2953, TC Memo. 1994-211
Mueller, TC, Dec. 48,225(M), 63 TCM 3027, TC Memo. 1992-284
Perdue, Matthew M. .... ¶ 38,963.40, 42,282.65
● TC—Dec. 53,729(M); TC Memo. 2000-28; 79 TC 1415
Pereira, Alfred v. Earle .... ¶ 25,124.95
● DC-Ore—51-2 USTC ¶ 9427
Pereira, Alfredo F. .... ¶ 12,014.304, 41,130.29, 42,322.84, 42,322.85
● TC—Dec. 33,698(M); 35 TCM 290; TC Memo. 1976-66
Losmann, TC, Dec. 46,475(M), 59 TCM 172, TC Memo. 1990-149
Litzenberg, David, TC, Dec. 45,114(M), 56 TCM 413, TC Memo. 1988-482
Lewis, TC, Dec. 43,072(M), 51 TCM 1072, TC Memo. 1986-211
Pereira, Alfredo F. .... ¶ 12,014.4055
● TC—Dec. 33,379(M); 34 TCM 1116; TC Memo. 1975-260
Whyte, CA-7, 88-2 USTC ¶ 9440, 852 F2d 306
Pereira, John (See Rodriguez, Rene R.)
Perel, Barnet (See Kolkey, Emanuel N. (Manny)
Perel and Lowenstein, Inc. ..... ¶ 8636.35, 8637.671
● CA-6—(aff'g TC), 56-2 USTC ¶ 10,035; 237 F2d 908
● TC—Dec. 20,999(M); 14 TCM 412; TC Memo. 1955-115
Pereles, Richard M. .... ¶ 29,335.591
● TC—Dec. 29,716(M); 28 TCM 872; TC Memo. 1969-174
Perelli-Minetti Estate, A. G. .... ¶ 8520.591
● BTA—Dec. 4190; 12 BTA 1082
Perelman, Howard H. ...... ¶ 20,620.142, 22,277.53, 29,225.1643
● TC—Dec. 26,399; 41 TC 234; A. 1965-2 CB 6
Campbell Co., TC, Dec. 29,889, 53 TC 439
Witte, CA-DC, 75-1 USTC ¶ 9477, 513 F2d 391
Campbell Co., CA-6, 71-1 USTC ¶ 9471, 443 F2d 965
Kaufman, TC, Dec. 26,786(M), 23 TCM 747, TC Memo. 1964-127
Phipps Industrial Land Trust, TC, Dec. 26,435(M), 22 TCM 1724, TC Memo. 1963-329
Perelman, Ronald O. (See Marvel Entertainment Group, Inc.)
Pereos, Alexander C. ...... ¶ 5507.4652, 20,620.608, 35,111.58, 39,651G.64, 44,419.10
● TC—Dec. 27,461(M); 24 TCM 949; TC Memo. 1965-180
Rector, TC, Dec. 35,179(M), 37 TCM 838, TC Memo. 1978-193
Pereos, C.N. .. ¶ 38,187.51, 38,519.71, 41,688.106, 41,688.546
● DC-Nev—2001-1 USTC ¶ 50,273
Perez, Angel P. .... ¶ 31,882.265
● DC-Fla—83-1 USTC ¶ 9106; 553 FSupp 558
Kraft, CA-6, 93-1 USTC ¶ 50,278, 991 F2d 292
Parks, DC-Pa, 96-2 USTC ¶ 50,645, 945 FSupp 865
Culley, CA-FC, 2000-2 USTC ¶ 50,662, 222 F3d 1391
Wang, Jr., TC, Dec. 52,937(M), 76 TCM 753, TC Memo. 1998-389
Perez, Augustin O. (See Fernandez, Augustin R.)
Perez, Carlos B. .... ¶ 38,967.29
● CA-2—(gov't's appeal dismissed pursuant to agreement of the parties), December 4, 1975
● TC—Dec. 32,725(M); 33 TCM 946; TC Memo. 1974-211
Forrest Cox, TC, Dec. 49,432(M), 66 TCM 1430, TC Memo. 1993-559
CMEM, Inc., TC, Dec. 49,390(M), 66 TCM 1241, TC Memo. 1993-520
Franklin, TC, Dec. 49,008(M), 65 TCM 2497, TC Memo. 1993-184
McNichols, TC, Dec. 48,870(M), 65 TCM 1943, TC Memo. 1993-61
Langworthy, Jr., TC, Dec. 52,747(M), 75 TCM 2501, TC Memo. 1998-218
AJF Transportation Consultants, Inc., TC, Dec. 53,220(M), TC Memo. 1999-16, 77 TCM 1244
AJF Transportation Consultants, Inc., CA-2, 2000-1 USTC ¶ 50,473, 213 F3d 625
Shaw, TC, Dec. 55,119(M), TC Memo. 2003-111, 85 TCM 1179
Proctor, TC, Dec. 42,404(M), 50 TCM 1166, TC Memo. 1985-503
Zack, TC, Dec. 38,481(M), 43 TCM 50, TC Memo. 1981-700

Perez, Carlos B.—continued
Rivera, TC, Dec. 36,275(M), 38 TCM 1338, TC Memo. 1979-343
Perez, Carlos B. .... ¶ 41,318.188
● DC-NY—70-1 USTC ¶ 9231; 310 FSupp 550
Biaustein, DC-NY, 71-1 USTC ¶ 9166, 325 FSupp 233
Perez, Daniel .... ¶ 41,318.132
● CA-2—(aff'g unreported DC), 78-1 USTC ¶ 9297; 565 F2d 1227
Klausner, CA-2, 96-1 USTC ¶ 50,173, 80 F3d 55
Iles, Sr., CA-6, 90-2 USTC ¶ 50,366, 906 F2d 1122
Cohen, CA-4, 80-1 USTC ¶ 9288, 617 F2d 56
Perez, Domingo ...... ¶ 3340.15, 4082.35, 8005.28
● TC—Dec. 52,992(M); 76 TCM 1004; TC Memo. 1998-442
Turay, TC, Dec. 53,555(M), TC Memo. 1999-315, 78 TCM 480
Perez, Edilio (See Brenniser, William)
Perez, John B. .. ¶ 3100.22, 39,475.23, 39,651G.305
● TC—Dec. 40,397(M); 46 TCM 1195; TC Memo. 1983-519
Perez, Jose A. .... ¶ 36,894.75, 41,758.10
● DC-Fla—85-1 USTC ¶ 9388
Perez, Jose A. . ¶ 37,514.26, 37,514.275, 37,544.20, 41,683.10
● CA-5—(aff'g DC per curiam), 2002-2 USTC ¶ 50,795; 312 F3d 191
Henry, DC-La, 2004-2 USTC ¶ 50,307
Porras, BC-DC-Tex, 2004-2 USTC ¶ 50,334
Abu-Awad, DC-Tex, 2003-2 USTC ¶ 50,716, 294 FSupp2d 879
Jones, CA-5, 2003-2 USTC ¶ 50,584, 338 F3d 463
Fletcher, CA-8, 2003-1 USTC ¶ 50,283, 322 F3d 508
Chase, CA-5, 2003-1 USTC ¶ 50,199, 55 FedAppx 717
● DC-Tex—2001-1 USTC ¶ 50,454
Hauck, Jr., CA-6, 2003-1 USTC ¶ 50,445, 64 FedAppx 492
Perez, Jose A. . ¶ 37,514.26, 37,514.275, 37,544.20, 38,079.60, 38,184.65, 39,032.17, 41,543.18
● DC-Tex—2002-1 USTC ¶ 50,259
Mortland, DC-Tex, 2003-2 USTC ¶ 50,572
● DC-Tex—2001-2 USTC ¶ 50,735
Perez, Jose A. . ¶ 37,514.25, 37,514.275, 38,079.60, 38,184.11, 38,184.12, 38,184.28
● TC—Dec. 54,924(M); 84 TCM 501; TC Memo. 2002-274
Casey, TC, Dec. 55,770(M), TC Memo. 2004-228, 88 TCM 332
Shireman, TC, Dec. 55,679(M), TC Memo. 2004-155, 87 TCM 1448
McIntosh, TC, Dec. 55,306(M), 86 TCM 406, TC Memo. 2003-279
Harrell, TC, Dec. 55,298(M), 86 TCM 378, TC Memo. 2003-271
Perez, Jose A. .... ¶ 41,653.76
● CA-5—(aff'g an unreported DC in an unpublished per curiam opinion), 2003-1 USTC ¶ 50,482
Perez, Pedro .... ¶ 41,333.192
● CA-5—(aff'g unreported DC per curiam), 74-1 USTC ¶ 9813
Perez, Salvador .... (Excise Tax)
● DC-Calif—72-1 USTC ¶ 16,031
Perez, Salvador .... (Excise Tax)
● CA-9—70-2 USTC ¶ 15,954; 430 F2d 669
● DC-Calif—69-1 USTC ¶ 15,877
Perez, Santiago . ¶ 27,348.141, 39,475.25, 39,560.34
● TC—Dec. 45,092(M); 56 TCM 312; TC Memo. 1988-464
Perez, Sergio (See Vial, Louis)
Perfect Window Regulator Co.
● CtCls—1928 CCH D-8283; 66 CtCls 147
Perfection Co. .... (Expired Excess Profits Tax)
● BTA—Dec. 4741; 14 BTA 1147
Perfection Foods, Inc.
● TC—Dec. 27,226(M); 24 TCM 61; TC Memo. 1965-15
Tidewater Hulls, Inc., DC-La, 68-1 USTC ¶ 9405
Perfection Gear Co. .... (Excise Tax)
● CtCls—1930 CCH ¶ 9429; 70 CtCls 422; 41 F2d 561
Perfette, Carman (See Marchionte, Louis)
Perfetti, Angelo .... ¶ 8550.30, 14,417.30
● TC—Dec. 42,525(M); 51 TCM 70; TC Memo. 1985-598
Perfetti, Angelo .. ¶ 8550.30, 8632.176, 9502.422, 14,417.30, 14,417.421
● CA-8—(aff'g, rev'g & rem'g TC), 85-1 USTC ¶ 9399; 762 F2d 638
Keirnes, DC-SD, 94-1 USTC ¶ 50,129
Quaschnick, TC, Dec. 50,451(M), 69 TCM 1781, TC Memo. 1995-45
Bailey, FedCl, 97-2 USTC ¶ 50,877
Lonsberry, FedCl, 97-2 USTC ¶ 50,888

Chart 11.1 Comparison of Cite Checking Sources

Source	Method of Organization	Citing Cases	Attributes
RIA's Citator Series	Case name	All citing cases.	For citing cases: • Provides the page on which the case is cited. • Lists cases by headnote.
CCH's Cases Finding List	Case name	Only those cases deemed relevant.	Cases Finding List works as a citator and as a reference to discussion in the Standard Federal Tax Reporter.
Shepard's Federal Tax Citator	Case citation	All citing cases.	For citing cases: • Provides the page on which the case is cited. • Lists any relevant headnotes.

2. Cite Checking IRS Documents

Actions on decisions, announcements, notices, revenue procedures, revenue rulings, Treasury decisions, and other government pronouncements can be cite checked.

RIA's Citator Series. In RIA's Citator Series the listing of government documents follows the listing of cases. In the Citator, any action taken on the government document will be indicated. First, locate the volume that covers the year in which the document was issued. Second, locate the document based on the type of document and number. The Citator provides subsequent action taken on the document and lists all citing cases. Finally, consult all subsequent volumes and supplements for later developments regarding the document.

CCH Federal Standard Reporter. The same documents can be found in CCH's Federal Standard Reporter through the Finding List. In the Finding List the government documents are listed in alphabetical order, then by document number. Any action taken on the government document will be indicated. In addition to providing any subsequent action on the document, the Finding List indicates all citing cases.

Example:

The following is an example of the information found in CCH's Standard Federal Tax Reporter:

Rev. Ruls.   **97,902**   ————CCH————

Rev. Rul.	Par. (¶)
1977 CCH ¶ 6935H	
77-420, 1977-2 CB 172	
. . . . ¶ 21,009.1967	
1977 CCH ¶ 6935 I	
Amplifying:	
Rev. Rul. 69-50	
Cited in:	
Minor, CA, 85-2 USTC ¶ 9717,	
772 F2d 1472	
Let. Rul. 8202002	
77-421, 1977-2 CB 188 . ¶ 22,299.88	
1977 CCH ¶ 6935J	
77-422, 1977-2 CB 307	
. . . . ¶ 29,650.408	
1977 CCH ¶ 6935K	
Cited in:	
Rev. Rul. 84-29	
77-423, 1977-2 CB 352 . . . . (Estate Tax)	
77-424, 1977-2 CB 481	
. . . . ¶ 40,720.293	
1977 CCH ¶ 6935L	
77-425, 1977-2 CB 383 . . . . (Excise Tax)	
77-426, 1977-2 CB 87 . ¶ 15,330.024; 15,330.1535	
1977 CCH ¶ 6937A	
Clarified by:	
Rev. Rul. 81-41	
77-427, 1977-2 CB 100 . ¶ 16,152.71	
1977 CCH ¶ 6937B	
Revoking:	
Rev. Rul. 58-79	
77-428, 1977-2 CB 117 . ¶ 16,753.43	
1977 CCH ¶ 6937C	
Cited in:	
Rev. Rul. 78-397	
77-429, 1977-2 CB 189 . ¶ 22,607.14; 44,390.134	
1977 CCH ¶ 6937D	
Superseding in part and obsoleting in part:	
Rev. Rul. 67-104	
77-430, 1977-2 CB 194	
1977 CCH ¶ 6937E	
Cited in:	
Let. Rul. 8303013	
77-431, 1977-2 CB 370 . . . . (Excise Tax)	
77-432, 1977-2 CB 375 . . . . (Excise Tax)	
77-433, 1977-2 CB 376 . . . . (Excise Tax)	
77-434, 1977-2 CB 420	
. . . . ¶ 34,107.437	
1977 CCH ¶ 6937F	
Cited in:	
Rev. Proc. 80-39	
Beneficial Foundation, Inc.,	
ClsCt. 85-2 USTC ¶ 9601, 8 ClsCt 639	
77-435, 1977-2 CB 491 . ¶ 26,960.35	
1977 CCH ¶ 6937G	
Modified and clarified by:	
Rev. Rul. 89-110	
77-436, 1977-2 CB 25 . . ¶ 5504.692; 11,620.209	
1977 CCH ¶ 6938B	
77-437, 1977-2 CB 28 . . . ¶ 5804.86; 16,753.483; 29,625.22	
1977 CCH ¶ 6938C	
Cited in:	

Rev. Rul.	Par. (¶)
Zappo, TC, Dec. 40,325, 81 TC 77	
77-438, 1977-2 CB 49 . . . . ¶ 5507.91	
1977 CCH ¶ 6938D	
Modifying:	
Rev. Rul. 76-519	
Rev. Rul. 76-518	
Rev. Rul. 76-99	
77-439, 1977-2 CB 85 . . ¶ 14,161.34	
1977 CCH ¶ 6938E	
Cited in:	
Widener, TC, Dec. 39,858, 80 TC 304	
77-440, 1977-2 CB 199 . ¶ 22,882.90	
1977 CCH ¶ 6938F	
Revoked by:	
Rev. Rul. 90-42	
77-441, 1977-2 CB 240 . ¶ 26,512.31	
1977 CCH ¶ 6938G	
77-442, 1977-2 CB 264 . . ¶ 8858.70; 15,612.304; 28,718.90	
1977 CCH ¶ 6938H	
Cited in:	
Upjohn Co., DC, 78-1 USTC ¶ 9277	
Woods Investment Co., TC, Dec. 42,315, 85 TC 274	
77-443, 1977-2 CB 327 . . . . (Estate Tax)	
77-444, 1977-2 CB 341 . . . . (Estate Tax)	
77-445, 1977-2 CB 357 . . . . (Excise Tax)	
77-446, 1977-2 CB 378 . . . . (Excise Tax)	
77-447, 1977-2 CB 384 . . . . (Excise Tax)	
77-448, 1977-2 CB 78 . . ¶ 44,427.14	
1977 CCH ¶ 6940	
77-449, 1977-2 CB 110 . ¶ 16,405.56	
1977 CCH ¶ 6941	
Amplified by:	
Rev. Rul. 83-156	
Rev. Rul. 83-34	
Cited in:	
Rev. Rul. 2003-48	
Rev. Rul. 2003-51	
Rev. Rul. 2003-19	
77-450, 1977-2 CB 175	
1977 CCH ¶ 6942	
Amplifying:	
Rev. Rul. 70-654	
77-451, 1977-2 CB 224	
. . . . ¶ 26,003.784	
1977 CCH ¶ 6943	
77-452, 1977-2 CB 226 . ¶ 25,736.77; 25,913.88	
1977 CCH ¶ 6944	
77-453, 1977-2 CB 236 . ¶ 26,157.41	
1977 CCH ¶ 6945	
77-454, 1977-2 CB 351 . . . . (Estate Tax)	
77-455, 1977-2 CB 93	
. . . . . ¶ 15,330.1323; 15,330.159; 15,452.48	
1978 CCH ¶ 6262	
77-456, 1977-2 CB 102 . ¶ 16,152.91	
1978 CCH ¶ 6263	
Cited in:	
Banc One Corp., TC, Dec. 41,985, 84 TC 476	
Let. Rul. 7906010	

Rev. Rul.	Par. (¶)
Obsoleted by:	
Rev. Rul. 2003-99	
77-457, 1977-2 CB 207	
. . . . ¶ 23,968.7232	
1978 CCH ¶ 6264	
77-458, 1977-2 CB 220 . ¶ 4760.22; 11,039.35; 25,202.20; 25,243.16; 25,282.089; 25,322.301; 25,343.18; 25,503.25	
1978 CCH ¶ 6265	
Clarified by:	
Rev. Rul. 90-17	
77-459, 1977-2 CB 239 . ¶ 26,512.37; 26,512.70	
1978 CCH ¶ 6266	
Cited in:	
Di Foggio, DC, 79-2 USTC ¶ 9448	
Rev. Proc. 2003-65	
77-460, 1977-2 CB 323 . . . . (Estate Tax)	
77-461, 1977-2 CB 324 . . . . (Estate Tax)	
77-462, 1977-2 CB 358	
. . . . ¶ 19,159D.60; 33,506.354	
1978 CCH ¶ 6267	
Cited in:	
Foil, Dec. 45,496, 92 TC 376	
Howell, CA, 85-2 USTC ¶ 9773, 775 F2d 887	
Rev. Rul. 87-9	
Rev. Rul. 81-36	
Public Employees' Retirement Board v. Shalala, CA-10, 98-2 USTC ¶ 50,726, 153 F3d 1160	
Distinguished by:	
Rev. Rul. 81-35	
77-463, 1977-2 CB 468	
. . . . ¶ 36,789.1175	
1978 CCH ¶ 6268	
77-464, 1977-2 CB 474	
. . . . ¶ 38,519.375	
1978 CCH ¶ 6269	
77-465, 1977-2 CB 61	
1978 CCH ¶ 6278	
Cited in:	
Arrigoni, TC, Dec. 36,758, 73 TC 792	
Rev. Rul. 80-1	
Superseding:	
Rev. Rul. 70-89	
77-466, 1977-2 CB 83 . . ¶ 14,054.26	
1978 CCH ¶ 6279	
77-467, 1977-2 CB 92	
. . . . . ¶ 15,330.0262; 15,330.1426	
1978 CCH ¶ 6280	
Cited in:	
Rev. Proc. 86-18	
77-468, 1977-2 CB 109	
. . . . ¶ 16,361.1936	
1978 CCH ¶ 6281	
Cited in:	
Rev. Rul. 81-3	
77-469, 1977-2 CB 196 . ¶ 22,795.85; 22,812.40	
1978 CCH ¶ 6282	
Cited in:	
Am. New Covenant Church, TC, Dec. 36,958, 74 TC 293	

3. Cite Checking Statutes and Regulations

Statutes, Treasury decisions, and regulations can be cite checked.

Shepard's Federal Statute Citations and Shepard's Code of Federal Regulations Citations. To cite check a statute, select the volume of **Shepard's Federal Statute Citations** that first contains the statute. Then check the supplements for any later developments. The statutes are organized based on the order found in the federal Code. Thus, most tax statutes will be found under Title 26.

Similarly, to check a regulation, select the volume of **Shepard's Code of Federal Regulations Citations** that first contains the regulation, then check the supplements for any later developments. The regulations are organized based on the order found in the Code of Federal Regulations. Shepard's does not indicate any action taken by the Tax Court. Shepard's provides some cite checking of regulations through the Federal Tax Citator.

Example:

The following is an example of the information found in Shepard's Code of Federal Regulations Citations, 4th Edition, 2004, Vol. 2, page 303:

CODE OF FEDERAL REGULATIONS   TITLE 26

§ 1.1502-31A(b)(1)(ii)
Cir. 5
430F2d1186*1969

§ 1.1502-31A(b)(2)
CtCl
608F2d471△1979

§ 1.1502-31A(b)(2)(ii)
Cir. 5
430F2d1186*1969

§ 1.1502-31A(b)(2)(iii)(a)
Cir. 10
417F2d293△1969

§ 1.1502-31A(b)(3)
Cir. 10
417F2d292△1969

§ 1.1502-31A(b)(6)
Cir. 7
444F2d1021△1971

§ 1.1502-31A(b)(6)(i)
Cir. 7
444F2d1021△1971

§ 1.1502-31A(d)
Cir. 7
444F2d1021△1971

§ 1.1502-31A(e)
Cir. 2
487F2d465△1973

§ 1.1502-32
Cir. 2
487F2d465*1967
Cir. Fed.
116F3d1462*1981
255F3d1360△2001
ClCt
Va 1ClC111△1983
34FedCl 767△1996
Ind
673NE1211*1988
78Geo1910△1990

§ 1.1502-32(a)
Cir. Fed.
116F3d1462*1981
ClCt
Va 1ClC111△1983
34FedCl 768△1996
Mass
415NE827*1980

§ 1.1502-32(b)
Cir. Fed.
116F3d1465*1981
Mass
415NE827*1980

§ 1.1502-32(b)(1)
Cir. Fed.
116F3d1462*1981
76VaL691△1990

§ 1.1502-32(b)(1)(i)
Cir. Fed.
116F3d1462*1981
i 116F3d1464*1981
ClCt
34FedCl 768△1996
78Geo1909△1990
76VaL691△1990

§ 1.1502-32(b)(2)
Mass
415NE826*1980

§ 1.1502-32(b)(2)(ii)
Mass
415NE827*1980

§ 1.1502-32(b)(2)(iii)
76VaL691*1966

§ 1.1502-32(b)(2)(iii)(b)
Cir. Fed.
726F2d1570△1984
ClCt
Va 1ClC111△1983

§ 1.1502-32(e)
ClCt
Va 1ClC111△1983
Ind
673NE1211*1988
66ChL861△1999

§ 1.1502-32(e)(1)
Cir. Fed.
726F2d1571△1984
ClCt
Va 1ClC111△1983

§ 1.1502-32A
CtCl
405F2d1304△1969

§ 1.1502-33
ClCt
42FedCl 181△1998

§ 1.1502-33(c)(1)
76VaL691△1990

§ 1.1502-33(d)
ClCt
42FedCl 188△1998

§ 1.1502-33(d)(1)
ClCt
42FedCl 188△1998

§ 1.1502-33(d)(2)
N D
552NW789△1996

§ 1.1502-33(d)(2)(ii)
Cir. 8
462FS516△1978
ClCt
42FedCl 188△1998
Mo
580SW245△1979
652SW687△1983

§ 1.1502-33(d)(3)
ClCt
42FedCl 188△1998

§ 1.1502-33(d)(3)(ii)
ClCt
42FedCl 188△1998

§ 1.1502-34
Cir. 2
199FS473△1961
78Geo1910*1966
136PaL10*1966
76VaL690*1966

§ 1.1502-34(a)
Cir. 2
199FS472△1961

§ 1.1502-34(b)
Cir. 2
199FS473△1961

§ 1.1502-34(b)(1)
Cir. 2
199FS472△1961

§ 1.1502-34(b)(2)(i)
Cir. 2
199FS472△1961

§ 1.1502-34(d)
Cir. 2
199FS472△1961

§ 1.1502-34A
Cir. 2
487F2d465*1967
617F2d944△1980

§ 1.1502-34A(b)(2)(i)
Cir. 2
487F2d465△1973
617F2d951△1980

§ 1.1502-35A
Cir. 2
617F2d944△1980

§ 1.1502-36
Cir. 6
220FS439△1963

§ 1.1502-36(a)
Cir. 6
220FS439△1963

§ 1.1502-36(b)
Cir. 6
220FS439△1963

§ 1.1502-38A(b)
Cir. 5
433F2d310△1970

§ 1.1502-40
CtCl
371F2d849△1967

§ 1.1502-40A(a)
Cir. 2
487F2d466△1973

§ 1.1502-41A(b)
Cir. 2
963F2d564△1992
Cir. 7
687F2d1116△1982

§ 1.1502-43A
CtCl
608F2d464△1979

§ 1.1502-43A(c)(2)
CtCl
608F2d465*1962

§ 1.1502-44
Cir. 9
345F2d768△1965
522F2d1057△1956

§ 1.1502-44(a)
Cir. 9
345F2d768△1965

§ 1.1502-44A
Cir. 9
522F2d1057*1967

§ 1.1502-47(a)(2)(ii)
Cir. 6
260F3d640△2001
Va 260F3d642△2001

§ 1.1502-47(d)(12)(iv)
Cir. 1
2003USApp LX14203△2003
336F3d33△2003

§ 1.1502-47(m)(3)
Cir. 3
177F3d144△1999

§ 1.1502-47(m)(3)(vi)
Cir. 3
177F3d145△1999

§ 1.1502-47(m)(3)(vi)(A)
Cir. 3
177F3d140△1999

§ 1.1502-47(m)(4)
Cir. 3
177F3d140△1999

§ 1.1502-72(a)
Cir. 5
594F2d124△1979

§ 1.1502-75
Cir. 5
126BRW722*1989
Cir. 6
2003USApp LX21111△2003
347F3d189△2003
Cir. 9
193BRW930△1995
ClCt
2003USClaims LX146△2003
56FedCl 714△2003
Mich
315NW520△1982

§ 1.1502-75(a)
Cir. 6
375FS126*1965

§ 1.1502-75(a)(1)
Cir. 3
515FS551△1981
Cir. 5
594F2d122△1979

§ 1.1502-75(a)(2)
Cir. 6
508F2d1221△1975
ClCt
2002USClaims LX137△2002
2002USClaims LX137*1993
2002USClaims LX191*1993
52FedCl 603△2002
52FedCl 603*1993
53FedCl 202*1993

§ 1.1502-75(b)
Cir. 2
928F2d569*1990

§ 1.1502-75(b)(3)
Cir. 3
515FS551△1981

§ 1.1502-75(c)
Cir. 2
435F2d922△1970
928F2d569*1990
Cir. 6
375FS126*1965

RIA Citator Series. RIA's Citator Series does not provide cite checking for statutes. However, regulations can be cite checked based on Treasury decision number. The Treasury decisions are included with the government documents after the listing of cases.

First, locate the volume which covers the year in which the Treasury decision was issued. The Treasury decisions are listed chronologically. Next, consult all subsequent volumes and supplements for later developments regarding the Treasury decision. In addition to providing any subsequent action, the Citator indicates all citing documents.

CCH Federal Standard Reporter. CCH's Federal Standard Reporter does not provide cite checking for statutes. However, regulations can be cite checked through the Finding Lists based on Treasury decision number. Treasury decisions are included with the other government documents. The Finding List also includes Committee Reports Finding Lists organized by Code section.

Example:

The following is an example of the information found in CCH's Federal Standard Reporter:

T.D.s   98,132   ———CCH———

T.D.	Par. (¶)
Ann. 95-107	
Notice 96-33	
8619, 1995-2 CB 41	¶ 17,925A.01;
	18,210B.01; 18,217C.01;
	18,277A.01; 18,922.0366;
	33,586.01; 33,620A.01
1995 CCH ¶ 47,049	
8620, 1995-2 CB 63	¶ 19,064.01;
	19,261.01; 19,261B.01
1995 CCH ¶ 47,050	
Cited in:	
Ann. 98-87	
8621, 1995-2 CB 261	¶ 36,964B.01
1995 CCH ¶ 47,051	
8622, 1995-2 CB 237	(Excise Tax)
8623, 1995-2 CB 28	¶ 11,685.01;
	11,700.023
1995 CCH ¶ 47,052	
8624, 1995-2 CB 258	¶ 35,131.01
1995 cch ¶ 47,053	
8625, 1995-2 CB 284	¶ 42,711.01
1995 CCH ¶ 46,560	
8626, 1995-2 CB 34	
1995 CCH ¶ 47,055	
8627, 1995-2 CB 86	¶ 27,881.01;
	27,900C.01
1995 CCH ¶ 47,056	
8628, 1995-2 CB 253	¶ 34,240B.01;
	34,301.01; 35,126.01; 36,703.01;
	36,803.01; 36,808.01; 37,536.01;
	37,541.01; 37,546.01; 40,432.01;
	40,461.01; 40,521.01; 40,522.01;
	41,674B.01; 41,686.01; 42,912.01
1995 CCH ¶ 47,058	
8629, 1995-2 CB 315	¶ 43,180B.01
1995 CCH ¶ 47,057	
8630, 1996-1 CB 339	¶ 42,782F.01;
	42,782H.01
1995 CCH ¶ 47,059	
Cited in:	
Harrison Est., TC. Dec.	
54,015, 115 TC 161	
Gribauskas Est., TC. Dec.	
54,267, 116 TC 142	
Corrected by:	
Notice 96-22	
8631, 1996-1 CB 54	
1995 CCH ¶ 47,060	
8632, 1996-1 CB 85	¶ 22,282B.01;
	22,282Q.01; 22,283.036;
	43,083.01
1996 CCH ¶ 47,006	
Cited in:	
T.D. 8670	
8633, 1996-1 CB 119	¶ 24,685.01;
	35,146.01; 36,964.01
1996 CCH ¶ 47,013	
8634, 1996-1 CB 230	¶ 33,589A.01
1996 CCH ¶ 47,005	
Corrected by:	
Ann. 96-19	
8635, 1996-1 CB 52	¶ 17,932.01;
	18,100.01; 18,904.01
1996 CCH ¶ 47,007	
Cited in:	
Schoof, TC. Dec. 52,501, 110	
TC 1	
Corrected by:	
Ann. 96-28	
8636, 1996-1 CB 308	¶ 35,124.01;
	36,421.01; 36,423.01; 36,702.01;
	36,783.01

T.D.	Par. (¶)
1996 CCH ¶ 47,014	
Corrected by:	
Notice 96-21	
8637, 1996-1 CB 232	
	¶ 33,640AA.01; 33,640B.01;
	33,640BD.01; 33,640C.01;
	33,640D.01; 33,640F.01;
	33,640H.01; 33,640J.01;
	33,640K.01; 33,640L.01;
	33,640M.01; 33,640N.01;
	33,641.01; 33,641AC.01;
	33,641B.01; 33,641C.01;
	33,641D.01; 33,641E.01;
	33,641F.01; 33,641G.01;
	33,641H.01; 33,641K.01;
	33,641L.01; 33,641M.01;
	33,641N.01; 33,641P.01;
	33,641Q.01; 33,641R.01;
	33,641S.01; 33,641T.01;
	35,132.01; 35,133.01; 35,867.01;
	35,909.01; 36,032.01; 36,300B.01;
	36,424A.01; 36,964.01;
	38,752B.01
1996 CCH ¶ 47,018	
Corrected by:	
Ann. 96-29	
8638, 1996-1 CB 43	
1996 CCH ¶ 47,021	
Corrected by:	
Ann. 96-35	
8639, 1996-1 CB 283	¶ 34,025.01
1996 CCH ¶ 47,008	
8640, 1996-1 CB 289	¶ 22,791.01;
	35,422.01
1996 CCH ¶ 47,009	
8641, 1996-1 CB 103	¶ 23,810A.01;
	23,810B.01; 23,810C.01;
	23,810D.01; 23,810E.01;
	23,810F.01; 23,810G.01;
	42,671.01; 42,679.01
1996 CCH ¶ 47,017	
8642, 1996-1 CB 126	¶ 25,134C.01;
	25,426.01; 25,426B.01;
	25,426D.01; 25,426F.01;
	25,426H.01
1996 CCH ¶ 47,022	
Corrected by:	
Notice 96-17	
8643, 1996-1 CB 29	¶ 15,401C.01;
	15,401E.01; 15,401G.01
1996 CCH ¶ 47,015	
8644, 1996-1 CB 200	(Estate Tax)
	¶ 44,019.01
Corrected by:	
Ann. 96-90	
8645, 1996-1 CB 73	¶ 21,961.01;
	21,964B.01; 21,965D.01;
	21,965F.01
1996 CCH ¶ 47,020	
Cited in:	
Pungot, TC. Dec. 53,764(M),	
TC Memo. 2000-60, 79	
TCM 1558	
Kosonen, TC, Dec.	
53,821(M), TC Memo.	
2000-107, 79 TCM 1765	
8646, 1996-1 CB 144	¶ 27,138.01;
	27,149.01
1996 CCH ¶ 47,019	
8647, 1996-1 CB 193	¶ 32,781.01;
	32,785.01; 32,788.01
1996 CCH ¶ 47,011	

T.D.	Par. (¶)
8648, 1996-1 CB 37	¶ 16,552.01;
	16,552F.01; 29,624.01; 33,179.01
1996 CCH ¶ 47,016	
Corrected by:	
Ann. 96-36	
8649, 1996-1 CB 179	¶ 31,127.01
1996 CCH ¶ 47,012	
8650, 1996-1 CB 4	¶ 9051B.01
1996 CCH ¶ 47,010	
Corrected by:	
Notice 96-14	
8651, 1996-1 CB 312	¶ 36,793.01;
	39,472.01
1996 CCH ¶ 47,025	
8652, 1996-1 CB 295	¶ 36,200A.01;
	36,202.01
1996 CCH ¶ 47,023	
8653, 1996-1 CB 67	¶ 20,614.01;
	30,424.01
1996 CCH ¶ 47,026	
Corrected by:	
Ann. 96-34	
Ann. 96-40	
8654, 1996-1 CB 298	¶ 36,310B.01;
	36,311B.01
1996 CCH ¶ 47,024	
8655, 1996-1 CB 351	¶ 27,941.01
1996 CCH ¶ 47,027	
8656, 1996-1 CB 329	¶ 39,651A.01;
	39,653B.01; 39,653C.01;
	39,660A.01; 39,660G.01
1996 CCH ¶ 47,029	
Corrected by:	
Notice 97-55	
8657, 1996-1 CB 153	¶ 27,184.01;
	27,189.025; 27,189.032;
	27,340.01; 27,541.01; 27,542.01;
	27,542C.01; 27,543.01; 27,545.01;
	27,546.01; 27,701.01
1996 CCH ¶ 47,031	
Corrected by:	
Ann. 96-51	
8658, 1996-1 CB 161	¶ 27,140.01;
	27,500B.01; 27,508.01
1996 CCH ¶ 47,032	
Corrected by:	
Ann. 96-58	
Ann. 96-50	
8659, 1996-1 CB 264	(Excise Tax)
8660, 1996-1 CB 195	¶ 14,156B.01;
	33,158.01; 33,168.0285
1996 CCH ¶ 47,033	
Corrected by:	
Notice 97-25	
8661, 1996-1 CB 319	
1996 CCH ¶ 47,034	
8662, 1996-1 CB 101	¶ 23,632.01;
	23,634.01
1996 CCH ¶ 46,405	
Corrected by:	
Ann. 96-84	
8663, 1996-1 CB 34	¶ 16,403.01
1996 CCH ¶ 47,045	
Corrected by:	
Ann. 96-82	
8664, 1996-1 CB 292	¶ 33,641M.01;
	36,025.01; 36,029.01; 36,032.01;
	36,036C.01
1996 CCH ¶ 47,039	
Corrected by:	
Ann. 96-86	

4. Electronic Cite Checking

LexisNexis. A case can be cite checked via Shepard's on-line through LexisNexis. Click on the "Shepard's" button, then enter the citation of the case. After clicking on "Check," the service will bring up the full treatment and history analysis as well as a complete listing of authorities that have cited the case. It will also list sources such as annotations and law reviews. A statute, regulation, or government document also can be cite checked. Click on the "Shepard's" button, then enter the citation of the statute or regulation. Click on "Check" and the service will bring up the relevant information.

In addition, if the researcher is already viewing a case, he can cite check the case by simply clicking on the Shepard's Signal indicator at the top of the case. Cite checking a case on-line using Shepard's is faster and more efficient than using the print version.

WestLaw. WestLaw's on-line citation service is called "KeyCite." After logging onto WestLaw, the KeyCite function can be accessed without entering a database. Simply type the citation in the "KeyCite this citation" text box in the left hand corner of the screen and click "go." To access the KeyCite function from a database, simply click on "KeyCite" on the toolbar across the top of the screen. When you click on "KeyCite," the "KeyCite this citation" textbox will appear in the left hand corner.

The "KeyCite" page provides a description of the type of information that can be retrieved through KeyCite. Once a citation has been entered, the KeyCite function provides the case's direct history and citing references. In addition to the citation history, KeyCite also provides "status flags." A yellow flag warns that the case has some negative history but has not been overruled. A red flag indicates that at least a portion of the case is no longer good law.

If the researcher is already viewing the case, he can cite check the case by clicking on the KeyCite status flag in the left hand corner of the screen or in the header of the document.

Other Electronic Services. Various other electronic services, whether on-line or through CD or CD-ROM, provide a means to cite check cases and government documents.

C. Main Points

- Cite checking a case is important for determining if a case has been overruled, reversed, criticized, limited, or distinguished.

- Cases that cite to the case being checked are referred to as citing cases.

- Cases can be cite checked by using Shepard's, RIA's Citator Series, or CCH's Federal Standard Tax Reporter.

- Government documents, regulations, and statutes also can be cite checked.

D. Problems

1. Cite checking is important for the following reasons:
   a. To assure that a higher court has not overruled the decision of a lower court.
   b. To assure that another court has not disagreed with the court's opinion.
   c. To determine if another case has followed similar law, perhaps with facts similar to those the researcher is considering.
   d. All of the above.

2. Consider *Banks v. Commissioner*, T.C. Memo. 2001-48.
   a. What was the holding of the trial court?
   b. What was the holding of the appellate court?
   c. What was the holding of the Supreme Court?
   d. Were any law review articles written about the case?

3. Consider *Selfe v. Commissioner*, 778 F.2d 769 (11th Cir. 1985).
   a. In what jurisdiction would the holding of the court be persuasive?
   b. What result if the taxpayer resided in the Fourth Circuit?
   c. What result if the taxpayer resided in your jurisdiction?

4. You are interested in finding law on the rules relating to the valuation of financial derivatives. In your research, you have found *Estate of Maddox v. Commissioner*, 93 T.C. 228 (1989). Can you find other cases that have cited *Maddox* and that discuss the valuation of derivatives?

5. Mr. Plum came to you, wanting help regarding some tax levies. His primary concern involves collection due process and the hearing provided for under section 6330. He had one telephone conversation with the assigned appeals officer and they discussed Mr. Plum's case. The appeals officer indicated that it was his position that Mr. Plum was not entitled to relief and that the determination to levy should be upheld. Mr. Plum wants to know if he would be successful on a suit seeking review of the determination made by the appeals officer. He would like to take the position that the IRS cannot establish he was notified that the conversation constituted his hearing. Through your research you have discovered *Montijo v. United States*, 2002-1 U.S.T.C. 50,321 (DC Nev). Does this case support Mr. Plum's position?

6. Consider Revenue Procedure 2000-1, 2001-1 I.R.B. 1. Have any actions been taken with respect to the Revenue Procedure since it was issued?

7. What is the status of Revenue Ruling 2004-43, 2004-18 I.R.B. 1?

Chapter 13

Related to Research

Law Reviews, Journals, and Other Publications

Law Reviews, Journals, and Other Publications

- *Which law reviews publish tax articles?*

- *Which journals focus on tax issues?*

- *What other publications might be important?*

- *How can articles be located?*

Amber stepped inside the door to the law firm's library and stopped. She didn't even know where to start. Terry, one of the senior partners, had asked her for an explanation of how the new market tax credit worked. He said that he didn't need anything in writing, just an explanation. Their meeting was scheduled for tomorrow at 10 a.m. How was she going to figure out the credit by then, she wondered.

"Can I help you?" she hadn't realized that Nick, the librarian, had come up to where she was standing.

She explained her problem to him. "I know I could look up the Code section and find information in various treatises, but I really want something that provides the big picture. Because I know so little about it, I could really use something that puts it all together for me, explaining it from the beginning to the end. And, if it could explain some planning strategies and traps for the unwary, that would be great. After I understand the big picture I can dig into the Code, regulations, and legislative history, and find the specifics for what I need to be able to explain the credit to Terry."

"I have just the thing," Nick said and moved toward the stacks where the periodical indexes were kept.

Contents

A. Key Terms

After completing this chapter, you should be familiar with the following key terms:

➤ Law Reviews
➤ Seminar Material
➤ Journals
➤ Index to Federal Tax Articles
➤ WG&L Tax Journal Digest
➤ Federal Tax Articles
➤ Current Law Index
➤ Index to Legal Periodicals & Books
➤ Shepard's Federal Law Citations in Selected Law Reviews
➤ Shepard's Law Review Citations

B. Discussion

Law reviews, journals, and other publications contain a wealth of information. A researcher could use an article in a number of ways. The researcher could use it to jump start

his research. An article may explain how a particular Code section works. Or, the article may explain a case and the ramifications of the case on the state of the law. Or, the article may address planning issues. Or offer suggestions for statutory changes.

Regardless of the focus of the article, it will likely contain references to applicable Code sections, Treasury regulations, other cases, or even other law review articles. As such, it can be used as an excellent starting point for research into other relevant sources. By considering relevant articles, the researcher can reduce the chances of spending valuable time re-inventing the wheel.

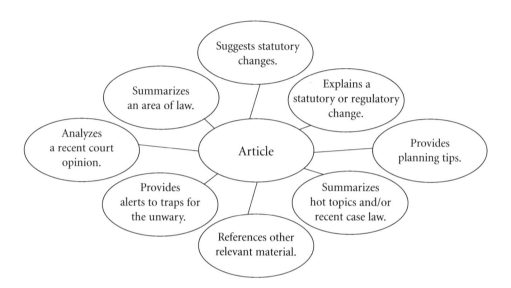

1. Law Review Articles

Almost every law school publishes a **law review**, and law review articles tend to be longer in length than journal articles. A tax article could be included in any law review publication. However, some publications specialize in tax issues.

Beyond any topic the law review may specialize in, each law review has its own attributes and characteristics. For example, some law reviews utilize students to review the articles, while others utilize peers. Some accept articles only from lawyers. Some law reviews focus on practitioner-oriented articles.

Chart 13.1 The Following Is a Summary of the Law Reviews that Focus on Tax Topics and Different Attributes of the Reviews

Law Journal	Publisher/Editor	Student-Edited or Peer-Reviewed	Accept Submissions from Students?
Akron Tax Journal	University of Akron School of Law	Student edited	No
Florida Tax Review	University of Florida (LL.M. students)	Peer-reviewed	No
Major Tax Planning	University of Southern California Law School Tax Institute (LexisNexis)	Peer-reviewed	No
National Tax Journal	National Tax Association	Peer-reviewed	Yes
Pittsburgh Tax Review	University of Pittsburgh School of Law	Student edited	No
Tax Law Review	New York University School of Law	Peer-reviewed	No
The Tax Lawyer	American Bar Association (Georgetown Law School)	Peer-reviewed	No (except some case notes)
Virginia Tax Review	University of Virginia School of Law	Student-edited	No (except some case notes)

In recent years, law review articles have increased in length and complexity. Several publishers are encouraging the submission of shorter articles or are restricting the size of articles accepted for publication.

Quote:

"As you may have heard, a group of law reviews, including Columbia, Cornell, Duke, Georgetown, Harvard, Michigan, Stanford, Pennsylvania, Texas, Virginia, and Yale, recently announced their intention to limit the length of articles. For example, Harvard Law Review will not publish articles longer than 70–75 law review pages 'except in extraordinary circumstances.'

The Fordham Law Review, the seventh most cited legal periodical in the country according to the Washington & Lee study of law journal citations, disagrees with this policy. We believe that quality is more important than quantity. Therefore, we will continue to focus only on merit in choosing what articles to accept. We seek to publish outstanding articles that will have a substantial impact on scholarly or public debate, without regard to rigid page count."

Letter from Elizabeth F. Gallagher, Editor-in-Chief, Fordham Law Review

2. Tax Conferences, Seminars, and Tax Institutes

The American Bar Association, other associations, and several law schools present tax conferences or seminars. As part of the presentation, the sponsors collect and publish the presenters' materials. These materials can be an excellent source of information on specific topics, such as estate and gift tax or real estate tax. Oftentimes, these seminars will include a presentation on recent case law or hot topics. These articles can be an excellent source for the researcher to stay up to date or get ideas for his own law review article.

Chart 13.2 List of Some Tax Conferences or Seminars

Title	Sponsor
CLE Meeting	Section of Taxation of the America Bar Association
Annual Federal Tax Conference	University of Chicago
Annual Institute of Federal Taxation	Tulane Law School
Cleveland Tax Institute	Cleveland Bar Association
Great Western Tax and Estate Planning Conference	National Law Foundation
Heckerling Institute on Estate Planning	University of Miami School of Law
Institute on State and Local Taxation	New York University
International Taxation Conference	Asian Development Bank Organization
Major Tax Planning Institute	Law School of University of Southern California
New York University Institute on Federal Taxation	New York University
Non-Profit Legal and Tax Conference	Washington Non-Profit Tax Conference, Inc.
Penn State Annual Tax Conference	Penn State University
University of Montana Tax Institute	University of Montana
William and Mary Tax Conference	William & Mary Law School

> **Practice Note:**
>
> Tax-Talent has an exhaustive list of on-going tax seminars on a wide variety of topics. You can find them at www.taxtalent.com. Click on "Career Tools," then "Tax Training Events."

3. Journal Articles   *RTA checkpoint*

Journals can provide an excellent source for information and updates on the latest tax issues. Because the articles generally are shorter than those found in law reviews, they are often more usable and practical as an aid for keeping current. Sometimes, a journal may include information from a tax conference. For example, each year the March issue of *Taxes: The Tax Magazine* includes the papers presented at The University of Chicago Law School's Annual Federal Tax Conference, making that issue particularly in demand.

Chart 13.3 List of Some Tax Journals

Law Journal	Publisher/Editor
Business Entities	Thomson Reuters RIA (WGL)
Compensation Planning Journal	BNA
Corporate Business Taxation Monthly	CCH, Inc.
Corporate Taxation	Thomson Reuters RIA (WGL)
Estate Planning	Thomson Reuters RIA (WGL)
International Journal	BNA
International Tax Journal	CCH, Inc.
Journal of International Tax	Thomson Reuters RIA (WGL)
Journal of MultiState Taxation and Incentives	Thomson Reuters RIA (WGL)
Journal of Pension Planning and Compliance	Aspen Publishers, Inc.
Journal of Practical Estate Planning	CCH, Inc.
Journal of Tax Practice and Procedure	CCH, Inc.
Journal of Taxation	Thomson Reuters RIA (WGL)
Journal of Taxation of Investments	Civic Research Institute
Journal of Taxation of Financial Products	CCH, Inc.
Practical Tax Strategies	Thomson Reuters RIA (WGL)
Real Estate Taxation	Thomson Reuters RIA (WGL)
Tax Advisor	AICPA
Taxes: The Tax Magazine	CCH Inc.
Taxpro Journal	National Association of Tax Professionals
Valuation Strategies	Thomson Reuters RIA (WGL)

Practice Note:

Some articles can be found free of charge at:

- www.accessmylibrary.com
- www.findarticles.com

4. Weekly and Other Publications

Several of the publishers of commercial treatises include a weekly supplement as part of their service. These publications are an excellent source of up-to-date material.

Tax Analyst provides both a weekly and a daily publication. Tax Notes Today is an extremely broad and comprehensive source of information. Even though it is published weekly, it contains anything from articles of the length of a traditional law review article, generally on a current topic, to short articles providing updates on the latest in the tax world. Each week it contains topics under a variety of headings, and it is not unusual for one issue to exceed one hundred pages.

BNA publishes the Daily Tax Report. It is an extensive daily publication that covers a variety of topics.

5. How to Find the Articles

a. Index to Federal Tax Articles

The **Index to Federal Tax Articles**, published by Warren, Gorham and Lamont, covers articles on federal income tax, estate and gift tax, and tax policy since 1913. Its data base includes not only tax journals, but also accounting and economic journals. A complete list of journals searched for the Index is included in the Index.

Volumes I through III include a listing of articles by topic. Volume IV includes a listing of articles by author. Under either listing, the articles are arranged in reverse chronological order. The main index covers approximately from 1913 to mid-1974. For later years, the supplements must be consulted. The Index includes the following supplements:

- 1974–1981 Cumulation
- 1982–1983 Cumulation
- 1984–1987 Cumulation
- 1988–1992 Cumulation
- 1993–1996 Cumulation
- 1997–2004 Cumulation
- Current Supplement

The Supplements also include a listing of journals searched, a topical index, and an author index. On occasion, summaries or digests of the articles are provided.

b. WG&L Tax Journal Digest

The **WG&L Tax Journal Digest** indexes articles appearing in only the following journals:
- The Journal of Taxation
- Practical Tax Strategies
- Estate Planning
- The Journal of International Taxation
- The Journal of Multistate Taxation and Incentives
- Taxation of Exempts
- Business Entities

The articles are organized by topic, and the Index provides a summary of the article. It also includes an index of the articles based on Code section. Finally, it contains a listing of articles organized by journal and then by topic.

c. Federal Tax Articles

Federal Tax Articles, published by CCH, covers articles on federal income tax, estate and gift tax, and tax policy since 1954. Its data base includes not only tax journals, but

also accounting and economic journals and major tax institutes. A complete list of journals searched for the Index is included.

The Index is organized in a looseleaf binder, primarily by Code section. Summaries of the articles are arranged under the Code section principally addressed in the article. If the article relates to more than one Code section, it is indexed only under the Code section most on point. One of the best attributes of the Index is that it includes an abstract of each article included under the listing by Code section.

Articles are also indexed by topic and author. The paragraph number in the topic or author index cross-references to the location in the Code section index, where the article summary can be found.

Bound volumes cover years 1954 through 1989. The bound volumes include:

- 1954–1967
- 1968–1972
- 1973–1978
- 1979–1984
- 1985–1989
- 1990–1996

The more current material is placed in the looseleaf binder, which includes all articles published after 1986.

The Index is updated monthly, with new pages either replacing existing pages or otherwise adding to the Index contents. Every six months, the reports are consolidated and assigned new paragraph references.

Example:

The following is an example of the information found in the Federal Tax Articles:

CODE SEC. 7443: MEMBERSHIP

.01 **"The Tilted Table: Penalties and Interest on Federal Tax Deficiencies."** Marvin J. Garbis and Miriam L. Fisher. 7 Virginia Tax Review, Winter 1988, pp. 485-505.

Describes the expansion of the additions to tax applicable to an understatement of tax liability, elaborates on the matter of interest which is said to be pertinent to every federal tax controversy, and elaborates on the tax penalty structure, which includes the negligence penalty, the fraud penalty, the substantial understatement penalty, the valuation overstatement penalty, and the valuation understatement penalty. Provides a survey of the penalty structure of the Internal Revenue Code, and examines the penalties that are applicable to tax professionals who may cause, or contribute to a taxpayer's understatement of tax liability. Addresses the principal criminal tax offenses, which include the willful attempt to evade or defeat tax, the willful failure to file returns, supply information or pay tax, the making, aiding or assisting in the preparation of false or fraudulent statements or tax returns, and the disclosure or delivery of such statements to the Internal Revenue Service.

CODE SEC. 7453: RULES OF PRACTICE, PROCEDURE, AND EVIDENCE

.01 **"Appendix G: Are the Claims Court's New Pretrial Procedures Working in Tax Cases?"** F. Brook Voght and J. Bradford Anwyll. 67 TAXES, September 1989, pp. 589-591, 594-595.

Focuses attention on Appendix G to the Claims Court Rules, provides an overview of Appendix G, and notes that Appendix G contains the newly adopted uniform pretrial procedures to be used by Claims Court judges. Sets forth the results of a survey of counsel regarding the effectiveness of the Appendix G procedures in tax cases, and states that while the pretrial procedures are self-executing, the parties must refer to Appendix G to determine their responsibilities subsequent to the commencement of a case. Contends that while Appendix G has provided useful and effective procedures, additional improvements may be of use.

.012 **"Forum Selection in Federal Tax Litigation."** William J. Falk and Richard L. Lawton. 33 St. Louis Bar Journal, Summer 1986, pp. 17-23.

Emphasizes the importance of forum selection in federal tax litigation. Describes courts available to hear federal civil tax cases, and explains their individual functions, geographic locations and personnel. Contends that factors that may affect the outcome of each case must be evaluated in depth prior to forum selection, such as forum precedent, jurisdictional limits, convenience and publicity. Notes that a federal tax jury trial is available only in the U.S. District Court, and focuses on the different rules of procedure affecting discovery, stipulations, burden of proof and subpoenas. Concludes that regardless of outcome expectation forum selection must be based on an in-depth analysis of the factors that may affect case resolution, such as the facts of each case and the law and procedures of the available courts.

.014 **"Litigation in the U.S. Tax Court."** William J. McNamara. 33 St. Louis Bar Journal, Summer 1986, pp. 24-30.

Describes the U.S. Tax Court, listing factors to determine requisite tax court jurisdiction. Explains that although no formal statutory rules for notice exist, once a deficiency is determined, statutory notice must be given. Evaluates difficulties of determining the last known address for such notice. Outlines IRS handling of docketed cases, pre-trial procedures, trials and resulting decisions, and notes the jurisdictional amount and procedure for small tax cases. Addresses Rule 60(a) regarding proper parties and the applicable rules of procedure and evidence for the U.S. Tax Court, and emphasizes the constant change in the court to accommodate an increasing caseload.

.016 **"The Real Estate Appraiser in Tax Court."** Deborah W. Thomas and Terry Gregson. 56 Appraisal Journal, July 1988, pp. 375-380.

Outlines the step-by-step procedure by which a tax controversy will make its way to the tax court, and explains the role of the tax court in valuation cases. Reviews real estate valuation cases, and addresses issues, which include those concerning the burden of proof, the use of expert witnesses, and the criteria used in the evaluation of the impact on the court's ultimate decision of a real

d. Current Law Index

The **Current Law Index**, published by Thomson Gale, indexes all types of articles, not just tax articles. It covers over 875 law journals, including academic reviews, bar association journals, specialty journals, and some journals from other disciplines. A complete list of journals searched for the Index is included.

The articles are organized by subject, author, title, case name, and statute. Only articles where the treatment of the statute is substantial are included in the listing by statute. The first volume includes the index for subject; the second volume contains the remaining indexes. No summary of the articles is provided. The Index is comprehensive and is available in the majority of law school libraries.

e. Other Indexes

The Index to Legal Periodicals & Books, published by H.W. Wilson Company, indexes all types of articles, not just tax articles. It covers legal periodicals, books, and annual institutes. The articles are organized by subject and author, case name, and statute (organized alphabetically). It does not contain an index based on Code section.

Shepard's Federal Law Citations in Selected Law Reviews indexes citations to Supreme Court cases, lower federal court cases, the Constitution, Code, rules of various federal courts, and regulations cited in a select group of articles. It indexes articles only from the following law reviews:

- California Law Review
- Columbia Law Review
- Georgetown Law Review
- Harvard Law Review
- Law and Contemporary Problems
- Michigan Law Review
- Minnesota Law Review
- New York University Law Review
- Northwestern University Law Review
- Standford Law Review
- Texas Law Review
- UCLA Law Review
- University of Chicago Law Review
- University of Illinois Law Review
- University of Pennsylvania Law Review
- Virginia Law Review
- Wisconsin Law Review
- Yale Law Journal

Example:

The following is an example of the information found in Shepard's Law Review Citations 2004 Vol. 1, p. 429:

CHICAGO LAW REVIEW, THE UNIVERSITY OF

62LCP(2)56
101McL
[1141
54MiL454
75SCL659
33SeH67
52VLR353
43VR548
77WQ713

—873—

266BRW921
PR
2001JTS732
89Cor191
75ILJ1317
73StJ349

—925—

191FS2d
[1193

—1175—

43BCR1
43BCR863
64BR1083
49Buf249
51Buf1
84BUR301
89CaL1665
90CaL1203
67ChL169
67ChL648
74CK1569
74CK1599
49CLA1
85Cor718
85Cor739
88Cor583
89Cor269
100CR1965
103CR1700
48Cth15
34Cum11
49CWL105
50DR67
91Geo67
54HLJ1375
114HLR430
114HLR448
115HLR
[1217
1999IILR56
1999IILR448
2000IILR237
2001IILR211
2003IILR337
2003IILR507
87ILR1213
89ILR495
66LCP(2)
[196
98McL2072
59MdL129
93NwL1143
95NwL1141
97NwL267
97NwL1165
97NwL1315
97NwL1497
74NYL633
59OhLJ339
62OhLJ1333
79OLR45
79OLR65
63PitL589
33RLJ799
74SCL1275

72StJ141
56StnL1
69TnL317
80TxL219
51VLR1499
51VLR1541
51VLR1729
51VLR1765
56VLR1663
56W&L580
39W&M
[1191
43W&M
[1907
38WFL1
2003WLR
[1115
30WmM273
112YLJ1577

—1197—

88CaL1061
86Cor1
99CR1259
49DuLJ1428
55FLR1221
36HUL416
77ILJ1
1999IILR61
80NCL465
95NwL443
97NwL351
78NYL1669
146PaL1185
146PaL1419
152PaL129
72StJ141
45StLJ1243
56VLR1663
42W&M
[1367
78WQ113
110YLJ625

—1215—

63LCP(1)
[292
93NwL215
72StJ141

—1225—

78BUR813
78BUR903
81BUR333
88CaL404
90CaL1889
67ChL615
67ChL1227
69ChL2007
73CK1257
74CK1537
100CR1965
48Cth15
31FSU509
91Geo757
72GW547
98McL2072
98McL2126
100McL
[1708
102McL71
94NwL77
149PaL2027
43SAC389
73SCL3
77SCL215
80TxL1
72UCR455

84VaL1069
86VaL794
86VaL1625
86VaL1690

—1337—

310F3d397
Wis
263Wis2d
[532
665NW750
75NYL383

—1425—

W Va
213WV485
583SE108
73TLQ123

—1457—

Wis
248Wis2d
[541
636NW478
77BUR925
101McL
[2706
74NYL1606
46WnL1215

Vol. 65

—1—

144F3d370
44AzL829
33AzSJ429
55BL956
80BUR635
104CR363
67FR239
67FR273
69FR83
69FR2741
70FR747
30FSU659
37GaL1167
53HLJ769
77ILJ469
69JBK28
87KLJ1165
83MnL116
84MnL1217
81NbL1320
77NDL1449
76NYL665
63PitL347
4SeH1042
31SeH1042
34SeH1
32SMJ423
41SoTR69
51StnL1534
82TxL227
87VaL1619
54VLR1955
24VtL268
57W&L951
2000WLR39
2001WLR
[1291

—35—

181FRD419
NM
129NM82
2P3d283
36Akr491
65Alb147
43AzL135
120BLJ779
80BUR1227
87CaL332
90CaL1635
46CLA784
72CUR201
73CUR943
40Duq77
48EmJ1359
66FR2649
30FSU679
53HLJ1217
37IDR641
76ILJ525
1999IILR430
2000IILR462
33JMR243
55MiL81
69MLJ377
64MoL249
79NbL711
77NYL1776
62OhLJ1409
149PaL1295
60PitL334
56StnL571
34Suf511

31TTR245
74TuL1409
47VR839
47VR897

—115—

46AzL117
33AzSJ491
46CLA699
50CLA903
24Day405
53DuLJ79
76ILJ1
76ILJ29
76ILJ49
62LLR1165
84MnL898
51NYCn352
51NYCn474
52NYCn133
52NYCn
[1125
44StLJ693
51StnL102
33Tol847
84VaL1620
86VaL463

—179—

Okla
995P2d1094
20AkLR195
50Buf103
87Cor743
48DuLJ696
86ILR1601
35LoyC479
87MnL583
94NwL153
36SFR411
54SMU1827
67TnL653
75TuL459
70UCR873
87VaL587
24VtL324
76WsL995

—345—

52AU173
24Day215
1998IILR909
87ILR909

—365—

68ChL1089
68FR1107
63LCP(1)56
63LCP(1)69
1999UtLR
[972
52VLR235
41W&M
[1463

—387—

50HLJ456
97NwL675
29ONU111
55TxR555
44W&M487
36WFL657
113YLJ269

—433—

Calif
80CA4th812
95CaR2d363
66BR1207
50Buf819

78CK1249
51CLA705
86Cor1131
48DuLJ1175
88Geo263
67GW786
28Hof741
36HUL455
86ILR1601
62LCP(2)51
62LCP(2)
[144
101McL
[2409
76NYL1164
152PaL33
77TxL361

—501—

51AU1135
32AzSJ1347
43BCR863
100CR702
101CR1312
104CR633
28FSU137
50HLJ408
54HLJ603
1998IILR
[1133
89ILR863
101McL
[2637
82NbL365
97NwL1115
73NYL1579
26ONU183
29ONU111
150PaL1473
73SCL1347
55StnL679
78TxL235
81TxL1443
1999UtLR
[958
52VLR1703
40W&M365
40W&M471
35WFL751
111YLJ547

—571—

204FRD180
49AU327
31AzSJ1278
58BL147
68BR959
68BR1055
2003BYU
[1239
88CaL1096
66ChL1191
74CK655
74CK1569
34CnL453
85Cor723
85Cor745
85Cor782
86Cor777
87Cor616
87Cor671
88Cor583
103CR1035
34Cum11
51DeP435
51DeP987
51DuLJ1397

Continued

429

Shepard's Law Review Citations indexes law reviews and periodicals cited in a reported opinion by a district court, the Court of Federal Claims, a bankruptcy court, appellate court, Supreme Court, military justice court, or state court.

Example:

The following are examples of the information found in Shepard's Federal Citations, 9th Edition 2006, Vol. 8, p. 237:

FEDERAL REPORTER, 2d SERIES   Vol. 372

798F2d[5]853	j) 468F2d[2]41	s) 424F2d20	N M	cc) 352US879	386FS1046
Cir. 6	477F2d[2]281	Cir. 2	80NM719	cc) 1LE80	Ala
399F2d[16]662	430FS[1]134	401F2d[6]672	460P2d249	cc) 77SC101	482So2d1211
466F2d[7]1185	430FS[2]134	534F2d[11]1023	Ohio	cc) 199F2d732	D C
683F2d[9]977	Cir. 6	319FS[6]1018	14OS261	cc) 233F2d148	424A2d89
86F3d[13]79	851F2d[3]129	319FS[4]1019	237NE894	cc) 247F2d940	Ill
Cir. 8	2006USDist	Cir. 3	Okla	cc) 254F2d470	117IlA96
f) 377F2d[17]967	[LX2737	297FS[6]920	453P2d286	cc) 273F2d936	253NE902
385F2d[2]51	Cir. 7	313FS[6]498	—996—	cc) 105FS886	Md
400F2d[6]567	437F2d[1]1148	Cir. 4	Scheuber v	cc) 121FS490	325Md726
401F2d[9]609	492F2d[3]1338	d) 454F2d[6]778	Commissioner	cc) 131FS119	328Md677
d) 421F2d[11]614	426FS[2]1019	Cir. 5	1967	cc) 148FS340	602A2d1212
d) 421F2d[12]614	521FS[3]96	385F2d[5]38	Cir. 4	cc) 159FS582	616A2d872
e) 428F2d137	Cir. 8	406F2d[3]936	540F2d[2]1252	cc) 161FS345	Mich
e) 428F2d[16]137	445F2d[1]261	406F2d[6]936	Cir. 7	402US313	440Mch264
433F2d[9]1062	445F2d[2]261	408F2d[8]886	457F2d[2]235	402US[8]315	487NW216
533F2d[1]1038	e) 484F2d[3]1324	428F2d[8]1020	Cir. 8	28LE794	N C
d) 592F2d[5]432	490F2d[3]315	648F2d[6]223	382F2d[2]187	28LE[8]810	142NCA513
603F2d[7]1317	517F2d1085	Cir. 6	Cir. 9	91SC1437	543SE221
739F2d[5]328	553F2d[1]40	274FS[3]420	d) 423F2d[2]502	91SC[8]1452	So C
14F3d[11]1261	553F2d240	Cir. 7	f) 438FS[2]373	Cir. 3	266SoC460
Cir. 9	574F2d[3]942	298FS[5]63	CtCl	604FS[4]560	224SE665
441F2d[7]883	729F2d[2]1156	Cir. 9	390F2d[2]919	Cir. 4	54NYL473
Cir. 10	954F2d513	422F2d[6]727	426F2d[2]382	332FS[8]421	47AL725n
381F2d[17]979	308FS[2]257	Cir. 10	182CCL668	342FS[8]535	—1018—
Conn	326FS[2]390	391F2d[3]438	192CCL74	352FS[8]428	Hurst v United
36CS27	326FS[2]611	419F2d[3]1318	63TCt165	Cir. 6	States
410A2d145	326FS[3]611	441F2d[6]1336	—999—	d) 601F2d[3]913	1967
Mass	460FS[2]76	456F2d[8]911	State Farm Mut.	f) 442FS[3]916	US cert den
7MaA830	537FS[2]710	668F2d[4]1122	Auto. Ins. Co. v	f) 442FS[5]916	387US910
391NE697	Cir. 9	734F2d[6]490	Automobile	Cir. 9	s) 370F2d161
Mich	527F2d[3]594	Cir. DC	Underwriters,	385FS[8]44	59LE972n
414Mch659	q) 550F2d[3]520	455F2d[6]1334	Inc.	Cir. 10	59LE986n
78McA286	Cir. 10	j) 455F2d[6]1335	1967	542F2d[13]542	—1019—
259NW462	558F2d[2]1378	Nev	s) 255FS404	601F2d[8]508	In re Low
327NW829	383FS[2]1155	83Nev520	Cir. 7	607F2d905	1967
58Cor29	436FS[1]596	436P2d15	374F2d[1]744	Cir. Fed.	(152PQ561)
17LE1081s	436FS[2]596	N Y	628F2d[2]1005	f) 736F2d[8]692	—1022—
12AL265s	439FS[3]890	69NYM852	385F3d[3]1098	CCPA	In re Hellbaum
2AL880s	645FS[1]919	331NYS2d171	318FS[3]1157	d) 392F2d[4]641	1967
112ALRF128n	Cir. DC	80CR1185	335FS1298	—1014—	(152PQ571)
113ALRF496n	2005USDist	77McL1436	Cir. 8	United States ex	CCPA
—981—	[LX35216	82AL265n	377F2d[2]331	rel. Meholchick	388F2d[2]1022
Brest v Cic-	2006USDist	82AL338n	Ind	v Rundle	467F2d[1]942
cone	[LX9734	82AL377n	148InA307	1966	
1967	358FS[3]136	—994—	168InA121	US cert den	**Vol. 372**
cc) 362US912	—983—	Davidson v	265NE426	386US986	—1—
cc) 4LE619	Kolod v	United States	341NE784	cc) 440Pa380	K-91, Inc. v
cc) 80SC662	United States	1966	485NE905	cc) 270A2d692	Gershwin Pub.
cc) 266F2d879	1967	Cir. 5	703NE692	—1016—	Corp.
cc) 23FRD103	US cert den	j) 569F2d[1]245	f) 703NE693	Piracci v	1967
488US[2]364	389US834	Cir. 7	769NE1177	Hearst Corp.	(152PQ375)
102LE[2]725	v) 390US136	j) 475F2d[2]214	4AL310s	1967	US cert den
109SC[2]650	v) 394US165	Cir. 10	20AL745n	s) 263FS511	389US1045
Cir. 2	v) 19LE962	380F2d[11]25	21AL1220n	Cir. 2	s) 389US805
541F2d[1]944	v) 22LE176	303FS[1]393	110AL473n	639F2d70	s) 19LE60
327FS[2]988	v) 88SC752	Cir. DC	—1004—	Cir. 3	s) 88SC43
450FS[2]207	v) 89SC961	419F2d[2]659	Tidewater	555FS203	422US[6]153
486FS[2]68	s) 389US966	14MJ686	Patent Dev. Co.	577FS331	441US[4]1
789FS[1]597	s) 390US985	Colo	v Kitchen	Cir. 4	45LE[6]88
Cir. 4	s) 392US919	171Col364	1966	557FS955	60LE[4]12
487F2d29	s) 19LE457	467P2d830	(152PQ36)	629FS761	95SC[6]2042
357FS[2]1132	s) 19LE1288	Fla	US cert den	162FS2d400	99SC[4]1559
360FS[2]24	s) 20LE1381	205So2d548	389US821	403FS2d432	
Cir. 5	s) 88SC459	Nev	s) 421F2d680	Cir. 9	
441F2d[2]385	s) 88SC1179	84Nev59		643F2d618	
j) 468F2d[1]41	s) 88SC2257	436P2d214			

In addition to those listed above, there are a number of business oriented indexes that include tax articles. Finally, there are a number of CD, CD-ROM and on-line indexes that are available.

Chart 13.4 Summary of Print Indexes

Title	Publisher	Organization	Comments
Current Law Index	Thomson Gale	• Subject • Author • Title • Case name • Statute	• Not tax specific • Available in most libraries • Does not provide a summary or digest of articles
Federal Law Citations in Selected Law Reviews	Shepard's	• Case citation • Constitutional provision • Code • Court rule • Regulation	• Lists where federal cases and Code sections have been cited in law review articles • Covers limited number of law reviews
Federal Tax Articles	CCH	• Subject • Author • Code section	• Tax focused • Provides a summary or digest of articles
Index to Federal Tax Articles	Warren, Gorham & Lamont of RIA	• Topic • Author	• Tax focused • Does not provide a summary or digest of articles
Index to Legal Periodicals & Books	H.W. Wilson Company	• Subject and author • Case name • Statute	• Not tax specific • Does not provide a summary or digest of articles
Shepard's Law Review Citations	Shepard's	• Law review or periodical citation	Lists where selected articles have been cited in court case opinions
The WG&L Tax Journal Digest	Warren, Gorham & Lamont of RIA	• Topic • Code section	• Limited coverage of journals • Provides a summary of the article

C. Main Points

* Invaluable information can be found in law review articles; Tax Conferences, Seminars, or Tax Institute proceedings; journals; and weekly and other publications.
* Some law reviews specialize in articles addressing tax topics.
* Journal articles are generally shorter than law review articles and can provide timely information.

- Articles on particular topics can be located through various indexes.
- The most well-known indexes of tax topics are the Index to Federal Tax Articles and the Federal Tax Articles Index.

D. Related Article for Further Reading

- William J. Turnier, *Tax (and Lots of Other) Scholars Need Not Apply: The Changing Venue for Scholarship*, 50 J. LEGAL EDUC. 189 (2000).

E. Problems

1. A law review article may be helpful for any of the following reasons:
   a. Interpretation of a recently amended Code section.
   b. Reference to other relevant and related information.
   c. Discussion of a recent court opinion.
   d. Discussion of a newly issued regulation.
   e. All of the above.

2. All of the following law reviews specialize in tax articles, except:
   a. Tax Law Review.
   b. Florida Tax Review.
   c. Yale Law Review.
   d. Journal of Corporate Taxation.

3. A journal article may be helpful for any of the following reasons:
   a. Interpretation of a recently amended Code section.
   b. Reference to other relevant and related information.
   c. Discussion of a recent court opinion.
   d. Discussion of a newly issued regulation.
   e. All of the above.

4. Which of the following indexes includes a digest or summary of each article included in the index?
   a. Index to Federal Tax Articles.
   b. WG&L Tax Journal Digest.
   c. Federal Tax Articles Index.
   d. Current Law Index.

5. Materials from a tax conference, seminar, or tax institute proceeding may be helpful for any of the following reasons:
   a. Interpretation of a recently amended Code section.
   b. Reference to other relevant and related information.
   c. Discussion of a recent court opinion.
   d. Discussion of a newly issued regulation.
   e. All of the above.

6. An article from Tax Notes may be helpful for any of the following reasons:
    a. Interpretation of a recently amended Code section.
    b. Reference to other relevant and related information.
    c. Discussion of a recent court opinion.
    d. Discussion of a newly issued regulation.
    e. All of the above.

7. Your client is interested in understanding how the Hope and Lifetime Learning Credits work (section 25A). However, you have only a basic knowledge of the credits.

    a. What articles can you locate that would help you understand how the credits work?
    b. Which indexes did you utilize?
    c. Which index did you prefer and why?

8. How many articles has your professor published? What are they?

9. You are interested in learning more about tax shelters.

    a. Select three indexes and locate articles on tax shelters using each index.
    b. Which index do you prefer? Why?

Chapter 14

*Watch video 16/31/2022
V.V.V._ Imf case Canlip v. Comm for exam*

Organizing the Research into a Finished Product

Preparing the Written Work Product

- *What types of written documents might you have to prepare?*

- *What are the differences between the potential types of documents?*

- *What responsibility do you have to your client under Circular 230?*

"Why do you have all these form books strewn about?" Mike asked, taking the seat opposite Kelley's desk.

"Mr. Darcy has asked me to prepare a petition for his client, Mr. Dashwood. They are both pretty certain that the IRS revenue agent is incorrect about a legal issue. But, since neither the agent nor Mr. Darcy can find a case on point, and the statute is a bit vague, it looks like the court will resolve this one," Kelley said.

"Wow, that sounds exciting. Getting to present a novel legal issue to the court doesn't happen every day. But, it doesn't explain why all the form books are here," Mike said, gesturing to the stacks of books that were threatening to tumble off of the desk.

"I've never prepared a Tax Court petition before. I am not sure what all must be included or how persuasively it should be written."

"Did you check the Tax Court rules to see what they said?"

"Well, not yet," Kelley said sheepishly. "Perhaps that is where I should have started."

Contents

A. Key Terms

After completing this chapter, you should be familiar with the following key terms:

➤ Memorandum

➤ Letter to the Client

➤ Response to Information Document Requests

➤ Tax Opinions

➤ Protest Letter

➤ Petition

➤ Brief

➤ Circular 230

➤ Best Practices

➤ Covered Opinion

B. Discussion

After the research is done, the practitioner generally must consolidate the information into a written document. The type of document will dictate, to some extent, what information must be included and whether any rules, whether formal or informal, must

be followed. Some types of documents are designed primarily to convey information. Other types of documents must be persuasive to fulfill their purpose. To get the best possible finished product, the practitioner must understand which type of document he is drafting.

Quote:

"There is such a torrent of words threatening to engulf us now that nobody should add to it unless it's absolutely necessary."

Ernst Jacobi, *Writing at Work: Dos Don'ts and How Tos* 19 (1979).

---

1. Types of Documents

a. Memorandum

If the research was conducted for another attorney, accountant, or business associate, the researcher will usually organize the research into a written product. For such in-house communications, the memorandum format is generally used. The facts should be succinctly stated, followed by the relevant rules and application of rules to facts. Finally, the researcher should set forth a conclusion, whether it be a legal conclusion or a suggestion of additional steps to be taken. The extent of detail included in the memorandum, both with respect to the recitation of facts and discussion of the law, will depend on the level of familiarity the attorney, accountant, or business associate has with the material and the extent of information the researcher intends to convey.

To the extent the memorandum is intended only to provide the recipient with information, it should be written as objectively as possible. Both sides of the issue should be presented adequately and fairly. Any weaknesses in the facts or issues should be identified. However, regardless of the purpose of the memorandum, the information should be conveyed in the most concise form possible.

b. Letter to the Client

If the research was conducted for the client, the results should be conveyed to the client, usually through a letter. Because a client rarely has the same degree of technical background in tax as the researcher, the information should be conveyed in a manner that is consistent with the client's knowledge of tax. In addition, the researcher should, to the extent possible, avoid using tax jargon. In all circumstances, the researcher should remember that short, clear sentences go a long way to creating a clear and easy to understand written document.

In the letter, the researcher should offer to speak with the client if the information is unclear. Oftentimes, a fifteen minute meeting or phone conversation with the client can clear up substantially more issues than a five page letter that takes five or more hours to draft.

To the extent the researcher needs the client to make a decision after having considered the information contained in the letter, that fact and a timeline for making the decision should be set forth. At a minimum, it should be made clear to the client what further steps, if any, need to be taken.

c. Response to Information Document Requests

During a tax audit, one of the primary tasks of the IRS revenue agent is the collection of information. Generally, the agent will collect information through a written **Information Document Request** (IDR). Each IDR issued by the IRS is numbered in sequence. IDR's are not the equivalent of a summons and are not self-executing. However, it is in the best interest of the taxpayer to respond to IDRs in an honest and timely fashion.

For purposes of determining whether civil fraud penalties should apply, courts have held the taxpayer's failure to cooperate with tax authorities, including the failure to reply to IDR's, is an indication of fraud.

Case on Point:

Padgett Coventry Price v. Commissioner
T.C. Memo. 2004-103

Over the years, courts have developed a nonexclusive list of factors that demonstrate fraudulent intent. These badges of fraud include: (1) Understating income, (2) maintaining inadequate records, (3) implausible or inconsistent explanations of behavior, (4) concealment of income or assets, (5) failing to cooperate with tax authorities, (6) engaging in illegal activities, (7) an intent to mislead which may be inferred from a pattern of conduct, (8) lack of credibility of the taxpayer's testimony, (9) filing false documents, (10) failing to file tax returns, and (11) dealing in cash. *Spies v. United States, supra* at 499; *Douge v. Commissioner*, 899 F.2d 164, 168 (2d Cir. 1990); *Bradford v. Commissioner*, 796 F.2d 303, 307–308 (9th Cir. 1986), affg. T.C. Memo. 1984-601; *Recklitis v. Commissioner*, 91 T.C. 874, 910 (1988). Although no single factor is necessarily sufficient to establish fraud, the combination of a number of factors constitutes persuasive evidence. *Solomon v. Commissioner*, 732 F.2d 1459, 1461 (6th Cir. 1984), affg. per curiam T.C. Memo. 1982-603.

The evidence establishing petitioner's fraudulent intent is overwhelming. First, petitioner was an attorney, and she took one course in taxation during law school.

Second, petitioner consistently and substantially understated her income. This is strong evidence of fraud when coupled with other circumstances. *Marcus v. Commissioner*, 70 T.C. 562, 577 (1978), affd. without published opinion 621 F.2d 439 (5th Cir. 1980). A pattern of consistent underreporting of income, when accompanied by other circumstances indicating an intent to conceal income, may justify the inference of fraud. *Holland v. United States*, 348 U.S. 121, 139 (1954).

Third, petitioner's explanations were implausible and inconsistent. She kept changing her story to fit the circumstances she was faced with. As the agents, and the Court, learned the truth, petitioner would change her story.

Fourth, petitioner attempted to conceal her true income by depositing it into her Merrill Lynch account.

Fifth, petitioner failed to cooperate with tax authorities. She attempted to prevent Merrill Lynch from complying with a summons. During the civil audit and criminal investigation, petitioner repeatedly refused to claim certified letters sent to her by the IRS. Petitioner explained that she refused the letters because they were addressed to "Padgett Price Ludlow" and not to "Padgett Price". Petitioner's name was listed on each of her returns for the years in issue as "Padgett Price Ludlow". Petitioner also instructed her representatives to be uncooperative. Petitioner lied to respondent's agents and attempted to persuade her employees to lie to the Government.

The IRS does not have the authority to force a taxpayer to create records or documents that are not in existence. However, when the taxpayer is providing documents that are already in existence, the representative should write a brief memorandum that describes the information being provided if it is not completely clear from the documents; if an agent receives documents that create questions, it could lead to additional IDRs.

In some situations it may make sense to draft a memorandum describing a particular transaction or issue in response to an IDR. However, the response should simply answer the question asked, nothing more and nothing less. The drafter must take great care in ensuring that information beyond that requested is not included. In sum, the drafter must walk the fine line between being cooperative and doing the agent's job.

> **Practice Note:**
>
> The IRS uses Form 4564 for Information Document Requests

d. Tax Opinions

For some tax issues and transactions, clients will want a formal **Tax Opinion** from counsel, rather than an e-mail, letter, or memorandum. Tax opinions set forth the lawyer's or the firm's written opinion of the tax consequences of a particular issue or transaction. Generally, a tax opinion will conclude that the consequences "should" or "more likely than not" will be favorable to the taxpayer.

Clients may seek formal tax opinions in those situations where the tax consequences from a transaction are less than clear and/or there is some risk of civil tax penalties if the taxpayer's position is incorrect. Under section 6664(c)(1), certain tax penalties will not be imposed on an underpayment of tax if it is demonstrated that there was reasonable cause for the taxpayer's return position at issue. In addition, the taxpayer must have acted in good faith. Traditionally, taxpayers could demonstrate reasonable cause if the return position were based on an opinion of counsel. As a result, tax opinions were often sought as an "insurance policy" against penalties.

> **Practice Note:**
>
> Treas. Reg. § 1.6662-4(d)(3)(iii) sets forth those authorities that are considered substantial authority for purpose of application of penalties:
>
> > Except in cases described in paragraph (d)(3)(iv) of this section concerning written determinations, only the following are authority for purposes of determining whether there is substantial authority for the tax treatment of an item: Applicable provisions of the Internal Revenue Code and other statutory provisions; proposed, temporary and final regulations construing such statutes; revenue rulings and revenue procedures; tax treaties and regulations thereunder, Treasury Department and other official explanations of such treaties; court cases; congressional intent as reflected in committee reports, joint explanatory statements of managers included in conference committee reports, and floor statements made prior to enactment by one of a bills managers; General Explanations of tax legislation prepared by the Joint Committee on Taxation (the Blue Book); private letter rulings and technical advice memoranda issued after October 31, 1976; actions on decision and general counsel memoranda issued after March 12, 1981 (as well as general counsel memoranda published in pre-1955 volumes of the Cumulative Bulletin); Internal Rev-

enue Service information or press releases; and notices, announcements and other administrative pronouncements published by the Service in the Internal Revenue Bulletin. Conclusions reached in treatises, legal periodicals, legal opinions or opinions rendered by tax professionals are not authority.

[handwritten margin notes: "Imp."; "1) Don't have sufficient legal analysis or"; "2) Opinion was not based on all of the client's facts"]

However, in some circumstances courts have held that the client did not reasonably rely on the opinion of counsel and therefore could not utilize the "reasonable cause" exception. Generally, courts have found a lack of reasonable reliance where the opinion of counsel was not based on all of the client's facts and circumstances or where the opinion did not provide sufficient legal analysis for the client to demonstrate reasonable good faith reliance.

Case on Point:

> Long Term Capital Holdings v. United States
> 330 F. Supp. 2d. 122, 211 (D.C. Conn. 2004),
> *aff'd*, 96 AFTR2d (RIA) 6344, 2005-2 USTC ¶ 50,575 (2d Cir. 2005)

In essence, the testimony and evidence offered by Long Term regarding the advice received from King & Spalding amounted to general superficial pronouncements asking the Court to "trust us; we looked into all pertinent facts; we were involved; we researched all applicable authorities; we made no unreasonable assumptions; Long Term gave us all information." The Court's role as factfinder is more searching and with specifics, analysis, and explanations in such short supply, the King & Spalding effort is insufficient to carry Long Term's burden to demonstrate that the legal advice satisfies the threshold requirements of reasonable good faith reliance on advice of counsel.

In the past it was not completely clear what must be included in a tax opinion in order to ensure penalty protection. Circular 230, discussed in more detail later in this chapter, has removed some of this uncertainty. Taxpayers can only rely on a "reliance opinion" to avoid the imposition of penalties if, first, the reliance opinion concludes at a confidence level of more likely than not (a greater than 50 percent likelihood) that one or more significant federal tax issues would be resolved in the taxpayer's favor.[1] Second, the reliance opinion must meet the following requirements:

- The opinion must identify and consider all facts the practitioner determines to be relevant.
- The practitioner must not base the opinion on any unreasonable factual assumptions. The opinion must identify in a separate section all factual assumptions relied upon by the practitioner.
- The opinion must identify in a separate section all factual representations, statements, or findings of the taxpayer relied upon by the practitioner.
- The opinion must relate the applicable law to the relevant facts.
- The opinion must consider all significant federal tax issues.
- The opinion must provide the practitioner's conclusion as to the likelihood that the taxpayer will prevail on the merits with respect to each significant federal tax issue.
- The opinion must provide the practitioner's overall conclusion as to the likely federal tax treatment.

---

1. 31 C.F.R. § 10.35(b)(4).

Circular 230 provides the opinion writer with a framework for the minimum information that must be included in an opinion drafted for the purpose of penalty protection. However, meeting the drafting requirements does not guarantee a client penalty protection. "[T]he taxpayer's good faith reliance on the opinion will be determined separately under applicable provisions of the law and regulations."[2] Undoubtedly, the persuasiveness of the opinion will go a long way in demonstrating the taxpayer's good faith reliance. In sum, the goal of the drafter must be to promote and protect the client's return position.

e. Protest Letter

beyond the scope of this class.

If a revenue agent has suggested changes to the taxpayer's income tax return, and the taxpayer does not agree with the proposed changes, the taxpayer should attempt to resolve his differences with the revenue agent. If the differences cannot be resolved, the revenue agent will issue what is generally referred to as a 30-day letter.

The representative can then appeal the taxpayer's case to the Appeals office, which is an independent, administrative office within the IRS. Conferences are informal and can be held through correspondence or through an actual meeting.

Practice Note:

- Information about the Appeals office can be found in Treas. Reg. § 601.106.
- The Appeals Office website can be found at www.irs.gov/appeals.

When an appeals conference is requested, a formal written **protest letter** must also be timely filed and must include:

- Taxpayer's name and address and daytime telephone number;
- A statement that the taxpayer wants to appeal the IRS findings to the Appeals Office;
- A copy of the letter showing the proposed changes and findings the taxpayer does not agree with;
- The tax periods or years involved;
- A list of the changes the taxpayer doesn't agree with and why he doesn't agree;
- The facts supporting the taxpayer's position on any issues he doesn't agree with;
- The law or authority, if any, on which the taxpayer is relying;
- If a representative prepared the protest, a statement that the representative has submitted the protest and accompanying documents; and
- Whether the representative knows personally that the facts stated in the protest and accompanying documents are true and correct.

Practice Note:

If the total amount for any tax period is not more than $25,000, a small case request may be made instead of filing a formal written protest. The information can be submitted using Form 12203, Request for Appeals Review.

---

2. 31 C.F.R. § 10.35(f).

A substantial number of cases are resolved through the Appeals process.

Practice Note:

The following Publications may be helpful in preparing a taxpayer's case for an Appeals conference:

- Publication 5, Your Appeal Rights and How To Prepare a Protest if You Don't Agree
- Publication 556, Examination of Returns, Appeal Rights, and Claims for Refund
- Publication 3605, Fast Track Mediation—A Process for Prompt Resolution of Tax Issues
- Publication 1660, Collection Appeal Rights
- Publication 4167, Appeals, Introduction to Alternative Dispute Resolution
- Publication 4227, Overview of Appeals Process Brochure

A protest letter is the representative's opportunity to explain to an independent party why the taxpayer's position is the correct position. It should be persuasively written, setting forth all the relevant facts and legal arguments in an organized manner. The followings rules should generally be followed:

- Do not attack the revenue agent as a means of trying to win the taxpayer's case.
- Assure that the facts included in the protest are all the facts necessary to support your legal position.
- Present the facts in a logical format.
- Present the legal arguments in an organized manner, using headings as appropriate to outline the arguments for the Appeals officer.
- Provide authority for any argument that you present.
- Write using simple, short, and clear sentences.
- Because this document provides the means for ending the tax controversy, allow time to create a polished, finished product by allowing time for many re-writes and edits.

f. Tax Court Petition

If the IRS proposes changes to the taxpayer's income tax return and the taxpayer does not agree to the changes and the disagreement cannot be resolved through Appeals, he will be issued a statutory notice of deficiency. If the taxpayer wants to continue his challenge to the IRS's proposed adjustments, he has the option of bringing suit in the Tax Court. To do so, the taxpayer must file a petition, generally within 90 days from the date the statutory notice of deficiency was mailed to him.[3] The notice of deficiency will include the date determined by the IRS to be the last day on which the taxpayer may timely file a petition with the Tax Court.

---

3. I.R.C. §§ 6212, 6213.

The requirements for a petition are set forth in the Tax Court Rules of Practice and Procedure. In addition, the Tax Court rules specify the form and style for the petition, number of copies to be filed, and other important information.

Practice Note:

The requirements for a proper petition are set forth in Tax Court Rule 34. An example of a petition is provided in Form 1 and Form 2 of Appendix I. Information on the form and style of documents filed in the Tax Court can be found in Rule 23.

Practice Note:

The United States Tax Court has its own rules of practice and procedure. They can be obtained from the Tax Court website at www.ustaxcourt.gov under Rules or by writing:

Administrative Office
United States Tax Court
400 Second Street, N.W.
Washington, D.C. 20217

Enclose a check or money order to "Clerk, United States Tax Court" in the amount of $30.

All the requirements set forth in the Rules must be followed.[4] The first paragraph of the petition must identify the taxpayer, set forth his mailing address and legal address. For corporate taxpayers, it must also set forth the principal place of business. The second paragraph must identify the statutory notice of deficiency, the date it was issued, and the office that issued it. The third paragraph must identify the type of tax, years at issue, and the amount in dispute.

Case on Point:

O'Neil v. Commissioner
66 T.C. 105, 108 (1976)

The petitioner argues that pursuant to Rule 13(a) and section 6213(a), the Court acquired jurisdiction for all the taxable years contained in the notice of deficiency by filing a petition contesting some of such years. That Rule and section do not support the petitioner's argument; they merely provide that this Court has jurisdiction to redetermine a deficiency for a taxable year only when the Commissioner has issued a notice of deficiency for such year and when a petition contesting such deficiency is filed with this Court. "Each year is the origin of a new liability and of a separate cause of action." *Commissioner v. Sunnen*, 333 U.S. 591, 598 (1948). The fact that separate taxable years are contained in one notice of deficiency does not mean that each of such years is automatically raised by filing a petition contesting some of such years. See *Miami Valley Coated Paper Co. v. Commissioner, supra; Citizens Mutual Investment Association, supra; John R. Thompson Co., supra.* The terms of the petition must be ex-

---

4. *See, e.g.*, Tax Court Rule 34(b). Form 4 of Appendix I can be used to supply the taxpayer's identification number. See Tax Court Rule 20(b).

> amined to ascertain which of the years has been put in issue by an indication that the determination for that year is disputed.
>
> Accordingly, it is clear that we have no jurisdiction to redetermine the deficiency in and addition to tax for 1971 and must grant the Commissioner's motion to strike all references to the taxable year 1971 in the amended petition. If the petitioner wishes to contest his tax liability for 1971, he must do so in another forum.

The fourth paragraph must set forth the errors the taxpayer believes the Commissioner made and the legal basis for the disagreement with the notice of deficiency. If the taxpayer is raising any affirmative defenses, they must be affirmatively pleaded.

Case on Point:

The Nis Family Trust v. Commissioner
115 T.C. 523, 538–39 (2000)

Respondent has determined deficiencies in tax against each of the petitioners, and the petitioners have filed petitions. We have jurisdiction to redetermine the correct amount of such deficiencies. See sec. 6214(a). As set forth *supra* in section I.A.2., the petition in a deficiency case must set forth each and every error that the petitioner alleges to have been committed by the Commissioner and clear and concise statements of facts upon which the petitioner bases the assignments of error. Furthermore, any issue not raised in the assignments of error is deemed conceded. See *id.* A petition that makes only frivolous and groundless arguments makes no justiciable claim, and it is properly subject to a motion for judgment on the pleadings. See *Abrams v. Commissioner*, 82 T.C. 403 (1984); see also *Rodriguez v. Commissioner*, T.C. Memo. 1995-67 (judgment on the pleadings granted where petitions merely set forth frivolous "protester arguments that have been heard by this Court on many occasions and rejected"); *Wright v. Commissioner*, T.C. Memo. 1990-232 (frivolous argument in petition that petitioner was exempt from Federal taxation justified granting respondent's motion to dismiss for failure to state a claim); *Brayton v. Commissioner*, T.C. Memo. 1989-664 (taxpayer made meritless "tax-protester" arguments; quoting *Abrams*, the Court stated: "A judgment on the pleadings is appropriate where a petition raises no justiciable issues."). We may grant a motion for judgment on the pleadings as to less than all the issues in a case. See *Brock v. Commissioner*, 92 T.C. 1127, 1133 (1989); *Caplette v. Commissioner*, T.C. Memo. 1993-46 (partial judgment on the pleadings, except as to fraud penalty, where petition merely contained "tax protester arguments that have been heard and rejected by this Court on many occasions").

The amended petitions all contain the same arguments: (1) The petitioners have no tax liability "due to a lack of consideration", (2) "[i]t does not appear that the United States and the State of California (each a body politic with their respective governments) are under any legal obligation to protect our property and ourselves", (3) although petitioners may have accepted some commercial benefits, "it does not appear that the tax in question bears a fiscal relation to those benefits", and (4) "regardless of the fact that some commercial benefits may have been accepted, it does not appear that any *obligation* to pay any particular tax in return was ever disclosed".

Those are all frivolous arguments. On numerous occasions, courts have rejected similar arguments. See, e.g., *McLaughlin v. Commissioner*, 832 F.2d 986, 987 (7th Cir. 1987) ("The notion that the federal income tax is contractual or otherwise consensual in nature is not only utterly without foundation but * * * has been repeatedly rejected

by the courts."); *United States v. Drefke*, 707 F.2d 978, 981 (8th Cir. 1983) (taxpayer unsuccessfully argued that taxes are debts only incurred when individuals contract with the Government for services). The cases cited in the amended petitions are not relevant to the adjustments made in the notices of deficiency. None of those cases relates to the validity of the trusts involved or to the substantiation of expenses, which are the issues set forth in the notices. Furthermore, the statute cited in the amended petitions, 50 U.S.C. section 1520 (1982), has long since been repealed. When it was effective, the statute related to the testing of chemical and biological agents on humans. Clearly such a statute is not relevant to our redetermination of any deficiency in petitioners' Federal income taxes.

In the amended petitions, petitioners state that "[petitioners bring] only an issue of law before the court." In petitioners' responses (to the motions for judgment on the pleadings), petitioners claim that that no longer is the case. Nevertheless, petitioners have not moved to amend the amended petitions to aver any facts in support of their assignments of error. See Rules 34(b), 41(a). Indeed, in petitioners' responses to the motions, petitioners' claim: "[t]here is no evidence" (1) "to suggest that there is a bona fide political relationship between the petitioners and the 'UNITED STATES' and the 'STATE OF CALIFORNIA'" and (2) "that the petitioners are subject to the written will of individuals called 'CONGRESSMEN'". Those claims do not raise any factual issue relevant to our redetermination of the deficiencies determined by respondent. Those are frivolous claims of no merit. Petitioners have raised no factual issues for decision by us.

None of the petitions or amended petitions assign any error that we consider justiciable: Petitioners rely on meritless tax-protester arguments that demand no respect from the courts. Petitioners have failed to make any legitimate challenge to the deficiencies determined by respondent. They have not assigned any error that could possibly influence us to redetermine the deficiencies determined by respondent.

C. Conclusion

In the petitions, petitioners have failed to address any of the adjustments made in the notices of deficiency. We, therefore, consider petitioners to have conceded those adjustments. See Rule 34(b)(4). They have made no other argument of which we take cognizance. We shall grant the motions for judgment on the pleadings.

The fifth paragraph must set forth the facts on which the taxpayer relies.

Case on Point:

Perry v. Commissioner
T.C. Memo. 1997-489

Rule 34(b)(4) requires that a petition filed in this Court contain clear and concise assignments of each and every error that the taxpayer alleges to have been committed by the Commissioner in the determination of the deficiency and the additions to tax in dispute. Rule 34(b)(5) further requires that the petition contain clear and concise statements of the facts on which the taxpayer bases the assignments of error. See *Jarvis v. Commissioner*, 78 T.C. 646, 658 (1982).

The petition filed in this case does not satisfy the requirements of Rule 34(b)(4) and (5). Although petitioner states that he disagrees with respondent's determinations, there is neither assignment of error nor allegation of fact in support of any assigned error. After having been provided the opportunity to do so, petitioner failed to file a

> proper amended petition as he was directed to by the Court. The allegations contained in the petition that petitioner has not had an opportunity to meet with respondent to discuss his 1991 Federal income tax liability and that respondent has failed to respond to his request for information do not present justiciable issues. Furthermore, the Court does not have the power to grant the unusual relief requested in the petition.
>
> Because the petition fails to state a claim upon which relief can be granted, we shall grant respondent's motion to dismiss. See Rules 34(a)(1), *123(b); Scherping v. Commissioner*, 747 F.2d 478 (8th Cir. 1984).

Finally, the petition must contain a prayer for relief and be signed by the taxpayer or his counsel. A copy of the notice of deficiency should be attached to the petition.

Practice Note:

The original and two copies of the petition must be filed with the Tax Court. The filing fee is $60.

In sum, the petition should:

- Comply with the Tax Court rules;
- Contain complete and accurate information;
- Set forth all required factual information;
- Set forth all errors the taxpayer believes the Commissioner committed; and
- Set forth all facts which form the bases of the alleged errors.

Practice Note:

Some petitions are published by commercial publishers, such as Tax Analysts in Tax Notes Today, LexisNexis, and Westlaw.

g. Tax Court Brief

If a case is tried before the Tax Court, briefs generally are filed after the trial. Rules applicable to the format and filing of the brief can be found in the Tax Court Rules of Practice and Procedure.

Practice Note:

The requirements for a brief are found in Rule 151. Information on the form and style of documents filed in the Tax Court can be found in Rule 23.

A **brief** must include the following:[5]

- Table of Contents with page references.
- List of Citations arranged alphabetically as to cited cases and stating the pages in the brief at which they are cited.

---

5. Tax Court Rule 151(e).

- Statement of the nature of the controversy, the tax involved, and the issues to be decided.

- In the opening brief, proposed findings of fact based on the evidence in the form of numbered statements. Each statement must be a concise statement of essential fact and not a recital of testimony or a discussion or argument relating to the evidence or the law. For each numbered statement there must be a reference to the pages of the transcript or the exhibit or other source that is being relied on to support the statement. In an answering or reply brief, the party must set forth any objections, together with the reasons therefore, to any proposed findings of any other party, showing the numbers of the statements to which the objections are directed. The party may also set forth alternative proposed findings of fact.

- Concise statement of law upon which petitioner relies.

- The argument, setting forth points of law and any disputed questions of fact.

- Signature of counsel or party submitting the brief.

When drafting a brief, the Tax Court rules should be meticulously followed. For example, proposed findings of fact should be listed separately, with only one fact included in each paragraph number. The facts should be organized in a logical manner, often chronologically or by issue. In addition, the findings of fact should include only requested findings of fact, not legal arguments. Finally, the party should include in the requested findings of fact every fact necessary to support his legal argument.

All the issues the party wants to contest should be addressed in the brief. Any issue not addressed may be deemed conceded or abandoned.

Case on Point:

Nicklaus v. Commissioner
117 T.C. 117, 120 (2001)

n4 On brief, petitioners advance none of the other arguments and contentions that petitioners asserted prior to the filing of their brief in this case. We conclude that petitioners have abandoned those other arguments and contentions. See *Rybak v. Commissioner*, 91 T.C. 524, 566 n.19 (1988). Even if we had not concluded that petitioners abandoned the arguments and contentions which they advanced prior to the time that they filed their brief in this case, on the record before us, we reject those other arguments and contentions.

The brief should be persuasively written, from the researcher's selection of and presentation of facts to the legal arguments. In conjunction, the goal of the researcher should be to make the brief as easy as possible for the judge to read and understand. A poorly-written brief is an invitation to the judge to move on to other work, possibly the opposing party's brief. The following rules can be used as guidelines:

- Use the active, rather than the passive, voice.

- Do not attack the revenue agent or Appeals officer as a means of trying to win the taxpayer's case.

- Avoid using terms like "clearly." If it were indeed clear, the party would not have to tell the judge that fact.

- Avoid terms like "never" and "always." Unless it is absolutely true, these terms cause the writer to loose credibility.

- Assure that your requested findings of fact include all facts necessary to support your legal position.

- Eliminate any requested findings of fact that are not necessary to support your legal position.

- Organize the presentation of the facts into a logical format.

- Present legal arguments in an organized manner, using headings as appropriate to outline the arguments for the reader.

- Assume the role of advisor to the judge; give him the tools he needs to resolve the case in your party's favor (rather than focusing on attacking the opposing party's position).

- Write using simple, short, and clear sentences.

- Even though Tax Court judges are well-versed in the area of tax law, do not assume they understand basic elements of the party's position; walk the judge through your party's argument as if the judge had only the most rudimentary tax background. The judge should not have to put down the brief to look up a point of law or a fact from the record.

- For a polished product, allow time for many re-writes and edits.

- Ask a co-worker to read the brief; ask him if he could follow your argument, was persuaded, and if there were any perceived holes in the logic. Then, modify the brief based on the comments received.

Practice Note:

The party must file the signed original brief plus two copies, plus an additional copy for each person to be served.

Practice Note:

The customary procedure of the Tax Court is for opening and reply briefs to be filed simultaneously. However, in the discretion of the court, *seriatim* briefs may be filed.

For simultaneous briefs, opening briefs are generally due within 75 days after the conclusion of the trial and reply briefs are due 45 days thereafter.

For seriatim briefs, the opening brief is generally due within 75 days, the answering brief within 45 days thereafter, and the reply brief within 30 days after the due date of the answering brief.

The timeline set out in the Tax Court Rules is only a guide and the judge may use his discretion in setting due dates for briefs.

Practice Note:

Some briefs are published by commercial publishers, such as Tax Analysts in TAX NOTES TODAY, LexisNexis, and Westlaw.

h. Writing Competitions

Students may be interested in preparing papers to submit for writing competitions. The paper should conform to the rules and intent of the specific competition.

Competition	Sponsor	For More Information
Tannewald Writing Competition	Theodore Tannenwald, Jr., Foundation for Excellence in Tax Scholarship	www.abanet.org
Law Student Tax Challenge	American Bar Association Section of Taxation	www.abanet.org/tax/lstc
American College of Trust and Estate Counsel Mary Moers Wenig Student Writing Competition	The American College of Trust and Estate Counsel	www.actec.org
Writing Competition	Federal Bar Association Section on Taxation	www.fedbar.org

2. Circular 230

Treasury has the authority to issue regulations to regulate practice before the IRS. The regulations are set forth in **Circular 230**. Recently, substantial revisions were made to the regulations, incorporating specific rules that must be followed regarding the provision of certain types of written legal advice.

Quick Find:

Circular 230 is a publication issued by the IRS. It contains regulations that govern practice before the IRS. It can be found on the IRS website, www.irs.gov.

The rules of Circular 230 apply to all types of written advice, from the traditional letter or memoranda to electronic communication, such as e-mail. The regulations include both a list of best practices, which are suggested practices, and mandatory practices for covered opinions, which must be followed in most instances. Those who do not comply with the rules and standards may be censured, suspended, or disbarred from practice before the IRS.

Quote:

Explanation of Provisions

Tax advisors play a critical role in the Federal tax system, which is founded on principles of compliance and voluntary self-assessment. The tax system is best served when the public has confidence in the honesty and integrity of the professionals providing tax advice. To restore, promote, and maintain the public's confidence in those individuals and firms, these final regulations set forth best practices applicable to all tax advisors. These regulations also provide mandatory requirements for practitioners who provide covered opinions. The scope of these regulations is limited to practice before the IRS. These regulations do not alter or supplant other ethical standards applicable to practitioners. T.D. 9165, 69 F.R. 75839, 75840.

Best practices. **Best practices** are referred to as "aspirational." Failure to follow the suggested practices will not result in disciplinary action. The best practices are:[6]

---

6. 31 CFR § 10.33(a).

- Communicate clearly with the client regarding the terms of engagement;
- Establish the facts, evaluate the reasonableness of any assumptions or representations, and arrive at a conclusion supported by the law and facts;
- Advise the client regarding the import of the conclusion reached, including whether the taxpayer may avoid accuracy-related penalties if the taxpayer acts in reliance on the advice; and
- Act fairly and with integrity in practice before the IRS.

Practitioners overseeing the firm's practice should take reasonable steps to ensure that the firm's procedures are consistent with the best practices.[7]

Covered Opinions. A **covered opinion**[8] is written advice that concerns one or more federal tax issues arising from specific types of transactions.

> A **covered opinion** is written advice that concerns one or more federal tax issues arising from listed transactions; plans or arrangements the principal purpose of which is the avoidance or evasion of income tax; or plans or arrangements a significant purpose of which is the avoidance or evasion of income tax if the written advice is a reliance opinion, marketed opinion, subject to conditions of confidentiality, or subject to contractual protection.

A federal tax issue is a question concerning the federal tax treatment of an item of income, gain, loss, deduction, or credit; the existence or absence of a taxable transfer of property; or the value of property for tax purposes.[9] Three specific types of advice come within the definition of covered opinions:

- A listed transaction.[10] A listed transaction is a transaction that the IRS has determined to be a tax avoidance transaction and has identified as a listed transaction by notice, regulation, or other form of published guidance.

> **Practice Note:**
>
> Transactions the IRS has identified as listed transactions can be found on the IRS website, www.irs.gov. Click on Businesses, then Corporations, then "Abusive Tax Shelters and Transactions." They can also be found through various Notices issued by the IRS. *See, e.g.,* Notice 2009-59, 2009-31 I.R.B. 170.

- A plan or arrangement, the *principal* purpose of which is the avoidance or evasion of income tax.[11] The principal purpose of a plan or arrangement is tax avoidance or evasion if that purpose exceeds any other purpose. The principal purpose is not to avoid or evade tax if its purpose is to claim tax benefits in a manner consistent with the statute and Congressional purpose.[12] An arrangement may have

---

7. 31 CFR § 10.33(b).
8. 31 CFR § 10.35(b)(2).
9. 31 CFR § 10.35(b)(3).
10. 31 CFR § 10.35(b)(2)(i)(A).
11. 31 CFR § 10.35(b)(2)(i)(B).
12. 31 CFR § 10.35(b)(10).

a significant purpose of avoidance or evasion without having the principal purpose of avoidance or evasion.

- A plan or arrangement, a *significant* purpose of which is the avoidance or evasion of income tax if the written advice is a reliance opinion, a marketed opinion, subject to conditions of confidentiality, or subject to contractual protection.[13]

  o *Reliance opinion.* A reliance opinion is advice that concludes at a confidence level of more likely than not that one or more significant federal tax issues would be resolved in the taxpayer's favor.[14] A federal tax issue is significant if the IRS has a reasonable basis for a successful challenge and its resolution could have a significant impact, whether beneficial or adverse and under any reasonably foreseeable circumstances, on the overall federal tax treatment of a transaction.[15]

  o *Marketed opinion.* A marketed opinion is written tax advice if the practitioner knows or has reason to know that the written advice will be used or referred to by another person in promoting, marketing, or recommending a transaction to taxpayers.[16]

  o *Subject to conditions of confidentiality.* There are conditions of confidentiality if the practitioner imposes on one or more recipients of the written advice a limitation on disclosure of the tax treatment or tax structure of the transaction and the limitation or disclosure protects the confidentiality of that practitioner's tax strategies.[17]

  o *Subject to contractual protection.* There is contractual protection if the taxpayer has the right to a full or partial refund of the fees paid to the practitioner if all or part of the intended tax consequences from the matters addressed in the written advice are not sustained or if the fees paid to the practitioner are contingent on the taxpayer's realization of tax benefits from the transaction.[18]

Advice that is not a covered opinion. The regulations provide that certain types of advice are not, by definition, covered opinions. It also provides opportunities for the practitioner to opt out of the covered advice rules.

The first exception to the covered advice rules applies to advice that might otherwise fall under any of the above three categories. A covered opinion does not include written advice provided to a client during the course of an engagement under which the practitioner is expected to later provide written advice to the client that satisfies the requirements for a covered opinion. This advice is referred to as "excluded advice."[19]

The second exception applies only to advice that otherwise would fall under the last category of covered opinions (certain types of advice regarding a plan or arrangement, a significant purpose of which is the avoidance or evasion of income tax). The following types of advice are not included in the definition of covered opinion:[20]

---

13. 31 CFR § 10.35(b)(2)(i)(C).
14. 31 CFR § 10.35(b)(4)(i).
15. 31 CFR § 10.35(b)(3).
16. 31 CFR § 10.35(b)(5)(i).
17. 31 CFR § 10.35(b)(6).
18. 31 CFR § 10.35(b)(7).
19. 31 CFR § 10.35(b)(2)(ii)(A).
20. 31 CFR § 10.35(b)(2)(ii)(B), (C), (D), and (E).

- ○ Qualification of a qualified plan;

- ○ State or local bond opinions;

- ○ Advice included in documents that must be filed with the SEC;

- ○ Advice provided to the taxpayer for his use after he has filed his tax return;

- ○ Advice provided by the taxpayer's in-house counsel; and

- ○ Negative tax advice (advice concluding that a federal tax issue will not be resolved in the taxpayer's favor).

The third exception applies to advice that otherwise would be considered a reliance opinion. A practitioner can opt out/legend out of the covered opinion requirements for a reliance opinion if the practitioner includes a prominent disclosure in the advice that it was not intended or written to be used and the taxpayer cannot use the advice to avoid penalties.[21]

The fourth exception applies to advice that otherwise would be considered a marketed opinion. A practitioner can opt out/legend out of the covered opinion requirements for a marketed opinion if he discloses that the advice was not intended or written by the practitioner to be used to avoid penalties, that the advice was written to support the promotion or marketing of the transaction addressed by the written advice, and that the taxpayer should seek advice based on the taxpayer's particular circumstances from an independent tax advisor.[22]

---

21. 31 CFR § 10.35(b)(4)(ii).
22. 31 CFR § 10.35(b)(5)(ii).

Chart 14.1 Covered Opinions

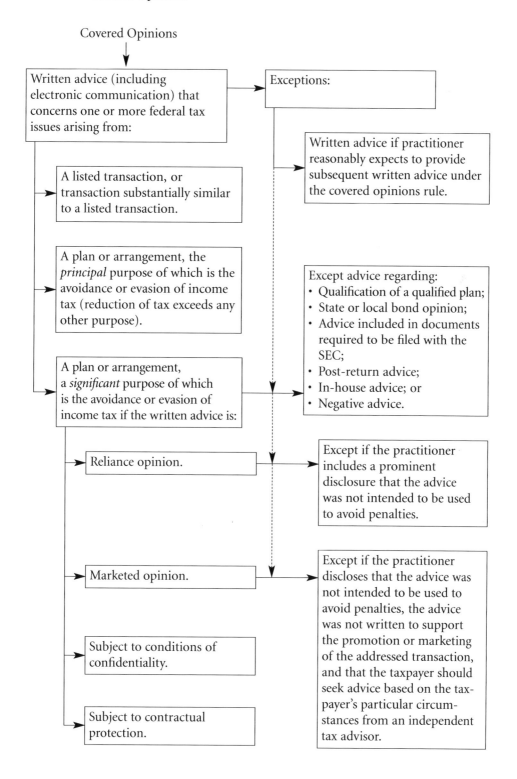

Covered Opinions

Written advice (including electronic communication) that concerns one or more federal tax issues arising from:

Exceptions:

Written advice if practitioner reasonably expects to provide subsequent written advice under the covered opinions rule.

A listed transaction, or transaction substantially similar to a listed transaction.

A plan or arrangement, the *principal* purpose of which is the avoidance or evasion of income tax (reduction of tax exceeds any other purpose).

Except advice regarding:
- Qualification of a qualified plan;
- State or local bond opinion;
- Advice included in documents required to be filed with the SEC;
- Post-return advice;
- In-house advice; or
- Negative advice.

A plan or arrangement, a *significant* purpose of which is the avoidance or evasion of income tax if the written advice is:

Reliance opinion.

Except if the practitioner includes a prominent disclosure that the advice was not intended to be used to avoid penalties.

Marketed opinion.

Except if the practitioner discloses that the advice was not intended to be used to avoid penalties, the advice was not written to support the promotion or marketing of the addressed transaction, and that the taxpayer should seek advice based on the taxpayer's particular circumstances from an independent tax advisor.

Subject to conditions of confidentiality.

Subject to contractual protection.

Standards for covered opinions. If the advice is a covered opinion, the practitioner must comply with the requirements set forth in the regulations.[23] If the practitioner willfully, recklessly, or through gross incompetence fails to comply with the standards, he could be censured, suspended, or disbarred from practice before the IRS.[24] The requirements are as follows.

Factual Matters:[25]

- Use reasonable efforts to identify and ascertain the facts and determine which facts are relevant. The opinion must identify and consider all facts that the practitioner determines to be relevant.

- Not base the opinion on any unreasonable factual assumptions. The practitioner must identify in a separate section all factual assumptions relied upon by the practitioner.

- Not base the opinion on any unreasonable factual representations, statements, or findings of the taxpayer or other person. The opinion must identify in a separate section all factual representations, statements, or findings of the taxpayer relied upon by the practitioner.

Relate Law to Facts:[26]

- Not assume the favorable resolution of any significant federal tax issue or otherwise base an opinion on any unreasonable legal assumptions, representations, or conclusions.

- Not contain internally inconsistent legal analysis or conclusions.

Evaluation of Significant Federal Tax Issues:[27]

- For each significant tax issue, contain either the practitioner's conclusion as to the likelihood that the taxpayer will prevail on the merits or a statement that the practitioner cannot reach a conclusion with respect to the issue;

- Describe the reasons for the conclusions reached or describe why the practitioner was not able to reach a conclusion.

- If the practitioner cannot reach a conclusion on a significant federal tax issue at a confidence level of at least "more likely than not," the opinion must include a prominent disclosure that the opinion fails to reach that confidence level with respect to a significant federal tax issue and that, with respect to that issue, the opinion was not written and the taxpayer may not use the opinion for the purpose of avoiding penalties.

- Not take into consideration the possibility that a tax return will not be audited, that an issue will not be raised on audit, or that an issue will be resolved through settlement if raised.

- *Marketed opinions.* The advice must provide the conclusion that it is at least more likely than not that the taxpayer will prevail on the merits with respect to each significant federal tax issue. If the practitioner is unable to reach a more likely than not conclusion with respect to each significant federal tax issue, the practi-

---

23. 31 CFR § 10.35(c).
24. 31 CFR §§ 10.50, 10.52.
25. 31 CFR § 10.35(c)(1).
26. 31 CFR § 10.35(c)(2).
27. 31 CFR § 10.35(c)(3).

tioner must not provide the marketed opinion, but the practitioner may provide an opinion that prominently discloses that the advice was not intended to be used and that it cannot be used by any taxpayer for the purpose of avoiding penalties, that the advice was not written to support the promotion or marketing of the transaction, and that the taxpayer should seek independent advice.[28]

- *Limited scope opinions.* If the opinion does not concern a listed transaction, a plan the principle purpose of which is tax avoidance, or a marketed opinion, a practitioner may render an opinion that considers less than all of the significant federal tax issues if both the practitioner and the taxpayer agree that the scope of the opinion and the taxpayer's reliance on it are limited to the federal tax issues addressed.[29] The opinion must disclose that it is limited to the one or more federal tax issues addressed; that additional issues may exist that could affect the federal tax treatment of the transaction and the opinion does not consider or provide a conclusion with respect to any additional issues; and that with respect to the significant federal tax issues outside the limited scope opinion the opinion cannot be used for penalty protection.[30] The practitioner may make reasonable assumptions regarding the favorable resolution of a federal tax issue for purposes of providing an opinion on less than all of the significant federal tax issues. The opinion must identify in a separate section all issues for which the practitioner assumed a favorable resolution.[31]

Overall Conclusion:[32]

- Provide either the practitioner's overall conclusion as to the likelihood that the federal tax treatment of the transaction or matter is the proper treatment and the reason for the conclusion or a statement that the practitioner is unable to reach an overall conclusion and the reasons for that inability.

- *Marketed opinion.* If the opinion is a marketed opinion, the practitioner must conclude that the treatment is proper on a more likely than not level.

Standards for written tax advice that is not a covered opinion. If the written advice does not come within the covered opinion provisions, it is still subject to the other written tax advice provisions.[33] The advice:

- May not be based on unreasonable factual or legal assumptions;

- May not unreasonably rely on representations, statements, findings of fact, or agreements of the taxpayer or any other person;

- Consider less than all relevant facts known or facts that should be known; or

- Take into account the possibility that a tax return will not be audited, that an issue will not be raised on audit, or that an issue will be settled.

The provisions also impose a heightened standard of care in the case of an opinion the practitioner knows or has reason to know will be used or referred to by a person other than the practitioner in promoting, marketing, or recommending to one or more taxpayers a partnership or other entity, investment plan or arrangement a significant purpose of which is the avoidance or evasion of tax.

---

28. 31 CFR § 10.35(c)(3)(iv).
29. 31 CFR § 10.35(c)(3)(v)(A).
30. *See* 31 CFR § 10.35(e).
31. 31 CFR § 10.35(c)(3)(v)(B).
32. 31 CFR § 10.35(c)(4).
33. 31 CFR § 10.37.

C. Main Points

Memoranda:
- Generally used for in-house communication.
- Used to convey information.

Letters to the Client:
- Used to convey information to the client.
- Should be written with the client's level of tax expertise in mind.

Information Document Requests:
- Written requests of the IRS revenue agent for information.
- Representative may want to provide an explanation in addition to providing the documents.

Tax Opinions:
- Set forth the lawyer's written opinion of the tax consequences of a particular issue or transaction.
- May demonstrate that the taxpayer had reasonable cause for a return position.
- Must comply with Circular 230.

Protest Letters:
- Must comply with the timeline set forth in the 30-day letter.
- A persuasive document intended to argue the taxpayer's position before the Appeals officer.
- Should follow the requirements set forth in Publication 5, Your Appeal Rights and How To Prepare a Protest If You Don't Agree.

Tax Court Petitions:
- Rules can be found under Rule 34 of the Tax Court Rules of Practice and Procedure.
- Sample petition can be found in Form 1 of Appendix A of the Tax Court Rules of Practice and Procedure.
- Tax Court rules set forth all the information that must be included in the petition.
- Intended primarily as an information document, advising the court and the parties as to the facts and legal issues present in the case.

Tax Court Briefs:
- Rules for preparing a brief can be found under Rule 151 of the Tax Court Rules of Practice and Procedure.
- A persuasive document, intended to argue in favor of the party's position.

Writing Competitions:
- Rules can generally be found on-line.
- Provide an excellent opportunity to practice persuasive and informational writing.

Circular 230:
- Regulations issued by the Department of Treasury to regulate practice before the IRS.
- Sets forth a list of best practices which are suggested guidelines for rendering legal advice.
- Sets forth rules that must be followed when rendering a covered opinion.

- A covered opinion is written advice that concerns one or more federal tax issues arising from listed transactions; plans or arrangements the principal purpose of which is the avoidance or evasion of income tax; or plans or arrangements a significant purpose of which is the avoidance or evasion of income tax if the written advice is a reliance opinion, marketed opinion, subject to conditions of confidentiality, or subject to contractual protection.
- Sets forth standards for written tax advice that is not a covered opinion.

Where can information on the various documents be found?

Guidance	Location
Protest Letters	• Publication 5, which can be located on the IRS website, www.irs.gov.
Tax Court Petitions	• Rule 34 of the Tax Court Rules of Practice and Procedure, which can be located on the Tax Court website, www.ustaxcourt.gov. • Form 1 and Form 2 (and Form 4) in Appendix I of the Tax Court Rules of Practice and Procedure, which can be located on the Tax Court website, www.ustaxcourt.gov.
Tax Court Briefs	• Rule 151 of the Tax Court Rules of Practice and Procedure, which can be located on the Tax Court web site, www.ustaxcourt.gov.
Writing Competitions	• www.abanet.org (Tannenwald Writing Competition). • www.abanet.org/tax/lstc (ABA Student Tax Challenge). • www.actec.org (ACTEC Mary Moers Wenig 2006 Student Writing Competition). • www.fedbar.org (Federal Bar Writing Competition).
Standards for covered opinions	• Circular 230, which can be located on the IRS website, www.irs.gov.

D. Problems

1. Ms. White, your client, has asked you whether the cost of obtaining an LL.M. in Taxation would be deductible.

    a. To answer Ms. White's question, what additional factual information would you need?

    b. Would you need to conduct any legal research?

    c. What form would your response to Ms. White take? What goals would you have in constructing the response?

    d. Assume the facts you need and draft a response to Ms. White.

    e. Is your response covered by Circular 230? If so, what is the impact?

2. Ms. Raymond, the senior partner, stopped you in the hall and told you that she had a research project for you. She was interested in knowing if there were any disclosure or registration requirements when participating in a tax shelter. And, she wanted to know if there were any penalties imposed when a taxpayer did not comply with the requirements. Before you could ask any questions, she was into the lobby and out the front door, mumbling something about being late for a meeting with a client.

    a.   To answer Ms. Raymond's questions, what additional factual information would you need?

    b.   Would you need to conduct any legal research?

    c.   What form would your response to Ms. Raymond take? What goals would you have in constructing the response?

    d.   Draft a response to Ms. Raymond.

3.   Ms. Foster has asked you to assist in the preparation of a brief to be filed in Tax Court. The firm represents the Andersons, who breed and sell race horses. One of the issues raised by the IRS is whether the Andersons engaged in the horse breeding activity for profit. Ms. Foster has provided you with a copy of all the documents filed in the Tax Court, including a copy of the transcript. You have read through everything and understand that the Andersons had been operating their business for five years and reported a loss each year. The Andersons' three children enjoy riding horses, but do not ride the horses that are used in the breeding activity. Over the past five years, the Andersons have sold five horses, all for under $2,000.

    a.   Prepare a statement of the nature of the controversy and the issue to be decided.

    b.   Prepare proposed findings of fact. For each requested finding of fact, could you explain why it is included in the requested findings of fact?

    c.   Prepare a concise statement of the law upon which your argument will rely.

    d.   Prepare the legal argument. What are your goals in drafting the argument? How do you intend to meet those goals?

4.   Mr. Matta, your client, owned and operated a small grocery store. On his income tax return he claimed a deduction for supplies, advertising expenses, cost of goods sold, and legal expenses. The IRS disallowed the claimed deductions on the basis that they were not substantiated. When asked why he didn't have any records of the expenses, Mr. Matta explained that a pipe had broken and flooded the grocery store, destroying most of his records. When Mr. Matta was unable to find other substantiation for the expenses, the IRS issued a statutory notice of deficiency, disallowing the claimed expenses.

    a.   What additional information would you need to prepare a protest letter?

    b.   Assume the facts you need and prepare a protest letter. What are your goals in drafting the letter?

    c.   What additional facts would you need to prepare a petition?

    d.   Assume the necessary facts and prepare a petition. What are your goals in drafting the petition?

5.   The Vice President of Tax for one of your large corporate clients is in your office and tells you that the company entered into a transaction in which the tax consequences were not completely clear. The Vice President further explains that the tax department for the company took a rather aggressive position when reporting the transaction on the company's tax return. He is now nervous that the company may be exposed to potential penalties if the company's reporting position is found to be incorrect. The client would like for you to research the issue and write an opinion for the client (assuming your research is in line with the client's conclusions).

    a.   What advice do you give your client with respect to the opinion?

    b.   If you are in agreement with the client's return position and provide the client with a "should opinion," will the opinion give the client penalty protection?

Index

@ U.S. Constitution
President
Negotiation is performed by Executive Branch
Tax treaties negotiated by Treasury Department
International Tax Office
Negotiation is conducted through written & oral communication.
Sending copy of U.S. model treaty to the treaty partner.
Partner treaty agree, sign the treaty by head of delegations.
Reviewed by Treasury Dept.
Draft is submitted to Secretary of State.
SOS forwards the treaty draft to President along with a letter of submittal
Senate submit the treaty to the Senate Foreign Relations Committee for hearings & comments
After hearing SFRC votes 2/3
ratification exchange the instruments of Ratification

How to do Research?

1) Start with secondary source and then jump into the primary authority.

2) Decide whether research is about individual, Partnership and corporation.

[Bittker and Lokken cover everything.]

3) Main research tools (i) RIA checkpoint and 2) Articles.

(for second exam)

1) Rothman article — writing tax opinion ⌣
2) Brook guide Pdf.
3) Circular 230 & AICPA article
4) Researching the Issue.
5) Chapter related to International tax.
6) Approach to tax research
7) Cite Checking → Purpose: — whether it has been overruled.
   a) To check if it is still a good law
   b) Get more primary authorities.
8) ch. 14 = Organizing the writing.
   a) Prediction writing v. husness writing.
9) Finished Product — Memo, Client letter, (IDR) Information document request)
10) Newman Ch. 16 – 19 / Chp. 2 of Memo
11) Model treaties, Purpose, Relationship of treaty & Code, competent authority.
12) First HW assignment
13) § 6662 and 1-6664-4d